W9-ABA-069

eBay the Smart Way®

Fifth Edition

Other Books by Joseph T. Sinclair

eBay Business the Smart Way®, Third Edition
eBay Motors the Smart Way®
eBay Global the Smart Way®
Building Your eBay Traffic the Smart Way®
eBay Photography the Smart Way®
eBay Inventory the Smart Way®

eBay the Smart Way®

Selling, Buying, and Profiting on the Web's #1 Auction Site

Fifth Edition

Joseph T. Sinclair

ΛMACOM

American Management Association
New York • Atlanta • Brussels • Chicago • Mexico City • San Francisco
Shanghai • Tokyo • Toronto • Washington, D.C.

Special discounts on bulk quantities of AMACOM books are available to corporations, professional associations, and other organizations. For details, contact Special Sales Department, AMACOM, a division of American Management Association, 1601 Broadway, New York, NY 10019.
Tel.: 212-903-8316. Fax: 212-903-8083.
Web site: www.amacombooks.org

This publication is designed to provide accurate and authoritative information in regard to the subject matter covered. It is sold with the understanding that the publisher is not engaged in rendering legal, accounting, or other professional service. If legal advice or other expert assistance is required, the services of a competent professional person should be sought.

Library of Congress Cataloging-in-Publication Data

Sinclair, Joseph T.
      eBay the smart way : selling, buying, and profiting on the Web's #1 auction site / Joseph T. Sinclair. -- 5th ed.
          p. cm.
      Includes index.
      ISBN-13: 978-0-8144-7451-8
      ISBN-10: 0-8144-7451-9
      1. Internet auctions. 2. eBay (Firm) I. Title.
      HF5478.S48 2007
      381'.177--dc22   2007002027
                                                              CIP

© 2007 Joseph T. Sinclair.
All rights reserved.
Printed in the United States of America.

"THE SMART WAY" is a registered trademark of Joseph T. Sinclair

This publication may not be reproduced, stored in a retrieval system, or transmitted in whole or in part, in any form or by any means, electronic, mechanical, photocopying, recording, or otherwise, without the prior written permission of AMACOM, a division of American Management Association, 1601 Broadway, New York, NY 10019.

Printing number
10   9   8   7   6   5   4   3   2   1

To my grandfather, Albert L. Hoener, Jr., and grandmother, Margaret Zoe Lorene Fellabaum Hoener, together the light of my life in my early years in Michigan

Contents

Acknowledgments

Many thanks to Don Spillane, who introduced me to eBay in 1998 and who is the quintessential retailer on eBay, first selling collectibles, now selling cars, and also my co-author for *eBay Motors the Smart Way*. Thanks to my agent, Carole McClendon at Waterside Productions and the Waterside support staff, who always do a fine job, and to Jacqueline Flynn and the folks at AMACOM, including Kama Timbrell, Bob Chen, and Andy Ambraziejus who have contributed to the book's success. Then too, I certainly don't want to overlook the clever people at eBay, who have done a great job of creating a new marketplace—a huge and dynamic new marketplace—which has expanded rapidly across the globe. And they continue to improve eBay each year. Good work! Thanks also to the many eBay entrepreneurs who have staked their resources and their futures on developing their retail businesses on eBay and have made it a more practical and attractive marketplace. And finally thanks to my wife Lani, daughter Brook, and son Thomas who endured with a minimum of grumbling the lengthy effort it takes to write a book. Wow! The fifth edition of this book and six other eBay books—that's a lot of endurance. Thanks.

I

Introducing eBay

1

eBay Overview

It's true that eBay holds auctions. It's also true that eBay operates only online. So what? Well, put the two together and you start to understand the dynamic new international marketplace eBay has created. It operates 24 hours a day, 7 days a week. It's not like anything that has existed before. The possibilities excite the imagination, and it offers you significant opportunities whether you buy, sell, or sell at retail.

How exciting is it? Quite exciting! In December 2004, eBay had 135 million registered users. The following statistics come from the third annual eBay Live conference, June 2004, in New Orleans, Louisiana, and from other reliable sources.

eBay's number of registered users, last quarter of each year:

1996	41,000
1997	341,000
1998	2 million

1999   10 million

2000   22 million

2001   42 million

2002   62 million

2003   94 million

2004   135 million

2005   181 million

2006   222 million

eBay members' sales for each year (in dollars):

1998   745 million

1999   2.8 billion

2000   5.4 billion

2001   9.3 billion

2002   14.8 billion

2003   23.8 billion

2004   34 billion

2005   44 billion

2006   52 billion

Additional statistics reprinted from my own eBay books show the number of items for sale on a typical day for various months:

Jul 1999   2.4 million items in 1,600 categories

Jan 2001   5 million items in 4,000 categories

Jul 2003   16 million items in 27,000 categories

Jun 2004   21 million items in 45,000 categories

Jun 2005   50 million items in 80,000 categories

Not bad, considering that the longest auction lasts only ten days, with many auctions lasting only three, five, or seven days.

Figure 1.1 The eBay home page. ©1995-2007 eBay Inc.

Markets

eBay is a great marketplace. It consolidates different markets for different types of products and brings them all to one place—a convenient online location.

Oddly enough, if you check prices on eBay, you will find that prices are often a bargain for buyers. Yet, sellers can get more money for their used products and closeout products on eBay than perhaps anywhere else. How can this be? How can both buyers and sellers come out ahead?

Used Goods

It's actually easy to explain. Local markets do not operate very efficiently; they're not large enough. Typically a seller takes a used product to a local dealer to sell. For instance, a seller might take a used Canon camera to a camera dealer. Because the local market is not huge, it will not include many buyers for the camera. The dealer takes a substantial risk that the camera will not sell in a timely manner.

Consequently, the dealer will not pay much for the camera. The seller sells to the dealer at a low price.

On the other hand, the dealer has to charge a lot for the camera. He or she must seek a profit that covers the risk of the camera staying on the shelf a long time. The profit must also cover the cost of doing business, which includes paying rent and employing sales clerks (overhead). The buyer buys from the dealer at a high price.

Thus, a low sales price (for the seller) along with a high purchase price (for the buyer) is the rule in a local market, particularly when most of the transactions take place through a local dealer.

Sometimes a local show (or flea market) offers an exchange (or swap) that brings together buyers and sellers more efficiently, and prices grow a little higher for sellers and a little lower for buyers, particularly for transactions that don't involve a dealer. For instance, at a camera show with a camera exchange, a seller can get a higher price for the Canon camera, and a buyer can buy at a lower price than in a transaction through a dealer. Nonetheless, even in a large city, for most products except the most popular, an exchange does not create the ultimate market. It simply never has a large enough population of buyers and sellers.

eBay has established an international marketplace with no peers except a few of the stock and commodity exchanges. The eBay marketplace rationalizes the sale and purchase of used goods (i.e., provides the best deal for both buyers and sellers). This is as much as such transactions will ever be rationalized (until more people join eBay). That is, eBay always has the maximum numbers of buyers and sellers compared to other markets, all of which are smaller. The auction feature of the eBay marketplace provides a mechanism that dynamically establishes market values quickly and efficiently. The transactions do not necessarily take place through a dealer. Consequently, a seller can usually sell for a higher price than in a local market, and a buyer can usually buy for a lower price than in a local market.

You can say that the eBay marketplace promotes *disintermediation*. This fancy word means that the dealer (the intermediary) has been eliminated. Again, referring to the camera example, the seller should be able to sell the Canon camera for more on the eBay market than to a local dealer, and the buyer should be able to buy the Canon camera for less on the eBay market than from a local dealer.

The Dealer

A dealer can still fit into the eBay environment. If a dealer can count on turning over used goods quickly, the economics of his or her business practices change. Consequently, a dealer who sells on eBay can afford to pay more for used goods to acquire inventory and sell such goods for less than in a physical location where overhead is higher and the market smaller.

Nonetheless, realize that every market is different. Dealers have been forced out of some markets by eBay and have thrived in other markets on eBay. What it comes down to, each time a dealer looks at an eBay market, is whether he or she can make money in that particular market. Sometimes the answer is yes, and sometimes it's no.

Keep in mind, too, that many dealers use eBay to sell new goods exclusively, or in addition to, used goods. Many dealers who sell new goods thrive. And many eBay members selling regularly have evolved into full-fledged dealers (retailers) themselves.

The more buyers and sellers for any particular product, the more the marketplace will rationalize the price. Thus, popular used items, such as common brands currently available, will be bought and sold at prices closer to the prices the items sell for at retail (i.e., at discount stores). Less popular used items, such as less well-known brands, may sell at prices well below their retail price at discount stores.

Law of Supply and Demand

Does the law of supply and demand work on eBay? Sure! When many sellers of a particular product want to sell to a few buyers on eBay, the price will go down. When many buyers want to buy a particular product from a few sellers on eBay, the price will go up. A huge market like eBay, however, has a maximum number of buyers and sellers compared to other markets. Due to the large number of buyers and sellers, the market will tend to be more balanced (more rational and stable) than a smaller market.

New Goods

Sellers sell new goods on eBay. In fact, new goods comprise about 30 percent of the goods sold today. However, sellers often do not sell new goods at full price or even at a discount price. More often eBay is a place to sell new goods at a deep discount. Consequently, buyers can expect to get a pretty good deal. But what about sellers? Can they get a good deal too?

Yes, a seller can sell a product new that he or she has not used or has decided not to use. These mistaken purchases happen to all of us sooner or later. What about that fishing reel you unwrapped at Christmas but never took out of the box? What about that food dehydrator you bought for making beef jerky but never got around to using? It's often difficult to return such merchandise for a refund, particularly after it sits in the garage for six months (or six years). But it's new, and if you sell it, you undoubtedly will sell it at a deep discount from the full retail price. eBay provides you the opportunity to sell it at the highest price you can expect to get.

Many sellers sell retail on eBay. This means they sell new goods as a business just like an offline retailer, albeit usually at lower prices. When eBay started its fixed price program, *Buy It Now*, the fixed prices gave eBay retailers a substantial boost. The fixed prices enable buyers to buy immediately just as they do in a retail store.

New goods also come from sources other than wholesale, such as distress sales and closeout sales by manufacturers and retailers. These are usually bulk sales. For instance, if an eBay retailer can buy 1,000 high-quality baseball caps for $500 (50 cents each) at a closeout sale and sell them on eBay for $4 each, that price is substantially below the normal $8–$16 price in the retail stores. Both the eBay retailer and the buyer can conclude a satisfying transaction. The buyer buys cheap, the eBay retailer makes a reasonable profit, and the closeout seller gets rid of excess inventory.

Moreover, if the seller does not have a retail store and an expensive website operation, she can afford to sell new goods on the eBay market in the regular course of business at even lower prices than a discount store (assuming she buys in more than token quantities). This provides a good deal for buyers and a profitable business for sellers.

Now, if you take a look at what's happening on eBay—if you haven't already—you will see the transactions described above occurring every minute of every day. eBay has built a huge marketplace. At any moment in time, tens of millions of items are waiting for bids, and tens of millions of potential buyers look over the merchandise. If you were to put all of this in a physical setting, no building ever built could house all of this commercial activity. It would take about one hundred football fields to accommodate a marketplace of only one million people. Indeed, eBay has created a huge and rational marketplace.

An Important Insight

The interesting thing about goods is that each product has its own market. It may have a much different market than something closely related. For instance, insulated winter boots with rubber bottoms and leather tops enjoy a thriving market in the outdoor labor force. They keep feet warm and dry in winter—just what the working man or woman needs. You can buy them in stores that cater to outdoor workers. Insulated boots made entirely of leather enjoy a thriving market among skiers. They keep feet warm and dry in snowy weather—perfect for use after a day of skiing. Known as apres ski boots, you can buy them in ski shops. Although similar, these two products have very different markets.

This phenomenon holds true on eBay too. Every type of item has its own market and means of being advertised and sold. That makes it misleading to generalize about eBay. What you might say about one product may not hold true for a similar but different product. Some product sales thrive on eBay. Some don't. This phenomenon misleads and baffles many people. But don't let it baffle you.

People want certainty. They want to know how to do it. They feel uncomfortable with the facts: 50 million items on eBay and hundreds of different standard ways to sell each of those items. But facts are facts. You need to become knowledgeable about any product you buy or sell to get the best deal for yourself, and you need to become knowledgeable about how such an item is bought and sold on eBay. Such knowledge leads to success. Generalizations do not necessarily lead to success on eBay.

Naturally, this book cannot cover the thousands of different ways of doing things on eBay. It has to make generalizations. Just be advised that the most this book can do is lead you in the right direction. Only your research will give you the insight you need for success with any particular product.

For instance, $300 digital cameras sell well on eBay, yet $300 couches don't. Digital cameras tend to be commodities. The one you buy on eBay exactly matches the one you might buy in a store. Couches tend to have much more variety, and you want to see them, feel them, and sit on them before you make a purchase. The $300 digital camera costs $8 to ship. The $300 couch costs $270 to ship. These differences seem obvious, but many other differences are more subtle, and only research will expose them.

The way a particular market relates to the whole market also varies. For instance, many previously successful dealers were driven out of the collectibles market by losing customers to eBay. Yet antique dealers have thrived using eBay to both buy and sell antiques. Again, research and experimentation lead to discovering the anomalies of any eBay market.

Naturally, if you are a consumer, you don't have the time to research every little thing you buy or sell on eBay. But it's undoubtedly worthwhile to research the more valuable items. However, if you are an eBay retailer selling in volume, product research is very worthwhile. Indeed, it's essential for success.

Fitting In

Where do you fit in? eBay is simple. You sign up for membership, fill in an online form with some information on an item, and suddenly you're a seller. To be a buyer, you don't even have to fill in the information for an item. Just bid on something.

Thus, the question comes up, Why a book? The answer is straightforward. The more you buy and sell on eBay, the more committed you become to making eBay commerce a part of your life. Then things become more complex. Your activities start to lead to significant dollars being at stake. Indeed, eBay commerce can add up to more than you expect whether you intend it to or not.

Many readers will buy and sell in volume for one or some of the following reasons:

Consumers

1. They buy and sell as part of their hobby (e.g., coin collecting).

2. They buy supplies and equipment for their business because they save money buying on eBay.

3. They use eBay as a convenient substitute for going to the local mall.

4. They wheel and deal in eBay items because it's fun, and there's lots of stuff.

5. They have eccentric tastes and use eBay to buy lots of offbeat stuff they can't find easily elsewhere.

Retailers

1. They sell on eBay to supplement their offline retail sales business in a physical location.

2. They operate a full-time retail business selling exclusively on eBay.

This book is a basic book for people who buy or sell occasionally as well as for people who sell at retail. It's for people who want to make the most of their eBay activities. Consequently, it's more for people who take eBay seriously than for those who play on eBay as a game or social activity. As you might expect, this book has a serious flavor to it. Hey! Saving money and making money is serious stuff.

Specifically, one purpose of this book is to be a primer for those who are serious about carrying on a substantial part-time or even a full-time business on eBay. My book *eBay Business the Smart Way, Third Edition* takes up where this book leaves off and expands on the business of operating as an eBay retailer.

If you use eBay regularly for whatever purposes, you will soon come to realize, if you haven't already, that eBay is a way of participating in commerce that requires skills and background knowledge to achieve your personal goals (e.g., saving money or making money). Thus, the serious slant of this book will give you the edge to be successful.

Other Online Auctions

What about other online auctions? eBay has had the lion's share of the online auction business. Most press accounts allege eBay's market share of the online auction market to be well over 90 percent. For any market to be highly rationalized, it must have a huge number of participants. As long as eBay has the major portion of the market, competitors (other online auctions) will have trouble competing effectively. The competitors will simply find it difficult to grow to a size where both buyers and sellers get the best deal. Size is perhaps the single most important characteristic of a successful online auction marketplace, and eBay got there first.

How did eBay get there first? That makes a fascinating story, but one which is beyond the scope of this book. Like other Web business success stories, eBay made customer convenience the primary goal for improving the eBay infrastructure. The result is a finely tuned system that works well and is reliable. But transactions require trust as well as procedures that work well. eBay outdistanced its competitors by using innovation to make auctions simple and effective and by creating a system that supports trust. Easy to use and trustworthy. What else do you need for a marketplace?

I encourage you to try other online auctions from time to time. Anyone can challenge eBay. Some specialty auctions will do well in spite of eBay. If someone can make a good market outside of eBay, it might be a benefit to you. But for the vast majority of consumer and general business goods, that seems unlikely.

Specialty Auctions

Because eBay has no effective competition, this book doesn't waste space covering other online auctions alleged to compete with eBay, even for comparative purposes. You can make the argument that some specialty online auctions will compete with eBay in their specific specialties. However, because market size is so important and because eBay caters to many specialty markets, you can expect eBay to dominate even individual submarkets.

Specialized Auctions

Some specialized auctions are different from the general auction market because of artificial restraints. For example, to hold a legally binding real estate auction, you have to have a real estate license and satisfy real estate regulations. Consequently, eBay can't take over that particular auction market easily. Nonetheless, eBay has held *nonbinding* real estate auctions online for years.

After becoming licensed in real estate in all the states, eBay has experimented with *binding* online real estate auctions in some states. If these binding real estate auctions work well, presumably eBay will expand its binding real estate auctions. Perhaps someday all eBay real estate auctions will be binding. But that has not happened yet, and eBay has not become a primary marketplace for real estate.

Will eBay continue to dominate? The eBay people are bright and innovative. They have well-financed potential competitors such as Google, Yahoo, and Amazon.com breathing down their necks, which will keep them running at full speed. eBay has the momentum and the market share.

eBay made a successful public stock offering in September 1998. (Its stock went up 3,900 percent in value by the end of June 1999. It went down after the dot com crash but went back up to its high in the summer of 2003 and then split again in the winter of 2005.) This has provided eBay with the capital to remain successful, and eBay has been profitable. All signs indicate that eBay will continue to dominate the Web auction scene for the foreseeable future. Indeed, the *Wall Street Journal* declared eBay "an institution" in 2004, something I have been saying in my books since 1999.

A Terrific Place to Shop

eBay is a terrific place to shop. Every time I forget this and go to the mall or somewhere else to shop, I am often disappointed. Customer service is too often terrible. Many minimum-wage store clerks seem to have no motivation to learn their retail merchandise, and they are all you have to rely on besides yourself. Stores are understaffed. Inventory is incomplete. Prices are sometimes unreasonably high. And more and more a significant amount of merchandise is on the shelves without price tags. Then too, you have to drive a distance to get such a unsatisfying buying experience.

It takes a long time to break old habits. I have been buying on eBay since 1998, and every year I buy more on eBay and other online stores and less locally. Now, I think of eBay first 75 percent of the time, and the other 25 percent of the time I usually wish I had. And whatever I buy is delivered right to my door! If you're new to eBay, start training yourself to think of eBay first when you want or need something. You won't regret it.

And what a terrific opportunity for sellers! The millions of people training themselves to think of eBay first constitute a huge market—all the potential customers you could ever hope for. It doesn't get any better than this.

What's Up?

What do you make of all this? eBay is a new marketplace like none ever known before. It features an efficient market for the exchange of used goods, good news for both buyers and sellers. It also brings with it new opportunities for those who want to wheel and deal in goods on a broader scale, especially new goods. In true capitalist spirit, it brings with it new opportunities to buy for less, sell for more, or make money, lots of money.

Indeed, things happen today on eBay faster than they ever have. The rate of change is accelerating. eBay is not stabilizing, so to speak, but rather reinvents itself often and continues to add features. A printed book cannot keep up with the changes. Therefore, I try to paint a general overview and point you in the right direction to find the current information you need to be successful. That's all a book can do today. But check the Epilogue for further sources of eBay information.

If you have a new idea about eBay or a new slant on eBay from personal observation—or an idea you dream up—and you want to share it, email me at *jt@sinclair.com*. If you mention it first and I use it in another edition of this book, I'll give you the credit. Thanks.

Final Word

As in every marketplace, the knowledgeable reap the profits. Although eBay is simple and straightforward, it provides the infrastructure for complex strategies and activities. And although eBay is simple to use, you need to know a lot in order to put it to your most profitable use. Whether you buy or sell one item, buy or sell in bulk, or buy or sell new or used goods, this book provides the information you need to operate intelligently on eBay. Even though easy to read, this book wasn't written for dummies. Indeed, it's for those who want to learn how to operate on eBay the smart way.

2

Buyers' Opportunities

The primary opportunity for buyers is to buy at the lowest possible price. That raises questions: Which buyers? What products? Tough questions to answer, because eBay evolves every day. Can an individual buy goods on eBay? Certainly. eBay got its start providing such a marketplace. Can a business buy goods on eBay? Again, yes. Today the potential for business purchases is greater than ever but still limited. Tomorrow, perhaps unlimited. See Chapter 25 for more information on business purchases; this chapter covers individual buyers.

Individuals

eBay attracts individual buyers (bidders) because such buyers can buy merchandise at good prices, sometimes at spectacular savings. A deal that's hard to beat! After all, this is the age of high-quality mass-produced consumer products. A Hoover vacuum cleaner works the same whether you buy it at full price from a retailer, at a discount price from a discount store, or at a deeper discount price on eBay. Fortunately for buyers, there are plenty of sellers. eBay has grown into a huge market consisting of tens of millions of people. Among those millions are many sellers. With a good balance between buyers and sellers, the market works well for buyers.

The bottom line is you can often buy things less expensively on eBay than you can elsewhere. This is a general statement that may not prove true in many cases. For instance, I usually price computer equipment on eBay and also at Fry's, my local discount computer store. Sometimes eBay offers lower prices. Sometimes Fry's offers lower prices. They both offer prices significantly lower than elsewhere. At the least, eBay provides a good reference for price comparisons, and if I couldn't make it to Fry's, I would have no reservations about buying computer equipment exclusively on eBay.

eBay offers a wide variety of merchandise. Although eBay commerce seems to be top-heavy in things like computers, consumer electronics, clothing, jewelry, and cameras, this hides the fact that there are millions of products for sale on eBay that have nothing to do with these categories. Likewise, if you don't like used (pre-owned) merchandise, a substantial and growing portion of the eBay merchandise sold is new, not used.

eBay's Role

eBay is just a marketplace to buy and sell, nothing more. eBay does not get involved in the transaction. The seller pays a small fee to eBay—analogous to renting a booth at a flea market. As a buyer, you make your own arrangement with the seller for payment and shipping. The eBay auction process sets the price.

The Time Factor

The transaction time doesn't necessarily favor buyers. If you want something right now, you can't buy on impulse, except for *Buy It Now* items (fixed price merchandise growing to be a substantial part of the eBay marketplace). You have to wait until the auction is over, and you have to be high bidder too. In addition, you have to tend your auction; that is, you have to have a bidding strategy and follow it through. Once you win the bidding, you must arrange payment and shipping with the seller. Often the seller will wait until your check clears before making the shipment (unless you pay by credit card or PayPal). Thus, the total time of a transaction tends to be measured in days or even weeks.

All of the above assumes that a seller puts up for auction the item you seek. The item may not be available on eBay. When looking to buy microphones over a two-month period a few years ago, I found that the number of microphones auctioned at any particular time varied between 110 and 215. When I looked for a copy of FrameMaker (specialized, expensive software) over the same two-month period, sometimes eBay had six copies up for auction and sometimes none. Consequently, you may have to wait to buy what you want to buy. It may not be continuously available on eBay. But due to eBay's huge size, sooner or later it will show up.

eBay Stores

Interestingly, you do not have to wait for some products. Some retailers running auctions have an eBay Store where they sell items at fixed prices. Look for the eBay Store icon (opened red door) by the seller's name. Many eBay sellers also have a URL (link) on their eBay *About Me* webpage to their independent website where you can order the merchandise immediately at a price comparable to the auction price. Don't overlook these opportunities when in a hurry.

Buy It Now

If you see the *Buy It Now* (fixed price) label on an auction listing, you can buy the item immediately for the price indicated. Your purchase terminates the auction.

The Market

The market for buyers is a smorgasbord. You can find almost anything you want. The enormous scope of the eBay market sets it apart from its would-be competitors. In a real sense, you should think of eBay as your personal asset. You can always turn to it to buy merchandise at good prices, merchandise that you otherwise might not be able to afford. And think of it as a long-term asset. No reason it won't work just as well for you even five years from now as it does today. Probably better.

Risk

What risk do you take to buy merchandise on eBay? If it was risky, eBay wouldn't be so successful. Nonetheless, you need to keep your eyes open and always stay cautious. Never pay more for something than you can afford to lose, because you take a risk that you will lose your money to an ecommerce criminal (i.e., someone who doesn't deliver the goods or otherwise defrauds you).

If you can't afford to lose more than $500, you should take proper precautions for all transactions over that amount. Fortunately, online escrow companies will protect you (for a fee) by handling the transaction. The escrow company doesn't pay your money to the seller until the shipper delivers the specified goods in reasonable condition. See Escrow Services in Chapter 4 for more on this.

eBay offers its own free insurance program that covers goods up to $200. It covers fraud but not shipping damage or loss. Some sellers (PowerSellers) now offer fraud insurance up to $500 through eBay. Some sellers are even bonded (not by eBay), which means that the bonding company will pay legitimate claims against them.

Con artists will always work eBay seeking to con you with means other than non-delivery of goods. But con artists work your local community too. You take a risk just by opening your front door. eBay may have even less fraud because eBay fraud is usually easy to trace online to the criminals responsible.

The good news is that eBay has a superb system for establishing reputations. In many cases, you will have full confidence that the seller will deliver the goods. The reputation (feedback) system comprises the heart and soul of the eBay system—truly a work of genius. You need to learn how to use it when evaluating sellers. See Chapter 8 for details. The eBay feedback system provides eBay a great opportunity for buyers because it decreases the risk of fraud significantly.

Credit Card Chargeback

If you pay by credit card and get cheated, you can do a chargeback. That is, you can call your credit card issuer and request that the charge be removed from your account. This is, in effect, a reimbursement.

Transaction Overhead

Buying things on eBay entails some routine expenses. Although most of the items are nominal, they add up. What you thought you bought on eBay so inexpensively might start looking like a purchase from a store in your neighborhood by the time you take delivery.

Shipping and Handling

The shipping and handling charges are a fact of life on eBay just as they are for mail-order purchases. Don't forget to include them in your price calculations. Often a seller will charge a flat fee, so you don't have to ask for an estimate.

Insurance

What happens if an item you paid for is not delivered? At best it causes a mess. Insurance provides the best defense against this awkward situation. Unfortunately, insurance probably isn't cost-effective for cheap items. For costly items, request insurance. Or, if the seller offers insurance, take it (even though you may have to pay for it). Note that some shippers (e.g., UPS and FedEx) include a minimal amount of insurance at no additional cost.

Sales Tax

As with mail-order purchases, one of the attractions of buying on eBay is that the seller is likely to be out of state, and you don't have to pay sales tax. Nonetheless, the shipping and handling costs often negate this savings; taken together, the shipping (cost) and sales tax (savings) often result in a wash, particularly for items between $30 and $100.

Don't forget, however, that when you make a purchase in your state (i.e., buyer and seller live in the same state), you have to pay sales tax (if your state collects a sales tax). Also read about use tax in Chapter 7.

Escrow Fees

If you make a high-price purchase, make the effort to put the transaction in escrow. The fees seem expensive, but the process protects you from nondelivery of the merchandise. The escrow agent doesn't send payment to the seller until the buyer says that he or she received what was represented by the seller.

Payment by credit card may relieve you of the need for escrow because you can charge back the purchase (get your money back) within a certain number of days (e.g., 90 days) if you have good cause to be dissatisfied or have been cheated.

Payment

If you need to send a money order or cashier's check, you will have to pay at least a nominal fee for it (perhaps a relatively high fee). You will do better to use a credit card or PayPal (covered in Chapter 20). You can always ask for a chargeback to recoup your money if the seller doesn't deliver the merchandise as represented.

Rent or Buy on eBay?

Need expensive equipment for a project? Buy it used (in excellent condition) on eBay. Use it. Keep it in excellent condition. When you finish the project, sell the equipment on eBay (in excellent condition). You can probably sell it for about what you bought it for if you keep it in excellent condition. Looks like an inexpensive rental to me.

This idea works well for items such as boats, RVs, construction equipment, and many other big ticket items.

Summary

eBay provides solid opportunities for buyers to buy new and used goods, and even services, at low prices. eBay's system for establishing reputation takes much of the risk out of the auction transactions. In some cases buying, using, and reselling an item even simulates renting such an item at a low cost for a special project. eBay provides you with a new low-cost alternative for acquiring the goods and services that you need.

What About Businesses?

This chapter discusses individuals. To get some ideas about how businesses can buy on eBay, read Chapter 28 about eBay's business-to-business website.

3

Sellers' Opportunities

The primary opportunity for sellers is to sell at the highest price. After all, isn't that what auctions are for? eBay provides an excellent means of potentially getting the highest price because so many potential buyers look for merchandise in the eBay marketplace. On eBay, individuals can successfully sell to individuals, and retailers can successfully sell to individuals. This chapter covers such auction opportunities. For more information on business-to-business sales, read Chapter 28 about the eBay business website.

Individuals

Suppose you have a seven-year-old Audio-Technica AT3060 professional microphone in excellent condition you want to sell. This fine piece of audio equipment has a limited local market. If you sell this to a dealer, chances are you will not get a good price. If you sell it through classified ads, you may not get many calls. But if you auction it on eBay, a few who appreciate the quality of the equipment and need it will step up from among the tens of millions of eBay buyers to bid on it. Because of the immense size of the eBay market, you can find numerous people interested in what you have to offer. The more people interested, the more likely you can sell it for a higher price than elsewhere.

It doesn't have to be a specialized piece of equipment like the Audio-Technica microphone to get bids. Even more buyers will bid for a popular Sony consumer audio cassette tape recorder like the Walkman WM-GX552, and with the maximum number of buyers, you are more likely to get the maximum price.

With a quick trip to your garage, you can probably make $1,000 in the next week ridding yourself of things you haven't used in years by selling them on eBay. Maybe $5,000.

Advertising

How do you promote your auction on eBay? You advertise it. eBay provides you with an advertising section in your auction listing webpage (i.e., the middle portion of the listing webpage). You use this section to present whatever information you want. You can even use Hypertext Markup Language (HTML), the simple markup language of the Web. Although this might sound like a chore if you don't know HTML, it's just the opposite. It's a great opportunity.

You can put anything you want to in your auction ad. There's no limitation. Naturally, you will want to at least fully describe the item you offer for auction. Chapter 16 will show you how to use HTML templates for attractive ads without having to learn HTML.

The Time Factor

Don't look at eBay as a quick fix. You can take your Audio-Technica AT3060, put it in the car, drive to a dealer, and perhaps get cash today, albeit a small amount of cash. eBay takes more time. The shortest auction lasts three days, and you might want to use a longer auction just to make sure you get the maximum number of bidders.

Nonetheless, creating an auction on eBay does not take long, and you don't have to do anything during the auction period except perhaps answer a few questions via email from prospective bidders. Once the auction closes, you simply arrange with the winning bidder for pay-

ment and shipment, and the deal is done. The auction takes the negotiation out of the deal, and you will not have to waste time with offers
and counteroffers.

Although not immediate, eBay does provide for a reasonably short
sales period without a great deal of effort on your part.

The Market

Consider the market as at least national and at best international. This
means that you send the item being auctioned via normal shipping
channels, or in the case of a foreign sale, you ship the item overseas. In
other words, the buyer won't appear at your front door to hand you a
check and pick up the item. Thus, to sell this way requires an additional time commitment on your part. You have to pack the item in a
box and go to the post office or elsewhere to ship the item. But strang-
ers won't knock on your door (as they might with classified ads), perhaps a greater benefit.

You can assume that the market is full of serious buyers. Occasionally
buyers will not complete the transactions for which they were the high
bidders. Fortunately, eBay provides a system that discourages such
behavior, and you shouldn't have to repeat an auction often due to a
non-paying buyer.

The best news is that eBay has a vast market. Tens of millions of buyers bid, and eBay keeps growing. You will always find a significant
number of potential buyers for common goods in this market, and you
will likely find buyers even for uncommon goods. This huge eBay
market, always waiting for you, provides a convenient way to sell merchandise no longer useful to you.

Retailers

Retailers are businesses that have new merchandise (and sometimes
used goods) to sell to consumers. Most retailers sell inventory in their
stores at full price or run sales to sell at a discounted price. But retailers often have excess or outdated inventory that will not bring full
retail price. For such inventory, eBay provides a potentially profitable
new outlet. Indeed, many retailers do quite well auctioning on eBay,
which provides a golden opportunity for excess-inventory sales and
closeout sales. In addition, it provides a golden opportunity for retail-

ers to buy at distress sales or closeout sales offline and turn around and sell the inventory profitably at retail for discount prices on eBay.

For retailers accustomed to fulfilling mail orders, selling on eBay is a natural fit. Retailers who have not sold via mail will need to get organized to fulfill eBay sales, not an overwhelming task, but nonetheless one that needs to be taken seriously.

Online Retailers

Retailers that exist only online will find eBay to be a natural extension of their online sales. Retailers that handle online commerce well will welcome eBay as an additional outlet. They can use their existing infrastructure to handle and fulfill orders easily and quickly.

eBay Retailers

A new breed of retailers has appeared that sells only on eBay. These retailers don't necessarily even have the expense of an ecommerce website and certainly not the expense of a store or warehouse. These people seek inventory at wholesale, distress, closeout, or otherwise low prices and then sell it on eBay at discount prices. In some cases, their overhead is so low that they can afford to sell at deep discounts even while purchasing their inventory through normal wholesale channels. Don't look at these sales efforts as amateurish retail operations. Many are serious businesses making big profits in this new marketplace.

Off Welfare

In the spring of 2000, President Clinton at a televised press conference claimed that by becoming eBay retailers, 20,000 people got off the welfare rolls. I wouldn't have believed it if I hadn't watched it myself. Where the president got his figures or whether they're accurate, I don't know. But there are over 700,000 people retailing on eBay, that is, auctioning merchandise routinely on eBay, whether part-time or full-time, as a source of steady income.

See my book *eBay Business the Smart Way, Third Edition* to get information on how to sell at retail on eBay.

What is a fly-by-night retail operation? Is it one where a one-person retailer purchases a huge inventory of a closeout item for a low price, spends two months selling it on eBay, goes on vacation for a month in Bermuda, and then returns to start the cycle over again? If so, I want to be a fly-by-night retailer. Indeed, eBay makes such special retail sales projects possible. Nothing requires that you have to have a store, warehouse, ecommerce website, or permanent address to be a reputable and honest retailer on eBay. You do need to diligently find the inventory, run the eBay auctions, fulfill the orders, and keep after your travel agent to make the appropriate hotel reservations in Bermuda.

Offline Auctioneers

Some auctioneers, such as estate sale auctioneers, look to eBay to extend their auction activities. Why not? For certain types of merchandise, they may get a higher price on eBay than they can in a normal auction offline. They make more money for their clients and more money for themselves in higher auctioneering fees. With a larger pool of buyers, they can sell for higher prices with potentially lower overhead costs.

Buyers Become Sellers

Many people routinely buy things for very deep discounts at local estate sales and garage sales and turn around and sell the merchandise on eBay for a profit. There are many other local sources where someone with an entrepreneurial inclination can buy at low prices and sell on eBay for a profit. For more inventory acquisition ideas, read *eBay Inventory the Smart Way*.

Offline auctioneers who cannot take advantage of eBay tend to be ones who handle real estate or goods that require a lot of paperwork. For instance, state laws may prevent real estate from being auctioned effectively on eBay. In addition, real estate requires a lot of paperwork just to get ready for auction.

Another example is the Sotheby's type of auction. Sotheby's is an old line auction firm with offices in London and New York. The items (works of art and the like) to be auctioned by Sotheby's are so valuable that they require that written bills of sale, receipts, certificates of authentication, and other documents be provided for review by prospective bidders before the auctions take place. These kinds of auctioneers can extend their operations to the Web but perhaps do best sticking to their traditional offline auctions. However, eBay provides a separate auction just for these types of auctioneers. See Chapter 25, which covers Live auctions.

Service Providers

No rule says you can't sell your services on eBay. However, this is a tough sell. Suppose you're an accountant seeking to pick up new tax clients. What do you sell? If you sell your services at a 30 percent savings from your usual fee of $120 per hour, you might find that you won't get much interest. Try a workable strategy. Offer a package of services at a reasonable price. For instance, you might offer to do a complete tax return for a $300 fee. For someone with a complex tax situation, that might look like a bargain (i.e., the kind of client you want to have for the long term). You might work inexpensively this year, but next year you can charge your regular fee. However, if that fee looks too expensive to someone, they probably don't need your services and will always be happy having their tax return prepared by H&R Block at a lower cost—and wouldn't be a good client for you.

Marketing your services requires imagination and experimentation to find a magic formula that works on eBay. In the meantime, if you don't achieve success in selling your specific packages of services, you may find success in picking up clients just by the act of auctioning your packages (see *eBay Business the Smart Way, Third Edition*).

Risk

As a seller, risk does not have to be a compelling concern. So long as you collect payment before you ship, you will protect yourself as well as you can in most circumstances. If you choose to ship before collecting payment, you will incur more risk.

Keep in mind, however, that in purchasing via a credit card a buyer can always ask the credit card company for a chargeback on an item with which he or she is dissatisfied. That creates the risk that you'll end up refunding the purchase price. I know of one retailer who not only lost in a chargeback contest (monitored by the bank), but the buyer didn't even return the merchandise. And the seller had a 99.8 percent positive feedback rating after thousands of eBay transactions.

But for sellers like him, chargebacks are rare. They're simply a cost of doing business. After all, offline retailers get chargebacks too.

Perhaps the biggest risk you run is a dissatisfied customer. An unhappy customer can make considerably more trouble than he or she is worth. You will do well to make a refund or do whatever it takes to keep a customer from fuming. You risk your eBay reputation. With this consideration in mind, the threat of a credit card chargeback becomes almost meaningless.

Transaction Overhead

eBay auctions have their overhead costs. Some you can pass on to the buyer, and some you can't.

eBay Fees

Although modest, eBay auction fees paid by the seller still constitute a significant expense, particularly for items of low value (see fee schedules, Tables 6.1 and 6.2, Chapter 6).

Merchant Credit Card Charges

As they do at most retail outlets, eBay buyers like to pay by credit card, and credit cards cost sellers money. Although you can get away without taking credit cards on eBay, serious sellers will want to offer credit card buying. Retailers need credit card merchant accounts to receive credit card payments. You may be able to get away with using special online payment services such as PayPal (explained in Chapter 20), which enables you to accept credit cards, in effect, without a merchant account. However, you must still pay PayPal a fee for credit card transactions completed through PayPal.

Shipping and Handling

Normally shipping and handling charges are a wash. The buyer pays them, and it costs that much to package and ship the item. Sometimes, however, sellers take a loss on shipping and handling.

The shipping cost is easy to determine. Look at the shipping rates. You will have a tougher time with the handling. That includes packaging materials and labor. It won't be accurate to the dime, but you have to calculate it anyway to avoid losing money on shipping and handling.

Profit?

Rather than a business chore, some sellers use shipping and handling as a business opportunity. You will see a lot of items selling for $8 on eBay with shipping and handling charged at another $6. Depending on the merchandise, a seller can make profit on the shipping and handling.

If you make an obvious profit on shipping and handling, though, you will irritate potential buyers and reduce sales. But you don't want to lose money on shipping and handling either, unless you plan to do so as part of your sales strategy.

One time I checked out buying a large $10 item. The various sellers wanted $9 for shipping and handling. Due to the unusual size of the item, that seemed a reasonable shipping cost. But when I bought from a particular seller at the *Buy It Now* price, I neglected to inquire about the shipping and handling cost. I was charged $27 for shipping and handling on a $10 item. Clearly the seller made about $18 on the shipping and handling, and there was nothing I could do about it. (Have you ever felt really dumb?) But that seller will never get my business again, and he missed a chance to get mentioned in one of my eBay books as a resource.

Sales Tax

Don't neglect to charge sales tax to customers in your state, particularly if you are an eBay retailer. You will need a sales tax license too. If you make only an occasional sale, your state sales tax laws may exempt you from collecting sales tax on incidental items but probably not on expensive items. The buyer pays the sales tax, and the seller collects it and pays it to the state sales tax agency.

Customer Service

As a retailer, selling via eBay is no different than selling offline. The same laws apply. The same ethical guidelines apply. You need to be ready to take care of your eBay customers just as you would have to take care of your customers offline. Failure to do so may adversely affect your reputation on eBay (covered in Chapter 8). It doesn't matter whether you sell one item or dozens of items. Customer service is the name of the game. Read Chapter 14 carefully.

Responsibility

An auction where the buyer buys something used or something new at a low price has an aura of finality. If a buyer responds with a complaint immediately after receiving the merchandise, a seller needs to respond diligently. If a buyer complains two months later, however, unlike Target or other national retailers, few would expect a seller to take care of the problem, unless the seller had provided a guarantee. Thus, few buyers expect sellers to provide as much long term customer service on eBay as in a physical retail store.

An Individual

If you sell only occasionally, a buyer will not expect much in the way of customer support. A buyer will expect the item to be as the seller represented and to be usable (unless represented otherwise). But if a buyer receives something that won't work after you represented that it was in working order, regardless of the lack of guarantee you need to make it right. Otherwise your reputation on eBay may suffer. People have high customer service expectations when purchasing on the Web, even though such expectations may not extend to the long term.

The point here is that along with the opportunities on eBay come responsibilities. Buyers expect reasonable customer service from all retailers, even occasional sellers. Although overall customer service responsibilities may be less over the long term on eBay than in other markets, this does not mean customers don't have expectations. Failure to meet expectations can negatively affect your reputation.

Opportunity

Look upon customer service as an opportunity rather than a responsibility. As in any other market, if you offer great customer service on eBay, you will get repeat business. Never make the mistake of thinking of eBay as a one-shot deal or as a temporary retail selling effort. You may sell on eBay for years to come. Perhaps decades.

Cost

If you're a retailer, customer service is part of your overhead. You have to expend the time, energy, and money to provide customer service or your employees do. It's not free.

Summary

eBay provides solid opportunities for sellers, whether individuals or businesses, to sell used goods for higher prices than the same goods might bring elsewhere. In the case of services, auctioning can even mean inexpensive advertising.

Another aspect of eBay is *retailing*. Retail selling on eBay provides huge opportunities to anyone who wants to provide good customer service and experiment with online auctions as a new type of retail outlet. Capital requirements and overhead remain low. The results can be spectacular. This is truly a prime opportunity for many people, and *eBay Business the Smart Way, Third Edition* devotes much discussion to this topic.

What About Non-Retail Businesses?

Can non-retail businesses sell on eBay? Sure. Non-retail businesses such as corporations, service providers, and the like certainly have the need to sell used equipment, overstocked supplies, and other items from time to time.

II

Using eBay

4

Learning eBay Basics

An online auction can be generated hundreds of different ways. eBay was not the first auction online. Perhaps not even in the first hundred. But eBay has constructed a digital mechanism that accommodates both the potential of the new Web medium and the psychology of human commerce. It is this subtle mechanism—the heart and soul of eBay—which has made eBay so successful. eBay does not merely translate a traditional auction into an online format. To understand eBay, you have to start with eBay values.

Community Values

eBay wisely sets what it calls *community values* that it expects to guide the behavior of everyone participating in eBay:

We believe people are basically good.

We believe everyone has something to contribute.

We believe that an honest, open environment can bring out the best in people.

We recognize and respect everyone as a unique individual.

We encourage you to treat others the way you want to be treated.

These statements of values set the tone for the conduct of auctions and the transactions that follow. Should you have trouble dealing with other people on eBay, it might be wise for you to review these guideline values. You might find in them some ideas on how to resolve your conflicts.

Values alone are not enough, however, and eBay requires you to sign its User Agreement, which sets forth the rules of the road for eBay members.

User Agreement

The following is not a reprint of the eBay User Agreement (at *Help, Rules and Policies, User Agreement*), which does change occasionally. Rather it's my impression of the high points. Your impression of the high points might be different from mine, and I urge you to take the time to read the Agreement in its entirety.

1. The information you provide for registration, bidding, or listing must be accurate and must not infringe on another's copyright or trademark.

2. eBay is only a venue. This means that eBay is only a place for people to conduct their transactions. It does not take part in the transactions.

3. You release eBay from liability for any claims arising out of the transactions in which you take part on eBay. You indemnify eBay from any claims by third parties arising out of your breach of the Agreement.

4. High bidders have an obligation to buy.

5. Sellers have an obligation to sell once a bid above the minimum (or the reserve) has been made.

6. Bid manipulation or interference is prohibited for both buyers and sellers.

7. You may not use any software that will adversely affect eBay's website.

Additionally, the User Agreement incorporates the following documents by reference:

Privacy Policy

Outage Policy

Board Usage Policy

Nonbinding Bid Policy

Listing Policy

Half.com Policy

Investigations Policy

Prohibited, Questionable, and Infringing Item Policy

Real Estate Policy

Unpaid Item Policy

Read the entire User Agreement and its incorporated documents yourself to get a full and complete understanding of what is expected of you and of the people with whom you will deal.

Trust

If you're new to eBay, you should now understand after reading the preceding two sections that trust lies at the heart of the eBay system. When you deal with someone a couple of thousand miles away, you have to trust them. Without trust, eBay would cease to function. Chapter 8 covers the feedback system, which builds the foundation for trust on eBay. Chapter 9 covers recourse against those who don't deserve your trust.

In 2004, eBay claimed that only one transaction in 10,000 was fraudulent. This indicates that fraudulent transactions are hardly a commerce-threatening number. According to eBay, about 1,300 employees worked on security and enforcement in 2004, showing eBay's commitment to making eBay and PayPal safe. Thus, one must conclude that trust does work when reinforced with the proper rules, regulations,

and enforcement. The remainder of this chapter covers the general
website mechanism that makes eBay bidding work. But don't lose
sight of the fact that the most important ingredient of the eBay magic
formula for success in buying, selling, and Web commerce is trust.

Navigation

The words at the top of the eBay home page are links that take you to
various parts of the eBay website (see Figure 4.1).

Figure 4.1 Page-top links. ©1995-2007 eBay Inc.

Site Map

Above the navigation bar perhaps the most important link is *site map*,
which takes you to the eBay Site Map, a longer list of links. This map
shows you everywhere you want to go on eBay, and you will find it
quite handy (see Figure 4.2). This is only one of many ways to navigate the eBay website, but it's one that gives you a great overview for a
variety of eBay activities.

Figure 4.2 Site Map list of links. ©1995-2007 eBay Inc.

I often use the Site Map rather than the other links on the top of the page to find where I want to go on eBay.

Buy

When you're ready to buy something specific, you need to find it first. You can go down the category tree until you find the proper category, or you can use the powerful eBay search mechanism.

Categories

The Buy link takes you to a list of browse categories. This is a more detailed list of categories than is on eBay's home page—a list that's quite useful.

There are over 65,000 categories to help you pinpoint what you're looking for. In any particularly category, you will usually find a variety of brands.

Search

In addition, a search entry is above the list, a box called My eBay at a Glance, a menu for buying resources, and more, all designed to make this a convenient starting point to buy something on eBay.

There are also links to search eBay Stores and to advanced searches, which come in handy if you would rather search than use the categories to find an item.

Advanced Search

The Advanced Search link on the eBay navigation menu is handy because it provides you with a comprehensive searching mechanism. You can search by item number, words, price range, categories, location of seller, bidder, and eBay Stores. In addition, you can do an "advanced" search with even more comprehensive criteria including "completed items." This will help you do sophisticated searches without using the Boolean operators covered later in the Search Aids subsection.

Any Page

You can search from almost any eBay page, using either the normal search or the advanced search. The Advanced Search link (link in the navigation bar) takes you to a search webpage that is more complete.

You will find it useful from time to time. See Figure 4.3.

Words

Searching on "words" (i.e., keywords) is undoubtedly the most popular type of search. The eBay search engine searches through the item titles (see Chapter 16). You can elect, however, to include the item descriptions in the search too. Consequently, if a seller had a "5 megapixel Sony digital camera" in the title and you searched for a Sony DSC-V1, you might miss the auction. If the seller included the model number in the auction ad and you elected to include the item description in your search, you would find the auction.

Figure 4.3 eBay Advanced Search page. ©1995-2007 eBay Inc.

Search Aids

You can use certain symbols to help your search. Don't worry about memorizing them, because you can search well without them. When you get frustrated and can't find what you're looking for, however, you might want to try them.

No symbol Lists all auctions with all the included words in the auction title in any order. Thus, *Shure microphone* will list all auctions with both *Shure* and *microphone* in the auction title.

Asterisk (*) Use as a wild card. For instance, a search on *mic** will list all auctions that include *mic*, *microphone*, or *microphones* in the title. It will undoubtedly list some other unexpected auctions too (e.g., Mickey as in Mickey Mouse).

Quotations (" ") Restricts the search to the words in the exact order quoted. For instance, a search on *"Shure microphone"* will list only the auctions where *Shure* and *microphone* are contiguous and in the same order. Thus, such a search would miss *Shure dynamic microphone* or *microphone Shure*.

Minus Sign (–) Does not include titles with the word after the minus. For example, *microphone –Shure* would include all auctions with *microphone* in the title except the ones that also had *Shure* in the title.

Parentheses ( ) Searches for both words in the parentheses. Hence, *(microphone,mic)* lists all auction titles with either *microphone* or *mic* in the title (uses no spaces between words, only commas). You can use with a word outside the parentheses. For example, *microphone (Shure,Sony)* will list all auctions with *microphone* and *Shure* or *Sony* in the title.

Keep in mind that the searches are not case-sensitive; that is, it doesn't matter whether you use upper- or lower-case letters in your words. Don't use common words like *the*, *and*, *an*, and *or*. The search engine ignores these words unless inside quotations. To keep your searches narrow and fast, search inside specific eBay categories, not in all of eBay.

Find Members

Another election is the Find Members search. It simplifies your search to find another eBay member whose eBay ID you know.

Favorite Searches

This election keeps a list of your searches that you want to use again and again. One click, and you can add a search. It even uses some artificial intelligence to automatically list your favorite categories. I discovered this feature while writing the third edition of this book and have found it very handy for searching for rare items over long periods (e.g., a certain brand or model of electronic equipment).

Don't Give Up

Having trouble finding something you need or want? Don't give up until you've tried searching several different ways. The eBay search engine is quite powerful and makes it as easy as possible to find items. Taking a little time now to learn to use the eBay *Search* feature will save you a lot of time in the future.

Sell

The Sell link takes you to the input form (*Sell Your Item*) where you enter an auction. See Chapter 6 for more information on entering auctions. The sublinks under Sell take you to useful information. However, this section isn't nearly as useful as it used to be in prior times. Therefore, I recommend using the Help section to find specific seller information.

My eBay

This link takes you directly to an accounting of everything you do on eBay. It's very handy, particularly when you lose track of what you've done or what you're doing. If you sell regularly, you will find this invaluable, at least until you choose to use a third-party auction management service. See more on *My eBay* later in this chapter.

Community

The Community section provides access to news sources, Discussion Boards, Chat, and even an Answer Center. You can read about the newest devices and procedures on eBay. You can get support, even live support. You can read stories about other eBay members. The eBay community is alive and dynamic.

Help

The Help section, or Help Center (link in the navigation bar), has information for rookies and old hands alike (see Figure 4.4).

The Help Center has a lot of useful information. Time spent learning how to use it will save you lots of time in the future. Especially take a look at the A-Z Index. Perhaps most helpful is the quick access to information for buyers and sellers and to eBay rules and policies.

The Selling section link takes you to plenty of information on auctioning items on eBay. Use it to get started, and then use it as a reference. Go *Help*, *Selling* for seller's information.

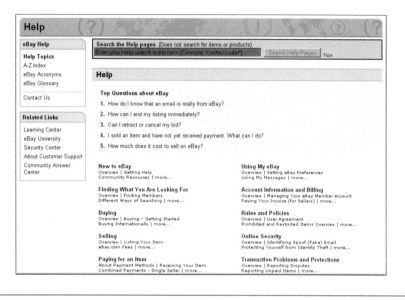

Figure 4.4 The Help window. ©1995-2007 eBay Inc.

The Buying section takes you to a substantial amount of information about bidding auctions on eBay. If you are primarily interested in being an eBay buyer, this is an excellent place to start learning about eBay. It's also a reference that you can use anytime you have any questions. Go *Help*, *Buying* for buyer's information.

Preparation

Starting with registration (discussed in the next section), you will be required to fill in forms on the eBay website for one thing or another. This section is a short tutorial to assist you.

If you have a broadband Internet connection, you simply fill out the form at your own pace while online. With broadband, you're always online until you turn off your computer. If you have a dial-up connection, however, you may feel uncomfortable spending a lot of time online. Perhaps your daughter wants to use the phone. Before filling out any eBay form, you can visit the form and save it. You can read it and even fill it in casually offline. In addition, with a few techniques, you can more effectively fill it in online.

Save As

Go *File, Save As* to save any webpage. This comes in handy for reading eBay information casually offline. After you save a webpage, remember where you saved it and what the file name is. Then access the webpage on your hard disk with your browser. With this technique, however, you cannot fill in the forms and submit them. You can simply read them leisurely offline.

Frozen Browser

After accessing an eBay form with your browser, simply go offline without closing the browser. The webpage will remain in the browser. You can fill in the forms at your leisure. Then get back online and submit the form. This usually works, but not always.

Paste In

You can write text almost anywhere (e.g., in a word processor), highlight it, copy it to the clipboard, and paste it into a form in a webpage. This technique enables you to read an eBay webpage (that includes forms) offline that you have saved. You can draft the input for the forms in a word processor offline. You can then get online, go to the forms, and copy and paste the text from the word processor into the eBay forms.

Registration

Registering to be a member of eBay is easy, fast, and free. Just fill in the registration form. You will choose an ID (your eBay name, which is a login name) and a password.

Welcome New Users

On the eBay home page you will notice the *register* link above the navigation bar. Click on the link to register. Under the navigation bar, there is another register link you can use too. Both of these are in small print.

There used to be a blue welcome banner that you couldn't miss containing the registration link, but now the register link is in the navigation bar.

Before You Register

eBay is a lifelong asset. Before you register, take the time to understand how it works. More importantly, take the time to understand what it means. If you register immediately, thinking that eBay is some sort of a game, that attitude may lead you to activities that are unacceptable to eBay and the eBay community. As a result, you may have your eBay rights terminated indefinitely. The loss of rights for the most dynamic and powerful commerce marketplace of the new century will undoubtedly be a loss that you will regret sooner or later. Read Chapters 8 and 9 to be sure that you know what you're getting into and what the consequences will be if you abuse the system.

Registering

To register, simply fill out the eBay online registration form. You'll know all the information requested except for your ID and password. You will have to dream those up.

Although you can navigate around the eBay website and even visit all the auctions, you cannot buy (bid) or sell anything unless you are a registered member. At least 200 million members have registered ahead of you. How difficult can it be?

ID (Log-In Name)

Pick an ID. Some people pick "cool" names such as *soaringeagle*. Others pick straightforward names like mine: *sinc* for Sinclair (sinclair wasn't available). Some use their email address so that people can always contact them. That, however, is no longer allowed.

Password

Don't take your passwords lightly anywhere, especially on eBay. If someone can find out your password, they can cause you much damage on eBay, financial and otherwise. Never use the same password for more than one website or service, and don't use short passwords (use a minimum of 10 characters). See Chapter 10 for more information about online security.

Registration Form

The registration is straightforward (see Figure 4.5). Choose your ID and password before you register so that you don't have to make a hurried decision. (Read Chapter 10 before you register.) The registration will ask you for the usual name, address, and phone number as well as some personal questions (optional).

Figure 4.5 Top part of the registration form. ©1995-2007 eBay Inc.

Confirmation

Click at the bottom of the form to submit your registration. Next you will have to wait. eBay will send you a confirmation number to your email address. You then take the confirmation number and follow the instructions (e.g., enter the confirmation number at the eBay website). The instructions will explain the remaining steps to complete your registration (e.g., enter ID and password). After you finish the registration process, you're legit. You can now buy and sell.

Using the Auctions

You can use four types of auctions for over 60,000 categories of goods and services.

Finding Items

The general categories are on the home page (see Figure 4.6). By clicking on a category, you get to lower-level categories (more specialized categories) as you go deeper and deeper into the category directory. The number of items currently up for auction are in parentheses after each category . Chances are you will find a low-level category that will fit well what you want to buy or sell.

For instance, a click on *Music* takes you to a level of subcategories in which a click on *CDs, Blues* takes you to auctions featuring blues music on CDs.

When you finally get to the category you want, you will see a list of auctions (see Figure 4.7). The listings you see are one-line each (eBay calls them "titles") from eBay auctions (a limit of 55 characters). This one line, created by the seller who entered the auction, should indicate exactly what is being auctioned.

Search

Once you have reached the lowest subcategory you can find, you can further refine your quest by using the search input near the top of the page on the left. For instance, suppose you have reached Blues and you see a long, multiple-page list of blues titles. But you're interested only in John Lee Hooker's music. Just type John Lee Hooker in the search input, and it will quickly and effectively search the Blues subcategory for John Lee Hooker's music.

The One-Line Title

As you read the list of titles looking for what you want, you'll find it helps quite a bit if the list is easily readable (see Figure 4.7). It helps you to skim through the listings quickly. Titles that have poor-quality typesetting (e.g., all caps) create an impediment to reading.

Sellers use poor-quality typesetting out of ignorance. They think that a technique like all caps will draw attention to their listing. Instead, it makes their listing less readable and creates a barrier to easily skimming the list. These sellers may think that if they are selling a Ford pickup truck, all caps will, by some magical attraction, draw in buyers who are looking for a Dodge van. Unfortunately, it doesn't work that way. Someone looking for a Dodge van will not buy a Ford pickup truck no matter what the title says and no matter how it is typeset. Instead, another person looking for the Ford pickup truck will have a more difficult time spotting the title because the title is all caps and more difficult to read.

The eye and brain together can easily pick out of a readable list whatever they look for. The more readable the list, the easier it is for you to find what you are looking for. The less readable the list, the more difficult it is to find what you are looking for. The one-line titles enable you to spot the auction of an item you are looking for. Then the specific auction page is just a click away.

Remember this when, as a seller, you enter your auction ad.

Figure 4.6 Categories on the eBay home and Buy pages. ©1995-2007 eBay Inc.

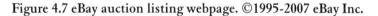

Figure 4.7 eBay auction listing webpage. ©1995-2007 eBay Inc.

Individual Auctions

Click on a title, and you will go to that auction. The auction is one webpage featuring one auction item. It has:

1. Standard information at the top

2. An auction ad (*Description*) created by the seller in the middle of the page

3. A place to bid at the bottom

For bidders, Chapter 5 covers the standard information and the bidding section. For sellers, Chapter 16 covers creating eBay auction ads.

Auctioning

The four types of eBay auctions provide you some flexibility for your auctioning activities.

Normal

The normal auction is similar to a silent auction. The seller sets a minimum bid to start things off. Some sellers set the minimum bid low, some set it high. If it's low, it will probably be bid up to market value. If it's high, it will probably be bid up to market value, too. If the minimum is over market value, it's unlikely to get any bids at all. The normal auction is for one item (or package) only.

Reserve

A reserve is like a secret minimum. You can still use a minimum bid just as in a normal auction, but the reserve is the secret minimum. As soon as the reserve has been exceeded by the current high bidder (assuming it ever is exceeded), eBay publishes the fact that the reserve has been met. It doesn't make sense to use a reserve unless the reserve amount is higher than the minimum bid. The reserve auction is for one item (or package) only. If no bidders bid the reserve amount or higher, the seller does not have to sell the item.

Dutch

The Dutch auction is for multiple identical items. Bidders bid in the normal way, specifying how many of the identical items they are bidding on. The top bidders win the auction but pay only the bid of the lowest successful bidder. For instance, suppose you auction five identical new toasters. The bids follow in Table 4.1:

Table 4.1 Bids on Five New Toasters at a Dutch Auction

Alias	Number of Toasters	Bid ($)
SinkLily	1	34
PunkyPete	1	33
LiveFive	2	32
LaxTrainer	1	31
ByNite	2	29
StoneRich	1	27
RainMore	4	26

The bids of SinkLily, PunkyPete, LiveFive, and LaxTrainer take all five toasters. All the winning bidders pay only $31 each for the toasters, the lowest bid of a successful bidder (i.e., LaxTrainer's bid). The seller sets the minimum bid, but no reserve is allowed in a Dutch auction. This type of auction used to be popular for the ongoing selling of popular mass products. However, eBay Stores provide a better place now for ongoing selling of such products. Consequently, Dutch auctions are no longer used by sellers as much as before the advent of eBay Stores.

Private

Anyone can bid at a private auction. What makes it private? The auction display keeps the bidders' identities secret. Of course, eBay notifies the seller of the winning bidder's identity, but that's the only bidder that even the seller will know. Private auctions are not widely used, but occasionally you will see one.

Comparison

The four types of auctions are briefly compared in Table 4.2, showing the advantages and disadvantages of each.

Table 4.2 Four Auction Types

Type	Advantages	Disadvantages
Normal	Lets market set price	No minimum guaranteed price (except minimum bid)
Reserve	Minimum guaranteed price (unpublished)	Item may not sell
Dutch	Can sell numerous identical items at once	If minimum price too high, no bids is a possibility
Private	For bidders who want anonymity	Fewer potential bidders

Restricted Access

This is not a separate type of auction. It's a restricted category. The only restricted auction currently is adult erotica. eBay attempts to ensure that anyone accessing this category is 18 or older by requiring a credit card number prior to access.

Auction Devices

There are several auction devices that modify the auction process. Because eBay is really a "marketplace" rather than an "auction," these devices modify the auction process to give it flexibility.

Fixed Price

One can sell on eBay with a fixed price. It's called the *Buy It Now* price. The seller doesn't have to set or sell at a Buy It Now price, but this device is available to those sellers who desire to use it.

If a buyer elects to buy and pay the Buy It Now price, the auction is instantly over. If the bidding goes above the Buy It Now price, the Buy It Now option ceases to exist.

Best Offer

This is eBay's newest bidding device. A seller can offer it, or not. If a seller offers it, a buyer can make a *Best Offer* only once during the auction. The seller has two days to accept or reject the offer. If the seller ignores the offer for two days, it's the same as a rejection.

If a buyer makes a Best Offer, the buyer is not otherwise prohibited from bidding in the normal way in the auction. One thing for buyers to remember is that when you make a Best Offer, the offer is in limbo for up to two days. You are stuck waiting to hear from the seller.

Advertising

Don't overlook the capability to advertise your auction item. There is an advertising section built into each auction webpage. All you have to do is to use it effectively is provide information. See Chapter 16 for further details.

Duration

Auctions run for three, five, seven, or ten days. They end exactly at the same time of day as they started. For example, a three-day auction that starts at 7:47 PM on Monday night ends at 7:47 PM on Thursday night. A seven-day auction starts and ends on the same day, same time. Consequently, you choose when you want your auction to end by entering it at the requisite time three, five, seven, or ten days earlier.

Prohibited Auctions

eBay has rules prohibiting certain things from being sold on eBay. The rules make sense, and eBay adds to the forbidden items as experience dictates. The list below includes some, but not all, of the items prohibited:

- Alcohol
- Child pornography
- Current catalogs
- Counterfeit items
- Securities (e.g., stocks and bonds)
- Human body parts
- Credit cards
- Drugs
- Prescription drugs
- Tobacco
- Forged autographs
- Embargoed goods
- Firearms and fireworks
- Locksmith paraphernalia
- Animals and wildlife products
- TV descramblers
- Surveillance equipment
- Government IDs and badges
- Stolen merchandise
- Lottery tickets
- Postage meters
- Items that infringe on a copyright or trademark such as Beta software, recorded media, OEM software, unauthorized replicas, and promotional items.

For an updated list, go to the Help Center and start with eBay Policies.

In addition, eBay treats some items as questionable. They are not prohibited absolutely, but you will have to be careful that you don't break any rules by selling them. A partial list of items includes:

- Used medical equipment
- Contracts
- Tickets
- Weapons and knives
- Autographed items
- Food
- Batteries
- Used clothing
- Offensive materials
- Artifacts
- Freon
- Pre-sale listings
- Police-related items
- Hazardous materials
- International transactions

If something on these lists catches your attention, you need to investigate the details. You need to seek out the reasons for and the degree of prohibition of each item on the lists that may affect your selling efforts.

The prohibition against infringing materials bears some additional comment. They include copyrighted items such as copies of music, movies, television shows, software, written works, games, photographs, artwork, images, and promotional items. But infringement is more complex than just stating a simple list of banned copies, and you will do well to read what eBay has to say about infringement, or potential infringement, if there is any possibility at all that you might be auctioning items for which this might be an issue.

VeRO

If you are an owner of copyrights—manifested in copyrighted materials—and sellers are auctioning infringing copies of your works on eBay, you can join the Verified Rights Owner (VeRO) program. This enables you to work together with eBay to curtail the infringing sales. Software developers and recorded music companies are active VeRO program members.

Gallery

eBay also presents auctions in a way different from just a list of one-line titles. It presents auctions in a photo gallery. Near the top of the listing page look for the double link *List View | Picture Gallery*. Click on Picture Gallery. This only applies, of course, to auctions that include a photograph and have been placed in the Gallery. If anything, the Gallery points out how important text is (which it does not have much of) in identifying items that people seek to purchase. Nonetheless, the Gallery is another place for your item to be displayed. But you can't get there without a photograph in your auction ad.

Keep in mind that, for certain items, looking at photographs is the best way to find what you're looking for. For instance, you might find it more convenient to look at Japanese prints in the Gallery than to hunt them down in individual auctions.

To have your auction listing (together with a photograph) included in the Gallery costs a little extra, but if your item justifies such a display, the Gallery may help you sell it.

After the Auction

eBay is not a party to the auctions. It is up to you as either buyer or seller to contact the other party to consummate the transaction. As a buyer (high bidder), I sometimes have an urgent need for the merchandise. Therefore, I contact the seller by email immediately to ask about exact payment, mailing address, etc.

However, contacting an eBay retailer can affect their follow-up system. Some sellers look upon unsolicited communications from buyers as an unnecessary interference with their auction management systems. Regardless, I still contact a seller when I need an item urgently.

Otherwise I wait for the seller's email.

Pay Immediately

One way to avoid communication as a buyer is to pay immediately. eBay's checkout is much improved today, and there's no reason not to use it. When you win an auction, go immediately to the eBay checkout and pay. You're done. The only further action required is for the seller to ship the item.

As a seller, you want to send a communication as soon as possible to the high bidder after an auction. This is especially important if you run many auctions. You need an email follow-up system that works so well that you discourage unsolicited email messages from buyers. Individual email from customers is time-consuming to handle, inefficient, and unprofitable, particularly for transactions involving inexpensive items. Naturally, when a problem arises, you are happy to get it sorted out by communicating with your customers. But otherwise, you don't have the time and energy to exchange email with them any more than is necessary.

Communication Management

Note that both eBay and most auction management services send email to the buyer immediately after the auction concludes. The official eBay notice is just background noise and will not keep a buyer from contacting the seller. However, the seller can elect to send the buyer an additional invoice via eBay. If the seller does so immediately after the auction, the invoice will keep the buyer from making an unnecessary communication. Best of all is an auction management service which will automatically and immediately send the buyer an invoice. Thus, the buyer will presumably not make any unnecessary communication to seller.

Escrow Services

eBay no longer provides escrow services. It recommends Escrow.com at *http://www.escrow.com*. (You can go to the Fraud Information Center at Escrow.com to learn how to avoid fraudlent escrow services.)

You must go through a series of steps, which Escrow.com spells out, to complete your escrow. Escrow.com will charge you 3.25 percent on the first $5,000 of value with a minimum of $25; $162.5 + 0.26 percent on the next $20,000 up to $25,000; and 0.89 percent over $25,000. If the buyer uses a credit card for payment, the fees go up substantially. This is not inexpensive, but it's worth it to a buyer who writes a big check.

What about sellers? Is it worth it? My position has always been that it is, indeed, worth it to sellers. If a buyer accepts an item in escrow, it's difficult for that buyer to come back later and claim that the merchandise is unacceptable. He or she has already accepted it. That's a decided benefit to sellers. Therefore, I believe that buyers and sellers should split the escrow fees. Nonetheless, many sellers disagree with me, as you might guess.

eBay recommends an escrow closing for transactions over $500. Everyone has their own opinion about this threshold amount, and the opinions of the buyer and seller will dictate the amount. Quite frankly, escrow closings are more trouble for sellers, and most sellers would like to see a higher threshold than $500. As a seller, one way to make yourself look good but raise the threshold is to put your escrow policy in your auction ad boilerplate. For example:

> No escrow closings acceptable for auctioned items with a sales price under $2,000.

A buyer of a $1,300 item might be disappointed, but he or she will still get a comfortable feeling that you don't make a blanket prohibition of escrow closings. A seller who does make a blanket prohibition of escrow closings is suspect and will lose some potential bidders.

Escrow Fraud

If you use an escrow company other than Escrow.com, be very careful that it is legitimate. Escrow fraud is running rampant on the Web. Websites that have tried to keep up lists of fraudlent online escrow services have given up. The lists become too long and too incomplete, in other words too much work to maintain. Try ScamFraudAlert for a user maintained website (*http://www.scamfraudalert.com*). And never use an escrow service recommended by the seller.

Wanted Page

Where do buyers without an auction to bid on go for assistance? If you can't find something you want up for auction, go to an appropriate Discussion Board and ask the Board participants. They can be helpful. Otherwise, go *Want It Now* on the eBay home page where eBay provides a wanted category with wanted postings. A buyer can post a wanted notice free. This is a relatively new feature for eBay (see Chapter 29). It shut down its wanted postings a few years ago, and this is a revival. Sellers can browse the wanted postings to find buyers.

Researching an eBay User

You can research another user's feedback (see Chapter 8 regarding analyzing a user's feedback). Go *Advanced Search, Find a Member, Feedback Profile*. You will need the user's ID.

You can also research another user's history of aliases and email addresses or contact information (in this case, eBay notifies the user). This type of search can provide you with a wealth of information on another eBay user for evaluating a seller or buyer or for making a transaction work.

Researching Market Value

Because market value is so important to success on eBay and because research is so important to determining market value, use the following list of sources to find the market value of items. Keep in mind that obtaining list prices is a good place to start in determining the used value of manufactured items.

Catalogs Look through printed catalogs and online catalogs of offline retailers and manufacturers.

eCommerce Look through the online catalogs of retail businesses that exist only online.

Completed Auctions You can access completed auctions on eBay where they are archived for a few weeks. You will find the winning bid amounts.

Shop Get in your car and go shopping.

Magazines Read specialty magazines. Many collectibles magazines feature compilations of values, and all specialty magazines have retail ads, many of which feature prices.

Manufacturers Go to manufacturers' websites. Often suggested retail prices are posted.

Books The library has reference books that are price guides. They are usually old news but still may be useful.

Appraisers Chat with an appraiser who knows market values.

Dealers Chat with a dealer who knows the market well.

eBay Resources Go *Community* on the navigation bar and try the following: (1) specialty Chat sessions where you can get advice from eBay retail experts; (2) Discussion Boards where you can also get advice.

Web Search Engines Use Google to look up items, and you will get to some of the sources mentioned earlier. It's a quick and efficient way to research.

Research—meaning the determination of market value—is the one most effective technique for success on eBay for both buyers and sellers. How do you know what to do unless you know the market value?

Completed Items

If you go through the categories and subcategories until you narrow down your quest for an item to a list of auctions, you can reach the eBay archives by doing a special search.

For instance, suppose you go *Jewelry & Watches*, *Jewelry Boxes & Supplies*, *Jewelry Boxes* and find 5900 items. You're looking for Lady Buxton jewelry boxes. In the search entry, type "buxton" and check the *in titles and descriptions* check box. You will get a more narrow selection of auction listings as a result of this search. In addition, look for *Search Options*, check *Completed listings*, and then click on *Show* Items.

You will get several weeks of completed auctions with winning bid amounts displayed. These are "comparables" for your appraisal purposes.

Representing Yourself

As you will read in Chapter 8, your reputation on eBay generates the trust you need to make successful transactions. If your reputation fails—due to your unfair or dishonest behavior—you will have a difficult time getting anyone to do business with you. You always want to be conscious of how you treat other people and be careful that you don't violate any eBay rules.

Feedback System

You can rate other eBay members with positive, neutral, or negative feedback and also make comments. Such ratings, however, are limited to transactions; that is, buyers and sellers rate each other.

There is no requirement that buyers and sellers rate each other for each transaction, but many do. So, there are plenty of ratings on each active member (except rookies) to establish a reputation. The feedback system works well. A person can't treat other people unfairly or with abuse without incurring negative feedback.

If One Doesn't Behave

The positive feedback ratings (for each positive rating you get a +1) and negative ratings (for each negative rating you get a −1) are added. If a person gets to a rating of −4, eBay automatically suspends his or her membership.

About Me

The feedback *comments* tend to be valuable when they are negative (assuming they provide the facts) and useless when they are positive (mostly ridiculous praise), although the *ratings* are always valuable. However, eBay gives you a place to tell people something about yourself. You can make an entry in *About Me*, and everyone can read it. If you do make an About Me entry, an About Me icon goes next to your name so that people will know that your information exists to be read. This eBay device gives you a chance to tell your story and increase your credibility.

If you sell regularly on eBay, your About Me webpage provides you with an opportunity to advertise. You can even include a link to your ecommerce website if you have one.

You can't be sure about trusting someone based on his or her About Me profile, but it's significant information that together with other information (e.g., feedback) you can use to make an reasonably informed judgment.

Be Prepared

Before you start your About Me entry, prepare your information ahead of time offline. Look at a dozen or more of other people's About Me presentations and decide how you want yours to read. Write the information. Find a graphic you want to include (e.g., a digital photograph of yourself). Then log onto eBay and go *Help, A-Z Index, A, About Me Pages: Creating.* You will eventually get to a handy form to fill in. Copy and paste the information you have prepared into the inputs in the form. Your photograph, if you use one, will have to be available on the Web somewhere (see Chapter 23), and you put the URL of your photograph in the appropriate input in the About Me form.

Create A Webpage

If you are not satisfied with what you can enter into the form casually, create a webpage about yourself instead. Submit the webpage into the input in the form. Remember to copy only the portion of the webpage between the *<body> </body>* markups when you copy and paste. (Do this the same way as when you submit the template for advertising as outlined in Chapter 16, or as covered in Appendix IV in regard to using a Web authoring program.) In other words, cut off the top and bottom of the webpage.

Submitting a Webpage

Because Chapters 16 and Appendix IV show you the general means of submitting a webpage for an input in a Web form, this chapter does not duplicate such information. You can also use the HTML tutorial in Appendix V to learn some basic HTML markups.

Edit

Don't worry about making your About Me perfect the first time. You can always go back and edit it or completely revise it.

Security

eBay has started a security program—ID Verify—wherein they check a member's application against the facts in an Equifax Secure, Inc., database to ascertain that a person is really who he says he is. It requires that a person submit via secured transmission (Secure Sockets Layer or SSL—built into Web browsers) certain personal information and a $5 fee. *This program is optional.* It is an excellent program that all honest and forthright eBay citizens should embrace. It provides an extra measure of protection against fraud and other criminal behavior. Although it's a voluntary program, eBay members can make it a compulsory program, in effect, by refusing to deal with anyone who isn't verified. That, of course, will not happen. Nonetheless, you can refuse and should refuse to deal with anyone for large transactions whose ID is not verified. This is part of eBay's SafeHarbor program to ensure that eBay is a safe place to do business.

Not a Credit Check

The eBay Equifax check is not a credit check. It's just a check to verify name, address, and other basic data.

The additional security fostered by the ID Verify program should encourage the growth of the membership and the additional participation of the members in eBay auctions, particularly auctions for more expensive items.

Naturally, people who are properly identified are more likely to behave well (i.e., be trustworthy). You would like to deal with people whose identities have been verified, and that works both ways. Buyers would like to know that sellers are who they say they are. After all, buyers are making payment and trusting that sellers will send the merchandise. Sellers would like to know that buyers are who they say they are. Invariably, sellers have problems with bogus bidding by people who hide behind their unverified eBay IDs. Accommodate both buyers and sellers. Have your ID verified.

ID Verify

To have your ID verified, go *Help, Rules and Policies, Identity, Identity: Overview, ID Verify.* The process takes you through a questionnaire that includes questions about your affairs that only you and Equifax would know. You are later notified as to whether you have been approved (verified).

This provides more assurance to other parties that you are unlikely to be a con artist. Most criminals do not want their true identities known. Unfortunately, for some reason this verification has not caught on. You can make it more popular—and perhaps eventually compulsory—by having your ID verified.

eBay does require ID Verify for buyers for transactions over $15,000. I believe this threshold should be lowered considerably ($500?) and applied to sellers as well. eBay has matured into an important national marketplace. eBay is no longer a place for con artists or miscreants who want to play games. ID Verify will go a long way toward reducing the number of both.

eBay requires a credit card or bank account from sellers. This is a sort of verification process, even though its purpose ostensibly is to ensure payment to eBay for seller's fees. If eBay cannot verify your credit card or bank account for some reason, you will have to use the ID Verify process instead in order to be permitted to sell on eBay.

Should you be afraid of the ID Verify process? My experience was that I didn't have to give any information that Equifax didn't already know. Giving your Social Security number is optional (and I didn't give mine), but, in any event, Equifax undoubtedly already knows it.

If you are a regular eBay user, either buyer or seller, I strongly recommend that you get ID Verify and require it of the other eBay users with whom you deal, particularly on high-dollar auctions. Widespread use of ID Verify will reduce the risk in the eBay marketplace for both buyers and sellers.

PayPal Verification

PayPal requires verification for you to become a PayPal member. This is a feature of membership that makes PayPal a safe payment system. There are various levels of verification, and you should opt for at least one level above the normal in order to increase your credibility. See Chapter 20 for more information on PayPal.

Privacy

An objection can be raised that ID Verify is an invasion of privacy—your privacy—by eBay. Indeed, you do have to trust eBay when you give bits of personal information. In my opinion, eBay has earned your trust, although everyone must remain alert to be sure it doesn't abuse your trust in any way. The risk of abuse compared to the advantage of greater security seems to be a risk worth taking.

Quality of Protection

A verification merely helps ascertain that a person is who he says he is. But John Larkspur (a name I made up) can be who he says he is and still be a Web ecommerce criminal. Therefore, all a verification does is identify a person.

I suppose if you start chasing a Web ecommerce criminal for recovery of stolen funds, it's best to know who he or she is. Presumably without the verification it might be difficult to know the true identity of the person you want to chase. But knowing the true identity of someone is no guarantee that you will catch them or recover stolen funds. In the final analysis, you have to rely on other indices of trust to do business with a person on the Web.

That's why the eBay feedback system is so valuable. It provides you with an eBay member's reputation. That, together with verification, is perhaps better protection than you get offline for dealing with someone you don't know.

By-Product

A by-product of the eBay verification and feedback system may be the use of eBay as a general commerce reference. In other words, suppose you want to do some business with an appliance dealer (either on or off the Web) that may involve a certain degree of trust (e.g., installment sale). The dealer can run a credit check on you. But perhaps that's not enough. The dealer can also look up your feedback on eBay. If you're verified, perhaps the dealer will have even more confidence that you are who you say you are. Will your ID on eBay be requested on credit applications in the future? That's something to think about.

Community

eBay is a community of people who are drawn together to take part in ecommerce. Many are just occasional community members, but others pursue communicating with other eBayers routinely for learning and even socializing. If you are one of those who uses eBay often, you may be interested in one of the communities supported by eBay.

Chat

To visit Chat on the eBay website, go *Community, Chat Rooms*. You will find a variety of chat rooms where people talk in real time with others currently signed into the chat room. The "talk" is in writing and appears on the chat board.

You can also use Discussion Boards (aka forums, mailing lists, discussion groups) to communicate with other eBay members (not in real time). Go *Community, Discussion Boards* to find a variety of online Boards. The Boards discuss various aspects of eBay and other topics. If you want more specific information regarding buying and selling, eBay also features Boards on specific ecommerce topics. If you deal in certain types of goods, eBay may sponsor a Discussion Board that has created a community in regard to such goods. For instance, there are Boards on jewelry, toys, and photography, to name a few.

And don't overlook the International Trading Board. It can help you expand your sales to other countries. See Chapter 30 for more information on selling abroad.

If you need help, need to understand a certain process, or want to help others, you can participate in the Answer Center, which covers a variety of topics regarding eBay operations. Go *Community, Answer Center*.

When you're having trouble contacting another eBay member, you can go to the Emergency Contact chat room and get some assistance. This is handy after the seller gets your check for $125 and is suddenly out of touch.

Finally, you can participate in a Workshop Board, a temporary Board on a very specific topic. You can even read past Workshop Boards. This is a type of Web-based training.

And that's not all. There are news, event schedules, and stories about eBay members all under *Community* on the navigation bar.

Help

It cannot be overemphasized that participating in an eBay online community when you need help can be very productive. You can return again and again as you run across new problems. Of course, don't forget that someday it will be your turn to give help instead of get it.

Is a Community for You?

Many of us do not have enough interest in the goods we use to join a community (unless we are professionals or collectors). Nonetheless, communities can be meaningful. As a buyer, you can join a community, albeit temporarily, to seek advice for making a purchase. Have your eye on a 30-year-old Nikon 300mm telephoto lens on auction and want to find out if you can use it on your 15-year-old Nikon camera body? Join the Photography Board and ask the experts. While you're there, have some good conversations, make some new friends, and enjoy the community in addition to getting the information you need.

As a seller, your participation in specialty Boards will put you in touch with prospective customers and increase your credibility. It's a natural for promoting your business so long as you don't practice blatant commercialism. Promote yourself and your business very subtly. Be helpful, be friendly, and give advice (based on your expertise as a retailer or user). People will recognize your contribution and remember you favorably.

Not Free

Being a member of an eBay community does not come free. If you participate regularly, it will take a lot of your time.

Education

Take advantage of eBay's user tutorials. Look for them via *Site Map*, *Resources*, *Learning Center*. That will take you to the eBay Learning Center where tons of fun and education await you. If you haven't used eBay before, it will help you to get going. In addition, you can attend eBay University in a city near you as eBay goes on the road.

Visits to the Auctionbytes (*http://auctionbytes.com*) website will keep you up to date on a host of eBay-related topics. Sign up for the two free email newsletters about online auctions. Ira Steiner, the editor and publisher, does a nice job of producing high-quality information.

Attend eBay Live, the annual eBay conference, which features three days of enlightening seminars and a great opportunity to meet other eBay members. In June 2007 it will be in Boston, Massashusetts. Check the eBay website for information on the conference.

eBay Customer Service

eBay seems a little weak in customer service for eBay users. True, it has a wide range of assistance features well presented. If, however, you have a special problem to solve, it's tough to find a place to get assistance. For instance, I signed up for ID Verify, went through the procedure, and was approved. Nonetheless, nowhere was it indicated that I had ID Verify. It's supposed to be noted with a special icon in your feedback section. (Eventually, many days later, it appeared.)

When I checked my feedback, not only was the ID Verify icon missing but I had at least four positive feedbacks ratings that were not mine. (They could have been negative feedback!) When I tried to get the mess straightened out, I spent a considerable amount of time trying to find where to contact eBay about these problems. Finally, I found a place to email eBay buried in a suggestion box somewhere on the site map. In other words, eBay doesn't encourage custom handling of user problems. Unfortunately, sometimes custom handling is the only way to solve a problem.

In answer to my email, eBay told me that the ID Verify icon would be added to my eBay persona immediately but that it was my problem to get the erroneously filed feedback straightened out. Since the erroneous feedback is positive, I had no incentive to correct it. Were it negative, I would have been incensed over eBay's unwillingness to take any responsibility for showing someone else's feedback ratings in my profile.

One strategy for finding the proper place to go for getting help when you need it is to consult the Answer Center. Go *Community Answer Center.* Ask a question and get an answer from a fellow eBay member.

My eBay

eBay is a great marketplace for buying and selling, and it does provide a variety of online customer service devices mentioned throughout this book. A very useful one is *My eBay*. Note that the link *My eBay* is found on the navigation bar on every eBay page.

My eBay is a customer service device that features the following:

- Bidding record
- Watch list
- Selling record
- Feedback record
- Account status
- Favorite categories and searches list
- Preferences
- And more

The records of your bidding and selling show what you've done on eBay. The watch list shows the auctions you've marked to watch.

Watching

In the basic information on each auction page, you will find a link labeled *watch this item*. You can put any auction on your "watch" list. You can see your watch list in *My eBay*. The list helps you keep track of items in which you're interested but have not yet bid on. When an auction's bidding starts to look interesting, you can join the bidding.

The recent feedback shows a partial record of your feedback. The account status shows how much, if anything, you have on deposit with eBay to pay your auction fees. It also can show a record of all your fees paid (going back to your first day, if you're willing to wait for the eBay database to crank out archived data). The favorites list gives you quick access to your favorite categories and saves you some navigation time. Try it. If you're a heavy eBay user, it can save a lot of time.

The sign-in preferences enable you to stay signed in. *This is especially valuable for automatically entering your ID and password for bidding; it saves time in bidding contests during the final minutes of an auction.*

Thus, *My eBay* provides you with convenient one-stop service to review your activities on eBay and even set up navigation and bidding shortcuts. Try the *My eBay* link over the navigation bar. You may find it's just what you've been looking for.

Anywhere

If your question is, Where can I access eBay? the answer is, Anywhere! Indeed, eBay even supports portable wireless devices including:

- WAP (wireless application protocol) cell phones
- Pagers
- PDAs (personal digital assistants)

Go *Site Map, Buying Resources, Wireless* (see Figure 4.8). This gives you the opportunity to keep up with your eBay commerce even when you're away from your home or your job. eBay's support for these technologies is through the normal vendors such as AT&T and Sprint.

Support for these devices means, of course, that as a buyer you never have to miss a final-hour bidding competition, nor as a seller will you miss answering questions by potential bidders in a timely manner.

Charity

Yes, eBay even provides you with opportunities for charity. Go *Giving Works* on the eBay home page. You will find information for buyers, sellers, and non-profit organizations.

eBay Evolves

eBay constantly experiments with everything on its website. Some things work, and some things don't. And eBay moves on. For every edition of this book, I have to make many changes to this chapter. Consequently, you are certain to find much of the information and the navigation different from that explained in this chapter when you use eBay. Nonetheless, this chapter provides you with a good overview to get you off to a good start in understanding and using eBay.

Summary

eBay works well and is easy to use as this chapter demonstrates. If you have difficulty getting started, you can get plenty of help. Once you get rolling, you can get even more help. Amazingly, almost everything discussed in this chapter is free. What a deal!

Trust is the foundation of the eBay system. Once you understand that and come to have confidence in eBay, you will feel free to sell or bid and then complete eBay transactions. But you must still be wary to protect yourself, and eBay provides some devices that you can use to do so.

Yes, the system does have some complexity. Much of the complexity, however, addresses problems you may never have. So, learn the basics, but at least skim over some of the exotic features; you'll know they're there when you need them.

Figure 4.8 eBay Anywhere. ©1995-2007 eBay Inc.

5

Buying

Bidding is where the fun is. It's a kick to bid and win, particularly when you have some competition. But the fun is the frosting on the cake for most people. Most people seek to purchase an item because it's at a good price or because they can't find it elsewhere. And no matter how much fun it is, it's also serious business just as any commercial transaction is serious business. Hence, enjoy your bidding, but don't lose sight of the fact that the winning bidder is obligated to buy the item auctioned.

Bidding

There is a string of steps to go through to bid on an auction. The first step is finding something to bid on.

Finding What You're Looking For

You can use the eBay auction categories, which are organized into a tree, starting on the home page. This is a good way to find what you are looking for and a good way to learn about eBay. The eBay search

71

mechanism is quite useful too.

Categories

Follow the categories from the most general on the eBay home page (or Buy page) to the more specific (see Figure 5.1). When you get as far as you can go, look at the listings. You will find some items that you are looking for.

For instance, to get to microphones, start with *Musical Instruments* on the eBay home page. Then select *Pro Audio*, *Microphones*, *Wired Microphones*. That will provide you with a listing of microphones. In many cases, you may find more items than you want to look through. You can narrow the search even further.

Searches in Categories

Once you get to a listing that contains the item you are looking for (e.g., wired microphones – see Figure 5.2), you can plug a keyword into the search input and narrow the listings even more. For instance, while at the *Wired Microphones* auction listing page, input *Shure*. Click on Search (see Figure 5.3).

You will get a new listing of auctions that will be all Shure microphones, or, to be more accurate, all the auctions in the listing will have *Shure* in the title (1,021 Shure microphone auctions the day I tried this search).

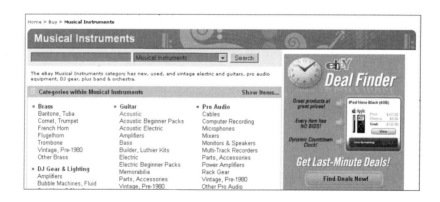

Figure 5.1 The eBay category *Musical Instruments*. ©1995-2007 eBay Inc.

Figure 5.2 Use the categories to narrow the listings. ©1995-2007 eBay Inc.

Figure 5.3 Narrow your results by using the search. ©1995-2007 eBay Inc.

You can refine your list with the search function as much as you want to. You don't necessarily have to do it in steps. Try *Shure new* to view only auctions that offer new Shure microphones.

Pure Searches

You don't have to begin with categories. You can use the eBay search engine right from the start. Go to the search entry in the upper right-hand corner, enter a keyword (search word), and click on the *Search* button. If you use the proper keywords, this works great.

eBay Search Tips

Sometimes the keywords for searches are obvious. Sometimes you have to figure out the not so obvious. And sometimes more than one keyword works. For instance, a microphone is also a *mic*. If you used *Shure mic* as the keyword in a search, you got 353 auctions. If you used *Shure microphone*, you got 1,044 auctions.

Misspellings

Sellers misspell words. Sometimes if you try some misspellings, you can find items that don't get much traffic specifically due to the misspelling. For instance, if someone misspelled *mic* as *mike*, they would have gotten only 6 microphones listed out of a total of 1,044 Shure microphones. If you can find items that are misspelled, you may find an auction with very little bidding competition. That means the item is likely to go for a low price.

Plurals

It used to be that plurals made a difference in eBay searches. Apparently eBay fixed this incongruity in its search engine. Today singulars and plurals get the same results.

Advanced Searches

Click on the *Advanced Search* link. You can make very specific searches based on a number of criteria.

Reminder

There's a more detailed explanation of pure searching in Chapter 4, which covers advanced searching techniques.

eBay Stores

Don't forget eBay Stores. You can search eBay Stores as well as eBay auctions. Go *Buy*, *Other Ways to Browse*, *eBay Stores*. Stores offer you fixed-price items for which you don't bid. You just pay your money to buy instantly. (eBay Stores is separate from eBay auctions.)

Reading the Listing

Many sellers, surprisingly, can adequately specify what an item is in 55 characters. Consequently, when you skim the list of auctions, you will be able to easily spot what you are looking for. Only the poor typesetting and bizarre titles will impede you. Auctions with photographs will have a picture icon beside the title.

New

You can have the listing arranged a variety of ways (e.g., ascending or descending based on closing date). New auctions have a new icon beside them. If you see the new icon at the top of the listing, you will know that the auction listing is arranged in descending order. However, the default is ascending order (oldest auctions first).

Reading the Auction

When you click on an auction title, the first thing you see is the basic information on the auction (see Figure 5.4). The basic information includes many links, which lead to more information.

- The words *Current bid* show the current bid. This is accurate. (The bid amount in the listing for a particular auction title is often inaccurate—a delayed posting.) If you want to know the latest bid, refresh the auction webpage (use the refresh button in your browser) and look at *Current bid*.

Reserve

If the auction is a reserve auction, once the reserve has been met or surpassed, the term (reserve met) will appear beside the bid amount. Until that happens, the reserve has not been met and the caption will read (*Reserve not yet met*). If you don't see either of these, it's not a reserve auction.

- The term *History* shows the number of bids and links to a list of bidders. There will be no bid amounts shown by the bidders, however, until after the auction is over.

- The words *Item Location* indicates where the seller lives or does business. That will determine whether you will have to pay sales tax if you win the auction. (It also places the auction in a regional auction, which may not be available when you read this.)

Figure 5.4 The basics are at the top of the auction webpage. ©1995-2007 eBay Inc.

- The word *Seller* shows the seller. Click on the seller's ID and you will get a screen that provides the seller's email address, after you log in. Sometimes a seller's name is an email address in which case a click on the name will bring up your email client. After the seller's name is a link, in parentheses, to the seller's feedback rating. A summary of the seller's feedback appears just below on the next line.

- The term *(View seller's other items)* links to a webpage that shows all the current auctions that the seller is running.

Note that the auction title and the auction number are at the top of the page.

These are the highlights, but there is other information there too.

Look around and check things out. And that's not all. Scroll down the page, and you will get to the auction ad. eBay provides space for an auction ad—a long one if seller is smart—created by seller.

Auction Ad

The auction ad is whatever the seller wants it to be. See Chapter 16 for details. This is a seller's chance to provide all the information necessary to help the buyer make a decision to bid. As a bidder, this is your chance to get all the information you need to make an informed decision. If you don't get the information you need, you have three choices:

1. You can pass, as will many other potential bidders.

2. You can bid without proper information, a choice you may regret.

3. You can contact the seller to get more information. If you have considerable interest in an item, contacting the seller is sometimes the only way you can get adequate information.

Making a Bid

At the bottom of the auction webpage, you can place a bid. Above the input is the current minimum bid. Your bid must equal at least this amount plus one increment higher. Click on the *Place Bid* button when you are ready to submit your bid (see Figure 5.5).

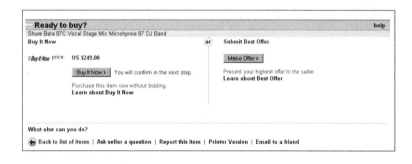

Figure 5.5 Bidding on the auction webpage. ©1995-2007 eBay Inc.

Then you get a webpage that requires your login and password. You need to input your ID and password before you sign in by clicking the

Sign In Securely button (see Figure 5.6). This step is not necessary if you signed in earlier.

Figure 5.6 The password page. ©1995-2007 eBay Inc.

Sign In

Once you have signed in, you do not have to enter your ID again for the duration of your eBay session for most procedures. (But you will still have to enter your password wherever it's required by eBay.) One advantage of signing in is not having to enter your ID and password to bid. This can give you an advantage in the final minutes of a contested auction.

See Chapter 11 for the Double Window technique that saves additional time submitting bids. The Double Window tactical advantage doesn't work unless you're signed in.

eBay sends you an email confirming that you have bid. However, this is not a good way to keep up on the bidding. You get the best information—and the latest high bid—by refreshing the auction webpage. In fact, this is essential to do in the last minutes of competitive bidding for an item in order to keep up with the bidding. This is the only up-to-the-minute source of the latest high bid.

Bidding Increments

The bidding increments are automatically enforced by the eBay system. You don't have to keep track of the increment level. The eBay system will let you know the minimum next bid. See Table 5.1.

Table 5.1 Bidding Increments

Bid ($)	Increment ($)
0.99 and below	0.05
1.00 to 4.99	0.25
5.00 to 24.99	0.50
25.00 to 99.99	1.00
100.00 to 249.99	2.00
250.00 to 499.99	5.00
500.00 to 999.99	10.00
1,000.00 to 2,499.99	25.00
2,500.00 to 4,999.99	50.00
5,000.00 and over	100.00

Buy It Now

After all this talk about bidding, sellers can now give you a fixed price too. Look for the *Buy It Now* icon (see Chapter 6).

After Your Bid

Chapter 11 provides much information on bidding, including strategies and tactics. After you bid, you will probably want to keep track of the auction in order to bid again or perhaps just to see the final outcome of the bidding.

Checking Your Email

When you bid, eBay sends you an email acknowledging your bid. This makes a good record. Don't discard it. You can find much information in this email message that you may need later.

Reviewing Your Activity

As mentioned above, you get the latest information by refreshing the auction webpage. But often you need to keep track of your bidding on a day-to-day basis too.

Current Auctions

You can always check the record of the auctions you have bid on (that are still open) should you lose track because you are bidding on several items. Go to the *Advanced Search* page and search *By Bidder* using your ID.

My eBay

Another place you can check is the more comprehensive record called *My eBay*.

Bidding

Go *My eBay* on the navigation bar. It features a record of your bidding. This is a good place to keep track of your bidding since other convenient eBay services are readily available there too.

Watching

eBay provides a way to make a list of auctions you want to keep track of but have not yet bid on. You put them on the watch list at *My eBay*. Thus, you can keep track of your bids and auctions you watch in one convenient place.

Being Outbid

As soon as you are outbid, eBay sends you an email message acknowledging you have been outbid. However, this is not a very good way to keep up with the bidding, particularly in the last hour of the bidding.

Winning the Auction

If you win the auction, eBay will send you a message informing you. Thereafter, it's up to you and the seller to get together to consummate the transaction.

Following Up

Traditionally, it's the seller who emails the high bidder to inform him or her of the details regarding payment and shipping. Nonetheless, if you don't hear from the seller in a timely manner, take the initiative to contact the seller. Keep following up until the transaction is completed.

For most transactions, the eBay checkout scheme works well. It's for your convenience. Use it unless the seller directs you to do otherwise. The checkout will lead you through the payment procedure.

Retracting a Bid

You can retract a bid if you desire, but you open yourself to negative feedback. You'd better have a pretty good excuse. Don't retract a bid. A little forethought will prevent unnecessary retractions. Go *Site Map, Buying Resources, Bid Retractions* for instructions on retracting your bid.

eBay Stores

eBay Stores have fixed price items, and no bidding is required. You simply click on the *Buy It Now* button, and you've bought it. However, all the current auctions of an eBay Store owner are included in her eBay Store. For those items, you will have to bid.

Optional eBay Bidding Features

This section mentions some of the eBay devices that are available to help you reduce your risk as a bidder.

This section is for collectibles, antiques, jewelry, and the like. It isn't for recently manufactured mass-produced consumer items. You don't have to have a Sony digital camera authenticated. No one is likely to counterfeit one.

Grading and Authentication

Although grading and authentication are not eBay services, they are services you can get from third parties and are well advised to do so in many cases. These processes require third-party experts and usually cost money. They are your best protection against receiving phony merchandise. If a collectible is worth more than you can afford to lose, have it authenticated before you pay for it.

A seller will usually take the position that he or she knows the item is authentic; thus, the buyer must pay for the authentication. Sometimes the seller will offer an authentication that's already been done. This may be acceptable, but be cautious.

Grading

Grading is simply the evaluation of the physical condition of a manu-factured item. Unfortunately, grading is different for different items. You have to know the market for a particular item to understand the grading. Grading is subjective (in the eyes of the beholder). And grading is subject to honest mistakes and, yes, even to dishonesty. This all adds up to a situation where a buyer has to be very careful. Investigate carefully the condition of any item being auctioned.

Quality

For some items, grading is a determination of quality, not necessarily physical condition, and should by done by an expert.

Some other books about eBay assume that there's an agreed grading scale on eBay. Don't believe it. Even if there was, most eBay users would not know exactly how to use it, and it would be unreliable. Always play the detective when it comes to ascertaining the condition of an auction item.

Authentication

Authentication is a process whereby an item is verified to be genuine (and in the condition represented). Is a Beanie Baby really a Ty Beanie Baby? Or, is it a forgery? A third-party expert verifies an item. A verification is an opinion by an expert and subject to being incorrect. Even experts make mistakes. If you are a collector, for instance, authentication is your best protection against forged or phony items. Go *Site Map, Selling Resources, Opinions Authentication & Grading* for a list of experts who provide authentications.

Verification

Verification is a means of establishing that an item is authentic in a way that "travels" with the item. For instance, suppose you have a Ty Beanie Baby authenticated by an expert. How can you make that authentication stick with the Beanie Baby itself? One way is to put the Beanie Baby inside a plastic display case. The third-party authenticator seals the case with his or her unremovable seal attesting to the authenticity of the Beanie Baby.

The Switch?

Unfortunately, the following is a common scenario based on an actual case (in the late 1990s). A person buys a rare Beanie Baby via eBay for $1,800. She receives it, and it turns out to be a forgery (worth $3). She informs the seller. The seller says it was authentic when he sent it and will not refund the money.

This is a sad case. The seller may not have known that the Beanie Baby was a forgery. Now he has the buyer telling him that it is. How does he know that she didn't switch it with a forgery and is pulling an $1,800 scam? The buyer is stuck for $1,800. She doesn't know whether it was an honest mistake on the part of the seller or a scam. But it doesn't matter. She's the one who is stuck.

Is a prosecutor going to pursue this case? (See Chapter 9 for more discussion on remedies for fraud.) Probably not. The case may be impossible to prove, and the prosecutor will not waste taxpayer resources on such a weak case.

Authentication would have protected the buyer in this case. Authentication is best set up as part of an escrow arrangement. Yet, the buyer could have protected herself in another way. Suppose, instead of opening the package received from the seller, she took the package directly to her local Beanie Baby dealer (expert). There the package was opened by both of them together. The expert examined the Beanie Baby and found it to be a forgery. Now the buyer has a witness. Assuming the dealer has a good reputation, she will be a credible witness. The witness makes a much stronger case, and the seller may find it prudent to take back the phony Beanie Baby and refund the $1,800.

Appraisal

It's tough to decide whether to put a discussion of appraisal into the buyer's or seller's chapter because it can serve both. An appraisal is an estimation of value that usually includes an authentication. Naturally, the estimate of value has a date. Market prices go up and down. Thus, an appraisal is good for only a limited period of time. Certainly an appraisal can be valuable to a buyer who may need to rely on a third-party expert opinion of value and who needs authentication as well. Then too, a seller can use an appraisal as a selling tool to verify market value for prospective bidders and to provide authentication.

With over 45,000 categories of items, a short list of appraisers in this book wouldn't make much of a splash. However, the following resource may be helpful: International Society of Appraisers (*http://*

www.isa-appraisers.org). What's It Worth to You (*http://www.whatsit-worthtoyou.com*) provides inexpensive appraisals on a wide range of items. It essentially acts as a clearing house for hundreds of experts who do appraisals.

Unfortunately, it's sometimes difficult to determine whether an appraiser is qualified. Certainly, membership in specialty professional organizations that certify appraisers provides some credibility, but for many categories of items, there are no professional organizations. Always look into an appraiser's credentials.

Physical Inspection?

Generally, if there is no physical inspection of an item, an appraisal is merely an estimate of value, based on information the owner has submitted to the appraiser, and it does not include authentication. For authentication, usually the appraiser must physically inspect the item. Keep in mind that in the absence of an inspection, the appraiser relies on the information the owner provides. As a buyer, you will want to know what that information was.

eBay Insurance

Currently eBay does furnish fraud insurance free. The insurance covers up to a $200 loss ($25 deductible). PowerSellers offer $500 of eBay fraud insurance for free. This insurance doesn't cover shipping damages or losses, only the nonperformance of the seller after payment has been made (e.g., seller fraud). This is a good program because it covers the inexpensive items where escrow would be relatively inconvenient. For the expensive items, eBay leaves the parties to make their own arrangements (e.g., escrow), which makes more sense for higher-priced items.

Escrow

eBay recommends the Escrow.com escrow services. This is your best bet to protect yourself against fraudulent sellers. Don't send a check for an auction item that's more than you can afford to lose. Put the transaction in escrow instead. You then send the check to the escrow agent. The funds are held by the escrow agent until you have received and examined the auction item. If everything is satisfactory (as represented by the seller), you inform the escrow agent, and the funds are released to the seller. If not, then you can return the item to the seller and get your money back.

Is Escrow Enough?

If you review the scenario under the preceding The Switch? subsection, you will find that an escrow by itself could not prevent that situation. However, an escrow together with an authentication is the ultimate assurance that you will enjoy a successful transaction in which you are well protected. In such a case, you make arrangements acceptable to the seller to have an expert authenticate the item before it is released from escrow.

Also take a look at eDeposit (*http://www.edeposit.com*). It provides services that make transactions safer for buyers and sellers and plans to offer an escrow service in the future.

Again, you need to be careful of what escrow service you use. There are many fraudulent escrow companies online.

eBay Toolbar

Try the eBay Toolbar, go *Site Map, Buyer Resources, eBay Toolbar*. It stays right in your browser, tracks your bidding, gives you desktop alerts, warns you of fradulent websites, and provides a search engine without being at the eBay website. This is a great tool for keeping an eye out for items that you want to buy. And it's free!

Let's Get Serious

OK now, let's get serious about online buying. Coincidently, the first day I received the manuscript for this book back from the publisher after the first round of editing, I had a purchase project. My beard was getting too long (for such a young man), and my beard trimmer quit working (dead internal battery). I needed to buy another. Thus, with the following experience fresh in my mind, I have added this section to the book.

Old habits die a long death. Time and time again I remind myself to buy it on eBay (or another online retail source). Yet I forget. So I rushed off to Retail Heaven (a made-up name for a well-know discount retailer – 10 miles away) to buy a beard trimmer without even thinking about eBay. Do you know what I found at Retail Heaven? They keep the merchandise locked up. No, this is not a misprint. Retail Heaven keeps beard trimmers locked up. Who knew? Who could have guessed?

In any event, after a half-hour wait and several attempts to get a clerk to open the beard trimmer vault (display case), I went home empty handed. I just couldn't wait any longer. I went to my computer and found nine pages of beard trimmers on eBay. It took me ten minutes to select one and pay for it via PayPal. Sure, I had to wait for delivery, but it came four days later.

It cost about $2.50 in gas to drive to Retail Heaven and an hour and a half of my time for a round trip. Let's say my time is worth $20 per hour. (I think it's worth a lot more, but that's a matter of opinion.) That means it cost me $57.50 ($2.50 + $30 + $25) to buy a $25 beard trimmer at Retail Heaven.

On eBay it took me ten minutes ($3.33 worth of my time) to select and pay for a beard trimmer. The price (including postage) was about the same as Retail Heaven. Thus, it cost me $28.33 ($3.33 + $25) to buy the same beard trimmer on eBay, a savings of $29.17 over Retail Heaven—not bad for a low-price purchase.

There is no doubt that there have been many spectacular buyer stories about great bargains on eBay. But the real eBay story is about buying things at a reasonable price *conveniently*. You have to train yourself. A lifetime of thinking, "I'll just run over to Retail Heaven and buy it," is costing you an unreasonable amount of time and money. Think *Online*! And if you think *Online*, eBay is one of your prime choices.

Illicit Merchandise

Sooner or later you will be presented with the opportunity to buy illicit merchandise. This is an opportunity you don't want to take. If you knowingly buy what you know to be stolen or pirated goods, you may be guilty of a crime in either your own state or the state in which the goods are offered.

In addition, such participation undermines the integrity of eBay. It's to your advantage to keep eBay a marketplace free of criminal activity.

After all, as a buyer, you can get great bargains today and for many years in the future. Why would you contribute to activities that undermine the marketplace that provides you such an advantage? Avoid illicit merchandise, and preserve eBay as a corruption-free, long-term personal asset.

The tougher test comes, however, when you have illicit merchandise sent to you unknowingly. For instance, there have been a lot of inexpensive CDs containing expensive software for sale on eBay. Many are legitimate, not pirated. Yet in one transaction, I bought a book via eBay (in a Dutch auction), and in the process of communicating with the seller, I was offered an unspecified version of Adobe PhotoShop, a $650 program on a CD, for just an additional $15. I had in the past bought legitimate expensive software (old versions) for very deep discounts on eBay (on CDs), just as I am able to do at local computer shows. So I accepted the offer without thinking much about it. When I received the book, the additional software (an up-to-date version of the PhotoShop) was on a recordable CD, not on a manufacturer's CD (i.e., the additional software was pirated). The seller maintains low visibility by not offering the pirated software on eBay. Rather she offers it via email in the course of arranging the payment and shipping of the book for a winning bidder.

The hard question is, What do you do? This kind of practice is very troubling and is not healthy for eBay and its legitimate users. In this case eBay accepts reports. So, you can file a report directly with eBay. Look in the SafeHarbor area of the eBay website for information on filing reports. By the time I got around to researching how to report this illicit offer, however, the incident was a few months stale.

Then about a year later I bid on a version of Adobe PhotoShop in a current auction. Afterward I received a deluge of email from people offering to sell me current copies of the program for $15–$50 (undoubtedly pirated). This is called *bid skimming*. I went to eBay SafeHarbor, which provides current guidelines on reporting violations. As per instructions, I forwarded copies of the email solicitations to SafeHarbor. Once you learn what to do, it's easy to do it.

Procedures

---

eBay checks the skimming email to see if the perpetrators are registered with eBay. I was notified in every case except one (sender warned but not kicked off eBay) that they were not registered.

eBay suggested that I forward copies of the emails addressed to *postmaster* at the ISPs from which the emails were sent. I didn't think that would generate any result. But I did it anyway (easy and quick to do). It did produce results. I received an email from Yahoo! indicating that it had kicked a sender off the Yahoo! email service. Ironic that Yahoo! kicked off the offender but eBay gave only a warning to another offender.

I also forwarded the illicit email to support at Adobe and received an automated reply, which meant that such was a wasted effort. Then I tried to find an email address at the Adobe website where I might forward the illicit email. That was also a waste of time. Adobe provided only a long form for reporting piracy. It would have taken me an hour to fill out the form for all the incidents of the illicit email. So I declined. Thus, I ended up not getting through to the one organization that might have done something about it.

Summary

Find what you're looking for. There are plenty of goods on eBay. Make your bids. The eBay system is easy to use. When you win an auction, follow up, and make your payment promptly. You'll find eBay to be a reliable source of things you need at reasonable prices, often at deep discounts.

6

Selling

The life of a seller is easier and more passive than that of a bidder—that is, until the follow-up. The follow-up is where the work is for sellers. This chapter covers the basics up to the follow-up. Chapter 14 (on customer service) provides considerable additional information on follow-up and fulfillment .

The selling opportunities on eBay are unlimited because the buyers are so numerous and have such varied interests, and the market is open 24 hours a day, 7 days a week. But many sellers run auctions, and you will not find a lack of competition.

Prior Chapters

Chapters 4 and 5 include many basics about auctions at eBay. Such basics are not necessarily repeated in this chapter. Consequently, you'll need to read Chapters 4 and 5, too, to develop a firm understanding of eBay auctions.

Sellers (Auctioneers)

The first step toward becoming a seller is registering to be an eBay member. Only members can auction (sell) or bid (buy). Chapter 4 covers registration, which is the same whether you are a buyer or seller. The next step for sellers is arranging payment to eBay.

Payment Arrangements

eBay makes its revenue by charging sellers at least two fees. The first is the Initial Listing fee. The second is the Final Value fee based on the winning bid.

You arrange to pay eBay by giving your credit card or bank account number to eBay. Then eBay immediately attempts to authorize your card or verify your bank account. Assuming you're approved, eBay will bill you via credit card or debit your bank account each month for the previous month's fees.

eBay requires a credit card (or other verification) to sell in order to:

- Ensure sellers are a legal age.
- Ensure sellers are who they say they are.
- Protect others from fraudulent or irresponsible sellers.

If you do not have a credit card or bank account, you can alternatively use ID Verify to establish your identity. See Chapter 4.

You calculate the Insertion fee based on the minimum bid or reserve amount according to Table 6.1.

Table 6.1 Insertion Fee

Minimum Bid or Reserve ($)	Listing Fee ($)
0.99 and below	0.30
1.00 to 9.99	0.35
10.00 to 24.99	0.60
25.00 to 49.99	1.20
50.00 to 199.99	2.40
200.00 to 499.99	3.60
500.00 and over	4.80

The spreadsheet formula for calculating the Initial Listing fee amount is:

```
=IF(E5<10,0.3,IF(E5<25,0.55,IF(E5<50,1.1,I
F(E5<200,2.2,3.3))))
```

In the spreadsheet, E5 is the cell where you enter the minimum bid or reserve amount. If you use another cell, substitute it in the formula.

You calculate the Final Value fee (cumulative) based on the high bid according to Table 6.2.

Table 6.2 Final Value Fee (Cumulative)

High Bid ($)	Fee
25.00 and below	5.25%
25.01 to 1,000.00	2.75%
1,000.01 and over	1.5%

The spreadsheet formula for calculating the Final Value fee amount is:

```
=IF(E8<=25,E8*0.05,IF(E8<=1000,((E8-
25)*0.025)+1.25,((E8-1000)*0.0125)
+25.625))
```

```
[Attributed to Eric Slone by author Neil J.
Salkind in eBay Online Auctions.]
```

In the spreadsheet, E8 is the cell where you enter the high bid again. Note that the fee calculation is cumulative; that is, it's 5.25 percent on the first $25, 2.75 percent on the next $975, and 1.5 percent on the excess. For the total auction fees, add the Initial Listing fee and the Final Value fee (see Figure 6.1).

Of course, you don't have to calculate these fees. eBay does it for you automatically and charges your account. The calculation formulas provided in the preceding paragraphs serve to educate you and provide you with a planning tool should you care to use it.

Figure 6.1 Spreadsheet calculates total eBay fees for running an auction.

This is a general view of the eBay auctioning fees. There are additional special fees for special features.

Bold Title in bold. $1.00

Featured Plus Auction placed in Featured list at the top of the page in its category. $19.95

Highlight Auction title highlighted with yellow. $5.00

Gallery Auction goes into eBay photo gallery (must have photograph). $0.25

10-Day Auction Longest auction gets a surcharge. $0.20

Reserve Price For reserve price, there's a surcharge; refunded if item sells. The fee is graduated.

Fixed-price For *Buy It Now*, add $0.05.

For a more complete review, go *Help, Selling, Listing Your Item, Fees.*

Setting the Minimum

Before you submit your auction, you must determine a minimum bid. If you run a reserve auction, you must determine the reserve. These decisions require general knowledge of the market for the item and, in particular, specific knowledge of the eBay market for the item.

One way to get this information is to research eBay auctions and past auctions. A survey of similar current auctions will tell you a lot. Use the archive of past auctions Completed listings to get a selection of completed auctions from which to derive market prices for items identical or similar to the one you will auction.

Research is a powerful means to get the appropriate information to set the stage for success. A minimum or reserve price too high or too low will probably not achieve the purpose of auctioning your item for the highest bid possible. Research can help you set the price at an intelligent value. See Chapter 4 for more details.

Rating the Condition of the Item

It's your job as the seller to accurately evaluate the physical condition of the item being auctioned. Misrepresentation could lead to disputes.

As Is

There are legal ways in many states to sell merchandise as a seller and have no further obligation to the buyer (e.g., the "as is" sale). Those ways may work legally, but they may not work on eBay as a practical matter. (See the detailed explanation of "as is" in Chapter 14.)

You get the impression from the verbiage in the auction ads on eBay that many sellers are selling merchandise "as is." So long as the merchandise works, there is no problem. But if something doesn't work and there's a resulting dispute, the dispute will be harmful to the seller regardless of the legalities.

The best advice is that if something doesn't work, don't sell it. If you choose to ignore this advice, at least indicate very clearly that the item doesn't work. Statements such as, "I don't know whether it works or not, sold as is," are an invitation to disaster. Statements such as, "Item doesn't work, being sold for parts," may be OK so long as they are prominently displayed.

Know the Market

Each item has a different market. Items within a certain market are often evaluated a certain way using certain terminology. Before you evaluate something, know the terminology. In many cases, you will have to know proper evaluation procedures too.

What's the penalty for ignoring proper evaluation? It might be a misrepresentation that carries liability. If you sell items outside your area of expertise, take a look at some of the auctions for identical or similar items on eBay to determine if there is special terminology or evaluation procedures you need to use.

Common Sense

Absent other terminology, you might use common sense terms. Don't stretch the truth.

New This means *unused*, not *used only a little bit*.

Like new or **mint condition** This means *in perfect condition* and *used only a little bit*. If an item has been used more than *only a little bit*, it's not in mint condition unless it's a heavy-duty machine (e.g., auto).

Excellent condition This means *no blemishes and works perfectly*. The assumption is that this item has been used considerably.

Factory refurbished or factory rebuilt This means that the item has been unused since being overhauled at the factory into *like new* condition. These items are usually in a factory-sealed box. If the item has been used since coming from the factory, that fact should be disclosed.

OEM This means *original equipment manufacturer*. OEM can be either the manufacturer or a reseller. Doesn't shed much light does it? Well, what the reseller does is add value to a piece of equipment bought from the manufacturer by putting a private label on it, bundling it with other equipment or intellectual property (e.g., software), or providing it bundled with set-up, service, or training. Such equipment is usually supplied in bulk to the reseller, not in consumer boxes with accompanying manuals, etc. Or, it might be a component inside another piece of equipment. Thus, when someone on eBay offers a piece of OEM equipment, it usually means that it does not come in a consumer box with all the marketing trimmings. That doesn't mean it's not new; it usually is new, or it should be described as used.

OEM Example

A reseller builds computers from components she buys from manufacturers. She buys DVD drives in bulk without consumer packaging to install in some of the computers she builds. She sells all the computers but has four DVD drives left over. She sells the DVD drives to consumers without consumer packaging. She advertises them as OEM DVD drives. They aren't in a pretty package. They may not even include an owner's manual or cables. But they are new.

These are my definitions. Others may have other definitions for the same words. Therein lies a significant problem.

Commonsense Words

By using commonsense words to describe the condition of an item, you may be inadvertently grading it. See the Grading section later in this chapter. Always provide further detailed explanation for the condition of an item that you auction on eBay, not just commonsense words, grading words, or grading abbreviations. Grading is best left to experts.

Blemishes or malfunctions should be disclosed. A photograph is a good means of disclosing blemishes. If you disclose something, it's unfair for a buyer to complain about the very defect that you disclosed. If you don't disclose blemishes, defects, and malfunctions, you are begging for a disputed sale and negative feedback.

Keep in mind that there are buyers for all items in whatever condition. The potential bidders looking for new goods probably will not buy used goods. The buyers looking for used goods are bargain hunting and probably will not spend extra money for new goods.

Misunderstanding

Some will tell you that there are standard words or abbreviations to use on eBay in describing items. Those are usually the eBay "in group" people who comprise a very small percentage of eBay members and who have no authority to establish any terminology. Such standard words will be understood only by a small percentage of all potential bidders. If they're not common sense words, they will be understood by few people. You don't have to use such words at all, and you are ill advised to use them without additional explanation. In fact, a detailed explanation of the condition of an item avoids problems with both grading and misunderstanding.

Don't use abbreviations for anything. You will lose a significant percentage of your market, OHPG.

Entering an Auction

How do you start an auction? It's simple. You just input the information in the Seller's section on the eBay website. Go *Sell* in the navigation bar. Follow the links and instructions you find there (see Figure 6.2 for entry of auction information).

Types of Auctions

Chapter 4 covers the types of auctions (normal, reserve, Dutch, and private) you can run on eBay. You will have to pick one (see Figure 6.2).

Input

You input all the basic information for your auction directly into the *Sell Your Item* form (see Figure 6.3).

Although the input is not burdensome, it takes time. If you run numerous auctions, the input requirements add up. You will start looking for a more efficient way of entering the auctions. Chapter 18 covers eBay bulk uploads.

Length

You control when your auction ends by entering it exactly three, five, seven, or ten days earlier at the same time of day. Those are your choices. It seems to make sense to have your auction end at a busy time on eBay. Perhaps that will get a last-minute bidding frenzy going.

Figure 6.2 Enter an auction and specify the category. ©1995-2007 eBay Inc.

Figure 6.3 Entering auction information. ©1995-2007 eBay Inc.

Auction Ad

One of the inputs is for the middle section of the auction webpage. This is the auction ad (*Description* – see Figure 6.4). This is your opportunity to sell your item. You should be well prepared ahead of time to enter the appropriate information here. Chapter 16 shows you how to make an HTML template (webpage template) to make your auction ads look professional. You can enter such a filled-in (completed) template in the Description input window in the form via copy and paste. (You can get free templates at *http://www.baysidebusiness.com*).

Figure 6.4 Auction ad (Description) input. ©1995-2007 eBay Inc.

Today things are more convenient than they were a few years ago. The eBay description entry form is a mini word processor (actually an HTML authoring program), which gives you increased capability. eBay also provides templates. The auction management services also provide templates. You don't need to use my templates nor create your own. eBay calls their templates "Themes," and you can choose one to use as you enter your listing.

Photograph

Photographs sell goods. Chapters 23 and 24 provide you with the skills and knowledge you need to successfully handle the digital photographs you need for your eBay ads—for successful selling.

Bulk Upload

The ultimate time-saver for numerous auction ads is a bulk upload. eBay provides the Turbo Lister (bulk uploading procedure), and Chapter 18 provides you with background on the bulk uploading process, which enables you to run many auctions with a minimum of effort.

Buy It Now

eBay gives sellers the option to charge a fixed price for their auction items as an additional feature to an auction, not in place of an auction. An icon indicating it's a *Buy It Now* item appears with the auction title, and the fixed price goes to the top of the auction webpage.

Sellers set the *Buy It Now* selling price higher than the initial bid. So long as no higher bids have been made, a bidder can elect to take the fixed price.

If the buyer has a credit card on file or has an ID Verify, the auction automatically terminates; the parties proceed to complete the purchase transaction at the fixed price. If not, the buyer is prompted to register a credit card or obtain the ID Verify. Once the buyer completes this procedure successfully, the auction automatically terminates. If a buyer does not or cannot qualify by registering a credit card or obtaining an ID Verify, the buyer cannot buy the item via the fixed-price procedure and will, instead, have to bid on the item.

Once the reserve price has been met, or once there is a bid in an auction without a reserve, the fixed-price alternative is no longer available to buyers.

Don't underestimate using a fixed price. Less than 250 years ago, a negotiated price was the common practice. The fixed price came along and started a retail revolution. Today both auction prices and fixed prices have their place in the eBay marketplace. Many buyers prefer fixed prices. Buyers especially like fixed prices when they're in a hurry and don't want to wait to make a purchase until the auction ends.

Usually, I'll wait until just before the auction ends to see if I can buy the item for less money. But like everyone else, sometimes I'm in a hurry. Then fixed prices look good, assuming they're reasonable.

Counter

Many sellers have used counters on their auctions ads (auction webpages) to determine how much traffic they get. That usually entails going to a counter website and following the procedures for installing a counter (try Andale at *http://andale.com*). eBay now offers a convenience. You can elect to have an Andale counter installed when you enter your auction information for your auction ad. There is no charge for this device.

Authentication and Other Protections

Chapter 5 covers authentication and verification. Review that chapter before reading this section. Pay particular attention to the subsection The Switch? which outlines a situation as potentially devastating to the seller as it is to the buyer.

Authentication

Authentication protects sellers as well as buyers. If you have your item properly authenticated as part of an escrow arrangement, the buyer will have a difficult time claiming that you sold counterfeit goods. You can avoid the situation outlined in The Switch? (Chapter 5) by endorsing authentication for expensive items.

Verification

Use verification wherever possible. Make sure that the verification is accepted within the particular market for the item. For instance, for the Beanie Baby example in Chapter 5, there were a number of verification services on the Web. If someone wants to know about the particular verification that travels with the Beanie Baby, you can point to a verification website.

Grading

It is a mistake to think that there is some agreed grading scale on eBay. Different types of items have traditionally used different words and different grading scales. Never use abbreviations for grading. Many eBay users won't know what you are trying to communicate. Abbreviations are a convenience for you but are terrible customer service.

Even words like "mint" and "excellent" do little to communicate properly except in the context of a particular commerce (e.g., antiques, stereo equipment, farm implements). The trouble is that different categories of items use different words or assign special meanings to common sense grading words.

The better practice is to explain the condition of an item you auction. The explanation is more useful to potential bidders and won't eliminate those who do not understand the jargon or abbreviations for a particular type of item.

If you are determined to use grading, make sure the grader is an expert in regard to the item graded. That might be you or an appraiser you've hired to authenticate the item. Explain that the item is being graded according to traditional custom for such items. *And then also provide an explanation of the grading as well as the grading words or abbreviations.* Thus, every potential bidder is informed.

The Penalty

The penalty for using grading that potential bidders don't understand is fewer bidders and consequently a lower sale price.

Appraisal

An appraisal can be a useful selling tool. It indicates market value for potential bidders and lends the authority of a third-party expert. Many appraisals also include authentication. See Chapter 5 for more information.

Shipping Insurance

Insurance that insures shipments against loss or damage is essential for both buyer and seller. If a package disappears or is damaged, who sustains the loss, buyer or seller? Who knows what the answer is to that legal question? It will depend on state law and the circumstances of the particular case. As a practical matter, however, the seller will probably sustain the loss. If not, the seller will surely get negative feedback. Don't try to split hairs here. Get insurance, or be prepared to be self-insured. Don't think the buyer (consumer) will sustain this loss.

On inexpensive items, self-insurance makes sense. That means you replace anything lost or damaged in shipment. For expensive items, buy the insurance. UPS and FedEx Ground automatically provide $100 of insurance, and additional insurance is inexpensive. US Postal Service insurance is relatively expensive. If you state your shipping policy as part of your auction ad, you can charge the entire cost of insurance (or half) to the buyer. But putting the responsibility for insurance on the buyer is not wise.

Receipt

Provide a receipt. Make sure it contains all the details of the sale, such as date, price, description of item, buyer's name, and shipping address. The receipt is a summary of the transaction. As such, it protects you as well as the buyer.

eBay Insurance

The insurance offered by eBay is insurance for fraud. Although free, the insurance does not necessarily benefit you. You know you're not fraudulent, and you don't need the insurance. But you have to keep in mind that such insurance is a customer service.

The insurance pays $200 with a $25 deductible. For PowerSellers only there is new eBay insurance coverage up to $500. This can be a convenient selling point.

Escrow

An escrow transaction protects the seller as well as the buyer, as the example in The Switch? subsection (Chapter 5) demonstrates. You are asking for trouble if you don't allow escrow transactions for expensive items. In contrast to the buyer, however, you have a different interest in the escrow arrangement.

Authentication and Escrow

Escrow without authentication is not important to sellers. However, an escrow arrangement can provide sellers with protection against credit card chargebacks and fraud. Go *Help, Buying, Buying - Overview, Knowing Your Seller, Payment, Escrow.*

Consequently, you have to ask yourself: Does this item require authentication? If the answer is no, then the escrow arrangement is not a priority for you as a seller.

As illustrated by The Switch? example, a Beanie Baby needs authentication. There are certainly plenty of counterfeit collectibles around. To do a transaction for an expensive collectible without escrow and authentication is asking for trouble.

Nonetheless, there are plenty of items that don't really require authentication. For instance, does a factory-refurbished brand-name camcorder need authentication? Probably not. It will come in a factory-sealed box and is very unlikely to be a counterfeit. For the buyer to claim it had been used or was a counterfeit would take a blatant act of fraud, which seems unlikely.

What about a used camcorder in excellent condition? Does that require authentication? Suppose the buyer claims it is in average condition and worth less? This is not a disaster as long as you have the serial number on record (and on the receipt) to identify it. Ask the buyer to return the item, and refund the purchase price. It's not like the Beanie Baby where the value goes from $1,800 to $3. Therefore, an escrow and authentication (that the camcorder is in excellent condition) may not be necessary from your point of view as the seller.

However, suppose the buyer runs out and misuses the camcorder (out of ignorance) the first day he or she receives it. Now the camcorder is not in excellent condition any longer, and the buyer blames you. In this case, it is possible that the camcorder is permanently inoperable and worth little. To escrow and authenticate, or not? In this case, there's no easy answer, but raising the question at least makes you aware of the risk. (Review authentication in Chapter 5.)

For expensive collectibles or even for expensive used appliances (are they in the condition specified?), an escrow together with an authentication will protect you as the seller as well as protect the buyer. For new or factory-refurbished items in sealed boxes, escrow and authentication may be unnecessary.

As a Practical Matter

As a practical matter, most buyers and sellers are careless and do not follow the guidelines I have set forth here. In most cases, things work out just fine. The fraud rate is low on eBay, and only a very small percentage of eBay members get defrauded. Why worry about it? Even so, fraud can happen, and you need to be careful, particularly when there's a lot at stake.

After You List the Auction

Once you have entered the input for your auction, you have nothing further to do. The bidding action is up to the bidders. You don't even have to watch. The auction will end three, five, seven, or ten days after you have entered it and at the same time. Only then do you have to follow up. In the meantime, you may get email from prospective bidders asking questions. If so, answer them promptly.

Changing an Auction

You can change anything you want to before the first bid. After the first bid, you can only add information to your auction listing. It will appear at the bottom of your auction ad, dated. You can change your item's category too. If you do something outrageous or unfair, expect to hear bad things from fellow eBay members.

Retracting an Auction

You can retract an auction for which there are no bids at any time. Who are you going to irritate? Probably no one. If there are bids, however, you face a different procedure. You must cancel the bids. There is a specific procedure for canceling bids. The cancellation goes on your record. Therefore, be very cautious about retracting auctions. It's probably not worth risking your reputation in most cases.

No Bids

When your auction runs its course and receives no bids, you lose the listing fee but do not have to pay the Final Value fee. If you want to run the auction again, you can take advantage of eBay's relisting policy for no additional fee. This policy, in effect, guarantees your first try. However, you need to be reasonable in your offering as there is no further fee-free relisting after the second auction fails.

When you're about to relist an auction for which there were no bids the first time, it's a good time to rethink the minimum bid or reserve. You may want to lower it.

Relisting

You can relist any auction automatically without going through the process of entering it again. This is a convenient service for relisting an auction without bids. (It's also convenient for auctioning the same item repeatedly.)

Follow-Up

Follow-up is the most important role of the seller. After all, you must contact the buyer and arrange payment. Then you must ship the item.

Accounting

Losing track of your auctions? You'd better get things under control, or your eBay operation will start to self-destruct. That will invariably result in negative feedback. See Chapter 22 for auction management services that will keep you efficiently organized.

Seller Search

Input your own ID and password in a *By Seller* search (via the *Search* link), and you will get a list of all your current auctions. This can be quite handy if you are running more than auction.

My eBay

Access *My eBay*, at *My eBay* over the navigation bar, and you will get a record of all your selling and bidding activities on eBay. This is an even more complete record than the Seller search. *My eBay* also includes recent feedback, your eBay account records, a list of favorite categories, your sign-in preferences, and other information. Thus, it makes a great place to hang out on eBay, a place where you have a lot of convenient information at your fingertips.

Customer Service

Chapter 14 covers customer service thoroughly. The fact that customer service occupies its own chapter instead of a section in this chapter indicates its importance.

For casual sellers, the quality of your customer service will directly affect your eBay reputation. Moreover, your success as a retailer on eBay will ride on the quality of your customer service. Customer service is not an activity to take lightly.

When an Auction Is Not a Sale

Why would someone want to hold auctions on eBay yet not necessarily want to make a sale? Advertising! eBay makes a viable advertising medium. Indeed, what many retailers do is to use a hybrid strategy. They offer one product a week at a serious discount as a draw to their auction ad. They sell the product at a small profit (or perhaps at a loss), but the effort is not really a selling effort. It's essentially advertising.

Then there are those who want to find out what the market is for a particular class of merchandise. What better way than to sell one item on eBay. In this case, the item is sold, but the act of auctioning is essentially for the purpose of appraisal, not necessarily to make a profit. This is an especially useful technique to use for test marketing.

Summary

Auctioning merchandise is as simple as inputting information into a form at the eBay website and including an auction ad (*Description*). Read Chapter 17 for more details on conducting eBay auctions. The more laborious task is the follow-up: corresponding with the buyer and shipping the goods.

7

What About Tax?

Questions about tax come up all the time in regard to eBay activities. When are you obligated to pay what tax? This chapter answers some of the the normal tax questions. However, this chapter doesn't pretend to offer you expert tax advice. You should get that from your accountant, lawyer, or other tax advisor.

Income Tax

If you make a profit, you have to pay federal income tax (to the IRS) and also to your state government (unless you live in AK, FL, NV, SD, TX, WA, or WY). How do you tell when you've made a profit?

Individual

Individuals don't pay much attention to income tax in regard to eBay auctions. Why? Because they don't auction items very often, and most of the time it's unlikely that they make a profit.

Basis

To determine whether you've made a profit in selling an item, you have to know your *basis* in the item. Suppose you bought a pair of new skis for $195 in 1997. You sell them on eBay in 2007 for $35. Your basis is $195. If you don't sell them for more than your basis, you don't make a profit. In this case, you took a $160 loss. You owe no income tax.

Suppose you collected comic books from 1975 to 1979. You paid 50 cents each for them, 300 in all. Your basis is $150 (300 × 0.50 = 150). You sell them to a collector via eBay for $2 each and a total of $600. Your income from the sale exceeded your basis. Your profit is $450 (300 × 2 = 600 − 150 = 450). You are obligated to pay income tax on $450.

Business Assets

Business assets are different. Suppose you had a side business mowing lawns. You bought a power lawn mower for this business for $525 in 1997 and got a great deal (40 percent off list price). Your side business lasts only a few years, but the mower is in great condition. You sell it on eBay in 2007 for $290.

Your original basis was $525. However, you probably either depreciated the mower (business asset) for tax purposes over several years or wrote it off all in the first year.

Depreciation

Suppose you depreciated the mower over five years at $105 per year. In 1997 you wrote off $105 on your income tax. In 1998 you wrote off $105 on your income tax. Finally, in 1999 you wrote off $105 on your income tax. But 1999 was the last year you were in the mowing business. Your basis in the mower is now $210 (525 − 105 − 105 − 105 = 210)

Since you sold the mower for a price over your basis, you made a profit of $80 (290 − 210 = 80). You have to pay income tax on $80.

One-Year Write-off

If you wrote off the entire purchase price ($525) of the mower in 1997, your basis is $0. Therefore, your profit on the sale is $290 (290 − 0 = 290). You have to pay income tax on $290.

Retail Business

For an eBay retail business, you usually buy at wholesale and sell at retail. The difference in the wholesale and retail price is your obvious profit for each item. But you also have other costs of doing business that you can write off. Your net profit is your gross income less your cost of sales (wholesale price) and less your other business expenses. You have to pay income taxes on your net profit.

Suppose you sold $105,000 of goods on eBay in 2006. The wholesale price you paid for the goods (cost of sales) was $55,000. You had $15,000 of other business expenses in 2006. Your net profit was $35,000 (105,000 − 55,000 − 15,000 = 35,000). You pay income tax on your profit of $35,000.

Note that this is a very simple explanation of a complex financial matter. I just want to give you a general idea of what is taxed. Many readers will have considerable knowledge of the tax rules and will find this information oversimplified.

Federal

The federal income tax is the most important simply because it is the highest rate, probably under 30 percent for most eBay retailers. Therefore, it is important that you and your tax advisor pay attention to the federal tax rules so as to minimize your income taxes.

State

Your state income tax is likely between 2 percent and 9 percent. Your state's rules may be different from the federal rules. Therefore, it is important you take the state income tax rules into account when doing your planning to minimize income taxes.

Sales Tax

Sales tax is collected by every state except Alaska, Delaware, Montana, New Hampshire, and Oregon. You pay sales tax when you buy something. You collect sales tax when you sell something.

In Your State

You must collect sales tax on all sales made in your state via eBay. To do so you have to have a sales tax license (or whatever it's called in your state). You collect the sales tax from the buyer and in turn submit it to the state.

Individual Sellers

Individuals who sell only occasionally seldom bother to get a sales tax license or collect sales tax. There may even be an exemption in your state for occasional sales. However, be advised that if you sell more than occasionally, you had better get a sales tax license and collect sales tax, or you may find yourself in trouble.

Retail Sellers

An eBay retail seller must get a sales tax license and collect sales tax on all sales within his or her state. If you don't do so, you'll find yourself in big trouble someday soon.

No Sales Tax

Retail sellers do not have to pay sales tax when they buy inventory for resale. For instance, when you are an eBay business buying inventory from a wholesaler, you do not pay sales tax on the inventory. But you do have to collect sales tax on all the inventory you sell at retail in your state.

Out of State

You don't have to collect sales tax on sales out of state. Since most of your eBay retail sales are likely to be out of state, you will not have to collect sales tax on most of your sales.

Change in the Wind

The US Congress is considering legislation that will require each retailer to collect sales tax for 7,600 taxing jurisdictions in 45 states. This might be something that you will want to learn more about and then have a heart to heart talk with your US Representative or Senator. *eBay Business the Smart Way, Third Edition* has a chapter on this issue.

Use Tax

If you don't pay sales tax on an item, in most states you are obligated to pay a use tax that's usually the same percentage as the sales tax.

Individual Buyers

Suppose you purchase a microwave oven online from a vendor in another state. You pay no sales tax. Therefore, you owe your own state a use tax that's the same percentage as the sales tax in your state.

The use tax is not understood by the general population. Most people don't know about it or don't understand it; and they don't pay it. It's practically impossible for a state to collect it from individuals.

Business Buyers

When a business buys business supplies or equipment in another state and pays no sales tax, it is obligated to pay a use tax on such supplies and equipment in its own state.

For instance, suppose you buy a computer printer online out of state for your eBay retail business. You pay no sales tax. You are obligated to pay a use tax on the computer printer to your state.

The state does have a way of enforcing this use tax for businesses. If you have a sales tax license, the state may audit your business to determine whether you are collecting sales taxes properly and honestly. In that audit, the state may find that you haven't paid use tax on your purchases from out of state. Then guess what? You'll have to pay the use tax plus penalities.

Other Taxes

We've covered the basics in this chapter. There are certainly other taxes you may be obligated to pay such as a local business tax, but other taxes are beyond the scope of this book and are usually nominal.

Summary

Again, let me stress that this chapter doesn't intend to offer you expert tax advice. You should get such advice from your accountant, lawyer, or other tax advisor.

Yes, if you're an individual, you're obligated to pay certain taxes. As a practical matter, most individuals don't bother to do so. Nonetheless, as your selling grows to be more than occasional, your selling activities begin to look like a retail business.

As a retail business (as an eBay retailer), you are most certainly obligated to pay various taxes. Unlike individuals, however, you are likely to get caught and penalized for non-payment should you choose to ignore the tax rules.

8

Giving Feedback

Reputation is often a subtle thing. A bad reputation doesn't keep you from doing business. Many business transactions are straightforward and essentially risk-free for each party. For instance, in an office supply store, you hand your $125 to the person at the counter, and you get a fax machine. The transaction takes place directly without much risk on either side.

However, if a transaction requires trust, a bad reputation creates an obstacle. For instance, suppose you take delivery of the fax machine but pay the $125 for it in installments over a six-month period. The seller has to trust you to make the payments. If you have a bad reputation (i.e., a bad credit rating), the office supply store will not make this arrangement with you.

Or, suppose you pay the $125 to the seller, who promises to order the fax machine and deliver it to you as soon as it comes from the manufacturer next week. You have to trust the office supply store. If the store has a bad reputation, you will probably not agree to pay for the fax machine until delivery regardless that the seller is an office supply store.

eBay transactions require trust. eBay sellers and buyers need good reputations. The idea of an international marketplace with a transaction mechanism that works well is great, but it won't work unless the buyer feels confident that he's going to get the Sony camcorder, for which he won the bidding, when he sends his $425 check to the seller. Why would anyone send a check to another person he or she doesn't know hundreds (or thousands) of miles away? For eBay, the answer is the eBay reputation system, the Feedback Forum. This is the heart and soul of the eBay system. This is the firm foundation on which the whole eBay transaction process rests.

eBay Feedback System

How does eBay establish reputations for its sellers and buyers? Simply, it enables sellers and buyers to rate each other. The ratings are simple: positive, neutral, or negative.

In addition, sellers and buyers can make comments. These comments often include fluffy praise resulting from successful transactions. When not fluffy, however, they can provide useful information of interest to the eBay community.

Positive, Neutral, Negative

Some of the following scenarios illustrate how you might enter feedback based on your eBay transaction experiences. These are solely my opinion. Everyone will have their own notions about the feedback that the other party deserves. I think, however, that you have to be reasonable above all.

For instance, suppose you visit eBay almost every day to pursue your hobby of collecting antique mirrors. In this instance, you buy a mirror, send a check to the seller, but don't receive the mirror immediately. Understandably, you get frustrated. The seller, however, happens to be a person who works long hours every day at a demanding job and only frequents eBay on the weekend as an occasional buyer or seller. She tends to think of eBay as a weekend activity. She gets your check and subsequently finds out on a Monday that the check has cleared. In all likelihood she is not going to get around to shipping the package until

Saturday. Is this unreasonable? Not for her. But if she were a person operating a retail business on eBay instead, it would be an unreasonable delay. Thus, one must determine reasonableness in an overall context.

Positive

Transactions often run into problems and are not always on time. *A positive performance by the other party is one that completes the transaction within a reasonable time (not necessarily on time) and according to the terms of the agreement (as defined by the auction offering).* Sometimes additional negotiation based on some reasonable circumstances may alter the agreement.

Case #1 Seller Enters a Positive

A buyer says he sent a check the day after the auction, but when the check gets to the seller, the envelope shows a postmark a week after the auction. Give the buyer a neutral or negative rating? No. Whenever a transaction consummates, rate the other party positive unless there is a compelling reason not to do so. A check sent a week late is not a compelling reason.

Case #2 Buyer Enters a Positive

The seller represents that he will charge the winning bidder $20 for shipping and handling. The buyer pays the bid plus $20. When she gets the product, she notices that the package has postage of $5 on it, not $20. She complains to the seller, but the seller won't budge. Give the seller a negative rating? No. Whenever a transaction consummates, rate the other party positive unless there is a compelling reason not to. The buyer has a right to complain perhaps, but it doesn't make sense to quibble with a charge that was stated before the auction closed.

Shipping and Handling

Note also that shipping and handling are different from just shipping. Handling does cost money; it's not free. If a seller states in advance a charge for shipping and handling, it doesn't provide the basis for neutral or negative feedback that the buyer thinks the seller set the shipping and handling charge too high. The shipping charge is just a portion of the total shipping and handling.

Neutral

Even when the transaction closes, a party may have caused so much distress that he or she does not deserve a positive rating. *A neutral performance by the other party is one that completes the transaction but not without a good deal of seemingly unnecessary frustration-causing or unpleasant behavior.*

Case #3 Seller Enters a Neutral

Here the story is the same as earlier (see Case #1 Seller Enters a Positive subsection) except that the buyer takes three weeks (instead of one week) before sending the check. The transaction closes, but the seller doesn't receive the check until almost a month after the auction ends. Give the buyer a neutral rating? It depends. If the buyer had some problems with making the payment but kept the seller informed, a neutral rating is probably not appropriate. If the buyer kept putting off the seller with misrepresentations or no responses, a neutral rating may be justified.

Case #4 Buyer Enters a Neutral

The seller represents that he will charge the winning bidder a reasonable shipping fee ("handling" is not mentioned). The transaction closes. The seller charges $20 and ships the product in an old cardboard box stuffed with newspaper. The buyer (high bidder at $45) sees the postage of $6.75 on the box and complains about the $20 shipping charge. The seller won't budge. Give the seller a neutral rating? Perhaps not. After all, the buyer could have tried to pin down the shipping fee via email before the auction was over, but she did not do so. Then too, the seller might mistakenly think that "shipping" really means "shipping and handling."

On the other hand, it looks as if the seller has attempted to augment his profit by unexpected gouging on the shipping charge. That deserves a neutral rating.

Negative

Negative ratings should be reserved for situations where the transaction does not consummate or grievous problems remain unresolved indefinitely or for a long period of time. *A negative performance by the other party is one that does not complete the transaction, completes it only after a very long delay, completes it only after causing a great deal of aggravation, or completes it according to different terms than defined by the auction offering.*

Case #5 Seller Enters a Negative

Here the story is the same as earlier (see Case #1 Seller Enters a Positive) except that after several promises to pay, which extend the transaction for three weeks, the buyer finally admits that he cannot scrape together the money to pay for the product. Give the buyer a negative rating? Whenever a transaction does not close based on the irresponsible or dishonest behavior of one of the parties, a negative rating is appropriate. The buyer should not have bid without the capacity and willingness to pay the winning bid, and now he deserves a negative rating.

Case #6 Buyer Enters a Negative

The seller represents that he will charge the winning bidder a reasonable shipping fee but nothing is said about handling. The seller charges the buyer (high bidder at $45) to pay $20 to ship the product (lightweight and not fragile) via the Postal Service (about $6). The buyer contacts the seller to complain about the high cost of shipping but never refuses to complete the transaction. The seller immediately reenters the item into eBay for another auction without giving the buyer a chance to pay after the buyer voices his complaint. Give the seller a negative rating?

The seller is not only gouging on the shipping but is apparently unwilling to be responsive to or to negotiate the buyer's legitimate complaint. The transaction does not consummate due to the seller's unreasonable behavior; he deserves a negative rating.

No Rating

No rule requires that a seller or buyer give the other party feedback. Unfortunately, failure to do so undermines the system. If a transaction does not reflect adversely on either party and neither party enters feedback, I suppose the system can survive without the information about that transaction. Indeed, such cases are the norm and not the exception, as many parties are too lazy or distracted to enter feedback. (I'm often guilty of that myself, I'm sorry to report.) When a feedback rating would be adverse to a party, however, and the other party (the offended party) does not enter it, that constitutes an irresponsible act.

For instance, suppose a seller operates a bait-and-switch scam. He offers one item of merchandise but substitutes another of inferior quality. A failure on the buyer's part to report such an offense via feedback undermines the system, particularly when it turns out that the seller routinely acts unfairly to other eBay members.

Special Cases

Special cases will always come along where the transaction did not close because the seller and buyer agreed that it should not close.

Case #7 No Closing

Suppose the seller auctions a model MX54-T chain saw. After the auction the seller informs the buyer that he has made a mistake. He has only the model MX54-C, which looks the same but is generally worth 30 percent less. He offers the different model to the buyer for the bid price less 40 percent and offers to ship it for free. The buyer decides not to close the transaction (not to buy the substituted item). Should the buyer provide negative feedback on the seller?

If the seller makes an honest mistake, don't rate him or her negatively. After all, in the above case the seller seems to have offered the buyer a favorable deal to atone for his "mistake." In such a case, assuming she believes the seller, the buyer will probably not enter feedback. Probably in most cases where the seller and buyer agree not to complete the transaction, no feedback is reported.

Unfortunately, feedback should be reported in such a case. It can be valuable to fellow eBay members, not for its rating value (e.g., neutral) but for its commentary. For instance, in this case, the buyer can rate the seller neutral but also include the following facts:

> **Proper comment:** He mistakenly did not have the item but made a reasonable offer to substitute.

If the mistake was sincere, this rating will not hurt the seller. If the mistake is routine, ratings like this will eventually expose the seller as a careless or shady operator.

Comments

Using positive, neutral, or negative feedback provides little information. Only a straightforward comment makes any sense out of a rating.

Just stating the facts gives your comment the maximum impact it deserves.

Negative or Neutral Feedback

Always just state the pertinent facts. Don't make any judgmental, accusatory, or speculative comments. If you do, you may be wrong, and you may lose credibility with other eBay members, presumably just the opposite of what you want to do.

If you make a judgmental, accusatory, or speculative statement, you may defame the other party, thus incurring legal liability. Seldom do you have all the facts you need to establish legally sound grounds to make such a statement. But you can state the facts as you know them. The truth is always a defense to defamation. If you stick to the facts that you know, you will make it impractical for someone to challenge you legally thereby making a lawsuit unlikely. Fairness also dictates that you cool down and determine what the facts really are before you make comments about someone.

The facts will damn the other person more in any case. Anytime you make an opinionated negative statement about someone else, people take it with a grain of salt. But facts are facts, and people pay attention to facts.

Improper comment (about seller): He intentionally aggravated me by taking far too much time to ship the vase.

Proper comment: He didn't ship the vase until 25 days after he received my money order.

Improper comment (about winning bidder): This gal's a deadbeat who needs a psychiatrist to get herself straightened out.

Proper comment: She promised to pay during the three weeks after the auction but never did.

Improper comment (about seller): This lowlife tried to triple his profit by gouging me on the shipping.

Proper comment: He required a huge shipping fee, refused to discuss it, and then killed the sale.

eBay provides you with only 80 characters (about 15 words) to make your statement. So, make it concise and factual. Save the expletives for telling the story to your friends.

Positive Feedback

Most positive feedback doesn't mean much. Just to give someone a positive rating is enough if the transaction went well. You see a lot of fluffy praise among the comments for positive ratings. Here again facts speak the loudest. Just state the facts.

> **Improper comment (about winning bidder):** Winning bidder is the greatest. Will do business again.

> **Proper comment:** Winning bidder paid promptly and was pleasant to deal with.

The improper statement boosts the bidder's ego, which is fine. Nothing wrong with that. And it does convey the message that the bidder did something right. But it doesn't tell us much. The proper statement has more impact because it conveys facts. Incidentally, the improper statement sounds canned, which it probably is.

Informational Feedback

Occasionally, the use of a comment is primary, and the rating is much less important. In the earlier Case #7 No Closing subsection example, the seller made a mistake and didn't have the item auctioned. He made an offer to sell a similar item at a good price and pay the shipping. On one hand, if the seller seems sincere, you don't want to give him a negative rating. Even a positive rating might be justified. On the other hand, if he's a con artist pulling the old bait-and-switch trick, you would want to give him a negative rating. You don't know for sure which he is. So, give him a neutral rating. Here the comment you make is more important than the rating, and the comment must be factual to be of use to anyone.

> **Proper comment:** He mistakenly did not have the item but made a reasonable offer to substitute.

When people look at this comment together with all the other comments, they will get a more accurate picture of the seller. If this situation shows up as an anomaly, people will excuse it. If together with other comments it shows a pattern of undesirable behavior, people will catch on quickly and will be reluctant to deal with such a seller.

Fairness

You can give a neutral or negative rating without making a comment, but fairness requires that you give a good reason to support neutral or adverse feedback. If you cannot give a good reason (state a fact or set of facts), then you should rethink why you are giving a neutral or negative rating.

Communication

Always attempt to work out any differences with the other party. Direct communication works well for resolving problems. Get the other party's phone number immediately after an auction finishes. Call or email him or her. Get the problems resolved.

Probably most adverse ratings result from a lack of communication or from one party's total failure to communicate. Make sure that you communicate. When the other party attempts to contact you, respond in a timely manner. When a problem arises, initiate communication.

Making a neutral or negative rating does not motivate the other party to live up to his or her agreement. It warns eBay patrons that you couldn't work things out with the other party because he or she acted unfairly, unreasonably, or fraudulently. Never threaten the other party with an adverse rating as a negotiation ploy (blackmail?). Reasonable people do not threaten others, and if the other person reports your threat, it will make you look like the bad guy.

Reporting negative feedback is not the last resort. You report negative feedback after you've reached the last resort to get the transaction completed and the transaction continues to have problems.

People make mistakes. In a transaction, reasonable people work together to minimize the impact of a mistake on each party. If that can't be done and the transaction doesn't take place, reasonable people walk away and get on with their lives. Getting angry at the other party doesn't serve much purpose. (By definition a mistake is unintentional.)

If the mistake happens beyond the point where the buyer and seller can cancel the transaction, reasonable people understand that life is

full of risks and try to work out the best solution to the problem.
Assume the other party acts reasonably until specific facts indicate the
contrary. If you do so, communication will serve you well when your
transactions run into problems.

Use Skype

For free or inexpensive telephone calls to the other party in an eBay
transaction, use Skype covered in Chapter 15.

Few eBay transactions end up with the parties unreconciled or involve
fraud where one party disappears. Yet one must assume that many
eBay transactions run into problems. When people communicate, the
problems get solved.

Negotiation

Interestingly, the auction process takes all the negotiation out of making a deal. Otherwise, a third of this book would have to be devoted to
negotiation. Nonetheless, problems sometimes arise. Buyers and sellers must negotiate. Good-faith communication gets the negotiation
done. But you need to be careful in your communication when you
negotiate. Always keep things open. Never close off communication
with unproductive statements like, "Take it or leave it." Never stop
keeping an open mind; never stop looking for a solution.

Name Calling

Some people deserve to be called names because they act so badly.
Still, you can never let communication degenerate into a name-calling
session. The only reason to communicate with someone you don't
know who lives far away is to complete the auction transaction. Name
calling will bring an end to the communication and is self-defeating.
Reasonable people don't resort to name calling.

Anger

When a transaction becomes frustrating due to the other party's abject
stupidity or felonious behavior, you can get pretty mad (I know I do).
Never take any action against the other party in the heat of the
moment. You will surely regret it. Cool off first. Then do something
rational. If the other party deserves the "worst," you will be better able

to administer the "worst" when you are rational. If it turns out that the other party really isn't that bad, you will save yourself some grief or guilt and will certainly save yourself from looking vengeful.

Public Record

The feedback ratings and comments constitute a public record. Anyone using eBay can see them anytime. The ratings are set in concrete. Once made, you cannot change them. You can add information to them later, but you cannot change them. They remain in the public record permanently for all to see. Consequently, a bad reputation on eBay will probably hurt you more in regard to eBay than a bad reputation where you live will hurt you in regard to your locale. Anyone who wants to know your eBay reputation can find it in one click.

The great genius of this system is that eBay doesn't care about anyone's reputation. eBay just makes a permanent public record of it. If you're a big eBay customer, eBay doesn't care. If it's your first time on eBay, eBay doesn't care. eBay just publishes the reputations in a public record, and it enables the sellers and buyers to make or break each other's reputations.

New Rule

eBay has changed the feedback rules. Now the parties can mutually agree to change or erase the feedback for a particular transaction.

eBay Action

If your feedback rating reaches a −4 (positives plus negatives), the eBay system will automatically shut you down as a member. You can have your case reviewed, but eBay can put you out of business (on eBay) permanently.

On the Positive Side

If you accumulate positive feedback, you earn colored stars, which go beside your name (see Figure 8.1).

It's Your Reputation

Does your reputation on eBay seem artificial? Does it seem more like an attribute in a digital game than the real thing? Can you break your agreements with impunity and walk away without consequences? If you develop a bad reputation on eBay, can you just erase the entire experience? Can you be sure your eBay reputation won't spread beyond eBay?

The answer to these questions is no.

Feedback Star Glossary

The feedback system is easy to understand. Feedback Stars are awarded to eBay members for achieving 10 or more feedback points.

You receive:

- +1 point to your feedback score for each positive comment and rating left for you.
- 0 points to your feedback score for each neutral comment and rating left for you.
- -1 point to your feedback score for each negative comment and rating left for you.
- A feedback star once you have 10 or more comments and ratings left for you.

Here's what the different stars mean:

Yellow Star (★) = 10 to 49 points
Blue Star (★) = 50 to 99 points
Turquoise Star (★) = 100 to 499 points
Purple Star (★) = 500 to 999 points
Red Star (★) = 1,000 to 4,999 points
Green Star (★) = 5,000 to 9,999 points
Yellow Shooting Star (★) = 10,000 to 24,999 points
Turquoise Shooting Star (★) = 25,000 to 49,999 points
Purple Shooting Star (★) = 50,000 to 99,999 points
Red Shooting Star (★) = 100,000 or higher

⚡**Tip:** In most cases, a high feedback score is a good sign, but you should always check a member's Member Profile to read comments and look for negative remarks.

Figure 8.1 eBay Star Chart. ©1995-2007 eBay Inc.

Your reputation on eBay is perhaps more real than your offline reputation. After all, more people can access it. It's the real thing. But how can a bad reputation on eBay hurt you in the world outside eBay? Easy to answer! What will prevent your banker from looking up your reputation on eBay before he or she loans you $23,000 for a new car? Nothing. In fact, a smart banker might do just that. (Will your alias on eBay be a question on future loan applications? Will the day come when you won't be able to get a loan unless you have a reputation on eBay?) Look at eBay as another credit bureau. Your reputation on eBay is not something to take lightly.

What about other creditors? What about potential employers? With 200 million people on eBay, you might have difficulty claiming with credibility that you don't have an eBay account.

It's Their Reputation

Reputation is not a problem for you because you're a good person who practices honesty, honors agreements, and treats others fairly. The good news: the eBay feedback system protects you against all the creeps who deserve bad reputations and get bad reputations on eBay just as they do offline. The system works for you, and you have a vested interest in maintaining the integrity of the system and making it work well.

The system relies on you to *tell it like it is*. This means that you must give people a negative or neutral rating when they deserve it just as you give people a positive rating when they perform as they are obligated to perform. By failing to give negative or neutral ratings when deserved, you undermine the system.

Retailers

The retailers on eBay who also sell at retail offline understand reputation. They know that reputation is everything when it comes to selling. They have built their businesses on their reputations. Ironically, many are reluctant to give adverse ratings to eBay buyers who abuse them. They reason that negative feedback given to a buyer who doesn't honor his or her agreement to purchase may result in retaliatory negative feedback. Thus, an aborted transaction can potentially hurt an innocent retailer perhaps more than a guilty buyer. This is an unfortunate weakness in the system, but the system has survived in spite of it.

Don't Hesitate

Give negative feedback in situations where the other party deserves it. The system depends on you to do so just like you depend on others doing so to support this wonderful ecommerce machine that eBay has turned out to be.

Non-Retailers

This situation is not limited to retailers. Almost anyone of goodwill who cares about his or her reputation might fail to post negative feedback on the other party. This natural propensity warps the entire feedback system.

Warp Effect

On one hand, if you see a retailer who has 79 positive ratings and 2 negative ratings, it most likely reflects a normal situation. You can't please everyone no matter how hard you try. Most likely those two negatives represent people who will never be happy with anyone.

On the other hand, if you see someone on eBay who has ten positives and four negatives, it seems probable that the warp (referred to above) has an influence. For each negative rating, there may have been one or more additional parties who should have given a negative rating but didn't. A person who has a substantial number of negative ratings is suspect, particularly when the ratio of negative to positive is high.

How the System Works

The system invites you to enter ratings on the people with whom you've done business in regard to an eBay auction. To access the reporting section, go *My eBay*. Under *Buying Reminders* or *Selling Reminders* you will find reminders to report fedback. (see Figure 8.2). Clicking on a Reminder link will start the procedure for giving feedback. For each eBay member requiring feedback, check the appropriate radio button to choose a rating. Then enter a comment in the input below.

If giving negative feedback, write your comment on a piece of paper offline before entering it as part of the rating. That will allow you plenty of time to avoid making a blunder you might regret. Remember, the rating and comment remain posted forever, and you cannot change them.

Figure 8.2 Leaving feedback. ©1995-2007 eBay Inc.

Comment on a Rating

Occasionally, you will need to comment on a rating you've already posted. eBay permits this, but it shows as an addition to the posted rating and does not take the place of the posted rating. Such a comment also becomes part of the permanent public record.

Comment on the Other Party's Rating of You

If someone makes an adverse comment about you, you can answer it. Never answer when you're mad. Cool down and carefully draft an answer. Follow the advice in the next section; just state the facts.

If the adverse comment by the other party is justified, you may be better off not making any comment. If you're guilty as charged but have a reasonable excuse, admit the charge but state why you felt you were justified in doing what you did. This will at least show you to be a reasonable and honest person.

Comment on Your Rating of the Other Party

There will be times when you want to comment on the other party after you've already commented once. Suppose as the seller you accepted a credit card for payment of the item sold. You rated the buyer positive for paying promptly. Later the buyer asks his bank for a chargeback on the credit card based on a complaint about the item bought. The buyer never contacted you to discuss the problem, if there really was a problem. This is a frustrating situation.

The buyer may be attempting to beat you out of payment for the item. If you can't get the matter straightened out with the buyer, you may want to add a comment onto the original rating you made explaining what happened after you thought the transaction had been completed.

A follow-up comment need not always be negative. Suppose you are the buyer in Case #6 Buyer Enters a Negative subsection earlier. Your negative rating of the seller catches the seller's attention. The seller tells you that the shipping costs so much because the sale includes a set of heavy batteries which have to be shipped separately, a situation of which you were not aware. You complete the transaction and receive the batteries as well as the item. At this point, you can reasonably add a favorable comment to your original negative rating.

Bickering

When the parties bicker back and forth with add-on comments to the original ratings, it usually makes both parties look like a couple of loonies. Never attempt to answer the other person's add-on adverse comment. Just let it go if you have nothing new to add. It has to stop somewhere. Sometimes broken transactions get to the point where the best thing to do is just move on. People looking at the public record of your ratings and comments can read between the lines very skillfully. If you have conducted yourself reasonably in a transaction, that fact will probably emerge from the comments, even if the other party has the last word. Don't risk your reputation (and your sanity) by getting into a bickering contest.

Public or Private

You can choose to make your feedback public or private. Why would you do business with a person who kept his or her feedback private? Why would anyone do business with you, if you keep your feedback private?

A few years ago, I communicated with a seller for a few days about an item (i.e., several emails). Then I didn't bid on the item as I had indicated to him I would. He sent me an email to ask why. I told him that just before I would have placed the bid, I checked his feedback. It was private, so I didn't bid. He took the time to reply and severely berate me for acting like a crazy person. What would you have done?

Liability for Defamation

eBay's permanent public record of feedback will generate lawsuits. If you make false or derogatory statements about someone, you may find yourself at the wrong end of a lawsuit. However, truth is always a defense. As long as you make factual statements in your feedback, you minimize your risk of being sued. So, if you find yourself heading for the feedback section on eBay very angry at someone, you'd better stop and cool off before you type in something you'll regret later.

Evaluating a Person's Reputation

You can easily and quickly evaluate a person's reputation. Just read his or her ratings. Start with the negative ratings. Then read some of the positive ratings. You will probably get a good idea of whether you want to do business with the individual.

Buyers Beware

When reading negative ratings, I am always struck by how many seem to be about winning bidders who just didn't understand their obligations and made unreasonable demands on the sellers, mostly out of ignorance. That leads me to advise that if you're a buyer, read the auction ad carefully, and don't complain if a careless reading gets you into a bind.

To fine-tune your analysis of a buyer or seller, pay attention to the percentage of transactions that are sales and the percentage that are purchases. Then look specifically at the feedback for each. It's possible that a person can be a great seller but a lousy buyer, or vice versa.

If you buy, remember that you're going to send the seller payment. The risk of the transaction is yours. If the seller proves unreputable, you're the one who's out the money. However, you must decide before you bid. Reviewing the seller's reputation and refusing to pay after you win the bidding will expose you to a justifiable negative rating.

If you sell, remember that if the buyer doesn't pay, you will waste your time and energy and become frustrated. In the end, you will have to put the item up for auction again with the requisite delay in selling the item. Also, remember that you don't have to sell to anyone so long as you have an acceptable reason. If the winning bidder has a poor reputation, you can sell to the next-highest bidder. Should you decide to do so, however, you should advise the winning bidder of your reasons and remind him or her of your right to refuse a sale. Be tactful. Keep in mind also that the second-highest bidder has no obligation to buy.

Up Front

If you want to be particular about who you will sell to, state it up front in your auction ad. For instance, you might say, "Will not accept a bid from buyers with a feedback rating below 10."

Security Center

eBay's security program exists to ensure that buyers and sellers can carry on commerce with the confidence that they will not experience an unreasonable level of the risk of fraud. The Feedback Forum, eBay's reputation program, may be considered a part of the security program. Take a look at the Security & Resolution Center to see what else this program offers. Go *Community, Security & Resolution Center*. Don't overlook the 23-page PDF booklet *Security & Privacy - Made Simpler*, a joint publication of the Better Business Bureau and eBay, available at the Security Center.

Conclusion

This chapter deals with a lot of negative situations. Does that mean they will all happen to you sooner or later? Not necessarily. Most transactions resulting from eBay auctions close eventually despite occasional neglect or slow performance by one or the other party. Most people act reasonably, communicate competently, and have the skills to conclude a long-distance transaction. Most deals close, and presumably the parties walk away happy. eBay provides you with a great way to sell stuff and buy stuff. But as for every public activity, the parties must follow rules of conduct. When an individual flagrantly violates those rules, you should warn the eBay community.

9

Reporting and Remedies

Report on the other party to eBay, and ask the other party to report on you via the eBay feedback system. Thereby, you build up your eBay reputation. Most transactions go smoothly, giving you your chance to pat the other party on the back and receive the same in return. Occasionally, however, transactions go bad. Chapter 8 covers eBay reputation and feedback. This chapter reports on what additional options you have when the other party treats you unfairly or commits fraud.

Most People Are Honest, But ...

Most people are honest, but occasionally a real loser comes along and grabs your money (or merchandise) and runs. eBay has seen scams in the past. eBay has scams today. And eBay will experience scams in the future. Kind of reminds you of real life, doesn't it? Well, cyber life ain't what it used to be.

If You Are a Bidder

How can you get zapped? Let me count the ways:

1. Merchandise damaged in shipment
2. Merchandise lost in shipment
3. Defective merchandise
4. Merchandise not in the condition represented
5. Merchandise substituted without your approval
6. No merchandise delivered

You should foresee a few of these and take the necessary precautions. For instance, merchandise lost or damaged in shipment can be covered by insurance.

If You Are a Seller

What can happen? After all, presumably, you control the transaction by withholding the merchandise until payment has been assured. But these four things constitute risk:

1. Insufficient funds for a check. You can get a report about a person's checking account (whether there has been prior trouble), but you will never know whether there are sufficient funds until the check clears.
2. Credit card chargeback. Any buyer can have his or her credit card bank nullify a purchase for good reason usually within a 90-day period. Some banks extend that period up to a year.
3. Forged or phony financial instrument (e.g., money order, cashier's check, certified check, traveler's check).
4. Shill bidding (see below).

Usually, prior trouble with a bank account warns you about a bad check. But when no prior trouble shows, you can still get stung when there are insufficient funds to cover your check. If a buyer does a chargeback on his or her credit card, you may have trouble getting your money or even getting the merchandise back. Then, of course, stolen credit cards cause ongoing problems. Counterfeit financial instruments cause problems offline. Online, where counterfeiters are easier to trace, counterfeit financial instruments do not cause as many problems, but beware. There is a booming traffic in counterfeit instruments.

Fraud Online

Interestingly enough, although fraud occurs at about the same rate online as offline according to some financial experts, more criminals get caught online than offline. Law enforcement can trace them easier online.

However, this observation does not apply to online criminal activity initiated abroad. Crime on eBay and the Web originating in foreign countries is running rampant. The Internet is no longer a safe place unless you take precautions to protect yourself. See Chapter 10.

Shill Bidding

Shill bidding is collusion between two or more bidders working an auction. Online, it can be one bidder working with two ISP (Internet service provider) accounts and two eBay accounts. Unfortunately, this probably happens more than anyone will admit. If you suspect shill bidding, report it to eBay.

Adverse to Buyers

Shill bidding affects bidders when the seller (with two ISP accounts and eBay accounts) bids up the price on an item. This is illegal and also is not permitted by eBay. Nonetheless, many people have second or third ISP accounts and eBay accounts. A seller with more than one eBay account can bid up an item without being discovered. If you have good reason to suspect this, report it to eBay.

Adverse to Sellers

Shill bidding affects a seller when the first bidder bids up the item to a high price to smoke out the reserve amount (the lowest price you are willing to accept) and to preempt honest bidders. The first bidder then retracts his or her bid late in the auction. The second bidder (who can be the same person using a different account) then bids slightly over the reserve. You, the seller, are left with the second bidder's lower bid. Anytime a high bidder retracts a bid, make an analysis to detect shill bidding. If you think it is, report it to eBay.

Negotiate

Should you find yourself in a situation where you have a problem, negotiate. Don't get mad. Don't make unreasonable demands. Don't threaten. Just keep asking the other party to do what he said he would do. Be monotonous. Discuss whatever, but always return to asking the other party to do what he said he would do. That means do what he advertised or what he represented he would do. In the alternative, ask for a refund and offer to return the item auctioned (buyer); or offer a refund and ask that the item auctioned be returned (seller).

It doesn't pay to quibble. As you will see from the remainder of this chapter, your remedies may not work well nor be cost-effective. Consequently, if the other party unreasonably disagrees with you, you may have to make the best of a bad situation and cut your losses.

eBay is not a moral forum; it's a commercial milieu. If you want to fight, blame, or determine right and wrong, you can probably do so better someplace else on the Web. For buyers and sellers, the marketplace has always been fraught with risk. eBay is no different. You have to roll with the punches. I recommend that you stand firm and insist that the other party perform as agreed, but you have to take a practical approach, too, due to the difficulty of finding an adequate remedy. For instance, you can't march down to small claims court and expect to get the matter effectively resolved when the other party lives 2,000 miles away in another state.

Remember the Telephone?

You don't have to negotiate by email. Pick up the telphone and call the other party. Get the telephone number from eBay. Go *Advanced Search, Find Contact Information*. eBay will email you the information. (Your request for the telephone number will be reported to the other party.)

Don't overlook Skype, eBay's new free telephone service, for use in your eBay activities. See Chapter 15.

Remedies

When negotiations fail to reach an acceptable solution to whatever problems arise, you must consider taking action. This section covers some things you can do.

Receipt

A receipt can protect each party to a transaction. It should specify the seller, the buyer, the date, the price, and the merchandise. The receipt should specify the merchandise in detail, and the specification should match the merchandise described in the eBay auction ad.

Absent a receipt, what do you have? Well, you have eBay's email notification regarding the winning bid for the auction. And you have the eBay auction ad itself. These documents establish the terms of the transaction absent a receipt.

Buyer's View

From the buyer's point of view, the receipt is a legal document that summarizes the transaction. If you have to go to court, it's handy to have. Always check the receipt for accuracy, especially in regard to the specification of the merchandise and the price. If the receipt is not correct—and the transaction is large enough—demand an accurate one.

Save all information in regard to the transaction, including the receipt. That means the eBay auction ad, the eBay email notification, and email correspondence. Alas, you may not remember to do so, but if you find yourself in a jam, you'll wish that you had done it.

Seller's View

Always provide a receipt that accurately summarizes the transaction. If a buyer does not dispute the accuracy of the receipt within a reasonable time, the receipt may come in handy later when a buyer starts making unreasonable demands. It also makes you look like a prudent and honest businessperson.

Just as for the buyer, save your eBay auction ad, the email notification, and all other information in regard to the transaction, such as any exchange of email.

Refund and Return

When there's dissatisfaction, a refund and a return of the merchandise often become a good remedy for both buyers and sellers.

Buyer's View

If something unacceptable goes wrong with the transaction and the seller doesn't cooperate, try to get back to the starting line. That means request a refund and return the item. Don't quibble about who will pay the shipping cost (but there's a difference between asking and quibbling). Make sure you send the item back in the condition in which you received it, if possible. This is often a disappointing remedy but a far more practical one than some of the others available.

Seller's View

Sure there are unreasonable buyers. Nonetheless, offer a refund when problems arise as the best way to preserve your reputation and build a following of loyal customers. That is not to say that if problems arise you shouldn't try to get them resolved in other ways, if possible. But a dissatisfied and determined customer will waste your time and sap your energy.

Occasional Seller

Even if you sell only occasionally on eBay, you may have to act like a retailer to preserve your reputation. Your auctioning of 15 or 20 items over the next five years makes you look like a retailer once the time element is removed (e.g., the Feedback Forum).

Oddly enough, it is the seller who usually suggests a refund and return. It's a good way to resolve a problem, keep everyone happy, and reserve your energy for other business endeavors.

The tough case comes along when you've sold something in an "as is" condition with a stipulation that it has defects, and then the buyer wants to return it because it doesn't work due to the defects mentioned. In this circumstance, you have plenty of reason to hang tough with the buyer. But you may find it more trouble to hang tough than to just make a refund.

When you offer or agree to make a refund, always insist that the buyer return the item as a condition of making the refund, even in those occasional cases where you don't want to get the item back. Faced with having to ship the item, the buyer may decide the perceived problem isn't quite as bad as imagined. Just offering to make a refund often defuses the buyer's anger and sets the stage for resolving the situation in another way.

Mediation

When you can't resolve a dispute, sometimes mediation helps. Now we have e-mediation? Well, whatever. Actually, SquareTrade (*http://www.squaretrade.com*) provides dispute resolution. It uses some online techniques to resolve disputes through mediation, but if such techniques don't work, SquareTrade stands ready to use a hands-on effort to resolve arguments. This service is available to all, but both parties have to agree to use it. This is an excellent service. Give serious consideration to using it, especially for serious disputes on large transactions.

The seller can pay a low monthly fee to SquareTrade for the use of their logo. The logo in the seller's auction ads signifies that the seller agrees to use SquareTrade should a dispute arise.

Report to eBay

Negotiated remedies don't always work, and sometimes you have to take action. In addition, nonperformance by one party (i.e., a buyer doesn't pay or a seller doesn't ship the merchandise) requires action.

Unresolved Dispute

When you have a dispute that you cannot resolve, you have to decide what you will do about it. Making a negative feedback that affects the other party's reputation on eBay may be appropriate, but it is not a remedy. However, it may force the other party to resolve the dispute just to make a credible reply to your negative feedback.

Report the problem to eBay as another step in seeking a remedy. Go *Community, Security & Resolution Center, Report Problem*. However, eBay has no interest in resolving commercial disputes. That's up to the parties. Only when an act clearly amounts to criminal behavior, or at least to a shady business practice, will eBay be interested in hearing from you. eBay's action against the other party, if any, will not provide a remedy for you unless it somehow forces the other party to resolve the dispute.

Nonperformance

If one party changes his mind about buying or selling in spite of the occurrence of a valid auction, you can usually convince the other party to perform just by standing firm and insisting. If nonperformance is due to fraud or a deliberate contracting with no intent to perform, you probably won't hear from the other party (i.e., they won't answer you).

Nonperformance is a deliberate act. In some cases, it may be a criminal act. In any case, it's unacceptable behavior, and you should make a negative feedback comment. In addition, if criminal behavior, you should report it to eBay.

Not Optional

Don't think of reporting nonperformance as an option. It's your duty as a good eBay citizen, so to speak, to report such behavior. Most (99.99 percent) of the people who use eBay act honestly and reasonably. If eBay works for you, you have an obligation to make it work for other people. Your feedback on nonperformance warns other eBay members. Your report to eBay on nonperformance (in the case of suspected criminal behavior) may help eBay eliminate bad actors sooner rather than later.

Whether such a report to eBay will result in a remedy for you is not certain. In some cases, it may force the other party to perform. In other cases, it will simply result in the other party being barred from participation in eBay or in no action at all.

Insurance

eBay does provide insurance against fraud. The limit is $200 with a $25 deductible. PowerSellers can offer $500 insurance through eBay. Although this insurance doesn't cover *very* inexpensive items, it does cover *moderately* inexpensive items on which you normally wouldn't willingly spend much money to get insurance. For items over $200 (or $500), eBay figures that the parties should protect themselves in regard to more expensive items; that is, they will act more carefully. This seems a reasonable assumption.

The insurance is automatic, and you collect on a loss by filing a claim. Although similar to filing a complaint, an insurance claim comes with a cash remedy. Too bad that the upper limit isn't $2,000 instead of $200 (or $500).

This insurance doesn't cover damage in shipment. You need to purchase shipping insurance to cover such a potential loss.

Better Business Bureau

Although not the appropriate place to register a complaint against an individual, the Better Business Bureau (*http://bbb.org*) provides a mechanism for filing a complaint against a business. First, the Bureau will refer you to a local Bureau organization if one exists in the locale where the company operates. Not being a governmental agency, the Bureau has limited power to pursue complaints, but for grievances against established businesses, this alternative might work.

Civil and Criminal Liability

Before the discussion of remedies goes further, you need to distinguish between civil and criminal liability.

Civil Claim

A civil claim is one between the parties to an eBay auction transaction. A court will resolve the dispute between the parties if one of the parties files a complaint. This provides the basis on which the court will resolve most transactional disputes. If the claiming party wins, the court usually grants an award of money to compensate for the damages incurred.

Criminal Complaint

Where one party commits fraud or theft, the act is an offense against the public (based on the victim's complaint). Once you file a criminal complaint, it's out of your hands. Only the prosecuting attorney (district attorney or DA) has the authority to prosecute or not to prosecute the complaint.

As a practical matter, the DA will probably not prosecute your complaint should you withdraw it. After all, you may be the only witness; if you don't cooperate, the DA may not find the complaint worth pursuing. If you don't withdraw your complaint, the DA might decide not to prosecute it for lack of adequate evidence or for other reasons. Nonetheless, the DA can choose to prosecute based on your criminal complaint, resulting in an arrest warrant being issued for the other party.

No Threats

Don't threaten the other party. Courts like reasonable people. Courts take a dim view of unreasonable people. You want to make sure a court always sees you as a reasonable person. This presents a dilemma: You always want to let the other party know that you intend to file suit; it may entice him or her to be more reasonable. But you don't want to threaten the other party because it will make you look unreasonable. Thus, you have to walk a fine line. In other words, tone down your threats so they seem like reasonable statements.

Improper: If you don't send my refund immediately, I'm going to sue you for everything you've got and report you to the Better Business Bureau.

Proper: Your refusal to be fair is forcing me to consider seeking remedies other than negotiation.

If you feel this low-key approach has had no effect, repeating it may make it more convincing to the other party.

In many states, a statement like the improper statement above is considered unethical for an attorney:

Improper (for an attorney): If you don't pay my client immediately, I'm going to sue you.

Proper (for an attorney): If you continue to refuse to be fair, you will leave me no choice but to recommend to my client that she file a lawsuit.

Remember, reasonable people file lawsuits only as a last resort.

Although not making threats is important in civil cases, it is particularly important in criminal cases. People who threaten to make criminal complaints if the other party doesn't do this or that do not favorably impress judges. Never overtly threaten to file a criminal complaint against someone if he or she doesn't agree to your terms. It will sound like you're abusing the criminal justice system for your own advantage. Be very subtle; the other party won't miss the point you make.

If you threaten, however subtly, to make a criminal complaint against the other party where such a complaint is not justified, it may have the opposite effect intended. The other party may become indignant and prove even more difficult to negotiate with. Moreover, as long as you can communicate with the other party routinely, chances are you cannot justify criminal action. Real criminals tend to disappear or become incommunicado.

Civil Suit

You can file a suit against the other party in your local small claims court without hiring an attorney. This makes a cost-efficient way of suing someone, if you have the time to handle the case yourself. You can use this kind of legal action particularly effectively against a resident of your state because when you get a judgment (award of money), you can collect it much more easily. As mentioned earlier in the chapter, however, you will have a difficult time using the small claims court to sue a party in another state.

If you need to conduct your own case in small claims court, there is plenty of information available. Nolo Press (*http://www.nolo.com*) publishes a series of self-help legal books that can assist you.

Small claims courts have an upper limit on the jurisdictional amount. In other words, if the damages you seek are over a certain amount, you cannot get full satisfaction in small claims court. For instance, suppose you seek a refund of $4,000 and the small claims court has financial jurisdiction for $3,000. You can't collect more than $3,000 in the small claims court. To recover the entire $4,000, you will have to hire an attorney and file your case in the regular court (the court of general jurisdiction).

Attorneys can be expensive. You need to make a determination as to whether it's worth it to pursue a lawsuit requiring the services of an attorney. With enough at stake, it may make sense. Otherwise a legal remedy may not be a cost-effective option.

Criminal Prosecution

When the other party makes a blatant misrepresentation or does not perform at all, it might be a criminal act. But criminal acts require criminal intent.

Suppose the seller represents that a computer printer prints at 12 pages per minute. It turns out the printer prints at only 4 pages per minute. The seller got the information from the manufacturer and then passed it on to bidders and potential bidders. The seller may have misrepresented the facts but presumably did so without intent. And without intent, there's no crime. This points out that you have to be very careful before you accuse anyone of a criminal act.

Suppose you send a check for the computer printer after exchanging email messages with the seller. You don't receive the printer in two weeks and you try to get in touch with the seller to no avail. How long do you wait to take action? Suppose the seller happened to go on vacation for three weeks just after your check arrived and was deposited, and the printer was mistakenly not sent. It may not be a good business practice to close the doors, in effect, for three weeks, but it's not a criminal act.

You need to consider it very carefully before you file a criminal complaint against someone. Make sure he or she has committed a criminal act, not just done something with which you don't agree. Make sure he or she intended to commit the act. Don't take filing a criminal complaint lightly. Keep in mind, too, that unless you have convincing evidence that the other party has committed fraud, the police will not have much motivation to take action.

However, when you've been had by someone, sooner or later it becomes painfully obvious. Don't be reluctant to file a criminal complaint. In such a case, it's not only your duty as a good eBay citizen, it's your duty as a good citizen of society. Usually, you will find that you are not the first victim. If you are the first victim, though, perhaps your complaint will save others the pain of being defrauded.

Is a criminal case a remedy for you? Not in most cases. You can probably best use it as a threat, albeit a subtle threat as explained earlier in the No Threats subsection. In a criminal case, however, the judge imposes a jail sentence, and that will not necessarily benefit you.

Out of Touch

If someone defrauds you, he will almost certainly take the money (or merchandise) and run. He will be out of touch, and your biggest clue that you've been bamboozled will be that you can't communicate with him. Can law enforcement eventually catch up with him? Apparently the police have an easier time finding criminals who have committed crimes online than offline, but it takes aggressive law enforcement to catch such criminals in any event. Whether you can enlist such aggressive law-enforcement investigators on your behalf is the question. Probably not!

Across State Lines

Conducting a lawsuit or even filing a criminal complaint across state lines is likely to be more complicated than filing one at home. It's probably not worth your time unless it involves a large amount of money. Attorneys typically charge well over $100 per hour.

State Court

For instance, suppose you are in Michigan and file a claim in small claims court against the other party who lives in New Mexico. You get a judgment in Michigan. What will you do next? You may have to file an action (which requires a hearing) in court in New Mexico in order to enforce the judgment in New Mexico. This will probably require an attorney. Then you have to collect the judgment, often the most difficult part of the process. And you have to do all this over a thousand miles from home. Note, too, that in some cases by law you may not be able to enforce a small claims court judgment in another state.

Suppose you want to file a criminal complaint against the other party in New Mexico. You will file the complaint from a long ways away. To get a conviction, the local DA will have to trust that you will travel to New Mexico to testify. The local DA may not show great enthusiasm about prosecuting such a case. Even if the DA prosecutes the person, a criminal conviction does not necessarily resolve the problems in the transaction (i.e., you don't get a remedy).

Attorney General

Many states handle fraud cases through the state Attorney General's office, not through the local DAs. The Attorney General may have a permanent fraud office or a fraud task force.

Federal Agencies

Under federal statutes you can file a complaint against the other party with the US Postal Inspection Service (*http://www.framed.usps.com/ postalinspectors*) if US mail was used by the other party, the Federal Trade Commission (FTC — *http://www.ftc.gov*), or the federal Attorney General. Again, this might result in penalties to the other party but no benefit to you. The subtle threat of doing so, however, may have an effect on the other party, if such a complaint is justified.

You can also file a report with the National Fraud Information Center (*http://www.fraud.org*). The Center transmits this report to the National Fraud Database maintained by the FTC and also to the National Association of Attorneys General. Where this will lead is anyone's guess, but it beats doing nothing if criminal behavior seems apparent.

You can file a criminal complaint in the federal court via the FBI (*http://www.fbi.gov*) if you believe that federal criminal laws have been broken. In fact, you can file a complaint online at the FBI website (see Figure 9.1). I have actually done this three times (non-eBay transactions). Whether the US Attorney will pursue the case is out of your hands, but often this is the most realistic way to prosecute criminals who operate across state lines.

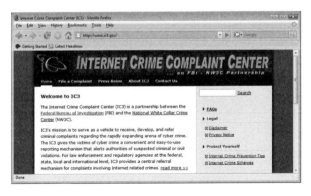

Figure 9.1 File a complaint online at the FBI website.

Federal Court

You can conduct a lawsuit between parties from different states in federal court. You will need an attorney, however, and conducting a lawsuit in the federal court tends to be more expensive than doing the same in a state court. To justify the expenses to conduct such a suit, the amount you seek to recover must be large.

eBay

Go to *Community, Security & Resolution Center* to report fraud to eBay. It's the best way to protect your fellow eBay members and maintain eBay as a viable and enduring marketplace.

Collecting a Judgment

Just because you get a judgment against someone doesn't mean that you'll realize a remedy. You still have to collect the judgment. Often this is impossible for any number of reasons:

- The other party disappears.
- The other party's assets disappear.
- The other party has no assets.
- The other party is difficult, and expensive, to locate.

You can go to all the expense of conducting a lawsuit (i.e., attorney fees), get a judgment, and then never collect a dime. This is a sobering thought when you consider initiating a lawsuit.

Prevention

This chapter will probably not help you much except to make you realize that prevention is your best defense against an unfair or fraudulent transaction. If you will recall, this book recommends that as a buyer you never bid more than you can afford to lose. If you bid more than that, make sure that you protect yourself with an escrow arrangement. If you're a seller, never deliver the merchandise until the buyer pays you.

Unfortunately, you cannot eliminate all risk. You can only take common sense precautions. If you go overboard as a buyer, you may be asking for negative feedback. For instance, if you insist on paying by credit card when a seller has stated in his auction ad that the only acceptable payment method is by money order, you're asking for trouble. The seller may not even have a credit card merchant account.

If you go overboard as a seller, you will put a damper on your business. For instance, if you take only money orders, you don't run the risk of chargebacks on credit cards. But you eliminate a lot of honest potential bidders who want or need to pay by credit card. And money orders have their own risks anyway.

Although precautions do not provide an absolute guarantee, they will considerably reduce your chances of becoming a victim of an unfair or fraudulent transaction. So, practice prevention as your best remedy for the acts of those unsavory predators lurking on the auction grounds.

Forget It

There comes a time when you may just have to forget it and get on with your life—not a pleasant thought when someone has treated you unfairly or defrauded you. But as you have learned from reading this chapter, conducting a lawsuit is expensive and time-consuming with negligible chances of collecting in most cases.

If you do get taken by someone, report it to all the proper places, but prepare to absorb the loss.

eBay Offenses

eBay lists a number of prohibited offenses in its eBay Security Center section of the eBay website. See an up-to-date list and more detailed information at *Community, Security & Resolution Center, Rules & Polices*. Some of these actions may constitute criminal activities; some do not. Regardless, eBay will take action (e.g., indefinite suspension of an offender) on any of these offenses reported. The following subsections list some of the eBay offenses.

Feedback Offenses

You cannot use second registrations or associates for the filing of positive feedback to boost your own feedback record (shill feedback).

You cannot use second registrations or associates for the filing of negative feedback to impact the feedback record of another person (shill feedback).

You cannot threaten negative feedback to demand from another person some undeserved action (feedback extortion).

You cannot offer to sell, trade, or buy feedback (feedback solicitation).

Bidding Offenses

You cannot use second registrations or associates to artificially raise the level of bidding to extremely high levels temporarily in order to protect the low bid of an associate (bid shielding).

You cannot email the bidders in a currently open auction to offer the same or similar item at a lower price (bid siphoning).

You cannot email bidders in a currently open auction to warn them away from a seller or item (auction interference).

You cannot retract a bid to manipulate the bidding.

You cannot use second registrations or associates to artificially raise the number of bids to the level required for a "HOT" designation.

You cannot chronically bid on items without completing the transactions for which you are the high bidder.

You cannot persist to bid on a seller's items after a warning from seller that your bids are not welcome (e.g., seller doesn't want to do business with you due to your negative feedback rating).

Selling Offenses

You cannot use second registrations or associates to artificially raise the bidding on your item up for auction (shill bidding).

You cannot represent yourself as an eBay seller (another person) and intercept the ended auctions of that seller for the purpose of accepting payment (auction interception).

You cannot manipulate the system to avoid paying fees.

You cannot sell items (accept payments) and not complete the transactions (not deliver the items).

Contact Information–Identity Offenses

You cannot represent yourself as an eBay employee.

You cannot represent yourself as another eBay user.

You cannot provide false information such as name, address, and telephone number to eBay.

You cannot use an invalid email address.

You cannot be an eBay user if you are under age 18.

Miscellaneous Offenses

You cannot use any device, software, or procedure to interfere with the proper operation of eBay.

You cannot send unsolicited email to past bidders or buyers.

You cannot threaten another eBay user with bodily harm via email.

You cannot publish the contact information of another eBay user on any online public area.

You cannot offer pirated intellectual property or illegal items for sale.

You cannot use profane, vulgar, racist, hateful, sexual, or obscene language on any online public area.

How Seriously?

Does eBay take fraud seriously, and if so, how seriously? eBay hired an ex-federal district attorney to oversee its security operations. Today it employs several ex-federal district attorneys and over 1,300 employees who work on security. That's serious.

Verified Rights Owner Program

eBay operates a program with publishers (software publishers as well as publishers of books and other intellectual property) that helps keep counterfeit or illegally copied materials off eBay: Verified Rights Owner (VeRO) program. If you are a victim of a fraud involving intellectual property (e.g., pirated software), a complaint to eBay (or to the copyright holder that is a VeRO) should result in some action.

Summary

This chapter does not attempt to define every transaction on eBay that is unfair or fraudulent. Indeed, when it comes to fraud, some criminals are ingenious. Nor does it attempt to define everything you can do to prevent someone from defrauding you or otherwise dealing with you unfairly. The chapter simply explores the potential of resorting to eBay or the legal system for a remedy. Unless large amounts of money are at stake, however, the prospects do not look good for recovering a loss through the legal system. Therefore, you have to be conscious that prevention provides your best remedy for the losses you would likely suffer, sooner or later, by being careless. But don't act so overly careful that you increase your potential for offending potential bidders.

Tens of millions of people use eBay each week. They include a few crooks who do their best to prey upon others for their own personal gain. But overall, nice people like you and me who just want to make mutually beneficial transactions comprise all but a very small part of the huge eBay marketplace.

10

Operating with Security

Security has become a topic that no basic eBay book can ignore, which poses a dilemma for me. I'm not a security expert, yet I need to include security information in this book. Thus, be advised to use this chapter as a resource that points you to additional security information, not as a complete online security treatise.

As mentioned in Chapter 9, the primary crime threat online is now coming from outside the country. Here's what I wrote in *eBay Business the Smart Way, Third Edition*, which has a longer and more robust security chapter:

> Don't underestimate this threat. Third-world countries have their share of highly trained digital experts, many of them trained in the US and other developed countries. In fact, there is no shortage of capable technology schools in many third-world countries either. Thus, there's an abundance of digitally knowledgeable people. Those who turn to crime in such countries have a risk-free, prosecution-free shot over and over again at your bank account, domain name (website), and other password-protected assets and networked financial processes. Such criminals work at it all day, everyday. It's their job. Sooner or later, they will get you.

Think of it this way. Cybercrime has now been outsourced to a pool of international cybercriminals that's larger than the pool of cybercriminals in the US. Cybercrime is going to get worse every year for a long time.

Indeed, whether you're a casual eBay user or someone who spends a lot of time on eBay buying and selling, the time has come to learn about online security before you suffer a big loss. That loss might be anything from money to merchandise to ID theft.

Equipment

You use a modem to get access to the Internet. For a normal telephone line, it's a dial-up modem. For a DSL telephone line, it's a DSL modem. For cable Internet, it's a cable modem. The question is, What should be the next piece of equipment between the access source and your computer?

Router

The answer is a router. Home (small office) routers are inexpensive and enable you to connect more than one computer to your Internet access (see Figure 10.1). Moreover, routers are an essential piece of security equipment. They go a long way toward keeping out the hackers. Don't use your computer without one.

Make sure you change the *Admin* password in the software that sets up your router, otherwise the router won't do you as much good. The hackers know the default password for your router set-up software.

Buy and use a router that includes a firewall. A firewall is software, but it runs faster when integrated into the router than it does as software running on your computer.

If you use a dial-up modem, you don't use a router. You will need software protection instead (e.g., a firewall).

Wireless

A wireless system for your home or office can be secure. But to make it secure, you have to set up encrypted transmission. Otherwise, anyone with a wireless NIC (network interface card) in their computer (e.g., laptop) can get into your local network so long as they are within range (e.g., in a car parked across the street). Without encryption you have no security, and a wireless network system is less secure than a wired system.

You may need to hire an expert (or the vendor) to set up encryption (a 10-minute job) for you if you can't figure out how to do it yourself.

Turn It Off

One protection of the dial-up modem is that a user is usually only online for a reasonably short time. No one can get into your computer when you're offline.

DSL and cable Internet access are full time. Hackers can always take a shot at your security. Consequently, you need to turn off your computer every night. That is, your computer goes offline for several hours everyday thereby potentially interfering with any long-term hacking processes.

Figure 10.1 A home (small office) router.

Software

Equipment security is not enough. You need software security too. The types of security software below are essential to minimize your risk online.

Firewall

If you use a dial-up modem or if your router doesn't have a firewall, use firewall software to protect your computer. This is not an option unless you want to appear naked on the Internet.

Anti-Virus

Viruses can invade your computer via email or program downloads. They can reek havoc with your computer. Well-proven anti-virus software is your best protection. Buy software that runs constantly.

Anti-Spyware

Spyware (see Figure 10.2) doesn't necessarily cause havoc with your computer, although it can slow down your computer. What it does is provide via the Internet information to someone outside your computer network. You can see where this could be hazardous to your ecommerce health. Indeed, most spyware is used today to gather legitimate ecommerce information for marketing purposes. But it is also used extensively to gather ecommerce information for crime. You can't afford to use your computer without anti-spyware software. Sooner or later, probably sooner, you'll suffer an economic loss.

Figure 10.2 Spybot website. ©2000-2007 Patrick M. Kolla.

Operating System

If you use Windows, you should be aware that when your computer is set to share with other computers, it is much more vulnerable to hacking than if not. Therefore, it is important to disable sharing. Since sharing is a default setting, you will have to take action to turn it off. If you can't figure out how to do it—and it's different for each version of Windows—hire an expert to do it for you (a five-minute job).

Updates

Make sure that all your security software and your operating system are updated regularly. That means almost everyday for anti-virus, anti-spyware, and operating system software.

Security Practices

It is difficult to separate security practices, equipment, and software. They are all part of an umbrella of protection for your computer. Each plays its role. With just one hole in the umbrella, you can get soaking wet. This section covers things you can do to increase your security online.

Passwords

Gone are the days when you could use the name of your dog as a password for access to a secure online account. Today you need passwords for access to many different accounts and websites, and names make terribly insecure passwords.

Never

Never give your password to anyone. Hackers con people into revealing passwords on the telephone or by email. Hackers don't crack passwords (assuming they're random characters) with some kind of digital magic.

The best passwords are random 12-character passwords with mixed numbers and alaphbetic characters. such as:

gTY92fd74H3c

If 12-character passwords aren't permitted, use as many characters as are permitted (e.g., sometimes the limit is eight characters).

But how do you keep track of these random passwords? You use a password database.

Password Databases

Password databases are convenient programs that enable you to store passwords, PIN numbers, and accompanying security information (see Figure 10.3). The database requires password access, so you only need to memorize one password. When you need a password, you can quickly look it up in your password database.

Pick a program that's easy to use, encrypts the password database, and requires its own password to access. You won't have to worry about anyone getting your password.

Password Agent, *http://www.moonsoftware.com*

Password Keeper, *http://www.gregorybraun.com*

Password Manager XP, *http://www.cplab.com*

Password Safe Pro, *http://www.passwordsafepro.com*

Password Security Vault, *http://www.hirtlesoftware.com*

Password Tracker Deluxe, *http://www.clrpc.com*

Figure 10.3 Password Safe Pro password database program.

Secret Question

Some accounts (including eBay) enable you to use a secret question to access your account under certain circumstances. How do you use it? This seems self-evident. You pick a question like: What's your pet's name? You enter *Portia*, your cat's name. No hacker could know this, right?

Wrong! A hacker might get this information over the telephone or someplace on the Web. The correct answer to this question is not *Portia*. It's *Shipwreck*. (Or, make up another equally obtuse name.) How do you remember this name? You keep it in your password database with your password.

eBay

Your eBay password protects you against someone else using your eBay account and ID. A bad actor could do you a lot of harm on eBay if you carelessly use your password and allow someone else to get it. With a well-choosen password that no one else can know, you can be confident your eBay account is secure.

PayPal

Your PayPal password protects you against someone stealing your money. Keep in mind that PayPal is essentially a bank. Treat your PayPal password as you would treat the password to your bank account online.

If a thief can get into your PayPal account, he can not only take all the money out of it but also send money to himself (his PayPal accounts). Then he can withdraw the money from his PayPal account and disappear. Consequently, it is important for you to give maximum security to your PayPal password.

Logging

You log in with a login name and a password. You don't have a choice. But do you log out?

When it comes to logging out, you do have a choice. You can simply close your browser, or you can log out. If you close your browser, your open account will time out (usually close within a half-hour). In the meanwhile, someone evil might be able to take advantage of your account being open.

The better practice is to always log out. When you log out, your connection to the account is broken, and no one can get access to the account without the password.

Secure Website

Never provide a password or credit card number except in a secure transmission. For instance, most online checkout mechanisms (on a secure webpage) take your credit card information and transmit it securely—by encrypting it—to the vendor's website.

How can you tell if the webpage is secure? Look at the URL window near the top of your browser. The URL of the website should start with *https://* not *http://*. Also, the padlock at the bottom of the browser should appear closed while a secure webpage is displayed. Do not deal with websites that do not use secure transmission for passwords, credit card numbers, and other secure information (i.e., that do not use secure webpages).

Free Email

Your ISP provides you with Internet service locally and knows your name, address, and perhaps your credit card number. When you use an ISP email account, your emails can be traced directly to you. Thus, people who use ISP email are easily traceable. Nothing wrong with this. It helps trace online criminals within the US.

A person with a free email account such as Hotmail or Gmail is not necessarily traceable. Anyone can sign up for such an account without paying and without giving personal information. Certainly there are legitimate reasons for using free email accounts, but anyone who uses such an account is immediately suspect until proven innocent. In other words, beware of people who use free email accounts. This type of email is used for fraud every day.

Social Engineering

Social engineering is simply a hacker gathering information about you. He might use:

- The telephone to call people.
- The Internet to research information about you.
- Commercial information resources to get your information.

Contrary to popular belief, hacking is not necessarily some mysterious digital activity used by computer programmers. It is programming skill used in tandem with social engineering to acquire enough information to gain access to one of your accounts.

For instance, a social engineer might contact ten potential sources by telephone to gain information about you. He gets a little bit of information from each of five sources and none from the remainder. Those five bits of information are enough for him to then contact your bank to pose as you and attempt to gain access to your bank account. That's social engineering, a very practical endeavor.

You can't control what other people will do in regard to social engineering with you as the target. But you can control yourself. Don't ever let anyone con you out of your personal information unless you are 100 percent sure they are legitimate. That's 100 percent, not 95 percent. And never give anyone your Social Security number unless required to do so by law.

Medical Industry

The medical industry is many years behind most other industries in using digital technology. Many medical businesses (e.g., doctors' offices, HMOs) still use your Social Security number as your account number. Don't stand for this. Don't give your Social Security number to any business that doesn't require it by law (e.g., employer, bank, stock brokerage firm). Insist that they use another account number for their records system.

It's outrageous that the use of Social Security numbers as account numbers still continues in the backwaters of our economy. With the huge amount of money that we spend on health care, you would think that the medical industry would not put our financial security at risk.

Phishing (Fishing)

Phishing is the practice of sending email to a person in an attempt to con the person into giving up personal information. In other words, the criminal is *fishing* for information that can be used to access an account or commit ID theft.

I get a dozen phishing emails everyday, many of them posing as eBay or PayPal. They look very authentic. They used to ask for information by return email, but the general public has caught on to that scam.

Now they ask you to click on a link to a website to provide the requested information. The link appears to be one where you have an account (e.g., eBay), but it really goes elsewhere to another website that appears to be authentic. If you fall for this scam, you will be giving away your personal information to someone with criminal intent.

You can tell where the link goes. Your email program will indicate where the link is going regardless of where the text of the email message states it is going. Thus, when the two are different, you are alerted to the scam.

Eudora 7, my email program, automatically alerts me when the visible text of the link and the URL for the link are different. That makes it easy, but somehow the feature doesn't always work. So I must stay alert and check it myself.

Phishing is a type of social engineering practiced on you. It's a criminal attempting to con you into giving up your personal information to assist the criminal in stealing from you. Don't fall for it.

Counterfeits

Modern digital technology (e.g., high resolutional computer printers) and the growth of ecommerce have revived the ancient art of counterfeiting. It is suddenly big business on the Web. What defense do you have against it? Not much! I am tempted to advise against accepting paper financial instruments (checks, cashier's checks, money orders) but many people still use them. All I can say is:

- Wait for the instrument to clear before shipping.

- Become familiar with the standard financial instruments (e.g., US postal money orders, Western Union money orders) so as to be able to spot a poor counterfeit. (You probably won't be able to spot a good counterfeit.)

An expert counterfeiter will print the name of the financial institution on the instrument but will print a different magnetic routing number on the bottom. Here's how that will work.

You get a check drawn on a bank in your state and region. You expect it to clear in two days. You expect your bank to notify you on the third day that it bounced if it is returned unpaid. If you haven't heard from your bank on the third day, you ship on the fourth day. (Substitute various time periods to make them appropriate to your situation.)

The problem is that the routing number has routed the check to some faraway financial institutional where clearing takes a long time. By the time the check is returned to your bank unpaid, it might be a week or three weeks later. You've already shipped the item.

You can check the routing number yourself. Look up the financial institution to which the routing number has been assigned. If it doesn't match the financial institution printed on the check, you have a counterfeit in your hands. (You can check routing numbers on the Web. RoutingTool.com at *http://routingtool.com* is one place.) If it does match, that doesn't mean it's not a counterfeit; but if it doesn't clear, you should get a notification that it hasn't cleared within the normal time period you would expect regarding the financial institution named on the instrument.

Prosecution?

The word I have received from my lawyer, who is a commercial specialist, is that the FBI won't work on a counterfeit case unless it's a loss over $50,000. This, of course, is unverified but believable. Commercial crime is running rampant now with a huge boost from abroad, and the FBI has to worry about terrorists as well as commercial criminals.

Resources

A problem with Web security resources is that individuals and small orginizations were pioneers in providing such security information online. Unfortunately, the amount of online fraud and crime overwhelmed those who choose to keep track of it, and many of the original security websites are no longer in operation. This section contains a few of the current resources deemed to be stable and enduring.

Scambusters

Scambusters (*http://www.scambusters.org*) provides a wealth of information on various scams with plenty of examples. The more scams you know about, the less likely you are to get taken by the next scam that comes along.

CyberSource

CyberSource (*http://cybersource.com*) publishes the Annual Online Fraud Report. Go to the website to get the latest copy. It will give you a good idea of the effect of fraud on online businesses and what the trends are. Study the report and you'll get a better idea of where you need to focus your anti-crime efforts.

OnGuard Online

This is a federal government website (*http://onguardonline.gov*) that seeks to educate the public to protect itself against Internet fraud. This has a wealth of information, and you will do well to work your way through it.

eBay Security & Resolution Center

Naturally eBay also publishes information about online fraud. You can find it at the Security & Resolution Center. Go *Community, Security & Resolution Center* and start reading.

Make sure you read the 23-page PDF booklet *Security & Privacy - Made Simpler*, a joint publication of the Better Business Bureau and eBay.

PayPal Security Center

The PayPal Security Center provides you with a wealth of information about online security too. It's worth your trouble going through it slowly and carefully from time to time to refresh your security knowledge and learn what's new. On PayPal go *Account Overview* and look for the *Security Center* link at the bottom of the page.

For information that you can print, look for the 20-page PDF *e-commerce Safety Guide*, an eBay-PayPal joint publication.

What About Being Online?

According to Interactive Software Solutions LP, there are more paper and mail based ID thefts every year than such thefts resulting from the use of the Internet. Electronic detection of ID theft comes sooner, and electronic losses are less. In other words, if you conduct all of your business online and follow proper security practices, you will have a lower risk of economic loss. (I have no way to verify this statement, but offline ID theft is certainly a significant and persistent problem.)

This statement, if accurate, indicates that you can be safer on the Internet than off. You can only be safer, however, if you learn about digital security (e.g., from security books and magazines articles) and religiously follow safe security practices.

Summary

Security is not just about eBay. It's a matter that concerns all your online activities as well as eBay and PayPal. Keep in mind, though, that eBay and PayPal are economic activities. If you don't use secure online practices for eBay and PayPal, you are likely to sustain an economic loss. Thus, security has become an important topic for a basic eBay book.

Again, let me say that you need expert information on this topic. This chapter is just an introduction, not an adequate source of complete information on security.

Don't try to eat the whole pie at once if you've never paid much attention to digital security before. First, get your equipment set up properly (e.g., buy a router). Next buy the requisite software and get it working properly. Make sure it's updated regularly. Finally, institute effective security practices such as using random-character passwords. I'm not suggesting you dally, but security is a lot to digest if you've ignored it. Don't try to do it all tonight after you've read this chapter. Take the time to do it right.

On the other hand, there is the urgency of protecting yourself before the worst happens. You might want to take a few days off to get your digital security in order. If you don't, you may find yourself taking a few weeks off to clean up the mess that some degenerate criminal left you with.

To end this chapter on a happier note, I will say that intelligent security practices work. They do protect you and lower your risk substantially of becoming a victim.

III

Using Bidding Strategies

11

Timely Bidding

There are no bidding guarantees, only strategies and tactics. This chapter will help you develop an eBay strategy and give you some tactics to improve your bidding success.

Realities

No bidding practices will guarantee that you will win an auction, except perhaps overbidding by a considerable margin. Another bidder can come in and outbid you at any time by offering a price that you do not wish to match.

At times eBay, the Internet, or your connection slows down, making the precise timing of bids difficult in the final moments of the auction. Then too, when you get set up ahead of time to carry on a last-minute bidding frenzy, you may unexpectedly get called away to do something more important and thereby miss the final minutes of the auction. I've done this on numerous occasions.

The bidding process itself may yield information about the item being offered—information that provides a basis for changing your bid limit at the last minute—but you may be unavailable or unprepared to make the adjustment necessary to win the bidding. Or, the bidding process in the heat of the last moments may overwhelm you; it's sometimes difficult to make decisions when the window of opportunity is measured in seconds.

The underlying assumptions of the prior paragraphs are:

That you will have bidding competition. The size of eBay tends to guarantee that you will. Nonetheless, you will find plenty of auctions where the expected competition does not materialize. You can often pick up valuable goods for even less than the minimum price you anticipated.

That your bidding competition will be tough, knowledgeable competitors. In fact, not everyone takes the time to bone up on eBay bidding, and your competitors may do some dumb things.

That your competitors who have already made competitive bids will also be there in the last few minutes of the auction. In fact, most bidders cannot appear at the finale of every auction they enter. Some of your competition might be missing during those last few minutes.

In conclusion, there are no guarantees, but nonetheless, there are opportunities to buy at significant savings.

Strategies

What is your strategy for making purchases on eBay? For most people it will be one of the following five purposes:

1. Buying goods (e.g., camera equipment) for less money than elsewhere. This is a *money-saving* strategy.

2. Buying from a large selection of goods (e.g., offbeat brands). This is a *consumer-buying* strategy.

3. Buying goods not otherwise available conveniently (e.g., old items). This is a *time-saving* strategy.

4. Buying for resale (e.g., buy at or below wholesale and sell retail,

that is, buy low and sell high). This is a *profit* strategy.

5. Having fun (e.g., last-minute bidding). This is an *emotional* strategy.

Some buy on eBay to save money, some to get a bigger selection, some to save time, some to make profit, and some to have fun. These are general strategies. Each eBay category may have its own special strategies, but with tens of thousands of categories, this book cannot cover them all. Thus, I don't provide strategies for buying any particular category of merchandise, but the general strategies above ought to work well in most cases.

Save Money

I can't speak for anyone else, but I can tell you my general strategies for buying on eBay.

- New items: These must sell at 40–55 percent of list price (i.e., a 45–60 percent discount). If you can't get the merchandise at such low prices on eBay, you should buy it at a discount store; it's less risky. You know the discount store, you know where it is, and the discount store usually provides a liberal return policy. Buying from an eBay seller, you usually don't get the same assurances.

- Factory-refurbished items: These are almost the same as new goods if they come in a factory-sealed box with a warranty. I will pay almost as much for these goods as for new goods (i.e., discounted price) under two conditions. First, the refurbished items are not generally available at retail. If they are, the price should be significantly lower than new goods. The scarcity of factory-refurbished goods makes them almost as valuable as new goods (i.e., new goods sold with a deep price discount). Second, the item is soon to be obsolete (within a few years). For example, a hard drive will last for ten years in a home office. You will use it for only three before you buy a bigger one. What difference does it make if you buy a factory-refurbished one instead of a new one?

- Used items in excellent condition: These must sell at 35 percent of list price (i.e., a 65 percent discount). When anyone can buy an item new at a discount store for 60 percent of list price, used items even in excellent condition usually aren't worth as much as one would think. Most people given the choice between buying a new item at 60 percent of list and a used item at 40–60 percent of list will choose the new item. Realistically, the market value for most used goods is normally below 40 percent of list (i.e., more than a 60 percent discount).

I won't pay more than the above guidelines indicate. That's my strategy. Of course, there are plenty of situations on eBay that do not meet my general guidelines. Often one brand leads the field in a category, and everyone wants it (e.g., Marantz for high-end stereo components). Items with the hot brand name often sell on eBay for what you might pay for them in a discount store, or even higher. This doesn't make sense, but it happens. You won't find me making such a purchase on eBay. However, I live in a metro area of seven million people with scores of specialty discount stores. Naturally, I would feel differently if I lived in a place where the nearest specialty discount store was 250 miles away.

For Sellers

I don't think my guidelines are unusually strict. If a person pays full retail for an item when anyone else could get it at a discount store for 60 percent of list price, the person takes an immediate 40 percent loss, in effect. Even if the item is still sealed-box-new, the person won't make up her loss by selling on eBay. She will take an additional loss, or she won't attract any bidders.

Some used goods are rare but in high demand. They can go at surprisingly high prices relative to their original list price (e.g., used Leica film cameras). For such goods, if I needed them, I would certainly bend my guidelines. But generally speaking, you can say that my strategy for buying on eBay is to pay less than I would elsewhere.

Every Item Different

General rules, like I've just stated above, sound great, but they are seldom useful unless used just as guidelines. The fact is that every item is different (and has its own market) even from similar items. The more you can learn about the market for each individual item you buy or sell, the better you will come out financially.

Not a Collector

Note that I'm not a collector. I'm a miser. Collectors tend to be time-savers.

Get a Bigger Selection

Many people live in rural areas where their local retailers don't offer the range of choices that people would have in metro areas. But they can find a wider range of choices on eBay. Catalog sales have thrived on this reality for over a century. Indeed, catalog sales remain high even in metro areas where people are too busy to shop or the specialty discount store is miles away on the other side of town. Keep in mind that a significant amount of the merchandise people sell on eBay is new. It's not all old stuff. The strategy here for buyers is to get a large selection. Low price isn't as important for this consumer strategy as it is for the money-saving strategy outlined above.

Save Time

There are two aspects of saving time: (1) saving yourself a long search for a hard-to-find item; and (2) simple convenience.

Saving Big Time

You have an old Shure microphone you bought ten years ago. Now you want an exact match for a special event at which your singing group will perform. But Shure doesn't make that model any longer. Where do you get it? You can hang out at the local rock band store or the audio equipment store hoping that a duplicate will turn up in the used equipment department. But eBay will offer a wider choice of used goods than is available locally, and eBay provides you with a good opportunity to find what you're looking for.

For this type of item, you have to price it at what it's worth to you, or you may waste a lot of your time. In other words, don't use your guidelines for money-saving purchases. This is a time-saving purchase. Will you really turn down a high price on eBay and continue to look for a cheaper price? For instance, suppose the Shure microphone listed for $150 ten years ago. Today, even in excellent condition, theoretically it should be worth about ten cents on the dollar (i.e., 10 percent of original list price). If you find one at 70 percent of list value ($105) on eBay, how much longer are you going to look around to find one cheaper? In fact, good microphones don't necessarily deteriorate if maintained properly and used properly, and the list price on a comparable new microphone today might be $250. So, as a practical matter, what you think *should* be the price (about $15) and what you are willing to pay (you want the exact duplicate) will probably be different. Keep in mind that eBay may be the only place where you can find this item without a lot of time-consuming searching in several nearby towns or cities. So, the strategy here is saving time. It's quick and easy to find it on eBay (if it's there).

Collectors

Many collectors fall into this category. They delight in finding something on eBay that they might never find in a decade of searching locally, and they will pay a premium price for an item that has no logical relationship to its original list price. The Beanie Baby phenomenon of the 1990s makes a good example. Collectors were willing to spend a lot for rare Beanie Babies on eBay to make their collections more complete because chances of happening across such a Beanie Baby locally were not good.

Convenience

And then there are those of us who look at eBay as a convenience machine. Why spend the time to drive to a faraway store to pick up an item you need but don't have to have immediately? Even if you don't save money buying it on eBay, at least it's delivered to your front door. I've been buying on eBay since 1998—a lot of new stuff for home and business. So far I have not had anything damaged in shipment.

Saving a long drive (i.e., gas expense) to a faraway store may pay for shipping costs in some cases too.

Yes, you see it online. You use PayPal to pay for it. And it magically appears at your front door. Not a bad shopping experience.

Make Profit

This is strictly a business strategy. For buying, you need to buy low, just as with the money-saving strategy, and sell at a profit. For arbitrage, you need to have the confidence that you can sell immediately at a higher price.

Retail

If you can buy new goods at or below wholesale on eBay and resell at retail (e.g., in your physical store), you can make a profit. However, presumably the risk of buying on eBay is higher than buying from a distributor. Thus, the price of new goods on eBay will normally have to be significantly lower than wholesale to justify the risk. Thus, the profit strategy is virtually identical to the money-saving strategy.

The exception is for goods in high demand that may be temporarily unavailable from distributors or manufacturers. If you can buy such goods on eBay, even for a premium above wholesale, and resell at retail (or even above retail), you can make a profit that you otherwise wouldn't be able to make. Here the strategy is to get the merchandise; but it's not that simple. You still have to get the goods at a low enough price to make a reasonable profit selling at retail. But be cautious. When the temporary shortage of goods passes, retail prices will fall quickly.

It's a little different for used goods. Some retailers enjoy a healthy market for used goods but cannot find enough inventory to buy for resale (e.g., antique dealers). However, eBay provides them with a major source of used goods that they can depend on for acquiring inventory. Here the strategy is to build up your used inventory, but you still have to get the goods at a discount deep enough to enable you to resell the goods and make a reasonable profit.

Arbitrage

Arbitrage is buying in one market and selling immediately in another market where the price is a little higher. In other words, if you can buy something on eBay and sell it immediately at a higher price somewhere else (another market that's not as efficient, either online or offline), you can make a small profit. Certainly, other online auctions do not operate as efficiently as eBay; that is, they do not have the volume to determine a stable price for a particular item. Perhaps you can engage in arbitrage between such auctions and eBay. If you can be sure of selling something immediately for a higher price in another market, buy it on eBay where it's likely to be cheaper, and then resell it in the other market.

Arbitrage is a stock-market technique. It does not work as well for the more erratic and less efficient goods market. The transfer of stocks is immediate. The cost of transfer for stocks is small. On the other hand, the transfer of goods usually takes time. The cost of transfer for goods involves shipping and sometimes sales tax and other costs. Nonetheless, where prices are out of sync enough and an immediate resale is assured, you can use arbitrage to realize narrow profit margins.

Arbitrage Is Not Retail

Buying at low prices on eBay and selling at retail is not the same as arbitrage. If you can buy at wholesale prices or below on eBay, which is quite possible, then you can sell at retail offline without having to sell immediately. There's more profit in a retail sale, so you don't have to make an immediate sale to minimize your holding costs.

Arbitrage can work two ways for you with eBay. First, you can buy elsewhere and sell on eBay, or you can buy on eBay and sell elsewhere. The principle is simply that the resale must be certain, immediate, and profitable.

An example is baseball caps with official major-league team insignias, about $8–$16 per cap at retail stores. If you can find a closeout purchase of 10,000 caps (in the closeout market) for $0.50 per cap and resell the caps easily to end users on eBay for $3 per cap, that's a retail operation. If you can resell the caps easily on eBay to sports distributors for $1.50 each (minimum order seven cartons—1,008 caps), that's more like arbitrage (between the closeout market and the wholesale market). The sale to the sports distributors is certain because they normally pay at least $4 per cap and would rather pay only $1.50. And the caps are always in demand. After all, the caps have the official major league team insignias.

In the example of selling to distributors, you would not want to take delivery of the caps. You would want to make the sales to the distributors so quickly that you could have your seller ship directly to the distributors. In other words, you would be strictly a middleman.

For arbitrage, the buying strategy is to buy low, but it must be coupled with a resale plan that can be carried out immediately. In other words, the price you anticipate for the resale determines the upper limit for which you can buy the goods and still make a small profit on the immediate resale. With arbitrage you have to be careful. Because the profits are usually small compared to the amount of money at risk. You can't afford to make a mistake.

I might also point out that arbitrage requires large transactions, significant amounts of capital, and extensive knowledge of the markets. The profit is small, so the transaction must be large to make the deal worthwhile. And unless you have excellent knowledge of the markets in which you deal, arbitrage is financially suicidal.

Why a section on arbitrage in a book like this? People dream up the idea of arbitrage by themselves without knowing anything about it. This section attempts to point out the significant risks.

Have Fun

Online auctions can be fun. They're like a game. It's perfectly legitimate to participate just for the fun of it. Don't forget, though, that legally an auction is not a game. An auction forms a legal contract between the seller and the high bidder. If you are the high bidder, you are legally obligated to buy the item. If you're not willing to complete the contract (i.e., pay for the item), don't play the game. Read Chapters 7 and 8 carefully.

Tactics

Naturally, your tactics will be different for different strategies. If you want to save money or make money, you will behave differently than if you just want to save time or have fun.

Tactics are things you can do to reach the goals implicit in your strategies. Once you have taken some time to develop your eBay strategies, you will have a clearer idea of what you want to accomplish on eBay. From what you read in this book and your own experience, you will come up with things you can do to reach your objectives.

Mixed Strategies

Many people have mixed strategies. I'm a money-saver. But I also appreciate the convenience factor. I keep both in mind when I choose my tactics.

Research

Nothing beats research as a tactic. If you want to use the money-making strategy, you have to know the list prices of the items you bid on. Then you can apply my percentage guidelines to estimate your high bid prices, or you can invent your own percentage guidelines. You can get list prices at manufacturers' websites, in online catalogs, printed catalogs, local stores, and the like.

You also need to know what identical or similar items have sold for on eBay in the past. You can click on *Completed Listings* on the left side of a list of eBay auctions and view the completed transactions going back a few weeks (with the highest bids displayed). Andale (*http://andale.com*) and other auction management services offer research services that covers back auctions. With enough of these transactions, you can estimate what the maximum bidders will bid for an item.

For more robust pricing information, try eBay's new *Marketplace Research*. You will have to pay a fee, but for big ticket items it could save you a ton of money (see Figure 11.1).

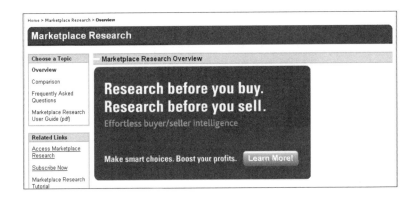

Figure 11.1 eBay's new Marketplace Research. ©eBay 1995-2007.

Know your offline markets too. It's silly to pay more for something on eBay when you can buy it with less risk locally (but see the Convenience subsection earlier). And that is the case for many items. eBay is not 100 percent effective in providing the lowest prices for all merchandise.

Check out the seller. Check his or her feedback. Check his or her other eBay auctions. If the seller has a commerce website, check that. You never know what you might discover that will help you in your bidding.

Without research, not only will you be prone to making significant mistakes, but you will have a difficult time gauging your success. Do your homework.

Research at Andale

For a modest fee, Andale, an auction management service covered in Chapter 22, provides an eBay research service based on past eBay sales. Some other auction management services provide similar research capabilities.

Buy It Now

This is a simple tactic and one I've come to use more and more. This is strictly convenience. Use *Buy It Now*, eBay's fixed price sales program. The *Buy It Now* program has been very successful for eBay sellers. As a buyer, take advantage of it if you seek convenience. You can make an immediate purchase and have the item delivered within a few days.

Sellers Be Careful

You might think that convenience is worth a higher price. To some extent that's true. But people still shop on eBay because they can find bargain prices. If *Buy It Now* prices cease to be bargain prices, it seems to me that eBay's fixed price program will no longer be successful. Convenience is great, but low prices are a primary consideration for many buyers.

Best Offer

Using this new eBay bidding device is iffy. You can make a best offer, but usually only one. If the first best offer doesn't work (doesn't get accepted by the seller), you can't make a second best offer on most items. The seller has two days to accept, reject, or ignore your best offer. This is probably best used on items that have been up for auction several times but haven't sold. I haven't had much luck with it, but it's certainly worth a try.

Once you've make your best offer, you're still free to bid normally on the item.

The Kill

If a seller does not follow the best practices outlined in this book, he or she will generally receive fewer bids for an item and will get a lower final bid. Look for sellers who have made one or more of the following mistakes in their eBay listing:

- Misspelling in the auction title
- Placement in the wrong category
- No photograph
- A poor photograph
- Too little information about the item
- Unreadable information
- Unreasonable terms
- An unfriendly presentation

When you find such an auction, you may be able to acquire an item at a bargain price. You have to know the item you are buying well enough to feel confident in your purchase, because the seller may not provide you or other bidders with the information or confidence you need to make a purchase decision. In other words, you have to have greater product knowledge than the bidders who will ignore this auction. You're like a vulture moving in for the kill on a crippled seller. Enjoy!

The Newbie Seller

Many buyers will bypass the auctions of new sellers who have no significant feedback, particularly for big ticket items. Who wants to take the chance? Consequently, with fewer bidders, the item usually sells for less. If you are a buyer who is willing to take the risk on a newbie seller, you can often buy for less.

Keep in mind, however, that the risk is real. If you get conned by a newbie seller, you won't be the first.

The Refresh

The Refresh is not only a tactic, it's a necessity. As you reach the final few minutes of an auction, you must keep informed of the bidding. To do so you refresh (reload) the auction webpage by clicking on the refresh button on your Web browser. This is the only way you can determine the latest high bid. The high bid amount for an auction in a list of auctions on eBay is hopelessly out of date—perhaps by hours. Keep this in mind when planning your last-minute tactics, and don't rely on the list of auctions for up-to-date bid information.

The Scare

This is a tactic to scare away potential bidders because they think the bidding is too intense. Suppose you will bid as much as $85 on an item that currently reflects a high bid of $23. The high bidder has bid $52 (but you don't know this figure). If you bid $24, eBay raises the high bidder to $25 (automatic bidding or proxy bidding; see The Bay Way later). You are now the second-highest bidder. There are three bids.

You bid again, this time $26; eBay raises the high bidder to $27. You bid again, this time $28; consequently, eBay raises the high bidder to $29. Now there are seven bids.

You can continue this procedure until you find the high bid. By the time you finally outbid the high bidder with a bid of $53, there will be 30 bids. That looks like a lot of activity, and eBay provides no way to analyze the auction except by looking at the number of bidders. Many bargain-hunting potential bidders will not take the trouble to look beyond the number of bids and will not bother to bid because of the apparent intensity of the bidding.

This tactic works best for standard items for which it is easy to establish a value. Potential bidders know the item and search for a bargain price. The bidding intensity will likely scare them away because they think the price will go too high.

Bidding intensity, however, attracts the curiosity of many bidders, particularly regarding nonstandard items for which it is difficult to estimate market value. Bidders may be curious to see what the intensity is all about. Therefore, this tactic may backfire for nonstandard items. The intensive bidding makes the items seem hot and attracts bidders rather than scares them off. Thus, this tactic works best for standard items such as new merchandise with well-known brand names.

Legal?

Is this tactic in violation of eBay rules? No. However, if you are assisting the seller (or if you are the seller operating under a different alias) by using this tactic as a means to artificially inflate the bidding, it is not only against eBay rules but is illegal in most states.

The Pass

Some items are just popular. Normally, new items sell for discounted prices on eBay. But for a few popular items, the high bid often exceeds the discount store price. Why buy the item from a distant seller on eBay that you don't know? Pass. Buy it at your local discount store instead.

The Bay Way (Proxy Bidding)

Set your highest price and walk away. eBay has it set up so that you'll win the auction if your high price is higher than any other bid; but the eBay system will only set your bid one increment higher than the second-highest bid. What a deal! With this tactic, you don't have to be at your computer in the final minutes of the auction. You only have to bid once. You will pay only one increment higher than the second-highest bidder. This automatic bidding (proxy bidding) is built into the eBay system.

Suppose the highest bid is $22, and you bid $46. eBay will now show you as being the highest bidder at $23. Another bidder comes along and bids $24. eBay will automatically make you the highest bidder at $25. And so it goes. The only way someone can outbid you is by bidding more than $46.

This tactic works when you are sure of yourself and sure of the value range. You know about how much the item will sell for, and you know definitely what you will pay for it. If the value range is lower than you will pay, you should win the bid in most instances. If the value range is higher than you're willing to pay, there will be some auctions, but not many, where you will have the highest bid. Take a shot at it; it doesn't take long to make one bid.

The Game

This is a nonfinancial tactic that enables you to enjoy the fun strategy mentioned above. Because bidding on eBay can be fun, you can play it as a game. The goal is to win the bidding, but the primary goal is not necessarily to win with the lowest winning bid possible. It's to win without an excessively high bid but have some fun doing it, that is, have some fun bidding.

In reality, when you bid in the final minutes of the auction, you might switch into game mode whether you intend to or not. The excitement of the final minutes may lead you to bid more than the high limit you set for yourself. Hopefully, however, you won't get excited enough to win at any cost. That could lead to a severe financial hangover.

If there is intense bidding in the final minutes and you're having fun, it's worth a few extra dollars to win. Go for it. The auction game is great fun to play.

Don't, under any circumstances, bid on auctions that you don't intend to complete when you're the high bidder. You will end up getting kicked off eBay and lose what will almost certainly turn out to be a lifelong asset: eBay membership.

The Smoke Out

You use the Smoke Out before you use the Bay Way; it gives you a better idea of what the winning bid might be. Sometime well before the auction ends, you attempt to smoke out the price range of the final bidding. This is especially important when you have trouble estimating the value of the item, and you won't be online at the auction's end.

Suppose you have a vague idea that the item might be worth about $120. You need it and don't have time to find it elsewhere. The current high bid is $42. When the final minutes of the auction come, you'll be across town on a business appointment. You don't have a snipe program (see the Snipe subsection later), so you'll make your final bid a few hours before the end of the auction.

This tactic requires that you bid in modest increments (e.g., $5) until you have the high bid (assuming it's under $120). Do this early in the auction. Then wait to see if anyone outbids you. If not, you may have reached the range of value for the item. Unfortunately, you won't know for sure until the end of the auction. But if someone outbids you immediately, it shows that you haven't reached the range of value.

Suppose you bid up in $5 increments to $75 to become the high bidder with three days to go. Two and a half days go by, and no one outbids you. That may indicate a value range lower than the $120 you anticipated. For your final bid you might want to try $85.

On the other hand, suppose you do the same, but within a day someone outbids you. You again bid up in $5 increments to $95 to become the high bidder. Another day and a half goes by, and no one outbids you. Now, you might want to try $105 for your final bid.

In both of these cases, you try to smoke out the value range because you're not sure what the value is. If you know what the value range is, you don't have to use the Smoke Out. In both of these cases, you make a higher bid at the end because you won't be around for the finale. You hope the higher bid will be enough to win in your absence.

Even if you will be present for the bidding in the last minutes, the Smoke Out can be a valuable tactic if you're not sure of the value range. It can help you anticipate the value range. For instance, if you're prepared to pay $120 and the value range turns out to be $90–$100, smoking out the value range early will give you confidence in the final bidding because you're psychologically prepared to pay a higher price than the value range indicates.

If you smoke out the value range and it turns out to be over $120, however, it gives you more information with which to further develop your tactics. You can drop out of the bidding and save what otherwise would be wasted time. Or, you can rethink your estimate of value. You may decide that a value range over $120 is not unreasonable. In that case, you'll be psychologically prepared to bid higher and stay in the game.

Obviously, the Smoke Out is not a perfect tactic. But it can help you in many circumstances. It gives you another way to gather information to prepare yourself before the final minutes of the auction.

The Reserve Smoke Out

The reserve is lower than the *Buy It Now* price. Of course, you don't know how much lower. But if there is minimal bidding activity and you suspect that the reserve might be substantially lower, it may be worth your effort to smoke out the reserve.

I was bidding on a four-year-old Lincoln Continental that had a Buy It Now price of $8,500. In the last 24 hours of the activity, the bidding was up to only $3,800. The seller hinted in the auction ad that the reserve was low. I was willing to pay $8,500, but it looked like I wouldn't have any competition in bidding lower. So, I started bidding at $7,400. I smoked out the reserve when I bid $7,800, and that was the winning bid. Consequently, I bought the car for $700 less than the Buy It Now price I was willing to pay.

The Snipe

The pure sniper never appears before the final minutes or seconds. Then he or she places the winning bid out of the blue at the last possible moment.

I make a bid of $40 to purchase a fiber-optic patch panel for my charter school's new computer network. It cost $500 at retail. Such items normally sell on eBay, when available, for less than $100. I was ready to pay $125 or more. I placed my bid six days before the end of the auction. No one else bid. I decided not to make another bid but was eager to get this piece of network equipment. So, just for kicks, I watched the end of the auction. Wouldn't you know it? Someone bid $41 in the last 10 seconds of the auction and bought "my" patch panel much to my chagrin. That's a pure snipe. And it's perfectly legal.

With Software

Many snipers use special software to do their sniping. You can buy it on eBay at various auctions. The software places a winning bid at a certain time before the auction ends, say 30 seconds before. In the software setup for the Snipe, you can put an upper limit on the bid so that you don't spend more than you want to.

Using the software seems like an almost foolproof way to win an auction. When you think about it, however, it doesn't do any more for you than the Bay Way, except it might come as a surprise to other bidders. In other words, when using snipe software, you can't change your tactic at the last minute, and the software is not infallible.

If you set the software to make a bid in the last ten seconds before the end of the auction and eBay takes 30 seconds before accepting the bid, you're out of luck. There are occasions when eBay may take 10, 20, or 30 seconds to crank out webpages. So, you might set the software to make a bid 60 seconds before the end of the auction. If eBay happens to be working fast at that time, you've given your bidding competitors plenty of time to place higher bids within the last 60 seconds.

Without Software

If you don't use software to snipe, you need to be at your computer ready to roll during the final moments. You don't know whether your last-minute bid will work because you don't know what the highest bid will be. You do know that you need to make a bid higher than the current highest bid, but you don't know how much higher you have to bid to win because of the way the eBay proxy system works. Consequently, the Snipe is theoretically a one-shot tactic. Maybe it'll work. Maybe it won't. That is, even if your snipe bid is higher than the highest bid showing, someone who has made a proxy bid higher than your snipe bid will win the auction.

However, you can combine the Snipe with the Smoke Out for an effective last-minute tactic. Perhaps we should call it the Last-Minute Smoke Out and Snipe. Give yourself a few minutes. You smoke out the value range in a hurry by making a series of quick bids. Once you find the value range, you have to decide what your last-moment bid will be and how long it will take to submit it (based on eBay's current operational speed).

No Smoke

If there is spirited bidding but there appears to be no proxy bidding, you won't have to do a Smoke Out. You can watch and then do a last-second Snipe.

Unfortunately, eBay sometimes runs at different speeds. When you try to snipe where timing is crucial, a lag time can frustrate you. You will have to test the response, estimate the lag time, and make your bids accordingly. For instance, suppose you test the response time and it seems to be about 20 seconds. You want to snipe within ten seconds of the close of the auction. Under these circumstances, you need to make your final bid about 30 seconds before the end of the auction.

Refresh

Remember the Refresh? Refreshing the eBay auction webpage is the only way you can keep up with the bidding. This is not a problem when eBay is fast. When eBay is slow, it compounds your sniping problems.

If you run into competition, you'll find yourself in the middle of a bidding war. The difference between sniping and a normal bidding war is that as the sniper, you will be a surprise competitor, perhaps disrupting the expectations of the other bidder(s). You will have to be ready to submit additional bids instantly in response to the competing bidders until time runs out.

The perfect Snipe is one that wins with zero seconds left. With eBay's varying speed and with such precise control normally out of reach, it's difficult to win with zero seconds left. But you might win with five seconds left under normal conditions.

The Double Window

How can you best submit those last-minute bids efficiently and responsively? Use double (or triple) browser windows. Open your browser, go to eBay, and open the auction at which you will bid. Next, for Firefox 2.0, go File, New Window to create a new and fully functional browser window that is, in effect, a second browser. For

Microsoft Internet Explorer (IE) 6.0, go File, New, Window; for IE 7.0 go Page, New Window. Now, as Figure 11.1 shows, you have two browser windows (two browsers, in effect) to make quick bids.

Actually, you can make as many browser windows as you want. I usually make about six to prepare for last-moment bidding. You add the bid price as you use each browser window to bid (see Figure 9.1).

Now, when you hurry in the final moments of the auction to compete with other bidders, you can make a bid quickly. After every bid, discard the window you just used, and move on to a fresh browser window (i.e., one prepared ahead of time). This works very effectively. You don't have to go backwards. (It worked more effectively before eBay changed the bidding sequence in the summer of 1999 from ID and password in the first window and price in the second window to the reverse. Apparently eBay did this either to slow down the intensity of the last-minute bidding or to prevent the more knowledgeable bidders from gaining an advantage.)

Figure 11.2 Two browser windows set up to bid.

The last few minutes of a hot auction can get very intense, and the Double Window tactic keeps you in the bidding. Don't worry about snipers. You can snipe better than any program can, particularly when eBay is not working at full speed.

Sign In to Save Time

See Chapter 5 for information on signing in. If you sign in, you don't have to enter your ID and password when you bid. This gives you an advantage in the final minutes of a hot auction because you can save the time it takes to enter an ID and password and can respond more quickly to sniping. Click on the sign-in link (either above or below) the navigation bar on any eBay page.

The Goen Technique

This is a tip from inventive reader LeeAnne Goen. She refreshes the *History* page when sniping because it's faster than the auction webpage. It has little text and no graphics. That is, she refreshes the *History* page in one browser, and bids in another browser. She can snipe more effectively this way.

The Ten Cents Difference

In order to make a bid, you must increase the amount of your bid by the requisite eBay increment (see Chapter 5). Presumably, most people submit a bid based on one or more increments. But you don't have to do it that way.

Suppose you bid $28. eBay proxy bidding automatically preempts you by a bid of $29 by someone who has bid $32. The incremental bid amount is $1. You want to smoke out the high bidder. You bid $30. The eBay proxy bids $31. If you bid $32, you will tie with the high bidder, but the high bidder—being first—will win the auction. If you bid $32.01, you will have the high bid and will win the auction. Thus, it's a good idea to always bid at least one increment plus a penny. I always bid at least one increment plus 10 cents.

Turn the above scenario around. Suppose you made the high bid at $32.10, and someone else is trying to outbid you in the last moments of an auction. They bid $32. You win by a dime.

Why bother with a few cents? Why not bid an extra dollar instead? Hey, the nickels and dimes add up. Look at the overhead for a buyer (see Chapter 2). You can get nickeled and dimed to impoverishment. Win the bidding by 10 cents and save 90 cents wherever you can.

The Routine Check

This puts the time-saving strategy into action. You will find eBay especially valuable if you can wait. Suppose you need the Shure microphone (in the Save Time subsection example) for a Christmas performance, but it's now August. Perhaps you can't find it today on eBay, but check every week. It'll turn up sooner or later. If you want to be diligent, you can check every three days because there are some three-day auctions. But check at least once a week. It takes just a little time to check the current auctions. When the Shure microphone does appear, keep in mind your strategy and act accordingly.

This is actually a good tactic to use for any merchandise, and I've used it to save money. But it's perhaps most valuable for the time-saving strategy. After all, for the time-saving strategy, there may be no viable alternative to the Routine Check other than going around looking for the merchandise at physical locations, which takes a lot more of your time.

eBay Implementation

eBay actually implements this tactic in *My eBay*. Your My eBay account will actually watch the auctions for the items you want to buy. When the items are put up for auction, eBay will inform you.

The Multiple-Auction Finesse

Sometimes you bid multiple auctions on the same item that end within a short time of one another. It seems to me this is dumb on the part of a seller. As a seller, you want to give the bidders plenty of opportunity and time to regroup, concentrate, and bid on each auction. But we've all seen two or three single-item auctions with the same item offered by the same seller end within a short time of each other. I've even seen three or four Dutch auctions, with the same items offered by the same seller, end within 40 seconds of each other. As a bidder, how do you handle this situation?

There are two rules. The first rule is forget the first auction (i.e., the one that ends first). The person willing to bid the highest will win that auction. Why be the high bidder if there is more than one auction? The second rule is figure out the most difficult thing to do, and do it. Everyone else will tend to pick easier tactics. If you pick the most difficult tactic, you have a good chance of winning.

The necessity for the Multiple-Auction Finesse, of course, depends on competition. If you don't have competition, you don't need to use the Finesse tactic.

Two Auctions

Because you will not bid the first auction, what do you do about the second auction? Well, you see the first auction through to the end, even though you don't bid on it. You need to know the winning bid amount. You have a pretty good idea of the value range because you witnessed the end of the first auction. The best tactic is to snipe the second auction. You will have an edge because you set up to snipe the second auction ahead of time. Don't forget the Double Window tactic. Presumably, your competition is now frustrated and busy trying to regroup in the short time between auctions. You, however, experience no frustration. You're ready to wrestle. It seems to me that you have the advantage. In this case, the most significant factor is to plan ahead.

Three Auctions

Bidders have the greatest difficulty regrouping for a second auction right after the final frenzy of the first auction. Again, you watch the first auction to the end. The bidders will tend to take the easiest path to winning a bid by skipping the second auction and bidding the third. That leaves the second auction with no competition or light competition. Because you set up to bid the second auction ahead of time, you have a good chance of winning the bid. The third auction will be a replay of the first, with higher bidding than the second. In this case, the most significant tactic is to bid the second auction.

If you don't win the second auction by some horrible accident of fate, you can easily snipe the third if you set up to bid the third auction ahead of time. Again, don't forget the Double Window tactic.

Why?

The intervals between auctions must be small (under two minutes) for the Finesse tactic to work. Why would a seller schedule auctions of the same item this close together? It might be ignorance. It might be the result of a bulk upload of auctions. It might be the result of a hurried entry of auctions. Whatever the reason, it happens more often than you might think.

If the intervals are too long, the bidders can regroup more easily and bid more effectively. Then the Finesse doesn't work.

Dutch Auction Bids

As explained earlier, at a Dutch auction, the high bidder wins but pays only the amount of the lowest successful bid. Suppose the seller auctions five identical items and five bidders bid on one item each. The bidding results in the last few minutes are as follows:

$77

$74

$73

$70

$68

If you bid $69, and no one enters another bid, you will be a winner and buy at $69. But if someone else bids, you may get knocked out of the winner's circle because you hold the last place at the bottom. However, if you bid $74, and no one enters another bid, you will be a winner and buy for a price of $70 (you knocked out the $68 bidder). And if someone else bids, they probably won't knock you out of the winner's circle, and the final low successful bid (the price to you) may still be lower than your bid of $74. Thus, the tactic is to bid in the middle of the pack and hope for a successful low bid that is less than your bid.

Organization

For one auction, you don't need much organization. You can keep everything under control just by following a plan and improvising. However, if you bid on multiple auctions, you need to devise a systematic way of keeping track of your bids.

First, you don't want to bid on multiple separate auctions for the same item. You could become doubly successful (triply successful, perhaps) and have to buy more than one item or possibly suffer negative feedback for the items you win but don't buy.

Second, you can't count on eBay's email notification system to keep track for you. While such a system is handy in certain ways, particularly for your after-auction records, it won't help much for successfully bidding on multiple unrelated items and for avoiding costly mistakes. I've bid as many as three different unrelated items at the same time. Even with just three auctions to manage, things start to get out of control without some kind of informal auction management system for bidding.

Summary

Think about what strategy you will follow for bidding on eBay. Then pick and choose your tactics to carry out your strategy. Invent some tactics of your own. There is never a guarantee that you will win an auction, but with a clear strategy and some useful tactics, you will do as well as you can on eBay.

And, remember, the bidder who bids highest wins. If you don't bid the highest, no strategy and no tactic is going to make you the winning bidder.

12

Systematic Bidding

Now that you know some techniques for bidding, don't get carried away until you devise a system for keeping track of your bids. It's so easy to lose track or get confused if you bid on different auctions simultaneously. If you do get confused and lose track, the end result is likely to be negative feedback.

Guidelines for Safe Bidding

One auction is easy and fun to keep track of. Two simultaneous auctions sometimes get a little confusing, but nothing gets seriously out of hand. With three auctions you start to lose it. Four auctions can become quite confusing. And five simultaneous auctions can put you in shock if not on feedback death row.

Keep Track

How do you avoid going berserk while bidding on multiple auctions (multiple items)? You develop a system to keep things straight. This is usually a paper system in which you keep notes on what you're doing.

The more auctions you bid, the more careful you have to keep notes. Should you make a mistake, it might result in negative feedback or the obligation to pay more for an item than it's worth. That's always in the back of your mind. So relieve the stress and get organized, develop a system, and get your bidding under control. This will make your bidding more enjoyable and more profitable.

Limit Your Volume

Without a system to keep track, keep in mind that you can bid on only two or three different items simultaneously at the maximum without getting confused. Until you have devised a system of keeping track of your bidding, keep your shopping volume low.

Don't Play the Field

If you want an item, don't bid more than one auction at a time for the item. Otherwise, you might be obligated to buy two or more of the same item. This can lead to a financial hangover. Moreover, if you back out of an auction as a winning bidder, it can lead to negative feedback. Not smart.

If you want to bid on more than one auction to be sure you get an item, schedule the auctions. They are not likely to all end at the same time or even within minutes of each other. With techniques such as sniping, you can easily bid on them in sequence until you win one.

I carelessly bid on three different auctions once to get a digital camera. Then I remained the high bidder in each auction with only a day or so left until the ends of the auctions. I panicked. But there was nothing I could do. Fortunately, in two of the auctions, other bidders outbid me several hours before the auctions ended, and I escaped without suffering any consequences while purchasing a digital camera in the third auction. But I've never let myself get in this situation again.

Use Auction Management Software

If you don't use your own system, try auction management software designed for bidders. Unfortunately, several auction management service vendors have offered bidder management software and found little demand for it. The offerings tend to disappear. Nonetheless, eBay encourages auction management services to offer it, and a few do so.

Check the services one by one to see what they offer for bidders. Go to *http://solutions.ebay.com*.

Use My eBay

My eBay is a series of eBay accounting systems (see Figure 12.1). eBay enables you to watch for new auctions (for a certain item) on which to bid, watch existing auctions for certain items on which to bid, track past auctions, and keep track of your other eBay activities. Try this system to see whether it can do the job for you of keeping track of your bidding. But you may find that My eBay isn't completely adequate. You may need to do some additional keeping track yourself.

Follow Up

Following up after you win an auction is necessary to complete the transaction. Wait for the seller to send you payment instructions. If you don't hear from the seller within a reasonable time, contact her to ask about payment instructions.

Figure 12.1 My eBay provides accounting for buyers. ©1995-2007 eBay Inc.

eBay Checkout

Perhaps the best way to handle the end of the auction is to use the eBay checkout mechanism. You simply pay, checkout, and let the seller handle the transaction from there.

The eBay checkout mechanism is much improved and works much smoother than in prior years. If you haven't used it lately, you might want to give it another try.

Pay Promptly

Pay promptly. Some means of payment are inherently slow (e.g., money orders). The more you delay, the more the inherent slowness is compounded. A seller likes to make sure she will get paid shortly after the auction. Help her by paying promptly or by notifying her that payment is on the way. If there is a problem, stay on top of it until you get it resolved. Sellers are very fussy about getting paid in a timely manner. Treat prompt payment seriously and avoid negative feedback.

Arrange Payment Ahead

For some items, you will have to arrange financing (i.e., get a loan). Make sure you get a loan approved before you bid. The seller will expect you to pay if you win the auction. The fact that you cannot get a loan is not a good excuse for not paying.

PayPal (through a national lender) does offer financing for consumer items purchased on eBay. If you use this lender, make sure you follow their guidelines and requirements ahead of time so that you are ready to pay the seller if you win the bidding. Otherwise, be ready to pay cash if you cannot obtain the loan.

Give Feedback

The best way to build your reputation on eBay starting out is to get positive feedback from purchasing items. However, many sellers will not give you feedback unless you give them feedback first. Sellers who are eBay retailers need a solid and voluminous feedback record to demonstrate to the world that they are trustworthy. Thus, make it a point to give sellers feedback as soon as you are satisfied that everything has gone well in the transaction. Most will return the favor.

Before you know it, you'll have an impressive feedback record.

Summary

There's more to being a bidder than just using bidding strategies and tactics. You need to bid safely and keep track of what you're doing, particularly at times when you are trying to buy numerous items. Stay organized and avoid negative feedback.

IV

Using Selling Strategies

13

Finding Things to Sell

Unlike *eBay Inventory the Smart Way,* which devotes 272 pages to find-ing wholesale sources of inventory, this book focuses primarily on per-sonal sources of items to sell on eBay. Also keep in mind that eBay isn't the only viable online marketplace. For large, heavy, or mobile items which are expensive to ship, Craig's List (see Chapter 32) provides you an alternative local marketplace that may be more appropriate than eBay.

Places

The first look at sources of items to sell is places in your house and outside your house.

Home Storage

It is in home storage places where you are likely to find items ripe to be disposed of.

Attic, Garage, Basement, and Shed

Most homes have an attic, garage, basement, or a shed out back where a wealth of items are stored. Some homes have all four. I think it is safe to say that many homeowners who do a systematic survey of the stuff they have in storage that can be easily sold on eBay can realize an income of $5,000 if they sell it. This can be a tax-free financial windfall (see the section below entitled A Little Is a Lot – Financial Planning). You might even be surprised to learn that your stuff in storage is worth more than $5,000. After you do a systematic survey, estimate the prices you can expect to get on eBay (or Craig's List). If the potential income is motivating, get organized to start selling.

Bedrooms and Closets

Don't overlook bedrooms and closets as places of storage. Did Grandma die three years ago, and nobody has been in her bedroom (full of stuff) since? Did your kids go away (to the Marine Corps, college, jobs in other cities) and leave behind stuff in their bedrooms in which they have no further interest?

Storage Unit

As families accumulate more and more stuff, they often rent inexpensive storage units close by where they dump their possessions that have the lowest use priority. Many of these items are good candidates for selling on eBay.

Convenience

The stuff in storage has been selected. That is, a decision has been made that there is not an immediate use for it, and it has been "put away." Taking a survey of the stuff in storage is convenient for two reasons. It has already been selected for low use priority, and it is all in the same place. The items in storage are prime candidates for profitable eBay sales. Don't worry about choosing items to sell from everything you own. Start with items in storage.

Activities

The items we use every day are not good candidates for selling on eBay until they break, wear out, or are out of date. It's the items related to activities in which we've lost interest that are the prime candidates for disposing of on eBay. Such items are often valuable.

Hobbies, Sports, and Activities

Reflect on your activities, past and present. Which have you de facto given up? Which do you intend to give up? Such activities might be hobbies, sports, recreational activities, sideline business endeavors, or other activities. Invariably, with each activity goes a set of items you may be able to sell for worthwhile income on eBay. If you have given up or intend to give up an activity, catalog all the paraphernalia that you have accumulated for this purpose and sell it on eBay. Activities might include anything from boating to stamp collecting, each with its requisite equipment, accessories, and even clothing.

Kids' Activities

Do the same for the kids' activities. This might include a lot of toys, for instance. Kids do involve themselves in activities that they will enjoy in their adult life (e.g., golf, camping). You don't want to necessarily get rid of items associated with life-long activities. But will they really play ice hockey again after quitting the recreational hockey league in eighth grade? Probably not. Sell those hockey ice skates and padding before they become obsolete.

Saved for Later Use

The primary reason for storage is to save things for later use. Sometime that later use materializes. Usually it doesn't. The problem is that it too often isn't worthwhile to sell something you've used. There's no market for it. You practically have to give it away to get rid of it.

eBay changes that. With a ready marketplace that makes it worthwhile to dispose of seldom-used things, you have more motivation to sell. You can make money by selling on eBay.

If you sell stuff on eBay today and put some money in the bank, you can always rent identical things later if you need them. But traditional renting is expensive. Is there another way?

Rent It

This is a great idea. Buy a used item on eBay to use. Use it. Then sell it after you're through using it. This practice becomes an ongoing source of items to sell. And this is almost identical to renting. In other words, if you want to rent something for an extended period, consider buying it on eBay, using it, and selling it on eBay instead.

Buy It

For instance, suppose you need an RV (e.g., motor home) for a one-time tour of the western states that will take two months. You know, Rocky Mountain National Park, the Grand Canyon, etc. To rent one for such a long period (60 days) would cost a fortune at $300 per day (i.e., $18,000). Instead, buy one a few years old in good condition for $24,000 on eBay.

Use It

Drive the used RV on your trip keeping it in good condition. Suppose it's ten years old and has 42,000 miles on the odometer when you buy it. You put 7,000 miles on it during your tour. It has 49,000 miles after you're done with it. So long as you keep RV in top condition, the miles you put on it in a few months will not change the value much, if at all.

Sell It

After your trip, sell it for $22,000 on eBay. A net loss of $2,000 is cheaper than renting for $18,000. It's also much cheaper than buying a new RV for $90,000 and taking a depreciation hit of $25,000 as soon as you drive it off the dealer's lot.

Any Equipment

The same concept applies for any type of equipment that you will have to use for an extended period. Renting for one day is usually reasonably economical. But renting for an extended period is usually prohibitively expensive. It's better to buy it on eBay, use it, and sell it on eBay. Your occasional "rental" equipment becomes part of what you sell on eBay.

Buy It

If you're going to "rent" it as described above, you have to buy it first. What makes this idea feasible is the size of the eBay marketplace. Prior to eBay, if you wanted to buy something used, you had to rely on your local marketplaces (classifieds, flea markets). Often you couldn't find exactly what you needed because the marketplace was too small to offer a useful variety of goods. eBay's national marketplace, however, offers a wide range of goods to purchase and use. And the same marketplace provides an "exit strategy" (i.e., a place to easily sell what you buy after using it).

Stuff

After looking at where we might find stuff to sell, what activities might yield stuff to sell, and the idea of buy-sell instead of renting, let's look at other sources of salable items.

Relatives' Property

Did your in-laws live with you for three months and then leave a lot of stuff in your garage when they moved to a city a thousand miles away? If so, offer to sell it for them on eBay. That may be the only way you ever get rid of it. Remind them of the normal consignment fee (10 to 25 percent) for making eBay sales.

Estate Sale

When relatives depart permanently, it may be time for an estate sale. If you enjoy selling on eBay, the estate (stuff) of a departed relative may be an opportunity to have some fun selling as well as to save some money in disposing of the property in the estate. The traditional alternative is to hire an auctioneer to conduct the estate sale.

Most estates aren't big enough to justify an estate sale. Yet, there still may be a lot of stuff to dispose of. Since it's not your stuff, you may feel it's worthless junk. Nonetheless, a little value research on eBay may reveal many valuable items that will make it worthwhile for you to catalog the items and sell them on eBay.

Friends' Property

A lot of your friends may want to sell on eBay but don't have the time or digital agility. If you like to sell, you can help them out by selling their stuff on eBay for them. And again, remind them of the normal consignment fee for making eBay sales.

Gifts

Do you get gifts occasionally that you have no use for? Someone else does have a use for them. And you can auction such gifts on eBay to reach those who want them. Of course, you have to be careful that you don't offend the gift givers. But that shouldn't be difficult. Use your imagination to dream up a story about why you don't have the sweater that Aunt Isadora gave you last Christmas.

Trash

Don't throw away that trash, and definitely don't pay to throw it away. Sell it on eBay instead. In my community in the San Francisco Bay Area, it's expensive to get rid of stuff. We are allowed one trash can a week for the normal trash removal fee. For anything more, we have to pay extra and make a call to arrange the pick-up. (The trash truck drivers actually keep track and won't pick up extra trash except by prior arrangement.)

Let's face it; some trash (not all) does have value. It's only trash because we don't know what else to do with it. Now, with eBay we have a place to get rid of it and make some money doing it.

Mobile Objects

Most mobile objects are vehicles, but some are self-propelled machines such as big lawn mowers that we don't normally think of as vehicles. These objects tend to depreciate fast but are nonetheless always useful to someone so long as they work. For instance, an all-terrain vehicle (ATV) may lose 70 percent of its value in the first five years regardless of how much it has been used. But so long as it works well, it always has some value to someone even after 10 or 15 years.

eBay is a great place to sell mobile objects. For example, it is the largest used car marketplace in the world. The trick here for selling smart is to recognize as early as possible that you are not going to use that vehicle any longer. The sooner you sell it, the less it has depreciated and the more money you will get for it. It's not unusual for people to have several mobile objects in the garage or shed that they would do well to sell immediately.

Large Items

Large items (e.g., sofas) are difficult to dispose of. If the Goodwill or the Disabled Veterans won't take them, you may have to pay to have them hauled away. eBay provides a limited market for such items. I bought a beautiful mahogany dining room table for a pittance, and the seller, who lived about 20 miles from me, delivered it. Nonetheless, eBay hasn't really done an adequate job of creating local marketplaces.

A better local marketplace online is Craig's List (see Chapter 32), which is now in hundreds of cities worldwide. If it's large or heavy or otherwise expensive to ship, an item probably isn't a good candidate for eBay's national marketplace. But it may be perfect for Craig's List, a strictly local marketplace in each city.

A Little Is a Lot – Financial Planning

Here's what I think. It may be a lot of trouble for you to sell your stuff from time to time on eBay. But if you make a project out of it, you may find it easier to do. So do a survey of what you have that you should sell. Then proceed to sell it on a project basis. My advice is to put the proceeds into an investment account (for retirement or for sending your kids to trade school or college).

Let's say you can sell the stuff you no longer need today for $5,000 on eBay. Remember, it is income-tax-free money unless you sell some stuff for more than you originally paid for it (unlikely). Let's also assume you can make an investment that earns a 5 percent compound annual rate of return. Where does your $5,000 get you?

Time Invested	Resulting Amount
5 Years	$6,300
10 Years	$7,200
15 Years	$9,300
20 Years	$12,000
25 years	$13,600
30 Years	$17,600

A more realistic scenario might be one where you do an eBay sales project every five years and invest the money. Each time you're a little more affluent and have a little more to sell. Here's a schedule that shows what the resulting investment amount will be at a 5 percent compound annual rate of return:

Year	Amount Sold	Resulting Amount
Beginning	$1,000	
5 Years	$3,000	$4,276
10 Years	$3,000	$8,457
15 Years	$5,000	$15,793
20 Years	$5,000	$25,156
25 Years	$7,000	$39,106
30 Years		$49,910

These analyses show you that cleaning out your garage and selling the stuff you don't need on eBay can be a worthwhile family project even if you don't need the money today.

If you put the money in an indexed mutual fund (e.g., indexed to the Standard & Poor 500), you may be able to achieve a 12 percent annual return. Here's what the same analyses look like with a 12 percent compound annual rate of return:

$5,000 Invested at 12 Percent Compounded

Time Invested	Resulting Amount
5 Years	$8,811
10 Years	$15,529
15 Years	$27,367
20 Years	$48,231
25 years	$85,000
30 Years	$149,799

eBay Sales Every 5 Years Invested at 12 Percent Compounded

Year	Amount Sold	Resulting Amount
Beginning	$1,000	
5 Years	$3,000	$4,762
10 Years	$3,000	$11,392
15 Years	$5,000	$25,076
20 Years	$5,000	$49,192
25 Years	$7,000	$93,693
30 Years		$165,119

This section is not meant to advocate a particular investment technique. Rather it is meant to demonstrate that you can use eBay to turn no-longer-useful assets into a little bit of cash which can turn into a lot of cash with some careful investing.

Although the sale of personal assets is not taxable for federal or state income tax purposes, to achieve a tax-free rate of return for your investment, however, requires careful planning. Otherwise the income taxes paid will reduce your rate of return. Consult with a financial planner or tax accountant on how you can set up an investment account that serves your purposes.

Sales Tax

Sales of personal assets may be subject to sales tax in your state or may be subject to sales tax above a minimum sales price. Check with your state taxing authority to determine what the laws are in your state.

Kids' Business Project

OK, if you don't want to do an eBay selling project yourself, how about setting one up for your kids? It will accomplish the following:

1. Clear out valuable space in your house.

2. Make money to fund a summer vacation trip or to buy a recreational asset.

3. Teach the kids about systematically organizing and operating a project.

4. Teach the kids business skills.

5. Introduce the kids to eBay, a life-long asset. (Yes, it will still be around in 50 years.)

High-Price Real Estate

Here's another way to look at all that stuff you store that you no longer need. Let's say your house is about 1,800 square feet, and you need to add 300 square feet to accommodate your growing family needs. At $100 per square foot, an addition to your home will cost you $30,000. Is it possible by selling stuff on eBay you can clear a 300-square-foot space in your house that will accommodate your family needs without building an addition?

Businesses

Businesses are no different from people. It may not pay to keep stuff around long term and store it. If a business doesn't need it, sell it on eBay. Take the money and expand the business or buy new business equipment.

Charities

Charities have run auctions and silent auctions locally forever to raise money locally. The sales proceeds are limited, however, because local sales don't bring maximum sales prices. Running charity auctions on eBay, however, will bring maximum prices.

Giving Works

Giving Works is a new section of the eBay website where you can go to sell items for charity. eBay offers a special Mission Fish program to aid sellers and a special catalog to appeal to buyers.

Donations Sold for Charity

Get people to donate their stuff to your charity. Then sell the stuff on eBay. You'll get the maximum selling prices you can get for the items and the maximum proceeds for the charity. The donors will get the maximum tax write-offs if appropriate.

Organizational Property

Charities (permanent organizations) are just like people. They own stuff they don't need any longer. It takes up storage space. Sell it on eBay, and put some money in the bank for the charity.

Conclusion

This chapter will give you some ideas on where you can find things to sell on eBay for fun and profit. Eventually, selling on eBay may lead you to considering the potential for running a retail business on eBay.

Many people who end up with a full-time or substantial part-time retail business on eBay get started with occasional sales of items that have to do with their hobbies, business, or other activities. eBay estimated in June 2006 that there were over 730,000 people running retail businesses on eBay. Thus, your selling on eBay can potentially lead to a new career. Indeed, the experience you get making casual sales on eBay can get you off to a flying start should you decide to make retail selling on eBay a sideline or full-time business. Such selling is beyond the scope of this book, but there are several books available on starting an eBay retail business that can help you including my book *eBay Business the Smart Way, Third Edition*.

14

Serving Customers

It doesn't matter whether you run five auctions a year, five auctions a week, or twenty-five auctions a day, the better you treat your customers, the more bids you will get and the higher the final bids will be. Consequently, this section of the book includes a chapter on customer service, an important activity crucial to selling successfully. The Web is an interactive medium that gives you the chance to serve your customers (buyers, bidders) well.

The Occasional Seller

Put yourself in a buyer's shoes. You want to make a bid for $520 on a used telephone system (retails for $1,849) for your small office. The seller represents the system as in excellent condition and wants a money order for the final bid price (no escrow).

You are faced with sending a money order for $520 to someone you don't know. You don't know whether you will receive anything for your money. If you do receive something, you don't know what kind of condition it will be in. Will you make the bid? Try the following four scenarios:

1. The seller has no history (i.e., no sales or purchases).
2. The seller has a history of 5 transactions, all rated neutral.
3. The seller has a history of 7 transactions, all rated positive.
4. The seller has a history of 153 transactions, 2 rated negative and the remainder rated positive.

How are you going to vote with your $520? Chances are you'll pass on number one, too much of an unknown. Number two looks as though he or she will be trouble of some sort; that's a pass. Number three looks like a reasonable risk. Number four looks like a low risk.

Each of the above sellers will lose a certain percentage of the potential market. Number one will get some bidders, but because of the low price, many potential bidders will pass because the risk is high. Few potential bidders will think it's worth the time and trouble to deal with number two, who obviously isn't making anyone happy. Although number three looks good, the information is a little thin, and some potential bidders will pass. Virtually all potential bidders will feel comfortable with number four; they've probably got more favorable information on number four than they do on many retailers in their own communities.

The point here is that your reputation is important as a seller, and your reputation depends on your customer service. It doesn't matter whether you sell occasionally or sell regularly. Make your customers happy, and you'll build a good reputation. A good reputation will bring more bids. More bids will bring a higher price.

Now, *as the seller*, what can you do to improve customer service for the auction of the used telephone system? Here are four plausible options:

1. Accept a credit card (or PayPal).
2. Offer to put the transaction in escrow.
3. Provide a warranty.
4. Throw in a gift certificate for a book (at a bookstore) on how to install and operate a small office telephone system.

If you accept a credit card, a person dissatisfied with the transaction can do a chargeback on the credit card transaction. That provides a buyer with a potential remedy. That will increase your bids. (PayPal has become an acceptable substitute for accepting credit cards.) If you offer to put the transaction in escrow, it makes everyone feel more comfortable because it lowers the risk. You'll get more bids. If you provide a warranty, it doesn't necessarily lower the risk, but it makes everyone feel more comfortable, and you'll get more bids. Even the book will broaden the appeal of the auctioned item, particularly if you name an appropriate book. Consequently, with a little customer service, you increase your potential for making more money. The four types of customer services listed above are a few among the many you can offer, and they work even if you are an occasional seller.

Credit Cards

Most buyers on eBay can use credit cards where sellers accept them. Debit cards from MasterCard and Visa are now a part of the credit card system, for all practical purposes, and many people with only checking accounts can therefore "charge" just like those with credit cards. (I was sent a MasterCard debit card by my bank without requesting it. I use it now much more than I use my credit cards.)

If you sell a lot or if you are an eBay retailer, perhaps the most common customer service you can provide is accepting credit cards. There are dozens more ways to get merchant accounts for Web ecommerce in 2007 than there were a few years ago. Get yourself a merchant account, and start accepting credit cards.

Occasional sellers need to read about PayPal in Chapter 20. PayPal makes a reasonable substitute for a credit card merchant account.

What can you do generally as an occasional seller to increase customer service? Respond to communications (e.g., email) promptly. Be prepared to ship promptly the item you sell. Think of yourself as a seller, and exercise some common sense. Follow the suggestions in the remainder of this book in regard to providing convenience for potential bidders.

The Part-Time eBay Business

If you have a part-time business on eBay auctioning merchandise at retail, pay close attention to customer service. Some of the things you can do are:

- Follow the guidelines in this book for running your auctions.

- Promptly respond to communications from potential bidders and customers.

- Organize a responsive follow-up system to track your customers through the transaction process. Read about auction management services in Chapter 19.

- Run your shipping operation in a professional manner.

- Accept payment in as many ways as possible.

- Provide guarantees where practical.

- Listen to your customers.

If you summarize the above list, it boils down to one idea: Get organized! Don't take selling on eBay lightly. Even selling just a few items a week can get out of control before you know it, if you're not prepared. If this happens, you will have some unhappy high bidders and other unhappy eBay members, and that does not bode well for success on eBay.

You can't conduct a part-time eBay business haphazardly and expect it to be as successful as it can be. If you take it seriously and provide good customer service, who knows? Your business may grow into something to which you can eventually devote your full time and energy; then you can quit your regular job!

eBay Biz Books

Before you make the commitment to operating a full-time retail business on eBay, read an eBay business book. Naturally, I recommend *eBay Business the Smart Way, Third Edition*.

Independent Contractors

If you have a full-time job and you are trying to supplement your income by selling on eBay, you may find it difficult to provide the customer service you need to maximize your success. Hiring employees to do some of the work is out of the question. Just the paperwork to employ a person is too demanding. One way to improve your customer service, when you don't have the time, is to hire independent contractors.

Shipping is a good example of something you can *outsource* (have done for you by another business). Some small businesses specialize in shipping merchandise for customers. Shipping is a chore. Have a shipping company do it for you. That will leave you time to spend on other customer service activities that you can do better, more efficiently, more quickly, or more easily. Obviously, the shipping company is an independent contractor.

Not so obvious is having a friend, neighbor, or acquaintance do your shipping for you as an independent contractor (e.g., out of his or her garage). Potentially, this can be a better service for you at less expense while providing more convenience. However, you need to consult the part of the tax laws that defines the difference between employees and independent contractors to make sure you can't be deemed by the IRS or state agencies to have an employee. Essentially, you will have to hand over your merchandise with a mailing label and let the shipping person do the rest. You can't exercise control. But this could be good part-time work for a stay-at-home spouse or someone who wants an extra part-time job for evenings or weekends.

If you don't follow the tax laws (and the labor guidelines of other governmental agencies), no one will ever catch you, right? Actually, that may not be the case. You can be reported by the person you contracted with. Potentially, it can happen a couple of ways. First, the IRS may go after the person for not paying income taxes, and the person will say that he or she thought you were withholding taxes (a lie, but that won't stop the IRS from coming after you). Second, the person may file for unemployment benefits after you stop doing business with him. Third, the person may file for workmen's compensation after getting injured in his own garage with his own equipment while doing your shipping. So it definitely pays to make sure that you really establish an independent contractor relationship with the person you contract with to do the shipping.

The details of this particular relationship are beyond the scope of this book, but it pays to research it thoroughly. You need to look into it because outsourcing via independent contracting can be a very practicable and cost-effective way for you to do business, and it will become even more viable in the future as more people work at home. See *eBay Business the Smart Way, Third Edition* (AMACOM 2007).

Fulfillment

Filling the order (the sale from the auction) is one of the most important functions you will provide as part of your customer service. Fulfillment means processing the order and getting the merchandise shipped in a timely manner. You need to have a speedy procedure to handle fulfillment. Today people expect things they have purchased to arrive quickly. You are not excluded from this expectation just because you don't have a website storefront or a physical retail location.

If you have a part-time retail business on eBay, you can't wait until the weekend to do your shipping. You have to ship as soon as payment is secured, or you will have some irritated customers. If you can't do the shipping part of the fulfillment every day, find someone to do it for you.

Drop Shipping

One clever way to do your fulfillment is drop shipping. Drop shipping means having your wholesaler ship the merchandise directly to your customer. Many wholesalers are set up to do this. Today, to be competitive many wholesalers give quick shipping service. Hence, drop shipping can solve your fulfillment problem at the same time that it eliminates your inventory warehousing problem. The only questions are, how much does it cost?, and can you do it more cost-effectively yourself?

Don't use drop shipping and then forget about the fulfillment service to your customers. It's your responsibility to make sure your customers get good fulfillment service via your drop shipping arrangements. That means you have to follow up with customer satisfaction surveys or otherwise assess the quality of service that your customers are receiving. You'll always hear from customers if the quality of your service is bad. But if your service (via the drop shipper) is just mediocre, you may not get the complaints that alert you that something is wrong. Therefore, you have to stay alert and keep testing to ascertain the quality of your drop shipper's service to your customers.

The drop shipper is no different from an independent contractor in regard to quality. The difference is that you can usually check up on a local independent contractor more easily than you can a distant wholesaler. As a result, you have to use other techniques to check up on the drop shipper.

If You're Small

If you're small, doesn't it mean that you can get away with not worrying about fast fulfillment and other customer service? The answer is yes, if you don't want to get bigger. But if you want to develop a strong business or expand your business, you'll have to provide good customer service today regardless of the size of your business.

The Full-Time eBay Business

If you operate a full-time business that conducts business on eBay, you will be expected to provide excellent customer service because there is so much Web commerce that does provide first-rate customer service. From dealing with Amazon.com and the like, people's expectations are high. If you do not provide such service, you will be an ongoing irritant to your customers, hardly an enviable position considering the eBay feedback system.

With a Website

If you sell at retail full-time on eBay as a business or if you are a retailer who sells a fair amount on eBay but who has a physical location too, you might seriously consider operating an ecommerce website. The question is, What is an ecommerce website? The following are some characteristics:

- Website catalog with inventory for sale
- Transaction system that takes orders, arranges payments, arranges shipping, and hands off the order to the fulfillment process
- Set up to receive payment in a variety of ways
- Organized to provide easy ways for people to communicate in regard to their orders or otherwise
- Attractive website with easy-to-use navigation

Perhaps the best ecommerce website of all is Amazon.com. The story of Amazon is one of pure customer service. The Amazon website may not win any awards for aesthetics or for technical flamboyance. But it sure creates an easy, interesting, and convenient experience to buy a book online (and other consumer items too).

If you do have an ecommerce website that functions intelligently, you can weave it into your eBay business. Here are some things you can do:

Include a link to your *About Me* webpage in your eBay auction ads. In *About Me* you can include a link to your ecommerce website to generate extra business.

Link to your eBay auctions from your ecommerce website to generate extra business.

Refer winning bidders in your eBay auctions to your website for routine, reliable, and convenient transaction processing.

Extend your customer service activities at your ecommerce website to your eBay winning bidders.

In other words, if you're a successful Web retailer with an ecommerce website, you probably already offer competent customer service. Why not extend it to your eBay customers too?

Without a Website

Having said all that, the fault in the plan to operate an ecommerce website is that you will have to market extensively to draw any traffic to the website. If you're thinking of starting an ecommerce website, however, you might consider a more cost-effective alternative. You are better off, in my opinion, to forego establishing an ecommerce website and focus your attention on other eBay-related sales mechanisms such as eBay Stores which do not require a huge amount of marketing.

Communications

If you do not operate an ecommerce website, you have to ask yourself how you can provide comparable services. The first reaction you might have is that you can communicate and provide customer service by telephone, snail mail, and email.

It seems to me the telephone may not work well. For instance, does someone whose only contact with you is via the Web, and possibly email, really want to start talking with you on the phone? Here are some reasons that the telephone may not work well:

Customer doesn't like to pay for long-distance phone calls. (Who does?)

Customer isn't available to talk on the phone during business hours.

Customer doesn't like to talk on the phone.

Customer wants a written record of entire transaction process.

You can handle a few of these things if you provide telephone ordering. You can get an 800 number so that the customer doesn't have to pay for the long-distance call. You can extend your business hours to cover evenings. Both are somewhat expensive, but your business volume may warrant such practices. And, after all, everyone talked on the phone before the Internet came into vogue.

Skype

With Skype, eBay's new telephone service, you may be able to offer your customers free telephone calls to you for a low price. The service is rudimentary now, but it will flower into a robust service in the next few years. Keep posted.

What about snail mail? Too slow! That leaves email as a primary means of communicating with customers. And that leaves you with the question, How can you provide customer service by email? The customer came to you (on eBay) via the Internet, not via email.

There is no simple answer to this question. Email is a capable, powerful, and even flexible means of communication. Certainly, you can use email efficiently to conduct business. Indeed, it's just people talking to people, but not in real time. What are some techniques you can use with email communication?

• Send a form(canned) email, like a form letter. This is important for handling various routine matters with standard form emails.

- Attach a file (e.g., word processor file) to an email message.

- Transfer lots of text into an email message via copy and paste.

- Put links to websites into an email message.

- Set up auto-responders to send automatic replies to certain email informational requests.

You will find that using email fits nicely into Web business practices.

Auction Management Services

Another way to provide customer services without a website is to use auction management services (see Chapter 22 for more details). Not only do these services provide you with enhanced customer communications and other services, but they also provide you with many of the ecommerce services provided on ecommerce websites with traditional ecommerce software. In other words, auction management services bring ecommerce services to your eBay selling activities. This is a legitimate breakthrough and provides a solid basis for operating without an ecommerce website.

eBay Store

The eBay Store has evolved to be a great substitute for an independent ecommerce website. For an eBay Store, eBay does the marketing and leaves you to concentrate on such important activities as great customer service.

A Little Bit More

As a seller, exceed expectations. Go the extra mile. Do a little bit more than you said you would. For instance, communication is so important. As soon as a buyer's check clears and you ship the merchandise, send an email notifying the buyer that the merchandise has been sent. It's not required, but it will be appreciated. If you are well organized, you can do it easily.

Guarantee

If you're an eBay retailer, there's nothing like a good old-fashioned guarantee. Why not offer one to your eBay customers? Many national retailers do. Sure it will cost something, but it will also give potential bidders the confidence to become actual bidders. And the more bidders, the higher the price. The guarantee works well for many retail sellers on eBay.

Packaging

Bidders probably don't expect much from occasional sellers, but from retailers on eBay buyers expect a professional job of presentation and packaging. That means an item needs to be cleaned and shined and then carefully packaged for shipment. If you don't do this, you will not maximize your retail business on eBay. Occasional sellers take note here; provide professional packaging too.

Goods That Don't Work

Many sellers sell merchandise in "as is" condition with no representation that the item will function or with a disclosure that the item does not function. Presumably such goods sell at low purchase prices because they are not in working condition. Clearly, eBay is an appropriate place to sell such goods, and buyers obtain such goods for parts or with the expectation that they can be repaired. However, if you're a retailer, you will do well to avoid such goods and only sell goods that function properly. Let someone else sell merchandise that doesn't work.

The Gift

Don't overlook the gift program that eBay operates. For $1 you can add a gift icon to your auction listing. Presumably you will reserve the use of this program for items that will make good gifts (almost anything) for the occasion. You have your choice of many icons representing different occasions, such as St. Patrick's Day, Mother's Day, and weddings. The items will be located in a special gift section as well as in the normal auction category.

The gift! Macy's, Neiman Marcus, Marshall Field's, Hudson's, and Nordstrom's. Does this ring a bell? Yes! Offer gift wrapping. Offer to enclose a card. Offer to ship direct to the gift recipient with some documentation sent to the buyer that the item was shipped in a timely manner. Offer a gift service. That's a nice touch for customer service.

Overnight Shipment

Sometimes customers want immediate delivery. The seller needs to provide a means. Unfortunately, this is out of the seller's hands. The best a seller can do is offer to ship overnight (for an extra charge) and then deliver the item to a reliable shipping service.

My personal experience regarding reliability for on-time delivery for express shipments is that FedEx is at one end of the spectrum and the Postal Service is at the other end. In 20 years of using FedEx (over a thousand packages), I have never experienced a late delivery (and never a missing package). My luck with the Postal Service is running about 50 percent (including at least one missing package). That is, the Post Office has delivered my Express Mail on time about half of the time in my experience, although the Postal Service claims an on-time delivery rate of 85 percent (according to a Postal Service representative at a trade show).

Here the seller's customer service obligation is to offer a reliable shipping service. If the package isn't delivered on time, the seller is at risk for negative feedback. Hence, if a seller uses the Postal Service, he takes his chances.

If you're a seller who offers overnight delivery service, specify which shipping service you use. That way buyers can make up their mind about the shipper's reliability, letting you off the hook.

I bought my wife a diamond bracelet for Christmas on eBay late on December 21 from an experienced eBay retailer who offered FedEx overnight shipping. The item was shipped on December 22 via Express Mail (i.e., Postal Service overnight service). I would not have bought the item had I known the seller would use Express Mail. The item was not delivered until late on December 24. Additionally, the Postal Service tracking service is apparently updated only once a day. I couldn't find out whether the package would show up on December 24. In a heroic last-minute effort, I was able to go to the mall before it closed and buy a substitute present for my wife thereby saving my marriage. The late-arriving diamond bracelet became a Valentines Day present.

This incident reflects very poor customer service that cannot be blamed on the Postal Service—and I was charged FedEx rates for the less expensive Express Mail. Shameful.

Payment

The acceptance of payment in ways convenient for buyers is an important customer service. For eBay, the more ways you accept payment, the better for your customers (bidders). Because this is so important, it is treated separately in its own chapter, Chapter 16.

Response Times

As you know, if you sell much on eBay, there are deadbeat winning bidders or non-paying bidders (NPBs) as they are called.

Get After Those Buyers

To protect yourself, you must deal with each buyer systematically. Depending on your eBay selling experience, you may want to give deadlines for responses. For instance, you may want to send a form email to winning bidders informing them that they have won, requesting payment, and setting a deadline for a reply (e.g., three days). If you don't hear from them via email in three days, you automatically send another email requesting a response within three days. If there's no response to the second email within three days, you might send a last, more strongly worded email. Most sellers seem to quit at three requests. Then it's time to relist the item or offer it to the second-highest bidder (and be sure to report negative feedback on the deadbeat buyer).

Is this customer service? Sure it is. You give every buyer a reasonable chance to perform because you're a reasonable person. This seems like common sense, but you'd be surprised at the number of sellers who have a short fuse and relist an item (or sell to another) when they haven't heard from a buyer within two or three days.

The Other Side of the Story

As the winning bidder you're ecstatic. You just won. It's something of an ego trip, particularly when the bidding was heated and you feel you got a good price anyway. Then you have to wait three days for the seller to contact you. This is a big no-no on the part of the seller.

As a seller, you need to contact the winning bidder(s) as soon as possible after the close of the auction, certainly no more than one day later and ideally immediately or in less than three hours. This is essential customer service. You've got a hot prospect who's ready to pay. All you have to do is arrange payment. Don't dally. As the transaction cools down, your chances of completing it (and getting paid) start to diminish. Be prompt in your communication to winning bidders.

Communication

Communication is the lubricant of the eBay mechanism. If you can stay in communication with the other party, you can usually work out almost any difficulties. Treat communication as a customer service.

Communication is time-consuming. Hope that you don't have to do anything but the routine communications (form emails) for every buyer. But when problems arise that need special treatment (i.e., special communication)—and they do occasionally, if not often—be ready to spring into action and exchange email messages.

Take the initiative in your initial email to winning bidders. Provide them with full information. Invite them to communicate with you if there are any problems. Be ready to handle those communications in a timely and efficient manner. The better organized and more systematic you are in handling your auctions and winning bidders, the fewer the problems and the less need for communications. The bottom line is that less of your time is taken by post auction administration.

How to Get Organized

How do you get organized? That's a question you have to answer within the scope of your skills and knowledge. Some ideas follow, but you know far better than I what's best for you.

Database Manager

Desktop database managers such as Corel Paradox, FileMaker, and Microsoft Access are fabulous and powerful programs. You will find them easy to use. They offer great potential and are very handy for keeping track of your inventory, auctions, and transactions.

Database Auction Management System

There's nothing better than a compelling project with which to cut your teeth on a new computer program. You can learn quickly and get better organized in the process. Learn some general database principles, usually available in books on the various leading programs, and forge ahead to build a custom application for yourself using one of the desktop database managers.

The best approach is to build one table into which you enter all your basic data as well as your follow-up data. When the table is open in front of you, you can easily and quickly go directly to the appropriate fields (column cells) and input data, delete data, or change data. You can cover a lot of territory in a short time. Or, a data entry and maintenance employee can do a lot of work in a short time.

Starting out with one easy-to-build table is an easy step to take, and a productive one. See *eBay Business the Smart Way, Third Edition* and *Building Your eBay Traffic the Smart Way* for more information on databases and datafeed marketing.

Auction Management Service

This database auction management idea is a great one. But it's already obsolete. Today eBay itself offers very capable auction management services at a low price, and dozens of other companies offer a full range of auction management services at low prices. All these services base their programming on the use of built-in databases. You don't have to reinvent the wheel. Take advantage of one of these services, and leave the creation of database auction management to someone else. Read more about these auction management services (used via the Web) in Chapter 19.

Spreadsheet

A spreadsheet such as Excel or Lotus 1-2-3 can help you account for your transactions. What you should know is that you often use the database capabilities of the spreadsheet program rather than the calculation capabilities. Why not use a database manager instead?

I don't recommend the use of a spreadsheet unless you are a spreadsheet expert and don't know or don't want to know how to use a database manager. For years eBay provided a spreadsheet solution to the bulk upload situation (Master Lister) and finally terminated it in favor of a database solution (Turbo Lister). Spreadsheets are great for calculations but not so adroit for accounting systems.

On Paper

Does anyone still use paper? Ultimately, pushing paper is not as productive as pumping digits. But sometimes the best move is one that's comfortable for you. A total paper system to handle Web commerce is insanity. But a hybrid system (paper–digital) makes sense. The goal is to get as close to 100 percent digital as is practical. Nonetheless, you don't have to get there immediately. Work toward that goal at a comfortable pace while still using some of your paper practices.

PowerSellers

The eBay PowerSellers program is for people who do a lot of retail auctions on eBay. It provides certain customer service benefits to you as an eBay customer. For example, as a PowerSeller, you can display the PowerSellers logo, which identifies you, in effect, as a high-volume eBay retailer.

This is likely to instill more confidence and trust in you by bidders than you would otherwise receive.

The program has monthly minimum sales requirements and several levels of participation based on sales. This program has evolved into something quite valuable for eBay retailers. Check it out at *Site Map*, *Selling Resources*, *PowerSellers*.

This is not a small program. eBay has over 100,000 PowerSellers. eBay provides $500 fraud insurance to the customers of PowerSellers, co-op advertising up to $8,000 per quarter, and other marketing programs. It has also arranged health insurance. This program for successful sellers gives some permanent sales structure to eBay and resembles a well-oiled selling machine. It's certainly something to aspire to if you're a high-volume eBay seller. Your PowerSellers logo shows that you are doing business successfully on eBay and therefore implies that you provide acceptable customer service. Indeed, one of the requirements to be a PowerSeller is a 98 percent positive feedback rating.

Amazon.com

If you want to maximize customer service at your website, study Amazon. Everything at Amazon is aimed at making it easy for customers to make purchasing decisions about books (and other merchandise) and then to easily purchase them. And sometimes at a discount! Navigation is easy. Searching is easy. Information access is easy. And ordering requires only one click.

One click does everything! It puts the book in your shopping basket and checks you out automatically. If you order another book within two hours, Amazon makes sure that both books (or more) are shipped together, if possible, to save shipping costs. It doesn't get any easier than one click.

This didn't happen haphazardly. The Amazon founder, Jeff Bezos, his wife, and a few employees spent a year designing and testing their website system before they opened on the Web for business. That means they spent a year on customer service before they took their first customer. (They could have easily opened in a month with off-the-shelf software.)

Try Lands' End (*http://www.landsend.com*), which enables you to try on clothes at its website via *My Virtual Model* (a model of yourself). Now that's customer service!

Ironically Speaking

Sears, the king of catalogs, discontinued its massive catalog just a few years before the Internet caught on in the early 1990s. It had the residual experience and expertise to quickly become a top Web department store like Amazon.com but lacked the vision. Not too long ago, a moribund Sears bought Lands' End to get back in the game. Then Sears itself was bought by K-Mart, another declining retailer. Can two obsolete retailers make one viable retailer? Will we see the Sears catalog again on the Web someday?

Do you have the digital control to do these fancy kinds of things on eBay? Certainly not. Nonetheless, you can develop your own brand of customer service within the eBay setting. In fact, eBay has established many customer service devices for sellers to use. Just learning and using all of them will put you ahead of the pack. In addition, the auction management services are replete with customer service devices. Just using *all* the features of one of these services will put you ahead of the pack.

Benchmarks of Customer Service

Of the Web as we will know it in 2020, probably only about 15 percent has been invented yet. Invent something you can do to improve your customer service on eBay (and be sure to let me know).

Even if you are an occasional seller, you need to provide good customer service. You have your own set of interests. The things you sell over the years will reflect those interests. The people you sell them to will tend to have similar interests. Despite the huge number of people using eBay, you may run across some of the same people in your eBay auctioning activities from time to time, if not regularly. Your reputation will count for something with such people.

So, to conclude, the following is offered as a baseline list of Web customer service benchmarks for eBay auctions:

- Easily readable text in auction ads
- Robust information on products for sale
- Guarantees (by eBay retailers for customers)
- Clear instructions on transaction procedures
- Multiple payment methods
- Quick service
- Professional fulfillment procedures
- Prompt communications

Don't feel too comfortable with this list. It's a good beginning, but it's not enough. If the above is all you have, some of your competitors are already ahead of you. Yet if you meet all the benchmarks above, at least you're ahead of most of your other competitors.

Where the Gold Is

In every gold strike (California, Colorado, Alaska), it never seems to be the miners who get rich. It's the store owners in the gold-mining towns that spring up who make the money. Similarly, you might consider providing services to eBay retailers. I know of an antique dealer in the Bay Area who provides the following package of services to other antique dealers she knows:

1. Puts their antiques up for auction on eBay.

2. Conducts the auction and communicates with bidders.

3. Receives the purchase payment.

4. Ships the antiques.

All an antique dealer has to do is stop by and leave the antique off at her office. She gets a percentage of the selling price. In other words, she does not only the fulfillment but also the auctioning.

Think up customer services you can perform for serious eBay sellers, and make a business out of it. For example, check out My EZsale (*http://myezsale.com*), an information service for eBay sellers (and other online retailers), and Craters & Freighters (*http://cratersand-freighters.com*) with shipping from 60 locations nationally.

Summary

Customer service is the essence of selling on the Web, whether it's via an ecommerce website or a series of auctions on eBay. As a seller, customer service should be in the front of your mind all the time. If a securities analyst on Wall Street can get together with a Web programmer and invent Amazon.com, you can probably come up with a few new ideas yourself for providing better customer service in regard to your eBay auctions.

15

Communicating with Skype

About a year before this book went to press, eBay bought Skype, a voice-over-IP (VoIP) telephone service. Why? Well, eBay has a long-range vision that buyers and sellers will communicate with each other someday by voice, that is by telephone. The difference between Skype and normal telephone service is that Skype goes over the Internet, and it's free.

VoIP

VoIP services are not new. I have been using Vonage since the spring of 2002. I've been very pleased with the service and the money that I've saved. (I also own a little stock in the company.) We installed an internal VoIP system in our charter school in 2003 when we installed a campus-wide fiber optic network. It has worked just fine. In other words, VoIP is a well-proven telephone technology.

As a VoIP system, Skype (see Figure 15.1) works several ways:

- Over the Internet completely (Skype's free basic service)

- Normal telephone to Internet (*SkypeIn*)

- Internet to normal telephone (*Skype Out*)

It is not a mature business telephone system yet, but it's quickly headed in that direction. It will soon be a robust telephone system quite suitable for customer service, exactly what eBay intends.

Figure 15.1 Skype home page. ©2007 Skype Limited.

Over the Internet

Over the Internet Skype is free. How do you use it? Simple. You download the free Skype software and install it in your computer. Now you're ready to talk free with anyone else in the world who has installed the Skype software on their computer. I talked business with a computer programmer in Australia for a half-hour—free—via Skype (both of us using Skype software).

Equipment

All that's required for using Skype at no expense is:

- A computer connected to the Internet
- A microphone
- Some speakers

You can substite a headset with a microphone for the microphone and speakers.

Software

The Skype free software is all you need, and it's quit spiffy. It has many advanced telephone features that make calling and receiving calls convenient. You can use Skype on your desktop computer or on your laptop.

Connection

Skype will work with a dial-up connection but will not perform at its best. It needs more bandwidth to approach the quality of normal telephone service. All the more reason to switch to broadband Internet access if you haven't already.

Normal Telephone to Internet (*SkypeIn*)

If someone wants to call you from a normal telephone at a real telephone number, they can with Skype. For this extra service, Skype charges you a fee. When you sign up for this service, Skype assigns you a telephone number. Anyone from any telephone anywhere can call you at that number, and you can receive the call via your Skype software.

You can also receive the call via special phone equipment wired to your computer. Using Skype with the proper equipment can be just like using a normal telephone. In fact, you can plug a normal telephone into one type of VoIP equipment and receive calls.

SkypeIn currently costs about $5 per month.

Internet to Normal Telephone (*SkypeOut*)

Ah-ha, the other half of the telephone service. If you want to call someone at their normal telephone, you can with Skype. For this extra service, Skype charges you a fee. You initiate your call from your computer, and it goes over the Internet as far as it can. Then it goes through a local telephone exchange to the local telephone, that is, the telephone of the call recipient.

The fee charged is in addition to the fee for normal telephone to the Internet.

Again, you can also call via special phone equipment wired to your computer. In fact, with the proper equipment, you can use a normal telephone via Skype to make calls to any other telephone.

At the time this book went to press, the fee for Skype Out was not available, as eBay was giving the service away free as a promotion. However, a review of the international rates showed a telephone service that's inexpensive. For instance, Skype costs about 2 cents a minute to France and 2.5 cents a minute to Japan.

Equipment

Note that Skype's services require that your computer be connected to the Internet. As you can see, you need to subscribe to both of Skype's paid services (SkypeIn and SkypeOut) in order to get normal telephone service via Skype's VoIP system. By normal telephone service, I mean actually using as normal telephone.

Here is some of the equipment you can buy today:

- A USB telephone that connects to your computer via a USB port. It is simply an extension of the basic free Skype service but gives it a physical capability. It can also work with SkypeIn and Skype Out. Most of such USB telephones sold are small and inexpensive. The one I bought for a trial did not work well. But the hour is early, and there will be good equipment by the time you read this book.

- A telephone that connects to your computer. This is simply a larger version the the USB telephone, aboout the size of a normal telephone (see Figure 15.2).

- A box that you can connect to your computer into which you plug a normal telephone. This will make most people feel comfortable using Skype. You will need to subscribe to the SkypeIn and the SkypeOut services to make the best use of this piece of equipment.

The equipment for Skype will improve rapidly. In addition there will be myriad other equipment available soon.

Figure 15.2 USB VoIP telephone.

Third-Party Developers

Skype was already successful when eBay bought it. Now with eBay behind it, you can expect it to grow rapidly into a well populated international communication system. It already has tens of millions of users.

Because it is destined for success and because it has an API (application program interface), many software developers will develop software that integrates Skype or provides new ways to use it. The API means that software developers can connect their software to Skype.

Look for an avalanche of software as well as hardware soon that uses or enhances Skype (*http://share.skype.com/directory*). This promised to be very exciting, particularly for customer service.

- Visit Multi-Link (*http://multi-link.net*) for a taste of what's coming down the road.

- Also visit VOX for Skype (*http://www.voxlib.com*), a service that you can use with any cell phone to make low-cost long distance calls via Skype through your PC (see Figure 15.3).

- And don't overlook the Skype website shop (*http://us.accessories.sk ype.com/direct/skypeusa/welcome.jsp*) for an exciting collection of equipment for sale.

Figure 15.3 VOX for Skype website. ©2006 VoxLib Corp.

Features

The Skype program that you use on your computer is very robust with features. Skype also offers some of the normal telephone services such as voicemail, conference calls, call forwarding, and speed dialing. And, get this: You can also make video calls with Skype. Both you and the person you talk with (see) will need a video cam.

But that's not all. You can also use chat via Skype with up to 100 other users. And Skype encrypts all transmissions for the trip across the Internet so that no one can eavesdrop on conservations.

That old monopoly AT&T is back together again. Skype makes a good antidote.

Summary

Skype was not ready for prime time eBay business use in 2006, although one could argue that some of the new equipment worked just fine. Look for 2007 and 2008 to be banner years for the enhancement of Skype.

And what's the point? The point is that voice communication—phone talk—is very powerful. People have used it and understood it for over 100 years. To bring it into eBay commerce at a very low cost is a very exciting development in customer service.

Also keep in mind that Skype is not limited to eBay. You can use it for anything, just like you can use any other telephone service. So Skype has exciting implications for all ecommerce, not just eBay. That is, it will be great for customer service for all ecommerce everywhere.

16

Writing eBay Auction Ads

eBay provides you with a webpage space (call it an "auction ad") with which you can do almost anything to advertise the item for your auction. Take advantage of this great opportunity. This is your chance to create some interest in your offering that will bring in a higher final bid. (Note that eBay Stores use essentially the same pages.)

eBay Advertising

Every medium has its own unique characteristics. The Web is an information medium. You can publish unlimited information on the Web at a small cost. It's not a medium like television where every time slot commands a premium price and where advertising is relatively expensive. Take advantage of the Web's strength and publish plenty of information on the item you auction.

Keep in mind that the Web (and eBay) is not a retail store where a customer can walk in, examine the merchandise, and talk to sales clerks. What you publish is what the customer gets. Your eBay auction advertisement has to create interest, then inform, and finally, close the sale.

An eBay ad has two parts: the one-line title that goes in the listing and the webpage section that is part of the auction page. This chapter considers the one-line title at the end of the chapter, but let's start with the ad itself.

The First Goal

The first objective of the ad is to create interest. A little hype is OK here, so long as you can back up the hype with facts a little farther down the page. The top of the ad should always include:

1. The specific identification of the item being auctioned

2. Condition of the item

3. One or two major benefits of the item to potential bidders

Put your strongest benefits here. You may get only one chance to hook the bidder/reader. Give it your best shot at the top of the ad.

Clearly and specifically identify the item being sold here, otherwise you will frustrate and anger potential bidders. Even worse, it may create a lot of unnecessary, undesirable, and time-consuming communication for you. If the item is a model XMT-5001 camcorder, not a model XMT-5011, you'd better get it right.

The condition of the item is important and should be stated at the top of the ad. *New, mint,* and *excellent* condition are prime selling points. Don't neglect to put them in up front. However, many people can't afford to buy a new product of the type you're selling. They look for bargains where the product is *in good working order but has a few cosmetic blemishes* (and other such descriptions). Express the condition as a prime feature, and you will draw potential bidders regardless of what the condition is.

Determine one or two major selling points that will draw the interest of the most likely bidders. Don't try to tell the whole story here. You have plenty of room later. Just mention one or two benefits to hook potential bidders.

Hook them into bidding? No. Your objective with the hype at the top of the ad is not to get them to make a bid. It's to get them to read more about your offering, that is, to get them to acquire enough facts on which to base a confident decision to bid.

> **Poor:** ActionCatcher camcorder with picture stabilization, flicker reduction, digital zoom, review/retake functions, and random editing

> **Better:** ActionCatcher camcorder XMT-5001, new, all automatic features, perfect for intermediate users and even novices

What's wrong with the information in the first example? Nothing. But it's too much information, and it doesn't seem directly tied to benefits. There's plenty of space to mention such information below. Action-Catcher has many different models of camcorders ranging in price from $300 to many thousands of dollars. Which model is it?

What's right with the second example? It mentions that the item is new and clearly identifies exactly what's for sale. Then it adds a little hype. It's probably not going to interest expert users, but then they won't buy the XMT-5001 anyway. It's not for experts. Novice and intermediate videographers will be likely to read more.

The Second Goal

The second part of the ad has two parts, the product information and the purchasing information.

Product Information

Now that you've hooked bidders into reading, provide them with the facts. The hype is over. Leave the hype to the television folks who only have a few seconds to hook potential buyers. And keep in mind that a television ad attempts to hook potential buyers into what? Into going to a local store to make a purchase, a local store where the potential buyer will interact with a sales clerk. On eBay there is no sales clerk. There's only your ad. Consequently, for the main body of your eBay ad, it's your job to supply the facts and benefits to enable the potential bidder to make a decision to bid (to buy).

On eBay, there's no limit on the ad. This circumstance requires facts. Provide as much factual data on the item for sale as you can find. Don't assume that anyone knows anything about the item. If you do, you'll be cutting out a significant percentage of your potential market.

What do you publish? Don't reinvent the wheel. A good place to start looking for information is the manufacturer's information and specifications. Get them off the box. Get them off the manufacturer's website. Get them out of the user's manual. Put in a link to the manufacturer's information and specification sheets on the manufacturer's website.

Hype, Information, and Specifications

The manufacturer's information and specifications usually contain some hype. Is that OK? Sure it is. So long as the ad is essentially informative, a little hype woven in is to be expected. Just a little hype, though. Overly hyped information loses credibility with potential bidders. Instead, they want facts and benefits.

A link to a manufacturer's website by itself is not enough. Such a link can cut your ad from seven paragraphs to one perhaps, but you still need a paragraph or two to keep readers involved in your ad. If you use a link, make sure it is a link directly to the specific webpage at the manufacturer's website that has the relevant information.

Express your personal enthusiasm for the item. If you have a positive opinion of the item, express it in terms of benefits to bidders. Honest opinions, even coming from the seller, are valuable. If you have a negative opinion of the item, don't say anything. Let the manufacturer speak for you. If the item is a lemon product, even if new, you'd better warn the bidders, albeit mildly. If you don't and you sell a lot of stuff on eBay, you may negatively affect your reputation. eBay is not a dumping ground for lemon products. If you treat eBay that way, you may adversely affect your reputation and fail to achieve your long-term objectives on eBay. Lemons can be sold honestly—albeit at lower prices—with happy sellers and buyers, but only with disclosure up front.

Don't make the ad too long. You could put the full text of three magazine reviews on the product in your ad, but that would be too much in most cases. Link to them instead. Beyond 1,000 or 2,000 words, you're bound to start losing people. However, it's different for every product. Bidders probably don't need 2,000 words about an office file cabinet. But if you're selling a $19,000 timeshare at a Steamboat Springs, Colorado, ski resort, 2,000 words may not be enough.

Losing Your Market

I was looking for a new camcorder on eBay. One person was selling two or three each week of the model I had decided to buy. He provided a generous amount of information (all the text from the manufacturer's website), enough to inspire a decision. He was selling the same model over and over again for an ongoing average price of about $550. I got ready to make my initial bid.

I reviewed what was being auctioned one last time. Surprisingly, I discovered another person selling the identical camcorder (also new). This person had posted very sparse information on the camcorder, only four sentences and few specifications. As a result, he had attracted few bidders. I put in my bid at this person's auction, won the bidding, and got the new camcorder for $450. The same day the other person sold three more identical camcorders at his Dutch auction for $550; the bids were $550, $600, and $600.

The moral of the story is that if you're a seller, it pays to provide plenty of information. If you're a buyer, it pays to look for the lazy sellers.

Purchasing Information

To build the bidder's confidence in purchasing from you, you must give complete information on how the transaction can be closed. How can the buyer pay? The more ways, the better. But whatever the acceptable payment methods, state them clearly. Don't forget shipping and handling. State specific amounts of such expenses up front.

Payment Methods

You will sell more if you accept credit cards (or PayPal). Do you know that you can take checks via the Web or via telephone? This is not popular, but it might be someday, and it's easy for you to do. See Chapter 16.

This is a golden opportunity to put in a link to your *About Me* webpage on eBay where presumably you have a lot of information about yourself or your eBay business. For some reason, a lot of sellers who should be doing this don't. You shouldn't miss this opportunity; it doesn't cost anything extra. However, don't put in a link to your website. eBay no longer allows it from your auction ad.

An alternative to operating a website for your business is to have an eBay store. You will certainly want to put in a link to your eBay store. eBay will automatically put a link (opened red door) to your eBay store after your name in your auction listing. But that's not enough.

Promote Yourself and Your Other Auctions

Promoting yourself works best after you have accumulated some proof that you're trustworthy. That is, as soon as you've built up some positive feedback, you can state, "Check my feedback." Make your self-promotion modest and factual. Do it, but don't overdo it. Also, use your auction ad to promote your other eBay auctions. You can put in a link in your auction ad to the eBay list of your other auctions. Although eBay does this for you, it's not enough. Do it yourself too.

The Third Goal

Ask for the order; that is, ask people to make a bid. Don't make a statement like "The lucky winning bidder will enjoy the CleanCut Estate Mower for many years." Rather say something like "Make a bid now. I think you'll be satisfied with the quality of this mower if you're the winning bidder, and I appreciate your interest in my auction." What you say doesn't have to be long or elaborate, but do ask for the bid.

Unique Products

Certain products do not lend themselves neatly to the preceding format, which is designed essentially for mass-produced goods with which many potential bidders will be familiar. Unique products and custom products require more explanation. Not only that, but in many cases, it may be appropriate and worthwhile to provide information expressed in a creative way.

Suppose you want to sell printing press prints of Van Gogh's self portrait. This is a well-known, inexpensive, mass-produced item that you find in college book stores for $20. Information about this work of art will help sell it, but the information isn't absolutely necessary. People will buy it because they like the way it looks, it's well known, and it's low cost.

However, suppose you want to sell numbered (limited edition), hand-made lithograph prints by an emerging new artist for $450 each. Providing voluminous information on the artist and the work of art as well as favorable art reviews and so forth will definitely help sell the prints. And if you can present this information in an attractive, unusual, and elegant way (i.e., with a template designed to sell art), you will realize even more sales.

Potential bidders who are looking for unique products will take the time to review a creative presentation of relevant information. It's not likely that someone who is only interested in comparing camcorder specifications prior to purchasing, instead, will take the time to read a lengthy creative presentation about a camcorder. But a limited edition print by an emerging new artist catches the imagination and will require a lot of information to make a sale.

Presenting the Ad

What's the goal for your presentation of the ad? The same as for the ad itself. You want potential bidders to read the entire ad. The best way to do this is to make it easily readable.

Text

Text is your most important medium. Remember, the Web is an informational medium. The most efficient way to convey the requisite information to potential bidders in most cases is via words.

The following subsections outline the format for the text. The penalty for neglecting to follow these guidelines is shrinkage of your potential market. Each guideline you fail to follow will shrink your market more. At some point, there will be no market left, and potential bidders will ignore your auction. In addition, if you do a sloppy job of publishing your ad, you detract from your credibility as a seller.

Grammar

Write the ad well. Check your spelling. Don't use acronyms or abbreviations; at least half the bidders won't know what those mean. Even if you use what you think are commonly understood acronyms having to do with the product or procedures on eBay, you will lose a lot of bidders, and you will never know it. Use good grammar and complete sentences. You are not writing a classified ad for which you pay by the word. Write something that's readable.

Don't be afraid to make mistakes. We all make spelling and grammatical mistakes. These are understandable and forgivable. What is irritating is the intentional cutting of corners (abbreviations, acronyms, incomplete sentences, all-lowercase, all caps, etc.) that makes reading more difficult for everyone and often makes the text itself virtually incomprehensible.

Paragraphs

Divide your text into paragraphs. It astounds me that some people put 1,500 words of information in their ad, all in one paragraph. That makes the text very difficult to read and comprehend. For example:

The ActionCatcher XMT-5001 camcorder with LCD color monitor. MSRP is $1,399. Features include: Built-in still camera with 140,000 pixels. LCD color monitor with 290-degree screen rotation for high- and low-angle viewing. Quick 44X Zoom with close-up focus. Picture stabilizing that differentiates between intentional and unintentional camera movements. Six-head mechanism for precision recording. Built-in head cleaner. Automatic system for recording, including auto focus, white balance, and auto exposure. Flicker reduction, flying erase head, and random editing. Floodlight built in that automatically turns on or off as needed. Review and retake functions with indicators for remaining tape time and remaining battery time. Remote control, editing, and dubbing. Image transfer and recording software. Special effects and titling. Languages: English, French, Spanish, and German. Fog and ND filters. Mic input. S-Cable output. Lens cover, dew sensor, 3-way power supply. New, sealed in box.

You can easily divide the above paragraph into separate paragraphs by using the HTML paragraph markup **\<p\>** at the beginning of each paragraph:

```
The ActionCatcher XMT-5001 camcorder with
LCD color monitor. MSRP is $1,399. Features
include:<p>Built-in still camera with
140,000 pixels.<p>LCD color monitor with
290-degree screen rotation for high- and
```

low-angle viewing.**<p>**Quick 44X Zoom with close-up focus.**<p>**Picture stabilizing that differentiates between intentional and unintentional camera movements.**<p>**Six-head mechanism for precision recording.**<p>**Built-in head cleaner.**<p>**Automatic system for recording, including auto focus, white balance, and auto exposure.**<p>**Flicker reduction, flying erase head, and random editing.**<p>**Floodlight built in that automatically turns on or off as needed.**<p>**Review and retake functions with indicators for remaining tape time and remaining battery time.**<p>**Remote control, editing, and dubbing.**<p>**Image transfer and recording software.**<p>**Special effects and titling.**<p>**Languages: English, French, Spanish, and German.**<p>**Fog and ND filters.**<p>**Mic input.**<p>**S-Cable output.**<p>**Lens cover, dew sensor, 3-way power supply.**<p>**New, sealed in box.

After you do so, the presentation will be more readable in a Web browser and will look as follows:

The ActionCatcher XMT-5001 camcorder with LCD color monitor. MSRP is $1,399. Features include:

Built-in still camera with 140,000 pixels.

LCD color monitor with 290-degree screen rotation for high- and low-angle viewing.

Quick 44X Zoom with close-up focus.

Picture stabilizing that differentiates between intentional and unintentional camera movements.

Six-head mechanism for precision recording.

Built-in head cleaner.

Automatic system for recording, including auto focus, white balance, and auto exposure.

Flicker reduction, flying erase head, and random editing.

Floodlight built in that automatically turns on or off as needed.

Review and retake functions with indicators for remaining tape time and remaining battery time.

Remote control, editing, and dubbing.

Image transfer and recording software.

Special effects and titling.

Languages: English, French, Spanish, and German.

Fog and ND filters.

Mic input.

S-Cable output.

Lens cover, dew sensor, 3-way power supply.

New, sealed in box.

Best Practice

To make the above list of paragraphs conform to HTML best practices, you will need to add the closing paragraph markup *</p>* at the end of each paragraph.

Although the above presentation is not as attractive as it can be with additional HTML coding (it needs bullets), it is definitely more readable than a solid block of text. Anyone can add the **<p>** markup without knowing HTML.

To add bullets, you must use more HTML markups. The **<ul>** and **<li>** markups are simple but not as simple as just **<p>**.

```
The ActionCatcher XMT-5001 camcorder with
LCD color monitor. MSRP is $1,399. Features
include:
```

<ul>

<li><p>Built-in still camera with 140,000
pixels.**</p>**

<li><p>LCD color monitor with 290-degree
screen rotation for high- and low-angle
viewing.**</p>**

```
<li><p>Quick 44X Zoom with close-up
focus.</p>

<li><p>Picture stabilizing that
differentiates between intentional and
unintentional camera movements.</p>

<li><p>Six-head mechanism for precision
recording.</p>

<li><p>Built-in head cleaner.</p>

<li><p>Automatic system for recording,
including auto focus, white balance, and
auto exposure.</p>

<li><p>Flicker reduction, flying erase
head, and random editing.</p>

<li><p>Floodlight built in that
automatically turns on or off as needed.</
p>

<li><p>Review and retake functions with
indicators for remaining tape time and
remaining battery time.</p>

<li><p>Remote control, editing, and
dubbing.</p>

<li><p>Image transfer and recording
software.</p>

<li><p>Special effects and titling.</p>

<li><p>Languages: English, French,
Spanish, and German.</p>

<li><p>Fog and ND filters.</p>

<li><p>Mic input.</p>

<li><p>S-Cable output.</p>

<li><p>Lens cover, dew sensor, 3-way power
supply.</p>

<li><p>New, sealed in box.</p>

</ul>
```

When the browser displays the code immediately above, it will have bullets, as shown in Figure 16.1.

Copywriting

What are we talking about here? We're talking about writing copy. Copywriters write copy. Some of the best copywriters working for large manufacturers, advertising agencies, and catalog companies make a lot of money just writing compelling copy correlating product features to consumer benefits. You can't expect to be a skilled copywriter without study and practice, but part of being a copywriter is writing clearly and in an organized manner. You can strive to do that much.

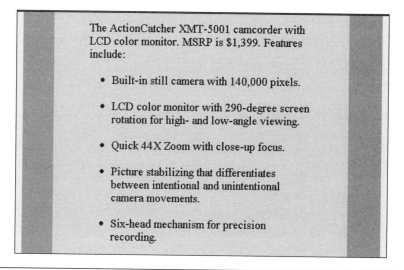

The ActionCatcher XMT-5001 camcorder with LCD color monitor. MSRP is $1,399. Features include:

- Built-in still camera with 140,000 pixels.
- LCD color monitor with 290-degree screen rotation for high- and low-angle viewing.
- Quick 44X Zoom with close-up focus.
- Picture stabilizing that differentiates between intentional and unintentional camera movements.
- Six-head mechanism for precision recording.

Figure 16.1 A bulleted list looks better than an unbulleted list for the information on this camcorder.

Read *Writing That Works*, Roman & Raphaelson, HarperResource, 2000, a small book that will improve your copy writing in a few pages.

Typesetting

The choice of fonts is quite simple. Use the browser defaults.

PC: Times New Roman, serif; Arial, sanserif; and Courier New, monospaced

Mac: Times, serif; Helvetica, sanserif; and Courier, monospaced

If you don't do anything, the text will appear in the browser default serif. This is your best choice. It's readable. It may be boring, because you see it all the time on the Web, but you're not trying to win a typesetting contest. You want your text to be readable above all else. Times New Roman and Times are easy to read on the screen.

If you use any font except the browser defaults, for the font to work, the website visitor will have to have the font installed on his or her computer. Chances of that may not be good. Therefore, your choices are limited to the fonts mentioned above.

Follow these eight standard typesetting guidelines:

1. Use italics for emphasis, not bold. Bold type is difficult to read through quickly. The use of bold for emphasis is appropriate only for warnings for equipment-threatening or life-threatening situations and for similar uses.

2. Make your lines between 9 and 11 words wide. This provides optimal reading. Wider lines are difficult to read. Narrower lines are difficult to read without special typesetting treatment (e.g., smaller type).

3. Avoid small type. Use at least 12-point type. Reading on a monitor is difficult enough. Don't make it worse. Space is not limited. (Note: 12-point type is the Web browser default, so you don't have to do anything in regard to specifying the type size.)

4. Avoid large type for text. Oversize type is difficult to read quickly.

5. Avoid huge type for headings. Headings are great, but keep their size modest. Use bold type.

6. Avoid centered text. Centered text is difficult to read. Make all text left justified (the default).

7. Avoid *all caps*. People cannot read all caps quickly. You don't need all caps for headings; you can use a larger-size font and bold.

8. Don't use all lowercase. It's difficult to read.

These rules are simple but nonetheless necessary for a professional look and readable text.

Layout

The width of the browser maximized is too wide for text. You need to narrow the text column to an easily readable size. There are a number of ways to accomplish this with HTML. If you don't use a template, you will have to learn a way to narrow the text column. The following code provides you two ways.

First Method

```
<table width="450"
cellpadding="10"><tr><td>

[your text paragraphs]

</td></tr></table>
```

This is the best way to ensure an accurate size of text column. This keeps the column 450 pixels wide. When you adjust the pixel dimension, stay under 550 pixels, or your presentation may not be readable.

Second Method

```
<dl><dl><dl>

<dd> [your text paragraphs]

</dl></dl></dl>
```

This shrinks the width of the column by expanding the left margin but is not an absolute measurement. Therefore, the column will expand and contract depending on the size of the browser window.

Each of your paragraphs should be marked with the **<p> </p>** markups. For example:

```
<p>The vase has a miniature hand painting
covering most of its midsection. The
painting has bright colors, which have not
faded, indicating that the vase has been
well cared for over the years. This is a
vase that museums would love to have.</p>
```

This is the proper way to do paragraphs. Avoid fancy and complex text layouts. Simple is best. Don't try to win a design contest. Just make your text readable.

Color

Color is a dangerous thing for webpages if not controlled carefully and properly.

Background Color

Some people change the background color of their ad using the *<body bgcolor="...">* markup. The result is that no one can read the auction information and make a bid. eBay is not going to stop you from shooting yourself in the foot this way.

Don't interfere with eBay's color scheme. Don't use the *<body bgcolor="...">* markup. The eBay auction section, both above and below your ad, together with your ad, comprises one webpage. If you change eBay's color scheme, you make it difficult for bidders to understand what's going on. In many cases, the eBay information will be unreadable if you change the background color.

Ad Background Color

To change the background color just for your ad without affecting the eBay color scheme, use the *<table>* markup. This means putting your entire ad in an HTML table. Use the first layout scheme mentioned above in the Layout subsection and add background color:

```
<table width="450" cellpadding="10"
bgcolor="#99ffff">
```

This will confine the background color to your ad, and the eBay auction listing color scheme will remain the same, as it should.

Color Combinations

There is nothing wrong with having your own color scheme in your ad. In fact, it can be quite attractive, if properly designed. Remember, it's readability you seek. There must be contrast between the background color and the text (foreground) color. The text default color is black, and you need a light background to go with it to make it readable. Here are some readable possibilities:

Black on white (default)

Black on light blue, light turquoise, light green, or cream

Browser-Safe Colors

Always use browser-safe colors. Not all colors appear the same in all browsers except the browser-safe colors. If you use browser-safe colors, what you see is what everyone else will see in their browsers. The browser-safe colors require three pairs of hex numbers and are limited to the following pairs:

00, 33, 66, 99, cc, ff

Thus, the color #00ccff is browser-safe. The color #01ccff is not browser-safe. The hex numbers correspond to RGB numbers (see Table 13.1).

Table 16.1 Hex Numbers and RGB Numbers for Browser-Safe Colors

Hex #	RGB #
00	000
33	051
66	102
99	153
cc	204
ff	255

Color Numbers

Browsers use hex numbers. Image editing programs use RGB numbers (and in some cases hex numbers too). RGB stands for red, green, blue. RGB numbers are easier for people to understand. Total dark is 000, and total light is 255. Thus, 000,000,000 is black; 255,255,255 is white; 255,000,000 is red; 000,255,000 is green; and 000,000,255 is blue.

Recommendation

For a useful collection of browser-safe colors that makes good background colors for reading, see Table 16.2, which gives the colors descriptive names. Unless you have experience as a webpage developer, stick with the default black type. If the background is too dark, there will not be enough contrast between the black type and the background with a resulting loss of readability. Use a light green (#ccffcc), light turquoise (#ccffff), light rose (#ffcccc), cream (#ffffcc), or another light browser-safe background color.

Table 16.2 Light Browser-Safe Colors That Provide a Good Background for Reading with Black Text (colors named by author, not official Netscape or Microsoft names)

Color	Hex #	RGB #
Cream	ffffcc	255,255,204
Tan	cccc99	204,204,153
Flesh	ffcc99	255,204,153
Light Gray	cccccc	204,204,204
Medium Gray	999999	153,153,153
Light Rose	ffcccc	255,204,204
Dark Rose	cc9999	204,153,153
Light Green	ccffcc	204,255,204
Fatigue Green	99cc99	153,204,153
Light Mauve	ffccff	255,204,255
Mauve	cc99cc	204,153,204
Light Purple	ccccff	204,204,255
Purple	9999cc	153,153,204
Light Turquoise	ccffff	204,255,255
Turquoise	99cccc	153,204,204
Light Blue	99ccff	153,204,255

Or, experiment to see what you like, always keeping readability in mind. Naturally, certain colors are more appropriate for some things than others (e.g., pink for women's items, blue for men's items), and maintaining good taste is always important. You don't want to get out of sync with your potential bidders.

Links

eBay offers you a wonderful opportunity to put links in your portion of your auction webpage. A link markup looks like this:

```
<a href="[URL]"> [text] </a>
```

What are the possibilities? They're limitless, but you need to limit them to what's relevant to your auction. The purpose of an ad is not "show and tell." It's to sell the item being auctioned.

eBay Link Policy

Regardless of what this book says, you need to occasionally consult the eBay link policies in the *Sell* section on eBay. eBay used to allow you to link to your website from your auction ad. That's no longer permitted. And the link rules are getting so complicated that you almost need a lawyer to decipher them. eBay evolves, and as it does, so do its policies. The thrust of the link policies is that eBay doesn't want you to link to your ecommerce website if it sells the same merchandise that you sell on eBay at the same or lower prices than you sell on eBay.

Your Website

You can't include a link to your independent ecommerce website in your auction ad. But can you include your website URL not as a link? Perhaps not. eBay seems to consider a URL as a "static link," whatever that is? Thus publishing the URL of your ecommerce website is apparently not permitted.

eBay Store

If you have an eBay Store, link to it in your auction ad. How do you get the URL? Go to your eBay store and look in the URL window near the top of your browser. Highlight and copy the URL displayed there. Paste it into your auction ad in a link markup. Link to your eBay Store even though eBay gives you a "opened red door" link automatically.

About Me

If you're more than an occasional seller, link to your *About Me* page on eBay. Your *About Me* page needs to present full information about you and your eBay activities or business. It will enhance your credibility as a seller. And eBay permits you to put a link to your independent ecommerce website from your *About Me* page.

Manufacturer's Website

If you do not have (or do not want to type) the manufacturer's information on the product being auctioned, you might find it on the manufacturer's website. If so, you can create a link from your ad to the place in the manufacturer's website where the information and specifications are posted. This relieves you of a lot of work in processing information for many products. But, in any event, you still need to put a paragraph about the product in your ad.

Review Website

If a Web magazine or other entity has favorably reviewed the product being sold, put in a link to the review. Don't copy the review and include it in your ad. That's a copyright infringement and may make your ad too long for casual reading. A link gets people who want to learn more directly to the review, and you don't have to get permission to publish the review.

Email

You might find it appropriate to provide an email link in your auction ad. This is a link that automatically pops up a potential bidder's email client with your email address already entered on the *To:* line. Although this provides a convenience to your potential bidders who want to contact you, it also has a tendency to clutter your auction ad with too many links. Experienced bidders know they can contact you through a link at the top of the auction in the eBay portion of the auction webpage.

To add an email link, use the code that follows:

```
<a href="mailto:[emailaddress]">[text]</a>
```

Here's how I like to do it:

```
<a
href="mailto:jt@sinclair.com">JT@Sinclair.
com</a>
```

This not only pops up an email client but also displays the email address (text) as a link.

Check with eBay

Before you add an email link, check the latest eBay rules. eBay tends to frown on buyers communicating with sellers except through eBay. And eBay continually changes its rules.

Auction List

You can put in a link to a list of your current auctions on eBay. Again, this is a convenience to potential bidders, particularly if the other items you auction on eBay are similar to the item featured in your auction ad. (Experienced bidders know that they can find this link at the

top of the auction in the eBay portion of the auction webpage.) You
may want to experiment with cross-linking to your other auctions.
Rather than putting in a link to your list of eBay auctions, try putting
in links to your specific eBay auctions that are relevant to the item
being promoted by your auction ad. Of course, this will require planning and ongoing maintenance because auctions last only a short
time.

Cross-Promotion Panel

Many of the auction management services provide a cross-selling
panel with three or four of your other auctions at the bottom of your
auction ad. Indeed, eBay itself now offers this service—for a fee.

Media

You can link to Web media too. This is a mixed blessing, as is
explained in the media subsections that follow. Media links use different markups.

Spanning the Web

It's one thing to go to another website via a link. That's easy to understand and easy to do with the link markup mentioned above. In addition, you can also bring media, such as images and sound clips, into
your ad (webpage). Such media doesn't have to be in the same place as
your ad at eBay. It can be anywhere on the Internet. Media is only a
URL away. Thus, you can span the Web to retrieve your media. You
can retrieve any media for which you have a URL, although the unauthorized use of someone else's media is a copyright infringement.

Photographs

Photographs sell merchandise. Always use them. They will increase
the number of buyers bidding on your item and are thereby likely to
increase the high bid. You take photographs with a digital camera and
make the JPEG file available at a place on the Web (a URL). You
retrieve it (put it in your auction ad) with the image markup:

```
<img src="[URL]">
```

The *src* is the *URL* of the image file. See Chapter 20 for a detailed
overview of using photographs in your eBay auction ad.

Use the logos of manufacturers, if you dare. They are trademarks, and you may be liable for violating the owners' trademark rights, although I suppose that you can get away with this most of the time. Many sellers seem to do so. However, never use a manufacturer's logo in a way that leads people to believe that you are the manufacturer or an official representative. That's sure to get you in trouble.

Logo

Use your business logo if you have one. It needs to be a digital image just like a digital photograph. It will add credibility to your ad if you are an eBay retailer.

Other Media

You can use other media in a webpage too. How about audio, digital video, Flash, animated GIFs, or clip art? These are seldom justified, although your ad can incorporate them just like digital photographs. (Again, the eBay link policies don't seem to cover this type of media. Better check the latest version of the policies before you use such media.)

Dancing digital doodads can be very distracting. They diminish the impact of the text information that sells the item being auctioned. They brand you as a Web amateur. Don't use them unless they directly relate to what you sell and unless they add to the information on the product.

Consider the Bidders

Remember, unless you are running multiple auctions, you may have a tendency to fancy up your one auction page. This can prove disastrous. What you think is *cool* and attractive may be a reading impediment to potential bidders. Serious bidders survey the offerings before they bid. Often it's tedious work. The faster and easier a potential bidder can glean the information from your auction ad, the happier he or she is and the more credibility you have as the seller. Potential bidders often read through dozens and dozens of auction offerings before they make a decision to bid. Before they make the decision, they invariably return to a few of the auction offerings to narrow the field. They make their decisions to bid based on adequate information, price, and the urgency of their need. They don't base their decisions on the coolness of your ad.

However, don't let me spoil your afternoon. If you want to run a cool auction ad because you're a wannabe website developer without a website, lavish your attention on your ad. It's great fun. But in your quest to make your ad cool, don't forget to make it readable too.

Using an Ad Template

If you have done some Web development, you will have no trouble creating your own ad. If not, and you want to learn, buy a basic book on HTML (see also the HTML tutorial in Appendix V). You can learn to do your own ads quickly and easily. Otherwise, use ad templates.

What Is an Ad Template?

An eBay auction webpage is an ordinary webpage constructed with HTML. A webpage is an ASCII document, a plain text document. You mark up the plain text with simple markups that tell the browser how to display the text, incorporate media, and make links (hyperlinks). It's a simple, straightforward system.

An ad template is an HTML document, a template webpage. All the markups already exist. You just put in the text, and your ad is done. You're ready to go.

Using a Template

Using a template is easy. You just fill in the blanks. The template often shows the blanks with the comment markup:

```
<!-- [instructions] -->
```

This markup provides instructions to you and has no other purpose. It does not show up in the webpage. By looking for this markup in the template, you will find the places where you need to enter text or URLs.

Sample Template

I created the following template for eBay auctions. Note that it has a comment line before and after every input.

```html
<table bgcolor="#99cccc"
width="100%"><tr><td>

<br>

<table bgcolor="#ccffff" width="520"
align="center"><tr><td>

<table width="400" align="center"><tr><td>

<br> <br>

<!-- add your short description of the item
BELOW this line to replace the xxx BELOW --
>

<center><h3>xxx</h3></center>

<!-- add your short description of the item
ABOVE this line to replace the xxx ABOVE --
>

<br>

<!-- add your text for your ad BELOW this
line to replace the xxx BELOW -->

xxx

<!-- add your text for your ad ABOVE this
line to replace the xxx ABOVE -->

<br>

<!-- add your shipping charge to replace
the xxx in the paragraph BELOW this line --
>

<p>High Bidder pays $xxx.00 shipping and
handling delivered anywhere in 48 states.
Higher outside the lower 48 states.</p>

<!-- add your shipping charge to replace
the xxx in the paragraph ABOVE this line --
>

<!-- add your boilerplate text BELOW this
line to replace the xxx BELOW -->

<p><b>Terms: </b>xxx</p>
```

```
<!-- add your boilerplate text ABOVE this
line to replace the xxx ABOVE -->

<br> <br>

</td></tr></table>

<br>

<table bgcolor="#ccffff" cellpadding="20"
align="center" border="0"><tr><td
align="center" valign="middle">

<!-- Put the URL of the photograph to
replace the xxx BELOW this line-->

<img src="xxx" border=0>

<!-- Put the URL of the photograph to
replace the xxx ABOVE this line-->

</td></tr></table>

<br>

</td></tr></table><br>
```

The first *xxx* to replace is for the short description of your item for auction. The second *xxx* to replace is for the text of your ad. The third *xxx* to replace is the shipping and handling charges. The fourth *xxx* to replace is the boilerplate. What is boilerplate? It's what you want to appear in every ad regardless of what you're auctioning. And the last *xxx* to replace is the URL of the digital photograph of the auctioned item.

Enter the template into a plain text file (e.g., use Microsoft Notebook or another plain text editor). Next you create your text in your word processor. Then you copy and paste it into the template. Save the template itself as a new file (e.g., *ad1.html*). Next test it; look at it with your browser. A digital photograph located somewhere on the Internet won't show up unless you're online. If the ad is OK, you're ready to go to the next step. If not, go back and adjust it.

When you're ready, go to eBay. Enter the ad into the proper input that's part of setting up an auction (see Chapter 6). You simply open *ad1.html* and copy and paste the contents (above) into the eBay input. It will appear on eBay just as it did in your browser.

Templates

As mentioned below, eBay itself provides templates now for your auction ads as do most auction management services. Consequently, you do not have to create your own template. However, if you're interested in experimenting, you can use the template above. Better yet, go to BaysideBusiness (*http://baysidebusiness.com*) and look for the templates there and use them.

Item for Auction

The first thing in the ad is a short description of the item for auction. This should be similar to the one-line title of the auction, but it need not be as short. However, don't make it too long either.

```
ActionCatcher camcorder XMT-5001, new, all
automatic features, perfect for novices and
intermediate users
```

This will appear in bold as a heading.

Body of Text

The body of the text is your opportunity to act as a salesperson. Give complete information. Anticipate questions, and provide the information that will answer the questions before they are asked.

```
xxxxxxxxxxxxxxxxxxxxxxxxxxxxxxxxxxxxxxxxxxxxx
xxxxxxxxxxxxxxxxxxxxxxxxxxxxxxxxxxxxxxxxxxxxx
xxxxxxxxxxxxxxxxxxxxxxxxxxxxxxxxxxxxxxxxxxxxx
xxxxxxxxxxxxxxxxxxxxxxxxxxxxxxxxxx

xxxxxxxxxxxxxxxxxxxxxxxxxxxxxxxxxxxxxxxxxxxxx
xxxxxxxxxxxxxxxxxxxxxxxxxxxxxxxxxxxxxxxxxxxxx
xxxxxxxxxxxxxxxxxxxxxxxxxxxxxxxxxxxxxxxxxxxxx
xxxxxxxxxxxxxxxxxxxxxxxxxxxxxxxxxxxxxxxxxxxxx
xxxxxx

xxxxxxxxxxxxxxxxxxxxxxxxxxxxxxxxxxxxxxxxxxxxx
xxxxxxxxxxxxxxxxxxxxxxxxxxxxxxxxxxxxxxxxxxxxx
xxxxxxxxxxxxxxxxxxxxxxxxxxxxxxxxxxxxxxxxxxxxx
xxxxxxxxxxxxxxxxxxxxxxx
```

Boilerplate

The boilerplate is the administrative information you put in each ad.

It covers procedures and policies.

```
We accept VISA, MC, money orders, checks,
and PayPal. Michigan residents add 8.25%
sales tax or send a copy of valid resale
certificate. Customers from outside the
United States are welcome. We ship anywhere
in the world. High bidder must pay within
10 days of auction or the transaction is
canceled. We will post positive feedback on
all finished transactions if the bidder
posts feedback. Please check out our other
auctions too. Bid now please, and thanks
for your bid! Camcorders for All, Inc.
```

Photograph Link

This is the URL of your digital photograph. It must be a complete URL.

```
http://www.camcordersforall.com/photos/
cam5001.gif
```

Changing Colors

In the template, the general background color is #99cccc, a medium shade of turquoise. The other background color is #ccffff, a light shade of turquoise. These background colors provide a neutral, unobtrusive appearance that does not detract from your information. Yet, they give your presentation a neat and professional look. If you want to change the colors, go through the template, find the numbers, and substitute your own hex numbers (colors). The subsection Color earlier in this chapter shows you how to use hex numbers.

Doing a Little HTML

You will notice that if you paste two paragraphs of text from your word processor into the body of the template, the paragraphs will merge together as one paragraph (browser view). You will have to add the HTML paragraph markups in your text.

```
<p>xxxxxxxxxxxxxxxxxxxxxxxxxxxxxxxxxxxxxxxxx
xxxxxxxxxxxxxxxxxxxxxxxxxxxxxxxxxxxxxxxxxx
xxxxxxxxxxxxxxxxxxxxxxxxxxxxxxxxxxxxxxxxxx
xxxxxxxxxxxxxxxxxxxxxxxxxxxxxxxxx</p>
```

```
<p>xxxxxxxxxxxxxxxxxxxxxxxxxxxxxxxxxxxxxxxxxxx
xxxxxxxxxxxxxxxxxxxxxxxxxxxxxxxxxxxxxxxxxxx
xxxxxxxxxxxxxxxxxxxxxxxxxxxxxxxxxxxxxxxxxxx
xxxxxxxxxxxxxxxxxxxxxxxxxxxxxxxxxxxxxxxxxxx
xxxxxxxxx</p>
```

This will display two paragraphs instead of one.

Definition

Note that the template starts with the *<table>* markup and ends with the *</table>* markup. The entire ad is inside an HTML table. The table defines the ad. It doesn't look like a table because we're just using the HTML table function for layout purposes, not to create an actual table.

The Ad

Voila! The ad completed using the template looks custom made. Observe how the template adjusted the ad to the amount of the text and the size of the photograph (see Figures 13.2 and 13.3). With a template, the design, layout, and typesetting are predetermined. You need only create the content that goes into the ad. Using any method of creating an auction ad, you still have to create the content; that is, you always have to write the ad and obtain or take the photograph.

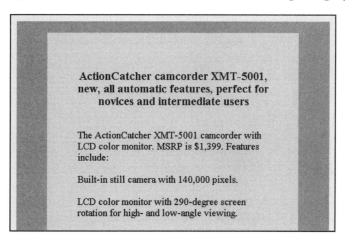

Figure 16.2 Top of an eBay ad made with a template.

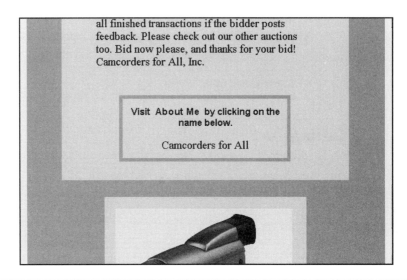

Figure 16.3 Bottom of an eBay ad made with a template. Note that the link to *About Me* will take buyers directly to your *About Me* webpage.

Alternatives

eBay now gives you a choice of themes (templates) to use for your eBay listing ad. Pick a theme that fits your item, and eBay will automatically generate a nice auction ad for you, free! You can do this when you provide the input for your auction listing on eBay.

Auction management services also provide ad templates (themes) for your auction ads. Your choices are usually greater than what eBay offers, and such templates are easy to use.

Don't Use My Templates

At the time I wrote the first edition of this book, readers needed templates, because templates weren't readily available. Now templates (themes) are available from a number of sources and most are easier to use than mine. I recommend that you use eBay's templates or those of an auction maanagement service, not mine.

Still, reading this chapter will give you a much better idea of how to put together an attractive auction listing ad.

For the templates available on my website, you don't have to worry about HTML. You just replace the *xxx* (via copy and paste) with the appropriate text wherever you see the *xxx* in the webpage. Go to *http:// baysidebusiness.com* for more of my templates.

You do not necessarily have to use the template in this chapter or ones from other sources. You can design your own; you can find a Web developer to design a template for you; or you can simply alter whatever templates you can find on eBay to suit your own purposes better.

The One-Line Title

Finally, at the end of the chapter we get to the beginning of the auction webpage, the one-line title. This is the one-line heading that eBay uses both as a heading (title) for the auction webpage and for the auction's listing on the page with the list of auctions. This line cannot be more than 55 characters long. The one-line title should:

- Include keywords for searches.

- Clearly identify the item.

- Be easy to read (traditional typesetting).

- Avoid using punctuation or symbols.

- Not include extreme adjectives such as *awesome*.

Searches

Some people search through the lists of items for sale on eBay. Many use the eBay categories to narrow the search first, then the search engine. Putting an item in two categories, if appropriate, gives you extra marketplace exposure, but it also costs more. People use keywords to search. If you're looking for a camcorder, life is simple. *Camcorder* is the keyword. The search result will be a list of camcorders for auction.

Word Order

The brand name, if it is important, should come first. The product should come second. The model identification should come third (second and third can be reversed). Condition, if new or mint, should come last; if not new or mint, the condition should not be included in the title.

```
ActionCatcher camcorder XMT-5001 new
```

A potential bidder probably searches on *camcorder*. He or she looks for known brands and known models.

Pop Quiz

What have I left out of the title in the example for this chapter?

When I wrote the first edition, digital camcorders were exotic. Buyers assumed that camcorders were analog unless specified otherwise. Today there are two types of camcorders widely sold: digital and analog. That should be specified in the title.

Not too far in the future, there will be few analog camcorders being sold. Buyers will assume that camcorders are digital unless specified otherwise. Times change.

For an unbranded item, the most compelling characteristic of the product should come first. Use your judgment. Always put the most important feature a potential bidder might look for first.

```
Eighteenth-century vase with miniature
```

A potential bidder probably searches on *vase*. He or she is already in the Antiques section, so there's no need to include the word *antique*. *Eighteenth-century* immediately categorizes the vase, although a more specific description would be better. Mentioning *miniature* indicates the vase has hand-painted art.

The line must be easy to read and specifically identify the item for auction. Review the one-line title for the camcorder:

```
ActionCatcher camcorder XMT-5001 new
```

ActionCatcher is a well-recognized name. (Actually, it's a fictitious name. Imagine that it's a well-known brand.) The fact that the camcorder is new, not used, is important enough to include. People looking for camcorders will find this item easily. Do not jazz up your title. It just makes it more difficult to read. Don't use exclamation marks or all caps to draw attention to it. It will be more difficult to read and more frustrating for a reader (potential bidder). Remember, an average reader looks at two or three lines per second.

Some products are more difficult to write titles for than others. For instance, if you are auctioning a microphone, you have a keyword problem. People will search both on *microphone* and on *mic*, so you have to include both in your title:

```
Shure dynamic microphone mic SM58
```

Each product has its own characteristics and jargon that you must consider. For instance, some people will even use *mike* for microphone.

If the item is new, always include that fact at the end of the line. New items command a premium price. Many people look for new items.

Sermon on the Title

I have always instructed that you should make your titles according to normal typesetting rules. No bold. No all-caps. No highlight. No jazzed up characters. Many other eBay authors disagree with me. And eBay statistics show that these typesetting treatments that I have warned against actually get more sales. Don't believe it.

First, eBay charges more for these treatments. They have a vested interest in publishing any statistics that support higher fees. Second, there are simply too many variables to take simple statistics like this seriously. For instance, aggressive sellers who make their living on eBay are more willing to pay extra for these treatments. But they do a lot of other things to increase sales that other sellers do not do. Is it the treatments or the other things they do that increase their sales? Third, every eBay category is different. The bold, all caps, and highlights actually work in some situations.

For instance, when people are window shopping—they don't know what they want to buy—the bold, all caps, and highlights might draw attention to an item. People aren't skimming the list. They're looking for something that might interest them.

When people know what they want, they look for it by skimming the titles. Bold, all caps, and highlights just make skimming more difficult. When people want a camcorder they often know the specifications of what they want, particularly what brand and model. Thus, in the camcorder category they will skim for brand name and model or perhaps a choice such as analog or digital. The more readable the title, the easier and faster it is to skim. It's the less readable titles that potential bidders are the least likely to read. Consequently, using bold, all caps, and highlights has just the opposite effect of that intended.

Now, there are no absolute rules for eBay selling, especially when there are 22 million items in 60,000 categories. But I believe that using good typesetting for titles is a more productive (profitable) general rule for sellers than using difficult-to-read typesetting in an ineffective attempt to draw attention to a product.

At the End, the Beginning

The reason this section (the one-line title) comes at the end of the chapter instead of the beginning is that it's the last thing you write. After you have thought through and have written your ad, you will usually have a better idea of what the title should say. Think about the keywords you will use. Think about exactly what potential bidders will be looking for. Then write the title.

Many sellers do a good job of writing one-line titles for their auctions. Consequently, good examples are not scarce. Nonetheless, there are plenty of bad examples too, so write with care.

Purpose

The purpose of the title is not to hook people. It's to identify items for which some potential bidders are looking. If I am not looking for a camcorder to buy, no matter what your title says about the camcorder you're selling, it won't interest me. If I am looking for a camcorder, you don't have to hook me to take a look. You just have to identify your item in such a way that I can find it easily (i.e., read it easily) on a list or via a search. Once I take a look at your ad, that's your opportunity to hook me on the particular product you have up for auction.

Summary

Your ad in your eBay auction listing provides you an opportunity to include all the information you need to sell one item effectively. Don't miss this opportunity. Present the information clearly and attractively. Don't overdo it with a lot of webpage frills. Above all, the information must be easily readable on the screen. And don't forget the photograph; photographs help sell merchandise on eBay.

17

Conducting Auctions

For people who will run only one auction at a time, this chapter will cover general auctioning strategies. Auctioning items one at a time may be fun and profitable, but it's no way to make a living, unless each item has a high price and a large profit. Most people who make a living on eBay make money by running multiple, simultaneous auctions—the more the better. Some retailers are running hundreds of auctions a week. So, for those who want to use eBay more productively, this chapter covers the handling of high volume sales.

General Auction Techniques

Although the general techniques this chapter covers below appear to pertain primarily to individual auctions, these techniques also apply to multiple auctions. Successful multiple auctions are always a collection of individual auctions that work well.

Timing

You do not enter an auction when it is convenient for you if you want to generate the most bidding action. You enter an auction so that it ends at a time when the most potential bidders will be online to pay attention to it. Consequently, if you think the most potential bidders will be online between 5 PM and 9 PM on Saturday evening, start your auction so that's when it ends.

This is easy to do because the auction will end at the exact time you entered it, either three days, five days, seven days, or ten days later. In other words, if you want a three-day auction to end Saturday at 7:30 PM, enter it at 7:30 PM on Wednesday evening.

Needless to say, there are complications. For instance, 7:30 PM where? There is a three-hour difference between New York and Los Angeles. There is an eight-hour difference between London and Los Angeles. Keep in mind, too, that eBay runs on Pacific Standard Time (PST), that is, the time in San Jose, California, where eBay headquarters is located (see Table 14.1).

As you can see in Table 14.1, eBay uses military time. And why not? It's unambiguous time; that is, it numbers each hour of the day uniquely. Thus, from the table, 19:00 hours (eBay time) is 7:00 PM Pacific time, 10:00 PM Eastern Standard Time (EST), and 3:00 AM Britain time.

Now, what if you are selling cases of Dr. Pepstop's Anti-Insomnia Elixir? The middle of the night might be a good time to have your auction end. Therefore, you have to enter it in the middle of the night.

Or, suppose you want to sell Arizona cacti (souvenir of the Old West) to Europeans. You might want to enter your three-day auction at about 11 AM PST on Wednesday. That puts the ending after dinner Saturday evening in Europe.

To set your computer clock, or your watch or clock, go *eBay official time* in the bottom left-hand corner of every eBay webpage.

Best Times
Most eBay sellers will tell you that evenings and the weekends, particularly the weekends when people are home from work, are the best times to have an auction come to a close.

Table 17.1 eBay Time and US, Japan, and Britain Time Zones

Japan	Hawaii	eBay	Pacific	Mountain	Central	Eastern	Britain
5:00	10:00	**0:00**	**12:00**	1:00	2:00	3:00	8:00
6:00	11:00	1:00	1:00	2:00	3:00	4:00	9:00
7:00	**12:00**	2:00	2:00	3:00	4:00	5:00	10:00
8:00	1:00	3:00	3:00	4:00	5:00	6:00	11:00
9:00	2:00	4:00	4:00	5:00	6:00	7:00	**12:00**
10:00	3:00	5:00	5:00	6:00	7:00	8:00	1:00
11:00	4:00	6:00	6:00	7:00	8:00	9:00	2:00
12:00	5:00	7:00	7:00	8:00	9:00	10:00	3:00
1:00	6:00	8:00	8:00	9:00	10:00	11:00	4:00
2:00	7:00	9:00	9:00	10:00	11:00	**12:00**	5:00
3:00	8:00	10:00	10:00	11:00	**12:00**	1:00	6:00
4:00	9:00	11:00	11:00	**12:00**	1:00	2:00	7:00
5:00	10:00	**12:00**	**12:00**	1:00	2:00	3:00	8:00
6:00	11:00	13:00	1:00	2:00	3:00	4:00	9:00
7:00	**12:00**	14:00	2:00	3:00	4:00	5:00	10:00
8:00	1:00	15:00	3:00	4:00	5:00	6:00	11:00
9:00	2:00	16:00	4:00	5:00	6:00	7:00	**12:00**
10:00	3:00	17:00	5:00	6:00	7:00	8:00	1:00
11:00	4:00	18:00	6:00	7:00	8:00	9:00	2:00
12:00	5:00	19:00	7:00	8:00	9:00	10:00	3:00
1:00	6:00	20:00	8:00	9:00	10:00	11:00	4:00
2:00	7:00	21:00	9:00	10:00	11:00	**12:00**	5:00
3:00	8:00	22:00	10:00	11:00	**12:00**	1:00	6:00
4:00	9:00	23:00	11:00	**12:00**	1:00	2:00	7:00

Greenwich Mean Time

PST is Greenwich Mean Time (GMT) less eight hours. GMT is a standard reference that you can use to calculate the difference in hours between a place (time zone) and PST. Consequently, if you know that PST is –8 and EST is –5, you know there's a three-hour difference that you need to consider.

Are there any good times of the month? Most offline retailers will tell you that sales are good around paycheck times. However, on eBay that phenomenon may not hold up. After all, someone can be the winning bidder on eBay and not have to buy a money order or write a check for several days after the end of the auction. Therefore, several days before payday (first and fifteenth) might work well in theory. And several days after payday may be prime selling time too.

Best Time of Year

What about time of year? Avoid holidays? Too many people traveling, right? But what about all those people who aren't traveling and who stay home looking for something to do? I remember that once while on vacation, I rushed to use someone's PC to make my final bid on an item. Consider most holidays OK for eBay auction action.

But tax time in April is always a tough time for most offline retailers. It's probably not a good time to auction your item on eBay either. The Christmas season, of course, is prime time to sell merchandise, especially an item that makes a good gift (just about anything). For the mail-order catalogs, the Christmas season starts in September or October. The closer to Christmas, the more success you'll likely have on eBay.

Yet eBay Christmas sales fall off well before Christmas due to the anticipated length of shipping times.

The Right Time

In truth, the right time depends on the item and the circumstances. A dozen authors can voice a dozen different opinions and you might even be able to get general statistics from eBay, but in the end each item has its own set of potential bidders that may or may not follow the normal bidding patterns in regard to timing. As a seller it's your job to experiment to find out what the best time is for each individual item you sell.

Did You Know?

The day before Valentine's Day is the end of the line to ship flowers and candy (FedEx), right? Not exactly. It turns out that if Valentine's Day falls early in the week (Monday, Tuesday, Wednesday), many working couples put off celebration until the following weekend. Therefore, Valentine's sales are brisk righ up until Thursday, that is, after Valentine's Day. Who knew? Experimentation in regard to auction timing is your best bet.

Who's There?

In reality, there is no one there in the final minutes of many auctions no matter when the auctions end. People make their bids earlier and forget about it. There is no last-minute frenzy. In such cases, the time the auction ends is irrelevant. All the theory, speculation, and observations of authors and other cognoscenti are for naught. Nonetheless, there are definitely some auctions that do have a lot of action in the last minutes.

Statistics

For a monthly fee you can access statistics kept by Andale, an auction management service. Such statistics are specific to individual products and can be very useful. Some other auction management services are now providing useful eBay statistics too. A review of such services will help you find statistics what will be useful to you. Even eBay now offers statistics. See Chapter 22 for a list of auction management services.

Convenience

The bottom line is that your best bet for timing may be an evening on the weekend with a seven-day auction. But that's a busy, and sometimes frustrating, time for everyone because eBay is so active. It may bring you the most bids, but the additional bids may produce negligible results on items that are not "hot." For many items, catering to your own convenience rather than to the perceived convenience of the potential bidders may bring a final bid almost as high. And if your convenience means more to you than the highest possible bid, enter your auction when it's convenient for you.

Multiple Auctions

Some people have run multiple auctions (same item) instead of a Dutch auction. That's not a bad idea. It gets bidders fired up. If they don't win the first auction, they still have more chances left. Where

I've seen it done, however, it was obvious that the seller conveniently entered the auctions one after another within a short time. Consequently, the auctions end very close together, usually within two minutes of each other. That does not allow enough time for losing bidders to regroup for a renewed bidding effort. As a result, the second and third items often have fewer bidders and often go for less than the first item. It is important to give bidders some breathing room. Multiple auctions for the same item should be spaced at least five minutes apart.

How Long?

The answer to, How long should an auction be? is another question: What's the purpose? If your primary purpose is advertising, the longest auction (ten-day auction) is for you. You're up the longest time for the least trouble and get the most exposure for the dollar.

What if you want to get the most bidders? The theory goes that the ten-day auction is the best because your auction is up longer and attracts more potential bidders. Hey! Enter your auction at 7:30 PM Wednesday evening and get exposure on two Saturdays. What a deal! This definitely appeals to a certain group of potential bidders, bidders with patience.

Another class of bidders, however—those without patience—will more likely bid on an auction with a shorter deadline. Whether because of circumstances or personal character, they can't wait. A ten-day auction goes well beyond their horizon. That's why *Buy It Now* has become popular.

The nice thing about the ten-day auction is that you rope in the patient bidders for the first seven days and the impatient bidders for the last three days and get the best of both worlds. That's why the ten-day auction makes good sense.

But what about you? You may not want to wait ten days. You need the money right now. Or you've got to get the stuff out of the garage right now before it drives you nuts. Or your landlord just gave you a ten-day notice, and you can't take your nine-foot wooden giraffe Tutmouse with you to your next apartment, which has only eight-foot ceilings. My god, what are you going to do with Tutmouse? There are lots of legitimate reasons to do shorter auctions, but most of them have to do with your wants, needs, or convenience rather than the quest to generate the most bids.

A general rule is that the more popular the item, the shorter the auction. In other words, a popular item (e.g., a recognized brand) will bring plenty of bidders in a short time. An obscure item needs all the time it can get to attract bidders. For instance, suppose you're selling a currently popular portable Sony television in the $150 price range. You will attract many bidders if the offering is reasonable. But, if you're selling an antique wooden soup spoon manufactured in Houghton, Michigan, you may have to wait longer than three days for a significant number of bidders to materialize.

Seller Control

In a real sense, a bidder's situation is out of his or her control. There are other uncontrolled competitive bidders with whom a bidder is sometimes funneled into a short bidding frenzy. In contrast, a seller has complete control over the setup of the auction. eBay's liberal policy of *almost anything goes* in the auction page provides a seller with a great opportunity to skillfully promote his or her item. As Chapter 13 explains in detail, everything you do properly works to attract more potential bidders (e.g., readable text). Everything you do improperly works to reduce the number of potential bidders (e.g., background colors that make text unreadable). Consequently, it pays to learn something about writing copy, advertising, typesetting, using HTML, and editing digital photographs if you're going to be a regular seller on eBay.

And never forget your reputation, which is also in your control. Would you send a money order for $750 to a seller who had obvious problems getting along with bidders and may even have cheated a few people? Would you send a money order for $750 to a seller who had made all his or her bidders happy?

Pricing

Presumably, your objective is to get the highest possible bid. To do so, you usually have to inspire some competitive bidding. How do you price your auction?

Low Minimum with a Reserve

The thing to keep in mind is that in the end, a bidder will bid only so much for an item. The price you set at the beginning has little effect on this reality. Low prices probably attract rookie eBay bidders, but rookies soon catch on that a low price in the beginning does not necessarily mean a low price at the end of the auction. Once rookie bidders realize their initial misconceptions, they look for signs that a seller is being reasonable.

A reserve, until it is met, is a hidden minimum allowable bid and doesn't tell bidders anything simply because it is hidden. If you use a reserve, bidders don't know whether you're for real or just another unreasonable seller. Many bidders will not bid on an auction with a reserve. (Many auctions do not get any bidders.) The low minimum adds an aura of unreality that may not be inviting to potential bidders. It's perhaps better to send a strong signal that you're for real. See High Minimum Bid (next section).

When does it make sense to use a low minimum bid and a reserve? When you want to test the market. You're not sure of the probable high bid, and you want the market (the bidders) to decide for you. If you set a high reserve, you won't sell the item and won't learn anything. But if you set a low reserve and get bids over the reserve, you may get a strong indication of the market value. You can use that knowledge in your next auction.

High Minimum Bid Without a Reserve

If you want to maximize the high bid, do your homework. Research what identical or similar items have sold for in past auctions. Chances are you're not going to get a bid that's higher. So set your auction with a minimum bid (no reserve) that attracts potential bidders. It must be high enough to live with should there be an abnormally low number of bidders and an abnormally low winning bid. It should be low enough to lure potential bidders to make a bid. It sends a message that you're serious about selling the item.

Other Authors

I've noticed that some other authors advise you to always start the bidding at one dollar. First, general formulas don't work on eBay with over

22 million items for sale each week. Second, who are you kidding when you offer an item worth $175 for a minimum bid of one dollar? On the other hand, when you start the bidding at one dollar, you pay a lower eBay insertion fee.

Being realistic about selling something is tough. You buy an item for 20 percent off list, use it once and decide it's not for you (although it's a popular item), and put it up for auction on eBay at 30 percent off list. You're an unreasonable seller because many people can buy the item for 35 percent off list at a discount store. To sell it on eBay new will probably require a price of 45 percent off list, if it's new. But it's not new (maybe *like new*), so you're going to have to offer it at even lower than 45 percent off list.

People selling items at retail on eBay are realistic about their prices. They have to be, or they couldn't stay in business. You compete with them. Thus, unrealistic pricing just wastes your time.

Research the market first. If you're not happy with the potential high bid, sell your item some other way. Or don't sell it.

Plenty of Stuff Not for Sale

There is plenty of small, expensive, high-quality stuff in my garage that I won't sell. It seems more rational to keep it, with the thought that someday I might need it again, than to sell it for the low price it will bring on eBay or anywhere else. However, one has more incentive to get rid of the large expensive stuff that takes up a lot of space.

Your main goal is to convey the message to people that you're a reasonable seller. They can buy from you at a market price and deal with a reasonable person to complete the transaction. Everyone is looking for a steal. Everyone finds one occasionally. But most of the time people pay the market price for merchandise, and that's something they're willing to do. You can usually find the eBay market price in your research.

Your auction setup, your advertising, your reputation, and the services you offer bidders all work to convey a message to potential bidders. That message should spell *reasonable*. The high minimum bid that's still lower than the market price is a good way to attract bidders because it seems reasonable.

The Market

Keep in mind that you don't decide price. The market does. For eBay, the market is eBay auctions; that is, eBay auctions for identical or similar items determine the market value of an item. It really doesn't matter what the price of an item *should* be. It doesn't matter what I think it should be according to my magic formulas expressed in this book. It really doesn't matter what you think the price should be. And it really doesn't matter what the price would be in a St. Louis flea market. The only thing that matters is what the market value is on eBay. Knowing and using accurate market values is the best selling technique you can use.

Research

Thus, the most important procedure you can use as a selling strategy is research. Research the market value of the item you want to sell. Use past eBay auctions to do an appraisal. Use offline data. Use list price as a reference for items that aren't very old. Use whatever reliable information you can find. At *http://www.worthguide.com* you can find auction data on some popular items. Using an accurate market price is all-important.

To use the eBay archives, go to a listing of auctions under a category or subcategory. On the lefthand side elect *Completed Listings*. Click on *Show Items* button to access the archives of completed auctions. This is an excellent means of doing your value research.

As mentioned before, Andale (see Chapter 19) has an excellent research system at a reasonable price that enables you to do very sophisticated price researching, and Andale has plenty of aggressive competitors.

Anomalies

Despite the fact that eBay has a high volume of both auctions and bidders and is a rational market, there will always be eBay market anomalies. How do you explain commonly available items selling auction after auction for 10 percent more than people would have to pay for them in a discount store? How do you explain a first-rate branded item selling new for as little as 70 percent off list price (30 percent of list price)? These anomalies happen by chance or due to some undiscernible force in the marketplace. Anomalies create the risk that no matter how careful your research, you won't get the high bid for your item that you aim for. Or, perhaps, you will get more for your item than anticipated.

Regional

I see so many auctions where the seller has put something cute for the *Location* entry in the auction listing. Don't shortchange yourself, be serious. Disclose where you're located. Many bidders search the auctions for just their locale to save shipping money or shipping time or to avoid sales tax. If your Location entry is a non-sequitur (e.g., the United States, East Coast), they'll bypass your listing.

Case Study

As it turns out, while I was writing the third edition of this book, I needed to sell my professional 35mm film camera on eBay. So, I decided to make a case study out of the project.

An Olympus OM-4 Ti and four professional OM lenses were to be auctioned. My research on eBay (reviewing the *Completed listings* archive) indicated that these were worth about $1,350 on eBay if each item were auctioned separately. (Unfortunately, I couldn't get direct comparables on the camera body and one of the lenses, so I used similar models. That turned out to be a considerable mistake.) Selling the items separately is more work than selling all in one package, and I anticipated that a package would sell for less. Since I wasn't looking for extra work, I decided to sell the camera and lenses as a package with a reserve of $985 hoping that bidders would get close to the aggregate $1,350 value for the components.

I took many photographs and selected four photographs of the camera body and three photographs of each lens for a total of 16 photographs to include in the auction ad. This may seem like a lot, but this is a big-ticket auction that requires generous photographs to maximize the sale price. My equipment was in "like new" condition, and the photographs demonstrated that fact. I even took care to enhance the photographs with image editing software to sharpen them a bit.

Next I wrote my auction ad text taking some care to make it useful to potential bidders. I'm not a copywriter (an advertising specialty) and cannot easily write compelling catalog text. But I can and did provide complete and accurate information on the merchandise to be sold. I also put in a link to an archive on the Olympus website (the camera was no longer manufactured) where bidders could get detailed information and specifications.

Buyers want to know why you are selling. This is a great chance for sellers to dream up any story that might help sell the item, and buyers know it. Nonetheless, buyers still want an explanation.

In my case, the real explanation was that I seldom used this camera. Although an excellent professional camera, it was too cumbersome to get out and use. I had discovered that digital point-and-shoot cameras are not only more convenient to use, but that in my hands, they take better photographs. I had become very enthusiastic about digital photography. The explanation in my auction ad, however, did not convey this enthusiasm. It stated simply that:

"Am selling because I use a point-and-shoot camera and never seem to have the extra time to get out this camera with all its lenses to use it."

The word "digital" did not appear anywhere in the auction ad.

Now I was ready to post the auction ad on eBay. I wanted to do a ten-day ad because that would catch more potential bidders. But it was Saturday when I contemplated this strategy, and a ten-day ad would finish on a Tuesday, not optimal. I could wait until the next Wednesday to post a ten-day ad to finish on a Saturday, but if I posted immediately, the auction would end on Memorial Day Saturday. Is that a good weekend to end an eBay auction? Many people go somewhere that weekend and aren't at home to bid on eBay. It might not be optimal. On the other hand, a long weekend is often a relaxed time for people when they might find the time to do some casual shopping on eBay.

To further complicate my situation, my wife was anticipating a possible business trip to Houston. If that fell into place, the whole family would accompany her, and we would leave shortly after Memorial Day weekend. Naturally, that would interfere with selling the camera and lenses on eBay after Memorial Day, and I anticipated using the money from the auction to buy a new digital camera that I could use in Houston.

This goes to show that the optimal situation for an eBay auction may not fit your schedule. When selling on eBay, sometimes life gets in the way. I opted to run a seven-day auction that ended the Saturday evening (about 5:00 PST) before Memorial Day weekend.

The first day five bidders bid my camera package up to $1,024 where the bidding stayed for most of the week. They were all experienced bidders with many transactions to their credit. Thus, the prospects of getting near the $1,350 goal looked good.

I had two people email me during the week saying that they wanted to buy the camera immediately. One offered to pay "substantially" more than the current bid; the other offered $2,000. I turned them both down explaining that an off-auction sale would violate eBay rules but at the same time encouraged them both to continue bidding. I got the idea that they weren't very knowledgeable bidders and that nothing would come of their interest in the auction.

Saturday morning, I checked, and the bids were up to a surprising $1,425. That was encouraging, and I figured that the bidding might even go a little higher. I missed the finale, however, and didn't know the result until I read the eBay email notification about two hours after the end of the auction. The final bid was $2,185. The buyer paid me via PayPal within two hours.

This was a rather substantial mistake, but I was lucky. I had obviously done a poor appraisal of two of the items for lack of comparables. I should have found direct comparables somewhere else since they weren't available in the eBay archives (Completed listings). Had it been a slow week for Olympus camera buyers, I might have sold the camera set for $1,000, apparently less than half what it was worth.

The moral of this story is that if you're a seller, make your value research (appraisal) precise. Get current comparable sales data somewhere other than eBay if you can't find it on eBay. If you're a buyer, look for dumb sellers like me who haven't done their homework and hope that not many other buyers make the same "find."

Package Value?

Another miscalculation in this case may have been my perception that the camera and lenses separately would sell for more than the package. There may have been some extra value in offering a set of camera equipment rather than individual components. This is a tough judgment call. Sometimes packages are worth more, and sometimes they're not.

Dutch Auctions

Selling in quantity makes sense sometimes, but not all the time. A Dutch auction offers something special.

Special Attraction

For instance, if you have a dozen new outboard motors (list $7,000 each) to sell at a high auction price (40 percent off list— i.e., 60 percent of list price), an eBay Dutch auction is probably not your best bet. But if you want to sell the outboard motors at a rock-bottom price (e.g., 70 percent off list—i.e., 30 percent of list price), a Dutch auction might work well.

A Dutch auction should offer something special to bidders so that it attracts enough bidders to be successful—that is, the auction sells the multiple items. If there is nothing special about the offer, you are better off selling the items in separate auctions over a span of time that enables the eBay market to absorb the offering.

Storefront

Sellers also use Dutch auctions in a special way. They use them as storefronts. What about a Dutch auction that offers AA battery packs (72 batteries) every week at a minimum bid of $10.95 each but always sells only about a dozen? This is not an auction. This is, in essence, a storefront on eBay. The price is always $10.95. The Dutch auction is run every week. It's a store where you stop in to buy an AA battery pack whenever you need some more batteries.

This offers you a real opportunity to sell large quantities at a fixed price. Always offer more items than the eBay market can absorb so that the price never goes up with competitive bidding. The special attraction of your Dutch auction is the low price for which you sell your items, and you don't want the price to go up even temporarily.

With eBay's fixed price option (*Buy It Now*), the Dutch auction used as a storefront is no longer as important as it once was. In addition, you now have the option of opening a real storefront on eBay via eBay Stores.

Featured Auctions

For a substantial extra fee, you can have your auction featured. For $99.95 you can have your auction featured on eBay. For $19.95 you can have your auction featured in its category. The featured auction appears at the top of its category. It also appears in the regular auction listings in bold.

Is it worth it? Probably not for most items. When potential bidders look for something specific, they probably don't look in the featured sections. Impulse items, however, may sell well in the featured sections. Many people visiting the featured sections are just out browsing around looking for something, anything, to buy.

If an item is difficult to search for (difficult to identify with keywords) and it's on a listing with a huge number of auctions, the featured section may be your best shot at selling it. If you are selling to novice eBay users, many of whom do not know how to search effectively, you might have some luck with the featured sections. And if you are selling a popular consumer item, you may sell well in the featured sections too.

I Never Look

As a buyer I never look at the featured section. Why? Because the featured items are selected by their sellers who pay money to get them featured. They are not selected by some objective panel that chooses outstanding offerings to alert bidders. The featured items (top of the listings) are repeated in the general listings (below). If I look at the featured listings, I end up reading them twice. Why bother? I always skip the featured section, and I believe many buyers do likewise. On the other hand, if buyers don't know what they're looking for, they might read the featured section.

Here, again, I am in disagreement with other authors and eBay about this. eBay furnishes self-serving statistics indicating that featured items sell better. I am skeptical. I don't think putting your item in the featured section is cost-effective in most cases. But don't let me keep you from experimenting.

Changing Auctions

You can always change your auction ad (*Description*). The change will appear tacked on the bottom of your auction ad. However, don't make changes that will upset bidders. You may get nasty email. For instance, don't auction a Cadillac Seville and then change it to a Mercury Tracer near the end of the auction period.

Check the Buyer

You don't have to sell to anyone you don't want to sell to. If you don't like a buyer, don't sell to him or her. Not selling to someone, though, has its consequences. For instance, suppose you check out the high bidder at your auction, and he has a feedback rating of +2 in eight transactions (i.e., five positive and three negative). You decide you don't want to do business with this guy. You refuse. On one hand, you may be saving yourself a lot of trouble. On the other hand, you may get negative feedback from the jilted winning bidder. Sure, you can explain the feedback. But do you want to go through that process?

If you don't want to sell to someone, make sure you tell him or her before the auction is over, not after.

Notify High Bidder and Set Deadline

As the seller, don't ever leave things ambiguous. Notify the high bidder (buyer) what to do and when to do it in complete detail. If the buyer doesn't meet deadlines, send reminders via email. Many people seem to agree, if you don't get any reaction from the buyer after two reminders (the initial email message plus two reminder messages reasonably spaced), consider the auction canceled. Perhaps you can sell to the second-highest bidder.

It's even better to announce a payment deadline in your auction ad (i.e., prior to the completion of the auction). That way a buyer has little grounds for claiming that your deadline is unreasonable.

Don't Flood the Market

Need to auction something, but there is a current auction offering an identical item? No reason to flood the market. Wait until the current auction is close to completion and then put your identical item up for auction.

Follow-Up

Chapter 14 on customer service covers follow-up for your auctions, and this chapter will not repeat such information except to say that systematic follow-up is an important part of your auctioning activity. There is a special type of follow-up, however, that can add retail sales.

If you have additional items to sell, you can use the auction follow-up to cross sell; that is, advertise your other items. The more similar or related the other items are to the item purchased, the more effective such advertising will be.

Database Techniques

You can enter multiple auctions in eBay by hand, but it's tedious and takes a lot of time. The more auctions you create, the more you have to keep track of. Pretty quickly things get out of control.

Multiple Individual Auctions

Although databases and other tools enable you to handle multiple auctions, don't forget that each individual auction must stand on its own and use the general techniques for auctions outlined earlier.

There's no reason to suffer such a demanding routine. If you are digitally adept, a desktop database can make your life easier. My book *eBay Business the Smart Way, Third Edition* provides some ideas for constructing your own database system.

But I don't recommend creating your own database application. As a practical matter, you will want to give serious consideration to using an auction management service rather than using a database program to create your own system. Why reinvent the wheel?

Summary

Conduct your auctions intelligently. eBay does not require you to be a genius to do well. Just knowing how eBay works and observing common eBay practices will give you a good idea of how you can make your auctions effective and rewarding, that is, get high bids.

When your auction frequency reaches a certain level, you're not a casual seller any longer. You're an eBay retailer. As such, you will probably find, sooner or later, that a desktop database, or better yet an auction manangement service, is a good way to keep track of your retail operation. In addition, they enable you to upload multiple auctions at once on eBay. Chapters 18 and 22 explain this in more detail.

18

Running Multiple Auctions

To manually enter individual auction listings in the eBay forms is fine for a few auctions. Many sellers, however, run dozens or even hundreds of auctions each week. Entering them all in the eBay form would take hours. There must be a quicker way. And indeed there is.

eBay first enabled bulk uploads of auctions via a strange system, essentially using an HTML template. Then came the eBay software, Master Lister, for making the procedure easier. The flaw was that the procedure itself didn't change. eBay simply offered software. Before Master Lister you were on your own. Master Lister at least made things easier but did not enable the use of a database.

In the meantime, the auction management services came on the scene and evolved into very useful tools. You no longer had to devise your own procedure or use the hobbled Master Lister. Most auction management services took care of your auctions regardless of the number, and who cares how they did it? (Hint: they did it with databases.)

It wasn't until Turbo Lister was introduced in late 2002 that eBay brought its bulk upload function into the 20th century. That is, you can use a database with Turbo Lister if you need to. And Turbo Lister is a reasonable database application by itself.

Moving on into the 21st century, Turbo Lister was too little too late. Many of the leading auction management services offer such comprehensive management systems for your high-volume eBay auction business that it's crazy not to use such a service. (See Chapter 22.) But today eBay also supplements Turbo Lister with other software services to make it more competitive with the auction management services.

Is this Chapter for You?

You can already tell that if you're only a casual seller, this chapter may not be of interest to you. It's for volume sellers.

Databases

The advantage of a database is that you can see large groups of information all at once in a table on one screen. Presumably each table row is an item, and you can see 40 or 50 rows at a time. This makes it easy to make data entries quickly and efficiently.

Indeed, TurboLister and its competing software from the auction management services are set up like database entry forms to enable the quick and efficient entry of data. The data in this case is the requisite information for eBay auction listings including auction descriptions (auction ads). Once you have entered the data, Turbo Lister will upload it for you. You don't have to sit at your computer and upload each auction individually.

Do we still need to consider using other database software such as Microsoft Access? The answer is yes and no. If you already use a database system for something else, TurboLister will enable you to integrate such a system into your auction management system with simple and straightforward techniques. If you don't have and don't need another database system for your business, one of the auction management services will provide you what you need.

Some reasons why you might want to use your own database application include:

1. You built a custom system a few years ago, and it still works great. Comment: You might check the auction management services to see what you're missing. Might inspire you to switch.

2. You use a typical sales and inventory control system (with a database core) for your physical store, and you want to integrate your store accounting with your auction management. Comment: This is a good strategy, but it's time to look for software that can manage your offline store as well as your online auctions.

3. You use ecommerce software (with a database core) for your ecommerce website, and you want to integrate that data with your auction management. Comment: This is a good strategy. Consider using an auction management service in place of your current ecommerce software thus serving a dual purpose.

4. You use the system I published in the first two editions of this book, and you're afraid to change anything. Comment: My system was a very contorted system due to eBay requirements that were necessary for efficiency at the time. It's outdated now. And it's time to switch to a more comprehensive and easier-to-use auction management service.

Consider using an auction management service to manage your eBay auctions and other processes. At the heart of every auction management service is a database application that maintains the data necessary for effective business and financial management. Such services are terrific software.

The word on the street is that auction management services take all the work out of an eBay business leaving you with only the problem of finding some inventory that you can sell profitably. There's a lot of truth in that.

How Many Auctions?

How many auctions can you run before you need a system? That's a tough question to answer. I ran four auctions simultaneously once without a system, and it drove me nuts. A paper system can work for a small volume, but probably not volume enough to make a worthwhile profit. Some eBay members think the fees of the auction management services are burdensome. But if you run a paper system instead, you just substitute a lot of your time for a little bit of money.

The following is one way to look at it:

> If you run an eBay retail business, you can't do it efficiently without an auction management service.

> Even if you run a sideline eBay business part-time, you need an auction management service.

> If you're a regular seller but don't sell as much as a part-time business, you're on the borderline. Maybe you need an auction management service, and maybe you don't. It probably comes down to your working style.

> If you're an occasional seller, you can get by with a paper system.

You owe it to yourself to at least investigate what the auction management services can do for you. One interesting aspect of such services is that many are available in modules. You can pick a few services out of a variety offered. In other words, you can use and pay for only what you need.

And what about eBay? Doesn't eBay offer free auction management services? It does offer some free software such as Turbo Lister. But it also offers some auction services for a fee putting it in direct competition with other auction management services. See more on these services in Chapter 19.

Turbo Lister

Turbo Lister is a good example of what software can do for you. It acts as a webpage-authoring program (like FrontPage and Composer) and in fact seems to be based on FrontPage. It enables you to create your auction listings (auction ads) offline at your leisure in an easy step-by-step procedure. It manages and schedule your listings. And it sends your listings to eBay. Because it works offline, the program works fast and you can work without delays. See three sections of the listing screen for Turbo Lister in Figures 18.1-3.

Figure 18.1 Listing screen for eBay Turbo Lister (top portion).

Figure 18.2 Listing screen for Turbo Lister (middle portion).

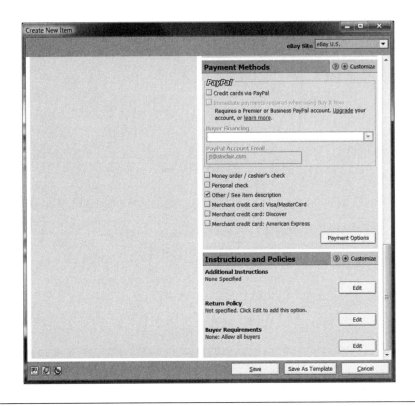

Figure 18.3 Listing screen for Turbo Lister (bottom portion).

Turbo Lister puts all the data in an Excel-like grid format that enables you to edit listings faster. It also enables you to duplicate listings (handy for similar items) and use other efficiencies. You can rerun and reschedule auctions, which is very useful when you sell a lot of the same inventory again and again. You always have a list of your auctions handy.

Turbo Lister also enables you to use eBay's fashionable auction templates (themes). You have a variety from which to choose. They will give your auctions a professional polish (see Figure 18.6).

A Real Benefit

How is Turbo Lister different than the online process to enter an auction? First, it works faster, particularly faster than a dial-up connection.

Second, it's more relaxed. If you're like me, doing data-entry work online always seems a little tense, even using broadband. Offline you don't have to worry about making a mistake that's irreversible. There's no pressure to complete anything. You can walk away in the middle of a task, have lunch, and come back and complete the task. It's probably all just a perceptual difference, but nonetheless it seems like the capability to work offline is a real benefit.

Database Considerations

Don't overlook the fact that Turbo Lister can import delimited data files. You can use almost any program with a database core (e.g., inventory management, order accounting, and the like) that can export a custom data file (a delimited file) and thereby integrate it with the eBay listing process via Turbo Lister. This is a real breakthrough for those who are using or want to use sophisticated retail software for their businesses.

Again, this makes my old database-mail-merge system obsolete. Or does it? The fact is that Turbo Lister data entry is still slower than entering data into a multirow, multicolumn database table. Turbo Lister is easier, especially for beginners. But a database solution can be much faster and more efficient for data entry. Consequently, you can applaud Turbo Lister as an efficient tool for its wide scope of capabilities, but for massive data entry, you might want to consider something else. Whatever else you use, Turbo Lister can accommodate it by accepting a delimited data file. Indeed, Turbo Lister can export a delimited data file too.

Auction Management Services

Is Turbo Lister a different process from an auction management service. No. In fact, several of the auction management services that provide all their programming via the Web actually use a desktop program for listing auctions. That is, every other function is accessed online except for the data entry function that resides in your computer.

To support data entry, a programmer either has to create a fairly heavy duty but lightweight program that downloads temporarily into your computer or a real heavyweight program that stays in your computer. The compromise that many programmers have found to be practical is a hardy but lightweight listing program that resides on your computer but that can be downloaded and set up automatically in a short time.

Thus, if you find yourself a hundred miles from your office without your computer, you can use someone else's computer, download the listing program quickly, and be ready to roll. All you need is your eBay login and password.

You can use Turbo Lister to do that. Turbo Lister is free as are many of the other listing programs offered by the auction management services. Try one.

Datafeed Marketing

Those who operate a retail business on eBay will want to explore the inexpensive possibilities for increasing sales using datafeed marketing as covered in my book *Building Your eBay Traffic the Smart Way*. An export from your database can put your items in many new online marketplaces through the magic of using a database (see Figure 18.4).

Figure 18.4 Datafeed marketing.

Conclusion

Don't try and go it alone without an auction management service if you're an eBay retailer. Find the software with the most database capabilities available that suits your needs and your pocketbook. This will enable you to handle 10 auctions or 1,000 auctions simultaneously with great efficiency and profit.

19

Making and Receiving Payment

Taking payment is so important to an eBay seller it deserves a chapter by itself. Why? Because payment is important to buyers. It's important to buyers for three reasons: capability, convenience, and safety. For instance, if a buyer doesn't have a credit card, he or she will not be able to pay if the only means of payment is via credit card. If the only means of payment is by money order and a buyer has to drive ten miles and stand in line to get a money order, the inconvenience will turn many potential bidders into passers (i.e., nonbidders). Of course, any means of payment deemed by a buyer to be unsafe will be likely to be avoided. Safety is a personal perception that varies from buyer to buyer.

Consequently, for sellers to provide adequate customer service, a variety of payment methods must be acceptable. Perhaps you don't have to accept payments by all means possible, but you do need to give buyers some choices.

PayPal has become such an important means of online payment that it has its own chapter, Chapter 20.

Payment Methods

The various payment methods follow. Accept payment as many ways as possible for maximum customer service.

Checks

Checks are the preferred way for Americans to pay. Yet the preferred way to pay online is clearly by credit card. What's going on?

I think the answer is that most buyers and sellers don't know that checks can now be used online as well as over the phone (since 1996). It works as follows:

1. The buyer gives the seller all the information from one of his checks via phone or email.

2. The buyer authorizes the seller to write a check for the purchase. The authorization is for a specific amount.

3. The seller inputs the buyer's information into a program such as TurboCheck (*http://www.turbocheck.com*). The seller uses TurboCheck to print the buyer's check using check forms and a computer printer. The seller signs the check on behalf of the buyer and deposits it. (TurboCheck software is inexpensive. The TurboCheck explanations of how online checking works serve as excellent resources to which you can refer or link your customers. This information helps overcome objections.)

4. The seller waits for the check to clear and then sends merchandise.

The biggest barrier to taking checks via the Web is that buyers have a difficult time understanding how the check-writing procedure works and why it's no more risky than sending a seller a check via snail mail. Therefore, they don't trust the method of payment, particularly if they don't have much reason to trust the seller.

The first two questions that come to mind are:

Seller: "How do I protect myself against a claim of fraud by the buyer?"

> Buyer: "How do I protect myself against the seller using the information from my check in a fraudulent way?"

The next two sections of this chapter answer these questions, but it will be a few years, if ever, before the public embraces the use of checks on the Web.

Major Corporations

Some of the largest and most reputable companies in the US are using checks this way primarily by telephone but also via the Internet. They make extra money by accepting a check over the telephone for payment on a delinquent account and then charging a service fee for doing so.

In the meantime, see PayPal in Chapter 20 for another workable means of using your bank account. It appears that PayPal has already preempted check writing via the Internet. In addition, debit cards, which one can use like a credit card, have become very popular for consumer purchases, and fewer people use checks every year.

Protection Against the Claim of Fraud by the Buyer

As the seller you can protect yourself against the claim of fraud by the buyer. Simply keep a record of the authorization. The authorization should include the check information plus a statement that the buyer authorizes the seller to write a check for a payment of a specific amount. If you take a check by telephone, you need to make a recording and archive it. If you take a check electronically, you need to archive the electronic text. Either way, should the buyer claim fraud, you can prove otherwise.

Protection Against Fraud by the Seller

As a buyer, every time you write a check, you present the check for a purchase. The seller takes possession. Any seller can use the information on the check to make additional checks and defraud you. Anyone at the drugstore, supermarket, video rental, telephone company, or elsewhere who sees your check has all the information necessary to make additional fraudulent checks. With that in mind, providing check information over the phone or electronically doesn't seem so ominous. Indeed, you have substantial protection against fraudulent checks because the bank will have to credit your account for any fraudulent checks or prove that you provided authorization for them.

What Does an Authorized Check Accomplish?

The most an authorized check accomplishes is reducing the duration of the transaction by the time it takes the check to get from the buyer to the seller via snail mail or FedEx. As the seller you must still wait for the check to clear before you can be sure of sufficient funds to cover it. There are electronic services that will inform you about a buyer's checking account (e.g., whether it has had problems), but they don't provide information about account balances, nor do they guarantee payment.

There If You Need It

If you're a seller, don't rule out electronic checks. This method of payment could be productive for you in certain situations. If you want to learn more about it, try the TurboCheck website, which has lots of information. This method may never reach its potential, but it's there if you need it.

Credit Cards

Any online transactions with a seller that accepts credit cards are—guess what?—merchant credit-card transactions. As a seller, this means you have to have a merchant credit account. This is a popular means of paying online, although PayPal has become a strong competitor. Thus, if you can obtain a merchant account that enables you to accept credit cards, you can expect to increase your eBay business.

Merchant Accounts

If you're not a volume seller on eBay, no one expects you to take credit cards. But if you're a retail seller, you may lose potential bidders by not accepting credit cards. In the past, merchant accounts were difficult to obtain, particularly for mail-order businesses, and then for Web commerce. But times have changed. Normal merchant accounts with their relatively low cost (about 2 to 3 percent of a sale) still may be difficult to obtain, but there are many higher-priced easy-to-obtain alternatives available for Web businesses. Research what's available at what price. Establish a track record, and work your way toward eventually getting a normal merchant account, usually from your bank.

What does it take to get a normal merchant account? A good credit rating and a banker who knows you and trusts you. But see PayPal in Chapter 20 for an easy alternative to accepting credit cards without using merchant accounts.

Money Orders and Cashier's Checks

Money orders and cashier's checks are reasonably safe payment methods. These are pretty secure for sellers to accept. However, they are easy to counterfeit, and it's probably getting easier rather than more difficult to counterfeit them. Fortunately, it's often easier to trace someone who's pulled a counterfeit scam online than it is offline. But that doesn't mean you won't get stuck. Be aware. Be careful. And be safe. Require a specific money order that you can recognize as not being a counterfeit (e.g., a postal money order).

Unfortunately, since the Fourth Edition of this book, counterfeit money orders and cashier's checks have become a substantial problem for ecommerce. This trend is yet another criminal attack on legitimate online business. Again, much of the counterfeiting is coming from abroad.

Easy Counterfeit

My bank (a huge national bank) issues money orders and cashier's checks that I wouldn't take. They are very plain and are printed on a laser printer. They don't even have a seal or a prominent logo, just a barely visible watermark. It looks as if anyone with a computer and a laser printer could easily counterfeit such a money order. However, most money orders are notoriously easy to counterfeit, even ones with complex designs, particularly when ostensibly issued by a nonstandard source (e.g., First International Monetary and Exchange Bank of Escalante). With a misleading bank routing number, a counterfeit money order could take several days (or weeks) to bounce. By then most sellers will have sent the merchandise.

Travelers Checks

Travelers checks are almost identical in concept to money orders and cashier's checks. Be careful of counterfeits (and forgeries). Otherwise there's no reason not to take them. When I returned from a long trip in prior years, I usually spend my excess travelers checks at the supermarket. But there's no reason I couldn't have spent them on eBay too. Today many people use ATM cards and credit cards instead of travelers checks.

Cash on Delivery

Cash on delivery (COD) is a time-honored means of collecting payment for mail-order merchandise (or Web merchandise). The risk to the seller is that the buyer doesn't pay, and the seller gets the merchandise back and gets stuck with high shipping costs too. Consequently, many sellers avoid this means of payment. Nonetheless, for certain markets, it may work well.

International Money Orders

How can you collect payment from abroad? It will take so long for the clearance of foreign checks that international money orders and credit card payments may work best. In addition, your bank may charge a special fee to clear foreign checks. This is a situation you need to research carefully. The potential of a global reach for your business is greater than you think. If you can work out a variety of payment methods to your satisfaction, you may get more business than you ever dreamed. Many retailers ignore this market, leaving it wide open for the more enterprising. Read my book *eBay Global the Smart Way*.

Cash

Never take cash. Taking cash is the best way to get into a knockdown-drag-out fight with a buyer. Cash leaves no record or proof of payment for either party. Cash has a wonderful way of disappearing in transit. It's almost humorous that people resort to using cash when they should know better. Don't be the object of the humor. Just say no.

Sales Tax

If you are an eBay retailer, don't forget to collect sales tax for items sold to people in your state (assuming yours is one of the 45 states that has a sales tax). You can find information at *http://www.mtc.gov/txpyrsvs/actualpage.htm* that will give you a start in getting your sales tax license in your state.

Special Payments for the Web

All the means of payment mentioned earlier are traditional. There are also many special means and schemes for making payments via the Web. Most are irrelevant because they are not widely used. One stands out, though, because eBay patrons use it. Indeed, eBay now owns it and has integrated it into the eBay system. It's PayPal, covered in the next chapter.

Escrow

Expensive items should go in escrow. Escrow is not a type of payment. It is a method of ensuring that the merchandise is delivered and payment is made. It's not cheap, but it's safe for the buyer.

Everyone has their tolerance level. Mine is somewhere close to $1,000. Certainly, for anything over $1,000, I would want to set up the transaction in escrow, at least with an unfamiliar seller. Other buyers less affluent than I might have greater tolerances and other buyers more affluent than I may have lesser tolerances, although generally one would expect tolerance to increase with affluence. At some level or another, any buyer with brains is going to want the transaction to go into escrow. As a seller, you need to be ready to agree to requests for escrow transactions at some reasonable level of purchase price.

Summary

The name of the game for eBay sellers is to collect payment via as many means as possible to provide maximum convenience to buyers. As an occasional eBay seller, you can only accept a limited number of means of payment. As an eBay retailer, you need to accept a wide range of means of payment. This is an important part of customer service. Fortunately, one of the easiest and most popular means of payment, credit cards, is now possible to offer to buyers through a variety of Internet services. And those sellers who do not have credit card merchant accounts can use PayPal instead to accept credit cards.

20

PayPal

The first edition of this book didn't cover PayPal because PayPal didn't exist when the book was being written. The second edition covered both PayPal, which had grabbed over two million users, and Billpoint which eBay created to compete with PayPal. Billpoint had about one-quarter as many users at that time. Why did eBay eventually buy PayPal? (Billpoint was a joint venture between eBay and Wells Fargo Bank, an innovative bank, which would have eventually proven an effective competitor for PayPal.) I think one reason is that eBay saw PayPal's potential to become not only a national but international means of exchange for consumer and small-business transactions. Another reason is that PayPal got a head start and was able to keep ahead through custom services and innovation.

Why PayPal and not credit cards? Unfortunately, credit cards are subject to a huge amount of Internet fraud in the Pacific Rim, Eastern Europe, and other places. In Indonesia, it is a rite of passage for college students to pay their tuition with credit card fraud; that is, using credit card numbers scanned from real credit cards or otherwise obtained. In contrast, PayPal has built-in verification that minimizes fraud.

PayPal now has 133 million members and offers accounts in 55 countries and exchanges 6 currencies. Let's take a look at how this convenient payment mechanism works.

Verification

Verification is a big deal. PayPal verifies your payment information before it gives you an account. Verification isn't foolproof, but it's an extra step that reduces fraud by a quantum leap.

Credit Cards

If you use a credit card, having the number and the expiration date are enough to use it online. But criminals compile lists of stolen credit card numbers and use them for online fraud. Lately a four-digit CVV2 number printed on the back of a credit card is used for verification. (Most credit cards have three-digit CVV2 numbers.) This extra step helps prevent fraud but isn't foolproof. It's new, and criminals will catch on to it quickly. Anyone who has access to your credit card (e.g., waitress) can copy it.

A separate PIN (personal identification number) can verify a credit card user too. But a user has to memorize it (together with a lot of other numbers in life); thus, it may not be practical for use for in everyday activities. Nonetheless, it is practical to use on the Web because you can store the PIN number in your password database (see Chapter 10). The use of a credit card PIN number on the Web is relatively new, but its use will grow rapidly.

Although credit card fraud online or offline is not a huge problem in the US, Europe, and many developed countries, it is a growing problem in other places abroad. Travel bulletins advise travelers not to use their credit cards in Indonesia (and other countries) because their numbers are likely to be stolen (e.g., by waiters and waitresses) and used fraudulently online, often to purchase merchandise in the US.

The bottom line is that online, credit cards are suspect. Although safe for cardholders to use online, credit cards are less safe for sellers to accept online, particularly when the merchandise is to be delivered overseas or to an address different from the billing address for the card.

Computer Vendor's Remorse

A computer vendor in California selling on eBay received an order by email for 12 PCs charged to a credit card in New York but to be shipped to Pakistan. (The transaction was not the result of an eBay auction but came in as a result of the seller's visibility on eBay.) The vendor being no dummy called the card holder to verify that the charge was not fraudulent. A nice conversation with the man on the other end of the phone line indicated that the order was, indeed, legitimate. The vendor shipped the PCs to Pakistan.

A month later the card holder requested a chargeback claiming that he never charged the computers. The vendor called the card holder again and asked what was going on. Yes, the same person at the other end of the phone line denied ever having verified the charge. The vendor reported this to the New York Attorney General who replied that it was the just the vendor's word against the card holder's word and that successful prosecution was unlikely. Therefore, no investigation would be initiated.

The vendor could not report it to eBay because the transaction took place outside the eBay marketplace even though the vendor's business was selling computer equipment exclusively on eBay. Consequently, the vendor took the loss without recourse.

PayPal Verification

When you apply for a PayPal account, your payment information is verified. You can use either a credit card or a bank account to finance your PayPal payments; that is, PayPal charges your credit card or your bank account whenever you pay someone. If you provide information on your credit card, your address is also verified—a significant additional level of verification attractive to sellers.

To make a payment, you must log into PayPal using your password. You send an email (notification) via PayPal to the seller, and PayPal deposits the money in the seller's PayPal account. Thus, both the payer (you) and the payee (the seller) must have PayPal accounts. (Any payee involved in a PayPal transaction for the first time can open a PayPal account quickly and easily.)

What's the bottom line for this crazy system? No one can use your PayPal account unless they have your password. It's unlikely a waiter in Indonesia will steal your password regardless of how many times you eat in the restaurant. But the waiter can easily steal your credit card number if you use your credit card to pay for a meal. (Yes, there has been a great revival in the use of travelers checks for those traveling in Indonesia and some other underdeveloped countries.)

So, credit cards have a fatal flaw in the new age of the Internet, and PayPal promises to be the new means of exchange for international consumer and small-business commerce.

How It Works

PayPal is the largest Internet payment service after the credit card companies. Once you get a PayPal account, you can use it just like a credit card to pay for something purchased from any seller that will accept PayPal. And PayPal is not restricted to eBay transactions.

Payments

You make payment by requesting PayPal to transfer funds from your account to the seller's account. PayPal notifies the seller by email that the payment has been made.

PayPal gets the funds you use for payment by debiting your checking account or by charging your credit card. So, to make a payment, you simply log into PayPal at *http://paypal.com*, elect to send a payment, and fill in the webpage form. It is simple to use and has become very popular.

Requests

You can also request that a payment be made to you. PayPal will notify the prospective payer (buyer) that you (the seller, payee) have requested payment. If the payer has a PayPal account, he or she can easily make the payment. If the payer does not have a PayPal account, PayPal instructs him or her how to open an account.

Seller Protection

PayPal has a Seller Protection Program to protect against chargebacks and fraud. It requires that sellers ship only to confirmed addresses; that is, only to buyers' addresses that have been verified.

Integration

eBay has integrated PayPal nicely into the eBay auction system. You can:

- Put a PayPal logo in your auction ad indicating that you accept PayPal.
- Invoice your buyer (send a request for payment).
- Use PayPal to pay for shipping with UPS.
- Manage your PayPal records of items sold and of payments made.

eBay and PayPal automatically generate all the necessary documents (primarily email messages) to make all this happen and manage your auctions too. In addition, you can even use PayPal as a checkout service for your non-eBay transactions.

Accounting

PayPal will even integrate with QuickBooks (accounting software), a handy capability for many.

As you can see, PayPal has evolved into more than just an online payment mechanism. And you can use PayPal to pay anyone. It's not just for use for eBay transactions. You can even use it in other online auctions and for other ecommerce.

eBay has also integrated PayPal into the eBay check out mechanism for payment after an auction. That makes payment by PayPal even easier for buyers.

International

Perhaps most importantly, you can now use it internationally. As mentioned above, PayPal is available in many countries and can exchange money in six currencies.

Countries

The countries currently are:

Anguilla

Argentina

Australia

Austria

Belgium

Brazil

Canada

Chile

China

Costa Rica

Cyprus

Czech Republic

Denmark

Dominican Republic

Ecuador

Estonia

Finland

France

Germany

Greece

Hong Kong

Hungary

Iceland

India

Ireland

Israel

Italy

Jamaica

Japan

Latvia

Lithuania

Luxembourg

Malta

Mexico

Monaco

Netherlands

New Zealand

Norway

Poland

Portugal

Singapore

Slovakia

Slovenia

South Africa

South Korea

Spain

Sweden

Switzerland

Taiwan

Thailand

Turkey

United Kingdom

Uruguay

Venezuela

This is a good enough selection to get you started in international commerce.

Note, however, that addresses are not yet verified some places abroad, a serious but presumably temporary shortcoming.

Currencies

You can pay or request payment in whatever currency you desire. The other party can do the same. When the choices of currencies don't match, PayPal will make the exchange at a very low exchange rate. The currently accepted currencies are US Dollars, Canadian Dollars, Australian Dollars, Euros, Pounds Sterling, and Yen.

What's the bottom line? You can make a payment to anyone in any participating country with a PayPal account easily and instantly, and they can make a payment to you as well. And the payments are safe. This new international system takes all the hassle out of international commerce. Unbelievable!

This alone opens up great new markets and fantastic opportunities for you. Start thinking how you can take advantage of this sudden elimination of the international payment bureaucracy (e.g., the banks).

Cost

A great service, but who pays for it? Buyers get off free. Sellers pay fees similar to credit card merchant account fees. Check the PayPal website for the current fee schedule and figure the fees into your overhead.

- Send money or withdraw funds: free.

- Receive funds: free when the buyer's funds are drawn on a bank account and about three percent when the buyer's funds are charged to a credit card (has to pay for the merchant credit card fee).

Special Services

PayPal also offers some special services. The first is a buyer complaint process. You can complain to PayPal about a transaction (about a seller), and PayPal will investigate, talking with both the buyer and seller. The second is a money-back guarantee program that PayPal offers through certain sellers. Buyers can pay a small fee and get satisfaction insurance. The third is a seller protection program. You have to qualify by doing certain things. It essentially protects you against chargebacks.

How about paying for UPS or USPS shipping and printing a shipping label via PayPal? Yes, you can do it. And PayPal will give you a weekly transactions report. PayPal is going wild with new services.

In fact, this book can no longer cover PayPal adequately. PayPal has mushroomed into a robust ecommerce service that almost requires a separate book. Many of its functions parallel those offered by eBay. You might ask, Why?, since eBay owns it. The answer is simple. PayPal is not limited to eBay members. Anyone can use it.

Retailer's Service

PayPal's Web Payments Standard merchants service (see Figure 20.1) is not only free but quite robust. It provides a shopping cart, taking payment by PayPal, taking payment by credit card, and accounting reports. You can combine that with PayPal's free shipping service, which includes creating shipping labels and packing slips, paying shipping fees to UPS or USPS and printing postage on labels, and tracking. What a deal!

Merchant Credit Card Account

And last but no least, you can use PayPal as your merchant credit card account. That is, you can accept credit cards from non-PayPal customers (without them having to become PayPal members). This is a major benefit for eBay retailers but probably not practical for casual eBay sellers. It's included with the Web Payments Standard merchants service mentioned in the previous section (see Figure 20.1).

Figure 20.1 PayPal Web Payments Standard service. ©1999-2007 PayPal

The Bank

As a seller, what happens to your money after someone pays you through PayPal? Well, PayPal holds it in your account. How do you withdraw it? Surprisingly, there are several ways:

1. Direct that the funds be transferred to your bank account.

2. Request a check be sent to you.

3. Shop offline (or online) with a PayPal debit card (MasterCard). that PayPal will issue one to you.

4. Get cash out of an ATM (with your PayPal debit card).

5. Shop online with a virtual credit card (MasterCard). This is an innovative arrangement.

6. Use PayPal as it was originally designed; that is, make payments online via email, even internationally.

PayPal sure looks like a bank, doesn't it? In fact, you can even deposit money into your PayPal account. PayPal performs the functions of a bank. Internationally, it performs the functions of several banks at once. Remember, you can use PayPal for much more than just your eBay auctions. Hey, your PayPal membership might be a lot more valuable than you thought. And they haven't stopped adding features.

One way to understand PayPal better and to make more effective use of it is to understand it as a bank, albeit a bank with unusual processes. It's a bank that doesn't charge you $40 for a wire transfer; an email transfer is free.

PayPal Shops

Join PayPal Shops where 100 million PayPal members might stop in. Don't believe it. Nonetheless, if you have an ecommerce website, it can't hurt. To join PayPal Shops you have to sign up for PayPal's money market arrangement (another financial function), which pays a return on any funds in your account. Then your shop and checkout are free. Or, if you have an eBay Store, your PayPal Shop is free. Don't get me wrong. I don't think PayPal Shops are a major retail force on the Web today, but you never know what tomorrow might bring.

And There's More

Although PayPal remains an easy-to-use service, it is no longer a simple service. It has become a set of multiple financial services and will develop into even more services in the future. Go to the PayPal website soon to study how PayPal works. Plan on spending some time doing so. Then it's worth an occasional visit thereafter to see what's new. Don't neglect keeping up to date on PayPal, or you will miss opportunities for greater efficiency in managing your financial affairs.

21

Shipping

Shipping is an important aspect of selling on eBay. Buyers expect prompt shipping by a reliable means. And, of course, they want to get shipping as inexpensively as possible. As a seller, you have a number of choices for shipping, and you need to match the shippers to the types of products you sell and to the needs of buyers.

Shipping and Handling

If you simply charge for shipping, then you have to wait until after the auction to quote a charge (depending on how far away the buyer lives). The buyer remains uncertain about what the charge will be until he or she receives a quote. If you quote a *shipping* charge in the auction ad and collect it, the buyer may be angry when the actual shipping charge turns out to be less.

One way to get around this frustration is to charge for *shipping and handling*. No one knows what handling is. It probably should be covered in your overhead. Yet, many sellers charge it. My policy is to quote a shipping and handling charge in the auction ad. That gives the buyer certainty. My shipping and handling charge is enough to cover shipping anywhere in the US, but no more. If the actual shipping charge to a place close to where I live is less than the shipping and handling charge, the buyer has no grounds for complaint. This is less trouble for both parties.

Some people make their profit on shipping and handling. They charge a lower price for the item and a high price for shipping and handling. So long as the charge is stated in the auction ad, buyers have little grounds for complaint. Still, this practice is irritating to buyers and not recommended. eBay also acts to curtail this offensive practice.

If you don't state a shipping or handling price in the auction ad, you'd better be ready to justify the charge. Otherwise you may get into a shouting match with the buyer.

Look at Zonalyzer (*http://zonalyzer.com*) for a program that you can embed in your auction ad, which enables bidders to choose and calculate certain shipping costs.

Packaging

Package well to minimize your shipping problems. Most people over-package perhaps. I've never received an item damaged that I've bought on eBay. But it's better to overpackage than to have to deal with damaged goods, collect insurance, and other nasty details.

Plastic Bag

Put the items you send in plastic bags to protect against moisture, unless there's a compelling reason not to do so. You never know when the package will get drenched in a rain storm. When it goes out the door, it's out of your control. eBay sellers in arid climates (i.e., the West) are the most likely to forget to do this. Rain does not enter into their daily equation. But when you ship everywhere, you need to keep rain and snow in mind.

Naturally, eBay is a fertile ground for selling packaging materials. Consequently, you do not have to look beyond eBay auctions to find materials you need to package well at good prices (see Figure21.1-2).

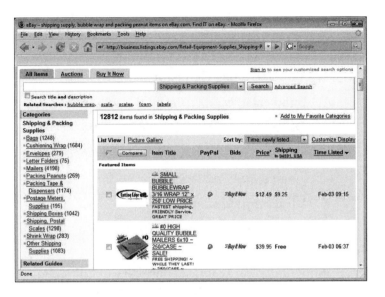

Figure 21.1 eBay shipping materials. ©1995-2007 eBay Inc.

Figure 21.2 eBay Shipping Center. ©1995-2007 eBay Inc.

Also ask your shipper (e.g., FedEx) what they provide free in the way of shipping materials (e.g., containers). The following are also sources of packaging materials and containers:

Associated Bag Company, *http://www.associatedbag.com*

Bubblefast, *http://www.bubblefast.com*

OfficeMax, *http://www.officemax.com*

ShippingSupply.com, *http://www.shippingsupply.com*

Staples, *http://www.staples.com*

Uline, *http://www.uline.com*

UPS Store (previously Mail Boxes Etc), *http://www.theupsstore* .com

iShip (*http://iship.com*), a subsidiary of UPS, offers an online shipping comparison website. You can use it to compare shipping costs by several different shippers. The UPS Stores also use it.

Free Packaging

Some shippers supply free packages for customers. The Postal Service is the leader offering a wide range of free packages. Go to *http://supplies.usps.gov* in order to see what they have.

Also try the eBay Shipping Center for links to shipping supplies. Go *Site Map*, *Selling Resources*, *Shipping Center*.

If It Doesn't Get There

What if you send it, and it doesn't get there? Who is responsible, the buyer or seller (you)? One way is to put the responsibility on the buyer and offer the buyer the opportunity to buy insurance. But what if the buyer doesn't buy insurance and it doesn't get there? Who is responsible, the buyer or seller (you)? Clearly, the buyer is responsible because that's the way you set up your sales requirements. This is terrible customer service, however, and you had better figure out another way to handle the missing package.

One way is to self-insure. If a package isn't delivered, you simply send another at your cost. Don't worry about getting and paying for insurance. Another way is to require mandatory insurance and require that the buyer pay for it. A third way is to use shippers that provide a minimal level of insurance (e.g., $100 for UPS) at no extra cost. Whatever your solution, don't overlook this aspect of doing business on eBay. And don't put the buyer in a losing situation.

Shippers

Any analysis of the different ways to ship that includes current costs would be instantly outdated. So I will leave you to figure that out for yourself. Keep in mind the following, however, in evaluating shippers:

Convenience How convenient is it for you to use a particular shipper? This is different for everybody. The shipper itself may offer different convenience options. How much paperwork does the shipper require?

Size and Weight What are the maximums? How do the maximums relate to what you need to ship?

Cost How much does it cost? Is it a flat fee or a fee based on distance?

Included? What does the shipping service include? Pickup? Insurance? Package tracking? Guaranteed delivery?

Reliability How reliable is the shipper? I believe FedEx is at one end of the spectrum and the Postal Service is at the other end. How far apart are they? (See the Chapter 14 section on overnight shipment for my comments on express shipment reliability.)

Customer Service A shipper's website where one can monitor shipping reliably 24/7 may be important for some buyers.

Shipping is currently very competitive and changes continually. Keep up to date on the options available to you by occasionally visiting the shippers' websites.. The less hassle your shipper causes you, the more smoothly your fulfillment operation will function.

There are other reliable shippers, but most people use one of the following:

Canada Post, *http://www.canadapost.ca*

DHL, *http://www.dhl-usa.com/index*

Federal Express, aka FedEx, *http://fedex.com/us*

Federal Express Ground, Home Delivery

Purolator, *http://www.purolator* (owned by Canada Post)

RedRoller, *http://www.redroller.com* (comparative website)

United Parcel Service, aka UPS, *http://ups.com*

US Postal Service, aka Post Office, *http://www.usps.com*

For large items, you may need to ship by bus (*http://www.grey-hound.com*) or truck (*http://freightquote.com* – see Figure 21.1). Go *Site Map, Selling Resources, Shipping Center, Freight Resource Center* for assistance with trucking.

Figure 21.3 For estimates on trucking costs, visit Freightquote.com. ©2006 Freightquote.com

Regional Shippers

There are now regional shippers in various regions of the US. They seem to becoming popular. You might try one of them if you can find one locally.

Postage

Postage meters are a must for those who use the Postal Service and have a busy fullfillment operation.

Ascom Hasler, *http://www.haslerinc.com*

Endicia, *http://www.endicia.com*

Stamps.com, *http://stamps.com*

Pelouze, *http://pelouze.com*

Pitney Bowes, *http://www.pitneybowes.com*

Pitney Works, *http://www.pitneyworks.com*

Postal Service, *http://www.usps.com*

Beware that for postage meters the monthly rent may be a modest portion of the overall cost. The hidden costs such as special ink, labels, and postage-via-telephone charges can make postage meters more expensive than the sales pitch tells. I rented a small postage meter essentially for letters, and just the special ink (in a cartridge) has cost almost as much as the postage.

You might try instead one of the Web postage services; you can print out postage on your computer printer.

Digital Shipping Systems

Don't overlook the digital shipping systems such as the PayPal system described briefly in Chapter 20. They print mailing labels complete with postage and packing slips via your computer printer. (You don't have to use postage meters.) They are now offered by the Postal Service, auction management software, PayPal, and even eBay.

The Whole Thing

What about a company that will do the whole fulfillment chore for you? That is, all the packaging and shipping. Unbelievably, for a reasonable flat fee, paDepot (*http://padepot.com*) in Allentown, Pennsylvania, will do it for you. In fact, it will even warehouse your inventory. Although there are other services that do this for corporate customers, paDepot does it for small businesses. Compare paDepot's service to

Craters & Freighters, mentioned in the section Where the Gold Is in Chapter 14.

Summary

As a seller, don't take shipping lightly. Shipping causes perhaps more conflict between buyers and sellers than any other issue. Ship intelligently and keep the buyer's needs in mind, and you'll avoid trouble.

22

Choosing Auction Management Software

Wow! Auction management services do it all for you. It doesn't get any better than this. These services take care of your retail business. eBay takes care of your marketing. You can find someone to do your fulfillment. And all you have to do is find some inventory that you can sell at a profit.

The first two editions of this book took the point of view that most of the software available for eBay auction management was inadequate. In fact, the first two editions offered a database scheme for keeping track of auctions that served multiple purposes. The auction management services were just starting to appear at the time the second edition was written and had not yet reached their potential.

What a difference today! Auction management services—software services delivered via the Web—are now quite robust. Sellers who don't use them will lose much more in lost time than they will save money by not subscribing to them. Even eBay has beefed up its auction management software imitating the excellent services offered by others.

Even eBay sellers who don't make a business out of their eBay activities can take advantage of auction management services for volume selling. I have no reservations today about recommending that you find an auction management service you like and use it. If you are an occasional seller, you can still keep track with a system on paper. But for volume selling or retail selling, an auction management service will be your best friend.

Andale

For the purposes of example only, I will illustrate the robust Andale (*http://andale.com*) auction management service in this chapter. But Andale has plenty of capable competition that you need to check out.

The eBay Industry

Growing up around eBay at an accelerating pace is the *eBay Industry*. Thousands of people are now working in one way or another to develop products and services to assist eBay members, primarily sellers, to work faster, easier, and more efficiently. Nowhere is that more evident than in the software business. As you will read in this chapter, there are now not only software programs but also online software services to assist people with their eBay activities. So, this is an appropriate chapter to introduce you to the eBay Industry. Watch it grow!

What to Do?

Were you to create the perfect auction management program, what would it do? The following are some ideas you might include:

Write Once You should never have to input data into the system a second time.

Inventory Control If you are an eBay retailer, you need to keep track of your inventory.

Product Descriptions Creating eBay auction ads in attractive templates (listing descriptions) should be quick and easy.

Auction Management You need a program to keep track of your auctions.

Customer Communication A special email program that keeps all your eBay email together in one place would make customer communication management more efficient.

Follow-up An automatic follow-up after each auction would save you much time and energy.

Transaction Checkout A transaction checkout just like an ecommerce website would provide convenience for your customers, although eBay's checkout now works very well.

Fulfillment A system that accounted for packaging and shipping would save time.

Documentation A system that created all your documentation, most of it automatically when needed, would be helpful.

Datafeed Marketing The capability to export selected data to other marketplaces (other than eBay or eBay Stores) could be used to increase sales.

Report Generation You need a program that analyzes your sales operations and provides reports to you. This capability can help you operate smarter.

Accounting Dovetail Transaction-accounting software that dovetails with your general accounting software (e.g., QuickBooks) would save you transferring data between programs.

eCommerce Software A system that would coordinate, integrate with, or substitute for your website ecommerce software would be helpful.

Retail Store Integration The capability to provide integrated robust retail programming for both your physical store and your online ecommerce is highly desirable if you have an offline store.

Use these ideas, add your own, and judge the numerous auction management services accordingly. Then choose one.

What Is a Service?

A provider delivers its auction management services to you via the Web. That is, you use the software in your browser.

How It Works

It's simple. You go to the auction management service website and log in. Then you can use whatever services you have subscribed to. You use the services through your Web browser. Sure, you have to learn to use each service, but this is simplified by the fact that you always work via the familiar interface of your Web browser.

As long as you remember your login name and password, you can use these services any time from any computer connected to the Internet.

Because you don't necessarily load these services on your computer in the form of resident programs, you don't buy the software. You subscribe to it (i.e., rent it) usually for a reasonable monthly fee.

What Are the Advantages?

We're all used to buying software and using it as much as we like for as long as we like on our computer without further cost. Thus, we need to try to understand the advantages of using software as a service.

1. You never have to update the software. That is done by the provider as soon as the improvement is ready to use. You get the upgrades sooner rather than later.

2. With some services you may not even have to store your data on your PC. You can store it on the provider's computer. Presumably the provider does daily backups relieving you of that task and worry.

3. You have unlimited use of the service for a flat monthly fee.

4. The fee per month is low considering the value of the software. When you buy software, sooner or later it becomes obsolete and you have to buy an upgrade. When you subscribe to a software service, it's like paying for software in small installments rather than all at once.

5. You never have to worry about installing the software on your computer or upgrading it.

What it amounts to is carefree use of software at a price that doesn't take a big investment up front.

What Are the Disadvantages?

Software services are not without disadvantages such as:

1. You need broadband to make the most effective and efficient use of a software service. Most services don't work as well with a dial-up Internet connection.

2. The monthly fee is an irritant, particularly when it is more than nominal. Unfortunately, an expensive software service would also be as expensive as a standalone program (i.e., one to be loaded on your computer), and you would have to pay the entire cost up front.

What's the Exception?

Even though you use the software service through your browser, sometimes it just makes better sense to have part of the software loaded on your computer and run on your computer. How is this different from normal computer programs? It isn't except for access.

Normal computer programs tend to be fat monsters that you install on your computer and that take a lot of space on your hard disk. Software service programs that you install and use on your computer tend to be lean programs that will download quickly. With your login and password, you can quickly download such software to any computer you use anywhere.

The truth is that many auction management services have a component that resides on your hard disk. It's usually the program that lists auctions. This is where you make the most data entries, and a desktop component (on your computer) works more efficiently than a server component (provider's computer). This is a hybrid approach, which seems to work well.

Andale

Andale is one of the leading third-party providers for eBay members and offers many different programming modules, some free and some by subscription. It's a good package to measure against the ideal auction management service outlined earlier in this chapter and against which to measure other auction management services. Below are some of the services it offers. Others are on the way.

Note that auction management services are generally for eBay retailers or eBay volume sellers. However, the modular approach gives other eBay sellers an opportunity to use auction management services for one thing without having to use an entire software suite.

Buying

Accounting systems for buyers didn't prove popular, but a few exist. Other buyer services are used by both buyers and sellers.

Research

eBay keeps weeks of completed auctions in its archives for research. Andale claims to keep months of completed auctions (known to appraisers as comparables). It provides detailed reports with statistics probably unavailable anywhere else.

Selling

The business people of eBay are primarily sellers, and Andale provides a broad range of seller's services.

Images

Like many other auction management services, Andale provides an image service to enable you to efficiently manage and store your auction photographs online.

Lister

This is an online service enabling you to create listings using templates (themes) that look professional.

Lister Pro

This is free offline software similar to eBay's Turbo Lister. You can use it for your whole organization. It has an Excel-like interface and will list and upload your auction listings.

Advertise

This is a service to account for your Google AdWord advertising making it simple to keep track of your ads.

Gallery

The Gallery is a great cross-marketing tool. The Gallery draws from all your auctions to present multiple photographs of items (in a gallery) in all your auction listings and even in email. It is, in effect, a mini catalog included to encourage additional product sales from an auction listing.

Email Manager

With a high volume of sales, it's easy to let the management of routine email communication with your customers get out of control. This new tool will help you.

Checkout

This is a typical ecommerce checkout that you can provide as a convenience to buyers. You can use this anywhere. It's not just for your eBay customers.

Stores

This is a fixed-price storefront in the Andale mall. I'm somewhat skeptical that this or the PayPal mall can be very successful. They are competing with eBay and eBay Stores and are probably not likely to garner a substantial market share. But who knows? We're still out on the Internet frontier.

Information for Decision Making

Andale is also in the information business. Thus, some of its services are information services.

Counters

Andale supplies counters. You can put one in your auction ad. A counter indicates the number of visits made to your auction listing.

Suppliers

Need a source of inventory? This service lists suppliers of merchandise and those looking for merchandise too.

Sales Analyzer

You need a reporting service that gives you reports on your sales and compares you to others selling the same products. It's a great way to know where you stand so that you can improve your sales.

ROI Reports

It's nice to have reports on how your eBay retail business is performing. Andale provides them.

New Services

Andale is committed, as are other auction management services, to providing a wide range of services for eBay members. Consequently, you can expect announcements of new services from time to time. It's an interesting time, because there is nothing static about what is emerging as the eBay industry.

eBay's Management Software

The eBay software service is the old Blackthorne software that has been around a long time. It competes directly with third-party software and services.

Seller's Assistant

This desktop software comes in two versions, basic and pro. With Seller's Assistant you can make attractive listing ads, automate your email, track sales information, generate invoices, and file feedback. Go *Sell, Seller Central, Advanced Selling, Seller Tools* for more information.

Selling Manager

This is eBay's latest and greatest tool, an online service. You use it in combination with Turbo Lister to create listings, manage listings, store customer information, manage email, manage feedback, print shipping labels and invoices, and create reports. It also comes in a *Pro* version, which does even more including inventory management and bulk process management. Go *Sell, Seller Central, Advanced Selling, Seller Tools* for more information.

Sales Reports

eBay can help you keep track of your selling performance. This service comes free with an eBay Store and by subscription otherwise.

Other Software

There is no shortage of other software and software services, and by the end of 2005 there will be at least an additional 20 percent of new useful products. This is a dynamic market that takes an ongoing awareness just to keep up. Check out the eBay Solutions Directory for a list of third-party software and service vendors. Go *Sell, Seller Central, Selling Solutions, Individual, Solutions Directory.*

Auction Management Services

These are online services like Andale that work through your Web browser. They include:

Andale, *http://www.andale.com*

AuctionHawk, *http://www.auctionhawk.com*

AuctionHelper, *http://www.auctionhelper.com*

Auctiva, *http://www.auctiva.com*

AuktionMaster, *http://www.auktionmaster.net*

ChannelAdvisor, *http://channeladvisor.com*

CoreSense, *http://www.coresense.com*

Dealtree, *http://www.dealtree.com*

DEK Auction Manager, *http://dekauctionmanager.com*

InkFrog, *http://www.inkfrog.com*

Kyozou, *http://www.kyozou.com*

ManageAuctions, *http://www.manageauctions.com*

Marketplace Manager, *http://www.infopia.com*

MarketPlacePro, *http://www.marketplacepro.com*

Marketworks, *http://auctionworks.com*

Meridian, *http://www.noblespirit.com*

MS Marketplace Services, *http://microsoft.com* (see Figure 22.1)

Mpire, *http://www.mpire.com*

StoreFront, *http://www.storefront.com*

Total Auction Management, *http://totalauctionmanagement.com*

Truition, *http://www.truition.com*

Vendio, *http://www.vendio.com*

Y.E.S. Software Suite, *http://www.yukonsoft.com*

Zoovy, *http://zoovy.com*

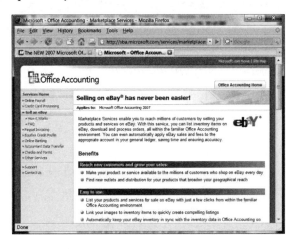

Figure 22.1 Microsoft Marketplace Services is aimed at eBay and PayPal. ©2007 Microsoft Corporation

Also consider PayPal covered in Chapter 20. PayPal has turned into more than just a payment service. It also provide certain auction management services for sellers.

Service or Program?

It is getting increasingly difficult to distinguish between programming delivered via the Web and programs that reside on your computer. Most auction management services provided via the Web also provide programs that reside on your desktop computer for part of their services, and some desktop auction management programs even perform certain functions with online assistance from a remote server. The important thing for you is to get the most for your money.

Auction Management Programs

If you prefer a more traditional software approach, you might consider one of these traditional auction management programs. Check out the following:

AuctionMessenger, *http://www.auctionmessenger.net*

AuctionTamer, *http://www.auctiontamer.com*

Auction Wizard 2000, *http://www.auctionwizard2000.com*

Blackmagik utilities (for Mac), *http://blackmagik.com*

Cricketsniper, *http://cricketsniper.com*

Easy Auction, *http://auctiontools.net*

EZLister, *http://www.ezlister.net*

Infopia, *http://www.infopia.com*

MarketBlast, *http://marketblast.com*

NetSuite, *http://www.netsuite.com*

ShipWorks, *http://interapptive.com*

ShootingStar, *http://www.foodogsoftware.com*

SpoonFeeder, *http://spoonfeeder.com*

Stone Edge Order Manager, *http://stoneedge.com*

Timber Creek Sold!, *http://www.timbercreeksoftware.com*

Shovelware CDs

If you're going to buy eBay software, *buy eBay software*. That is, don't buy a CD with everything else in the world on it. CDs with everything in the world on them are known in the industry as *shovelware*. You can get a shovelware CD on eBay or at a local computer show for $4-$8. That's what shovelware is worth. If you want to buy an eBay program on a CD with shovelware, subtract $4-$8 and you'll know what the eBay program by itself is selling for.

Ironically, you can probably find the software and information contained in most shovelware CDs someplace on the Web for free if you use the search engines briefly.

Anything offered as part of a shovelware package is suspect. If the eBay software seems to get lost in the hyped benefits of the shovelware package, it's probably not worth much.

As you have probably discovered in your reading, I don't favor traditional programs for auction management. Auction management services offer far more. Unfortunately, not everyone has a broadband connection to the Internet. If you don't have a broadband connection, you have a solid reason for using a traditional program rather than an online service. Nonetheless, obtaining a broadband connection should be your goal due to the wider scope of services it will bring.

Auction Analysis Software

Some eBay-related software provides you with analysis capability. It can be quite enlightening to use, particularly if you are a high-volume seller. Try Hammertap (*http://www.hammertap.com*) or Terapeak (*http://terapeak.com*) too. Some of the auction management services also provide analysis software (e.g., Andale).

eBay's Standard Software

What is standard eBay software? It's software that's part of the eBay website and that provides extracurricular eBay services. In other words, it's built-in software created by eBay, not by independent software developers.

For instance, the eBay proxy bidding (see Chapter 11) is built into the system and provides a solid service to the current high bidder in an auction. In addition, eBay provides services that enable you to keep track of your activities on eBay. *My eBay* provides you with an automatic record of all your activities on eBay. Consequently, any independent eBay software you consider buying should offer more than these built-in eBay devices.

Unless you're an eBay retailer or otherwise a volume seller, eBay's standard software is probably all you'll ever need.

Advertising Services

The cross-marketing advertising services were mentioned earlier. Andale offers its Gallery and eBay offers its similar Cross-Promotions. In addition, eBay now offers *Keywords on eBay*, a new advertising program for eBay members. This enables you to actually sponsor boxed advertising on eBay for products you auction related to keywords. If you're an eBay retailer, look for these ads and for information on how they work.

Buyers

And what about buyers? When some of the auction management services were starting out, they offered buyer auction management services. Apparently there isn't much demand, and it's rare to see such services heavily advertised today. Nonetheless, if you buy on a grand scale, you need to be well organized. You will need to devise a system to keep track of your auctions and purchases. Look at the Buying Solutions section of the eBay Solutions Directory to find buying software and services.

Summary

Well, there's no shortage of help, and more is on the way. The auction management services make running auctions on eBay and the entire process of selling as easy as it can be.

V

Taking and Using Photographs

23

Taking Photographs

Digital photographs sell merchandise. eBay enables you to embed images in your eBay auction ad. This is a wonderful opportunity to show what you're selling. People like to see the things they contemplate buying.

Photographs may seem unimportant for some products. For instance, how do you show software or other seemingly intangible products? It's simple. You show the box. Even showing the box will help you sell. In fact, showing the box or showing manufacturers' photographs and drawings will help you sell used products as well as new products. Where the merchandise is used, blemished, scratched, or otherwise damaged, however slightly, a good close-up photograph of the item will provide potential bidders with the information they need to make a bidding decision. The more disclosure you make, the less trouble you will have from buyers. A photograph is often the best way to disclose exactly what you're selling.

Surprisingly often, a photograph assists a seller to make more accurate disclosure. If you advertise one model but show another in a photograph, some knowledgeable potential bidders will set you straight. It's not unusual at all for a potential bidder to be more knowledgeable than a seller in regard to an item, and you see sellers being set straight routinely on eBay. Better to learn about your mistake before the auction is finished than after.

Photography Tips

Product photography is something of an art, but you're not taking pictures for the Buick brochure, so don't worry about it too much. Do, however, take the little bit of extra time to ensure that your photographs are appealing. And use a digital camera. Film is out, and digital cameras are now inexpensive and easy yet efficient to operate.

Here are some things you can do:

1. Photograph in color. Does anyone use B&W anymore?

2. Use diffused outdoor light—lightly overcast day or in the shadow of your house—if practical. If you shoot outdoors on a sunny day, you may need a flash to fill in the shadows.

3. Use a flash indoors. Diffuse the flash with a translucent cover (e.g., a piece of white plastic garbage bag taped over), or bounce the flash off the ceiling, to avoid glare. It's even better to use flood lights if you have them. Use two or three. Use one each to point at the item from the left and right about 45 degrees offset from center. Use the third to backlight the item (out of sight), if practical.

4. Use a plain, dull (not shiny), pastel one-color background. Cloth backgrounds (e.g., sheets and tablecloths) work well.

5. For large items, shoot against an appealing background. For instance, shoot cars in a residential neighborhood, not on an asphalt parking lot.

6. Get as close to the item as possible. Use a closeup lens, if appropriate. But be careful of overexposure from a flash.

7. Fill the frame when you shoot. The image of your item will be larger and higher quality. If you use a digital camera, use the highest resolution setting (minimum of 640 × 480).

8.   Use a tripod, and focus carefully.

Take multiple photographs for items that deserve multiple photographs in your auction ad (e.g., vehicles). Don't forget to take photographs of the blemishes and defects that bidders will want to see.

Close Up

Most digital cameras do not require a special close-up lens for shooting small items; you can get good photographs of small items easily.

Digital Camera

Inexpensive digital cameras can be surprisingly high quality today. They're perfectly adequate for eBay photos. Using a digital camera is the least expensive, quickest, and most convenient way to create digital photographs. Just shoot the photographs and load them into your computer. It couldn't be easier.

A good quality 2-megapixel digital camera (under $100) provides adequate quality for most purposes. If you sell antique Japanese prints and want to capture the subtle colors, don't use an inexpensive digital camera. Use one with at least a 3-megapixel image. But most items do not require such quality. With a 2-megapixel camera, you can take high-quality photographs (if you know how) of almost anything for eBay auctions. So, you don't need an expensive digital camera to produce even high quality photographs for your eBay auction ads.

Megapixels

Most digital cameras sold now exceed this minimum requirement by several megapixels.

Make sure that any digital camera you buy has the capability of taking close-ups. This is a feature you will use a lot. Fortunately, unlike film cameras, most digital cameras do have close-up capability without a special lens.

If you buy a digital camera used (e.g., on eBay), make sure you get the manual, software, and USB cable. Otherwise, you might spend a lot of time and money acquiring such items; and you will need them.

Avoid older digital cameras that don't use a USB cable to connect to your computer. They are likely to be troublesome.

Size

Don't make your photographs large. Seldom is a photograph larger than 500 × 375 pixels justified for an eBay ad. Make it smaller. Digital images larger than 400 × 300 aren't needed and take longer to download. Large photographs make your eBay ad photographs slow to appear, perhaps even slowing the download of your entire ad. They also may interfere with your auction webpage. However, don't think by recommending 400 × 300 that I'm saying you should enlarge smaller photographs to that size. If you have smaller photographs, use them in their smaller size. Digital photographs don't enlarge well.

Typically, adequate digital cameras use at least a 640 × 480 pixel format, and you don't want to use anything smaller. This is quite large. Since digital camera formats do not provide a proper size, you will have to shrink your digital photographs. The best way to do it is to reduce the size of the image with an image editing program (covered in Chapter 24) to make the image file smaller to download.

Image Markup

Regardless of the actual size of the digital photograph, you can set the size that it will show on eBay in the image markup. Suppose the image is 640 × 480 pixels. You want to shrink it to 400 × 300. Use the image markup:

```
<img src="[URL]" width="400" height="300">
```

The size of the digital photograph remains the same, but the browser reduces the image shown in the webpage (the ad) to 400 × 300. This does not reduce the download time but saves you the task of image editing. This is not a recommended procedure, primarily because it causes an unnecessarily long download time. Note that when you do shrink a photograph, you need to maintain the aspect ratio (the ratio of the width to the height), or your photograph will become distorted.

Photo Editing

You can use an image editing program such as Adobe Photoshop Elements to decrease the size of the image before you use it. There are hundreds of inexpensive photo editing programs that can resize digital photographs and also do much more. Such programs are usually bundled with digital cameras, scanners, new PCs, color cards for PCs, and even other software. Most will enable you to easily change the contrast, brightness, and sharpness. In other words, these programs act like a digital darkroom. You can make better photographs than you took. Whether you want to go to all that trouble is a personal matter, but if you have to change the size, it's usually little additional trouble to at least sharpen your photographs. You can see the photograph change as you make the adjustments. Chapter 24 covers image editing.

Format

All digital images must be in the GIF (.gif), JPEG (.jpg), or PNG (.png) format. Most digital photographs are in the JPEG format. The photo editing programs enable you to make conversions to other formats.

Tools and Services

Interesting photography tools and services are starting to pop up. You may find some of them useful.

The Boxes

Several vendors offer lighted boxes inside which you can shoot great product photographs. These range in price from $90 to $4,000, and some come with a digital camera included.

EZCube, *http://www.tabletopstudio.com*

Cloud Dome, *http://www.clouddome.com*

Coloreal eBox, *http://www.ortery.com*

MK Digital Direct, *http://www.mkdigitaldirect.com*

Why would you pay so much for a box? Well, if you have small expensive items to sell, the higher quality photographs and the efficiency will eventually pay for a box. You can, of course, build a box yourself with flat-white walls and lights inside. But some of these boxes have features that you might find it difficult to duplicate easily with a do-it-yourself project.

Outsourcing

Outsourcing means having someone else take your photographs. Auction 123 (*http://www.auction123.com*) will shoot your vehicle photographs for under $75 and provide you with a nice presentation for your eBay Motors auction ad. It's a useful service called Dealer Assist and is available to everyone. If you're looking for extra work, Auction 123 is looking for franchisees and photographers.

Making Photographs Available

You store digital photographs on your hard disk. When you want to make them available to others via the Internet, you have to upload them to a hard disk that's on the Internet such as a host Internet Service Provider's (ISP's) hard disk.

Storing Photographs

The reason you must store a photograph on a hard disk on the Internet is that it gives it a URL.

Website

Suppose you store your photographs at your website (*www.yourwebsite.com*). Your root folder (directory) at your website is:

```
/clients/yours/public_html
```

You can create a handy folder named *photos* just to store your photographs:

```
/clients/yours/public_html/photos
```

Suppose you need a photograph named *item41.jpg* (in your auction ad at eBay) that you have stored on your website in the *photos* folder. The image markup in the ad will look as follows:

```
<img src="http://www.yourwebsite.com/
photos/item41.jpg">
```

Thus, your image stored on your website will appear magically in your eBay ad. (See Appendix IV for ideas about using a Web authoring program to create your image markups.)

If you need help with creating folders and determining what the URL of your images will be, consult your host ISP.

ISP Account

If you don't have a website, you may be able to store your photographs on your dial-up ISP's hard disk in the space reserved for you. Your ISP reserves space for your email messages. Most ISPs also enable you to use such space for webpages too. If you can put up a webpage, you can store photographs. Suppose your Web address is *http://www.isp.com/ ~yours*. You can create a folder named *photos* and upload all your photographs for eBay auction ads to that directory. The image markup will be:

```
<img src="http:// www.isp.com/~yours/
photos/item41.gif">
```

If you need help with creating folders and determining what the URL of your photographs will be, consult your dial-up ISP. Or, your ISP may have instructions published online. Many ISPs do.

ISPs

If your dial-up and your host ISPs are the same, you have a combined dial-up plus host account. Most people who are serious about having a professional website will use a separate host ISP that caters to their needs, not their dial-up, DSL, or Cable ISP.

Special Services

There are a number of Web services that cater to auction users. They will store your photographs for auction ads for free or for a fee. Go to their websites to get instructions:

- Auctionimage, *http://www.auctionimage.com*
- FreePicHosting, *http://www.freepichosting.com*
- Imagehost, *http://www.imagehost.com*
- ImageHosting, *http://www.imagehosting.com*
- PennyThings, *http://www.pennythings.com*
- Picturetrail, *http://www.picturetrail.com*
- PixHost, *http://www.pixhost.com*
- Pongo's, *http://www.pongo.com*

- Webshots, *http://www.webshots.com*

These are not the only places you can store your photographs. eBay itself will allow you to store one photograph per auction without charge (see below). ISPs like AOL and MSN offer photograph storing services. And most of the auction management services include photograph storage too.

Make sure when you sign up with one of these services that you know how to upload your photographs to the service (to their website). Also make sure you know exactly what the URL of your image will be once you have uploaded the image. Many of these services also provide scanning and other image services.

eBay Picture Service

You don't have to use an outside service for storage. You can use the eBay Picture Service (*http://pages.ebay.com/help/basics/pictureservices.html*). The first photograph per auction is free. After that, it costs you a nominal fee. You don't have to do anything special. This service is integrated into the auction listing process. This is a convenient service that you will want to try. eBay automatically deletes your photographs after your auction ends.

Uploading Photographs

To upload your photographs to your storage place on the Web, you use the File Transfer Protocol (FTP). Consequently, you will need an FTP client to upload the images. There are many freeware and shareware FTP clients available. Try *http://www.cnet.com* and look for *downloads*.

I upload with WS_FTP, which is easy to use. It enables you to show a directory (folder) on your own hard disk on the left and a directory on the hard disk of your website on the right. After getting online, you simply highlight the file(s) on the left and click on the arrow pointing right to make the upload. You can also download by highlighting the files on the right and clicking on the arrow pointing to the left (see Figure 23.1).

Figure 23.1 WS_FTP uploading files to a website.

Get WS_FTP at *http://www.ipswitch.com/_ebay/index.html*. This URL also provides special instructions for eBay users. Other FTP clients include:

- CuteFTP (*http://www.cuteftp.com*)
- Fetch (for Mac—*http://fetchsoftworks.com*)
- FTP Voyager (*http://www.ftpvoyager.com*)

Pulling In Photographs

Through the magic of links, you can pull media into your eBay auction ad from other servers on the Internet. This is a little different from a link to another webpage. A link to another webpage will take you to that webpage. But a media markup will bring the media into the eBay auction ad in the auction listing (which is a webpage). The media can be images, sound clips, or even video clips (see Figure 23.2).

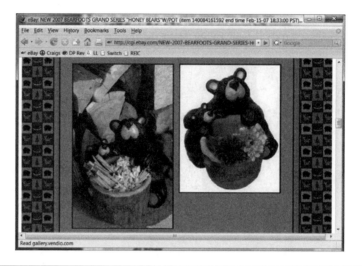

Figure 23.2 Photographs of products in auction ad made with template.

But we are concerned primarily with digital photographs. Store the photographs at your website, in your ISP account storage space, or at one of the Web services that offer to store photographs. Then pull it into your eBay auction ad with the HTML image markup.

```
<img src="http://isp.com/~yours/photos/
image12.jpg">
```

Making It Happen

So, you've stored your photograph where it's accessible on the Web. You have its correct URL. What do you do next?

At eBay

When you access the *Sell Your Item* form in the Sell section to enter your eBay auction ad, be ready to enter the URL of your image. The URL will start with *http://*.

If you don't add the URL at the time you enter the other information for your auction, you can add it later. If you add it later, however, the photograph will be tacked onto the bottom of the ad and will look like an add-on.

In the Template

In the template featured in Chapter 16, you add the URL of the photograph into the template. You then enter the entire template in the *Description* for the auction ad at *Sell Your Item*. (You also enter the URL of the photograph into the *Picture URL* for the eBay auction ad when you use a template. eBay needs the photograph for the top of the listing page and for other system purposes.) The template places the photograph in a special place. The whole point of using a template is to create an attractive auction ad with the photograph well integrated (see Figure 23.2 above).

Other People's Photographs

Other people may have photographs you can use. It's not difficult to get them and use them. But then there's the question of permission.

Manufacturers

More specifically, you can use photographs from manufacturers' websites; simply right-click on the photograph. You will see the file name of the photograph, and you can also save the photograph to your own hard disk. Once you have saved it, you can use it as if it's one of your own; that is, you can upload it to your Web photograph storage place.

Another way you can use it is to look at the Source for the webpage (Go *View, Source* in either the Firefox browser or the Microsoft browser) after right-clicking on the photograph to get the image file name (see Figure 23.3).

The source will show you the URL of the photograph. (Sometimes the URL is incomplete because it is a relative reference, and you will have to try to figure out the complete URL. This level of analysis is beyond the scope of this book, but this method is worth mentioning for readers who know HTML.) Once you have the correct and complete URL, you don't need to download the photograph and you don't need to store it at your Web photograph storage place; you only need to use it where it is. That is, you use the URL of the manufacturer's photograph at the manufacturer's website by putting the manufacturer's URL in the *Picture URL* in your eBay auction ad (i.e., *Sell Your Item*) or in a template.

```
Netscape                                                  _ □ x
<BR> 
<TABLE BORDER=0 CELLSPACING=0 WIDTH="100%" >
<TR>
<TD ALIGN=CENTER VALIGN=TOP WIDTH="20%">
<IMG SRC="truxton.jpg" HEIGHT=171 WIDTH=128>
<BR><B><FONT FACE="Arial,Helvetica"><FONT SIZE=-1>John<
<BR><B><FONT FACE="Arial,Helvetica"><FONT SIZE=-1>509-5

<TD WIDTH="2%"></TD>

<TD ALIGN=CENTER VALIGN=CENTER WIDTH="1" BGCOLOR="#0000

<TD WIDTH="2%"></TD>

<TD><B><FONT FACE="Arial,Helvetica"><FONT SIZE=+1>JOHN
<P><B><FONT SIZE=+1>M</FONT></B>r. Truxton grew up in E
first job after graduating from Santa Rosa Community Co
in 1962 was as a firefighter with the Lakewood, Colorad
Subsequently, he took a sales position in Denver with t
Company, a manufacturer of fire fighting devices. Then
employment in sales with IBM's Office Automation Divisi
returned to college to get a MBA in Real Estate at the
```

Figure 23.3 The source shows the entire webpage in HTML.

Now it's one thing to say you *can* use these techniques, but the fact that you can doesn't mean you should. In fact, you must consider everything on the Web to be copyrighted. If you use other people's copyrighted materials without permission, you are liable for copyright infringement. So, before you download a photograph or logo from a manufacturer's website into your eBay auction ad, you might first consider getting permission from the webmaster at the manufacturer's website.

Unfortunately, this is impractical, and many eBay sellers download and use manufacturers' logos, product literature, photographs, and other intellectual property for their eBay ads with impunity. A different approach is to provide a link to a manufacturer's website where bidders can find complete information on products and photographs too. This is a better practice.

eBay Sellers

You can also use the photographs taken by other eBay sellers. You can download or pull them in the same way as you do for manufacturers' photographs. Of course, such sellers are likely to be your competitors, and your pilfering is likely to upset them. It's not a good practice.

Nonetheless, I have always taken a mellow view of this. If someone wants to steal a seller's photographs, who is he to stand in their way? Like many sellers, he is likely to have pilfered photographs and logos from manufacturers. It seems a little hypocritical to get irritated at a fellow eBay member for doing the same to him. On the other hand, eBay retailers who make selling on eBay their livelihood disagree with me about this, and understandably so.

If you are an eBay retailer and use of your photographs by other sellers irritates you, you can probably find a JavaScript script somewhere on the Web that will prevent people from stealing your photographs out of your auction ad. The JavaScript script would go inside the image markup.

Graphics

A digital photograph is just a digital color graphic. You can use any color graphic just as if it were a digital photograph. Consequently, you may want to use a drawing or other art form rather than a photograph. Whatever graphic you use, however, you must first convert it to a GIF, JPEG, or PNG file format. Photographs are always best, but if you can't find a photograph or can't take one, a color graphic may be better than nothing.

Summary

A digital color photograph helps sell merchandise on eBay. It is well worth going to the trouble of taking one, editing it, and using it in your eBay ad. Use a digital camera as the most practical means of getting digital photographs. The seemingly toughest part of the procedure, image editing, is really quite easy, and it's a step you need to take just to resize or crop your photograph, if nothing else (see Chapter 24).

Once the digital photograph is ready, it's just a matter of posting it via FTP on a website and referencing its URL in your eBay auction ad. This is a pretty simple process, and a pretty powerful means of advertising. Of course, it's even simpler to use eBay to store your photographs if all you need is one photograph for each item.

24

Using Image Editing Software

Why have an image software tutorial in an eBay book? Hey! It's fun to touch up your digital photographs for your eBay auction ads. And you will find a few other techniques useful too. Image editors range from Adobe Photoshop at about $650 to freeware or shareware programs you can download from the Web. Some are quite easy to use. Some are incomprehensible. But we will attempt only a few simple things and leave the more incomprehensible programs to professional photographers and those who want to learn a lot more.

In fact, many image programs make easy-to-use darkrooms. Before you use a image program, however, you first have to have digital photographs. Digital cameras are easier to use than film cameras. You will shoot many more photographs without a care because the photos cost nothing except battery power. You will get better photographs too. And the photographs are already in digital form. You simply transfer them to your computer's hard disk, usually with a USB cable. Then you're ready for the digital darkroom.

The Digital Darkroom

The technology of using color graphics is impossible to understand without a lot of study. The top programs have extensive and robust capabilities. Using Adobe Photoshop proficiently, for instance, entails applying it to specific graphics activities. You can spend months, or even years, learning how to use it with photographs. Then, if you want to use it to create digital watercolor paintings instead of photographs, the learning begins all over again. Nonetheless, you can do amazing things with image editors with just a little learning.

This chapter will simply cover four things you can do quickly and easily to improve your digital photographs. The program to use is the freeware IrfanView (*http://www.irfanview.com*).

IrfanView

This program was picked because it is a freeware program that you can download from the website mentioned and it's simple to use. It's a capable program, but there are commercial programs that offer additional functionality and convenience. If you do a lot of image-preparation work, you might consider buying a program like the robust but inexpensive Adobe Photoshop Elements (*http://www.adobe.com*), a slightly less feature-laden version of the expensive Adobe Photoshop, or the popular PaintShop Pro (*http://www.jasc.com/products/paintshoppro*) each for about $80 street price.

Today a computer or a video card (powers your monitor) usually comes bundled with an image editor. If you know you have one, try it on some digital photographs. If you don't know whether you have one, look around your hard disk for an unfamiliar program. You just may find an image editor. Image editors usually have the word *photo*, *picture*, or *paint* somewhere in their name.

And, of course, if you buy a digital camera, it invariably comes bundled with an easy-to-use image editor.

Another free image editor is Picasa from Google. It's also a photograph album with many handy features. You can download it from Google.

Cropping

If you have the software to edit digital photographs, you don't have to frame your subject as carefully in your viewfinder when you take photographs. In fact, most inexpensive digital cameras take an image much too large for an eBay ad. Remember, anything larger that 400 × 300 will take too long to download, might be too large for your HTML work, and is much more than you need. That means you can crop a lot and still have a large image left.

Virtually every graphics editor has a cropper. You crop to get the right look for your photograph, not to reduce the size. After you do your cropping, you resize the image to the size you desire.

For IrfanView simply put the cursor on the photograph and hold down the left mouse button to create the cropping rectangle. Then go *Edit*, *Crop Selection*.

Contrast

When shades of black and gray are similar and when colors are similar, a photograph tends to have a flat, dull look. When you digitally increase the clash of the blacks, grays, and whites, particularly around the edges of objects, and when you digitally increase the clash of the colors, a photograph comes to life. This is contrast. You have to be careful, however, that you don't introduce too much contrast, or the photograph will look unnatural. But increasing the contrast just the right amount in a photograph will often make it look better. For Irfan-View, go *Image*, *Enhance Colors*.

How do you know what the right amount is? You can see it. As you apply the contrast, you will see the photograph change before your eyes (see Figure 24.1). Not all image programs will do this, but you want to use one that does.

You can move the Contrast control panel (Figure 24.1) off the program window in actual use, enabling you to see the full photograph. It's hard to find a photograph that doesn't seem to improve with added contrast. You will probably find yourself adding contrast to all your eBay product photographs.

Figure 24.1 Applying contrast in IrfanView.

Brightness

Adjusting brightness is less straightforward than adding contrast. Sometimes it works, and sometimes it doesn't. If you have a particularly dark photograph, you may want to increase the brightness. However, as you increase the brightness, the colors start to look increasingly bleached out. It's more likely that you will want to decrease the brightness just a little. The colors will often become richer and more saturated. You will notice that the brightness control is on the same panel as the contrast control in Figure 24.1 above.

You must use both of these controls to improve the look of photographs. More times than not, I reduce the brightness a little and boost the contrast to get a substantially improved photograph. Indeed, it's amazing how much you can improve the look of a dull photograph by changing only contrast and brightness.

Gamma

Gamma is the light intensity of the monitor. It is another way to adjust the brightness and works a little differently than the brightness control. It wouldn't be mentioned here except that IrfanView puts it on the panel with brightness and contrast. You can ignore it or play with it to see its effect. I recommend you ignore it.

How Do You Do It?

Again, as you adjust the brightness and contrast, the photograph will change before your eyes. Play with the controls (systematically). Have some fun. When you get a look that you like, it's time to save the photograph. (Click on *OK*.) The photograph is now the image that you adjusted it to be.

What if you want to go back to the original? That's OK. You haven't altered the original photograph until you save your work. That brings up an important point. You might want to keep all your original photographs somewhere special on your hard disk. When you decide to adjust one, make a copy first. Adjust the copy and save it. That way you'll always have the original.

Resizing

IrfanView has a resizing function wherein you enter the numbers (the dimensions) you want and IrfanView resizes to those dimensions. For IrfanView, go *Image, Resize/Resample* (see Figure 24.2).

Figure 24.2 Resizing by the numbers.

Remember to preserve the aspect ratio (ratio of the width to the height) by checking the box on the panel.

Suppose your photograph is 1600 x 1200 pixels. You crop it to an image 1320 x 956. You want to get it down to a width of 400 pixels. So, you resize it to 400 x 290. Resize your photograph after you do your cropping. Now you have only one final step: sharpening.

Sharpen

Sharpening is the last step in your photo editing. You don't want to sharpen until you have an attractive photograph exactly the size that you will use for your eBay ads. Sharpen enough to make your photograph look sharp but not so much that it starts to look funny. Some image editors don't enable you to sharpen by degrees. They do it for you automatically. For IrfanView go *Image, Sharpen* and it instantly sharpens your photograph without any effort on your part. Slick!

Note that if you happen to use an old image editor, it may not have a sharpening control. You will need to use a more up-to-date image editor. Sharpening is an excellent means of improving your photographs, so it's worth using the appropriate software to do your image editing.

Orientation

When you shoot, you sometimes use the camera in the portrait position. When the image is in digital form, you can rotate it 90 degrees to the proper viewing position. For IrfanView go *Image, Rotate Right.*

Work Flow

Busy people who sell in volume on eBay will want to set up a work flow for their photograph processing. This is nothing more than a uniform routine of processing digital photographs step by step. If you do it the same every time and work out an efficient process, you'll save time and energy.

Out of Focus

The one thing that's almost impossible for image processing to do is correct a photograph that's significantly out of focus. Sharpening can't work miracles. Thus, make sure that you focus properly when you shoot, and you will save yourself some wasted time. Cameras with automatic focusing don't always work perfectly, but overall they do a pretty good job. Use one to increase your efficiency in getting your photography work done.

File Formats

There are many graphics file formats. Whatever you start with, you must eventually convert your photograph to a GIF (.gif) or JPEG (.jpg) format. You can also use PNG (.png) format, but it doesn't work in early Web browsers. Most image editors will convert photographs from one file format to another. Simply save in the file format you want.

GIF

GIF files are compressed as much as 2:1 without loss of quality. However, they are only 8-bit files, that is, 256 colors. You need at least 256 colors to make a photograph look real, so GIFs work OK.

JPEG

JPEG files can be compressed a little or a lot. JPEG compression is "lossy," which means that quality diminishes during the compression process. The greater the compression, the smaller the file and the greater the loss of quality. But JPEGs are 24-bit files, that is, potentially 16 million colors. Consequently, JPEG files can look good, particularly when they're not compressed much. JPEGs work better than GIFs for photographs because they have more colors.

PNG

PNG is a relatively new graphics file format slowly starting to come into use on the Web. It's an advanced file format that can carry with it extra information regarding the photograph. However, using its advanced capabilities is well beyond the scope of this book.

There's More

Image editors offer a lot more than this chapter covers. Some offer much more than others. You can spend as much time and energy as you want processing photographs. You have two steep learning curves to climb. The first is technical. Color is highly technical as is the digital technology that makes color possible on a computer. The second is artistic. To make good graphics, whether photographs or anything else, you have to have some artistic skills.

Using this technology is great fun. At the same time, our objective is a simple one: just post some good photographs with our eBay auction ads. It's not much fun to get bogged down in digital-color technology just to accomplish something seemingly simple. Therefore, a good strategy is to stick with the simple approach of this book.

Summary

The procedure this book recommends for processing your photographs is simple:

1. Take a photograph with a digital camera.

2. Transfer it to your hard drive.

3. Adjust it (i.e., brightness, contrast).

4. Crop it.

5. Resize it.

6. Sharpen it.

7. Admire it—or redo it. See Figures 24.3 and 24.4 below.

8. Upload it to your storage place on the Web that you use for your eBay photographs.

9. Put an image markup in your eBay auction ad to pull it in.

This is a simple strategy and an easy one that will accomplish your goal of posting good photographs to get more bids and, therefore, higher winning bids on your eBay auction items.

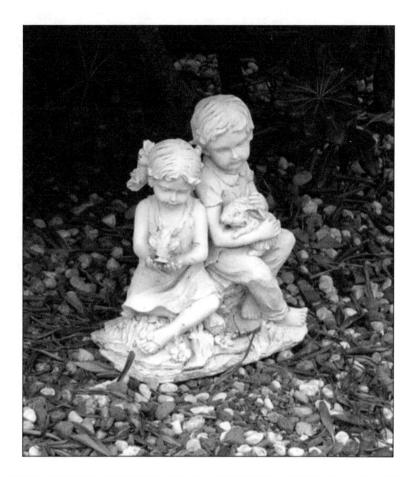

Figure 24.3 The product photograph before sharpening and cropping.

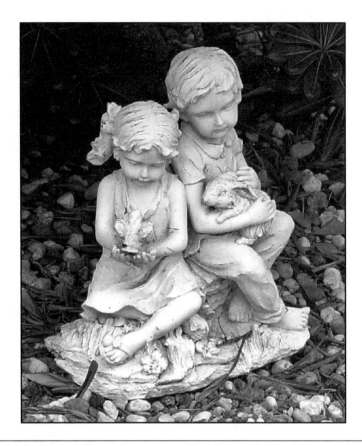

Figure 24.4 The product photograph after sharpening and cropping.

VI

Specialty Marketplaces

25

Specialty Auctions

If a nationwide auction makes sense, what about local auctions? After all, many items don't trade well at long distances but do trade well inside metro areas. eBay answered this question by creating "regional" auctions, which are essentially the leading metro areas (about 60).

Unfortunately, the local auctions have all but disappeared from the eBay scene. They have been relegated from the eBay home page to obscurity, if you can even find them the next time you look.

Regional Auctions

Local (regional) eBay auctions provide a convenience for bidders and extra exposure for sellers. They are designed to handle large or heavy inexpensive items or other items not appropriate for long-distance shipping due to size or cost. For instance, a desk worth $100 that costs $150 to ship almost anywhere will be difficult to sell nationally on eBay. But in a local auction, a buyer will drive across town in a borrowed pickup or van to take delivery.

Office equipment, hardware, garden supplies, livestock, and so forth are all good candidates for local eBay auctions. If it's large or heavy and inexpensive and if eBay has an auction for your area, sell it at a local eBay auction.

For Bidders

You used to find local eBay auctions for regional areas in the US named for their metro area. Each local auction used to have its own attractive home page. No longer. The local auctions became somewhat lackluster. They always were just a subset of the general eBay auctions. But the last time I looked, they looked like an unadorned subset. Now I can't find them on eBay.

In other words, eBay created the local auctions by filter (a database search technique). Everything was filtered out except auctions originating from within the local area. Consequently, this was a convenience for potential bidders rather than a truly separate auction.

eBay designed the local auctions this way to avoid blank lists for thinly traded items. Nonetheless, you could use the eBay search for specific local items productively if you decided the catagory directories were unproductive.

eBay local auctions have great potential, although eBay has never learned how to do them effectively. In a few years, as eBay expands its general membership, it will likely generate a critical mass for some of its local auctions. Perhaps then eBay will learn the magic formula for making local auctions work well.

In the Future

Why do I cover something that eBay apparently doesn't offer any longer? Local marketplaces are an important concept with huge potential in the future. For instance, Craig's List has created successful marketplaces in many cities around the country and even in cities in other countries. In 2004, eBay bought a 25 percent interest in Craig's List. Read Chapter 28 for more on Craig's List.

Today one can elect to have the listings on an auction listing page sorted according to the ones that are nearest first. I guess this is eBay's latest attempt at local auctions.

For Sellers

The local auctions gave a boost in marketing power for a seller's items, particularly the items that did not make sense to sell nationally. When a seller auctioned an item, she did not have to elect a local area, but she lost nothing by doing so. She gained by having her item appear in a regional auction as well as the national auction.

For local auctions the question comes up, What if potential buyers want to see the item? You need to handle this just like you would if you put an ad in the local newspaper; that is, if you don't want someone to come to your home, you may have to arrange to have the item inspected somewhere else. Keep in mind, too, that you can normally get more information on an eBay bidder than you can on someone who answers your classified newspaper ad by phone.

Street Address

eBay has stated that it will not give out your street address to anyone. Presumably no other eBay member can get your street address except from you.

For local auctions, use common sense and be clear in your auction ad what your policy is regarding inspection and shipping. For items appropriate for local auctions but inappropriate for shipping, you might want to indicate "For pickup only."

Keep an Eye Out for Them

Because the local auctions were just a subset of the total eBay auctions, eBay could easily and quickly reinstate the local auctions at any time.

Real Estate

Most states regulate real estate auctions, and you have to have a real estate license to hold such auctions. eBay is supposedly licensed in real estate in every state. Nonetheless, eBay runs mostly non-binding real estate auctions. It has experimented with binding real estate auctions. The complexity of real estate transactions does not seem to conveniently fit into the normal eBay procedures. Real estate auctions have a different eBay fee structure. In effect, running a non-binding real estate auction on eBay is essentially a form of advertising.

Real estate is a growing category for eBay, although its growth has been disappointing compared to many other eBay categories. More and more real estate sellers are finding their way to eBay to advertise by running auctions. In particular, Realtors are making good use of eBay to advertise their listings. Naturally, local auctions would give real estate sales a boost.

Strictly Local

Some other goods and services are strictly local. That is, it doesn't make as much sense to auction them on national eBay as it does on a local auction. For instance, most attorneys provide services only locally. An auction (advertising) effort for attorney services would get a boost from a local eBay auction.

A restaurant provides another prime example. It doesn't make much sense to auction off a dinner for two nationally, unless the restaurant happens to be in one of the top-ten tourist destinations in the country. But a local eBay auction might prove enough of a boost to make such an auction effective.

As this book goes to press, there are over 60,000 categories of goods and services being auctioned on eBay. There are a thousand ways to effectively sell these goods and services on eBay. (Many of them haven't been invented yet.) The local eBay auctions will eventually add even more ways to effectively auction goods and services.

If you think you've missed getting in on the ground floor of eBay, you haven't. The local eBay auctions will someday be the next ground floor. The local eBay auctions will develop different dynamics and new opportunities.

I must say it's bold of me to say this. I may have more faith in the future success of local eBay auctions than does eBay. When local auctions start to work—and they will—the local eBay auctions will indeed provide opportunities for greater sales and new ways to sell. But for now, you will have to look elsewhere for effective local marketplaces. That why I cover Craig's List (see Chapter 28).

Half.com

Wow! I discovered Half.com while writing the second edition of this book. It's a powerful and easy-to-use website that enables you to purchase goods at a fixed price—millions of items. The idea is that the goods are used and sell for less than half price. But the goods can be new, too, and sell for more than half price.

eBay originally bought Half.com to supplement the eBay consumer-to-consumer auction transactions with fixed-price transactions. Alas, perhaps we need to say goodbye to Half.com. eBay intended to merge it into eBay by August of 2004. The original problem was that since eBay had instituted its fixed-price system (*Buy It Now*), Half.com was redundant. The fact is, however, that eBay postponed the merger, and Half.com still exists. eBay attempted to integrate it into eBay but apparently has given up on that strategy. Consequently, today Half.com continues to operate in much its original form (see Figure 25.1) despite the fact that there are also eBay auctions for items that fall into Half.com product categories.

Figure 25.1 Half.com website. ©1999-2007 Half.com Inc.

Buyers' Benefits

Now, we're not talking about selling everything as eBay does.

Half.com limits its offerings to books (printed), music (CDs), movies (VHS, DVDs), and games (electronic). These are called intellectual property, although Half.com also sells computers, software, and other electronic equipment. The nice thing about some intellectual property is that once you've used it, you usually don't want to use it again (e.g., once you've read the book or seen the movie, you don't want to do it a second time). Yet the benefits are the same for the next person who uses it (i.e., the next person who reads the book or sees the movie). For digital intellectual property (e.g., CDs and games), the experience is just as high quality for the second user as the first. Half.com provides a mechanism that enables anyone to sell such goods at low fixed prices in an efficient and smoothly operating international market.

Half.com is not perfect. If you need a book in a hurry (e.g., a text-book), you may have to wait for media mail, which can take a couple of weeks. You may have no option for quicker shipment. Then too, the seller has to confirm that there is a transaction. If the seller sold the book to someone else, you will get an email informing you that you need to buy the book from another seller. That can cause a delay of a few days.

The first time I bought a used textbook (for my daughter and her friend), I didn't understand the problem. One day I had my choice of 9 different used copies of an $85 textbook for about $45 each. Three days later the number available was down to four. I immediately ordered two and was informed two days after my order that one textbook wasn't available. Then it was too late to get a second one at less than $67, and there was no assurance that that was available. So, I elected to buy the second one new in the college bookstore. I didn't want one of the girls to have to wait until one-quarter of the course was over to read the textbook.

Books

Think of Half.com as a used bookstore online, one that offers hundreds of thousands of titles.

Buying Books

Here's what I bought on my first try (see Table 25.1). I had been meaning to buy and read these books for a while.

The savings provided me with an incentive to buy. My savings were $42.82, that is, 64 percent off list. A shipping and handling charge of $6.85 was added to my order. Keep in mind, these are not impulse purchases that I happened to see on a table as I walked to the checkout counter of a bookstore and will never read. I actually read the first and third books and will read the second just as soon as I can break my indentured servitude to my publisher.

Table 25.1 Books and Savings

Title	Purchase Price	List Price
Passage to Juneau: A Sea and Its Meaning (Raban)	$6.37	$26.50
Passionate Sage: The Character and Legacy of John Adams (Ellis)	$6.47	$15.95
The Power Broker: Robert Moses and the Fall of New York (Caro)	$10.79	$24.00

Alas, I could not find the eighth and final volume of Page Smith's *People's History of the United States*. But Half.com has over 8 million items for sale, and it turned up later.

Since my initial purchase, I have purchased many additional books. Now, before I buy books I don't need immediately, I always check with Half.com first.

And If It's Not in Stock at Half.com

Half.com will display books from eBay itself (those listed at a fixed price – *Buy It Now*) at the bottom of the Half.com product page, if available. This gives you an additional source to purchase a book when it's not in stock at Half.com.

Out of Stock

For Half.com, "out of stock" means that no seller has submitted the book for sale. The catalog database for Half.com is huge, but Half.com cannot possibly have all titles in the catalog. Half.com depends on its sellers to provide the inventory. As soon as a seller provides a book, it is in stock and available for purchase. Half.com has millions of books in stock.

Music

Right from the beginning Half.com offered plenty of popular music. Today it offers all. Even J.S. Bach, who was invisible when I first tried Half.com, has 17 webpages of titles today. This is a great source of music CDs.

Movies

I found the Kenneth Branagh version of *Hamlet*, a favorite of mine, listed (along with nine other versions) as well as *Chariots of Fire,* about the 1924 Olympics, a wonderful movie. This is undoubtedly the largest selection of movies in the universe. I don't know that for a fact, but if it isn't, it's certainly close.

Games

Because I don't play computer games, I don't have much to report here. Keep in mind, however, that the digital-game industry is larger than Hollywood in dollar sales. We're talking big money. Any website that can save a kid a few bucks, or parents a few hundred, is a welcome relief to purchasing at full retail.

Searches

The search engine at Half.com at one time didn't work very well. You could only do a definitive search with an ISBN number. However, it is now much improved. But when all else fails, go to Amazon.com and search. Come back to Half.com with the ISBN or UPC numbers.

Numbers

The ISBN (International Standard Book Number) and the UPC (Universal Product Code) are standard industry inventory numbers, often expressed as bar codes, found on products in the Half.com catalog.

The Half.com database is independent of inventory. Therefore, you will find books that are "out of stock." This makes a very complete database possible, enabling you to order books that are not in stock. As soon as someone offers such books for sale, your purchase will automatically take place, and you will get the book. Or, rather than purchase automatically, you can elect to be notified when a book you want comes into Half.com's inventory.

Reputation

The feedback system works a little differently on Half.com. Only sellers get feedback. After all, the buyer buys for a fixed price immediately with a credit card. Therefore, why rate buyers? The Half.com feedback system has been integrated into eBay's feedback system.

The feedback is based on how quickly the seller confirms the order, how quickly the seller ships, how well the seller classifies the condition of merchandise, and how well the item is packaged for shipping.

Selling on the Half

As a seller, you have to be on your toes to remain successful. Just as in eBay auctions, good customer service is a must.

When you are just a casual seller, you may not worry too much about your reputation. Nonetheless, the system requires that you give good customer service. In the spirit of eBay and Half.com, you need to make an effort to take care of details and ship promptly. Most merchandise is shipped by the US Postal Service media rate, which is slow. Any delays you add to the inherently slow shipping will be agonizing to many customers.

Selling Procedures

It's easy to offer an item for sale. You just enter the ISBN number (for books) or the UPC number (for other items), the price, the condition of the item, and comments. You can also offer shipping by Priority Mail (faster than Media Rate). Your item goes into the vast Half.com catalog; that is, the item appears in stock.

It's your responsibility to ship the item adequately packaged. When someone buys your item, you are notified via email by Half.com and must confirm within 48 hours that you have the item and will ship it. You must then ship within 24 hours after confirmation. If you do not follow this procedure, the order may be canceled, subjecting you to a low feedback rating. If you're slow, you may not get a top rating.

Generally, you need to set your prices realistically. I recommend the following price structure (percentage of list retail price new – based on my observations, not a scientific study) for used books:

Like new 60%

Very good 45%

Good 35%

Acceptable 25%

Remainders, which are new books that did not sell in the bookstores, can be sold for more than 60 percent. In practice, however, remainders sell for lower percentages. Many books sell for below the suggested percentages.

Shipping

Unless you offer Priority Mail and the buyer elects it, you can ship the item any way you want. The media rate for books is the least expensive and is what will be expected by buyers. Half.com will reimburse you for shipping according to Table 25.2. The reimbursement is the same regardless of what the actual shipping costs are.

Table 25.2 Half.com Reimbursement for Shipping

	Media Rate	Priority
Hardcover		
First item	$2.33	$4.70
Subsequent items	$0.90	$2.75
All Other Items		
First item	$1.89-1.94	$4.70
Subsequent items	$0.65-69	$1.50

You need to send the bottom half of your order confirmation with the merchandise. You can also send a receipt. You are not permitted to send anything else (e.g., promotional materials) with the merchandise without Half.com's permission.

Fee

Half.com takes a 15 percent fee on sales. The fee is graduated. More expensive items over $50 are charged at a lower percentage. Half.com provides the Web catalog, completes the sales transaction, and collects the purchase price on all sales (via credit card). That doesn't leave sellers much to do. Sellers merely list the merchandise and ship it. Seems like a reasonable arrangement. Half.com takes no listing fee; listing is free.

Business?

Can you make a business out of selling on Half.com? Sure. In the publishing industry, books that don't sell in the bookstores are said to be remainders. Since books are sold on consignment (a practice started during the Great Depression), the bookstores return unsold books to distributors, which in turn return them to publishers. You may be able to get remainders from bookstores, distributors, or publishers at very low prices. Sell them on Half.com. Likewise, you can find sources of excess inventory for textbooks, music CDs, movie VHS tapes and DVDs, video games, computers, software, and electronics.

Live Auctions

eBay bought the old San Francisco auction house of Butterfields to acquire the expertise to auction valuable fine art and artifacts online. eBay Premier for offline auction houses and art dealers was the result. That didn't seem to work. Then eBay made a deal with Sotheby's. That didn't last either. Today eBay no longer owns Butterfields but continues the experimentation with its Live Auctions. These auctions are primarily for high class art objects that require lots of paperwork such as authentication documents. And they are held live online. Included in these auctions are collectors' books, antiques, fine arts, manuscripts, art, and the like.

It was bound to happen sooner or later on eBay, a live auction via the Web. And eBay Live Auctions makes a great place to experiment with live auctions. Fine art auctions handle the expensive items that make it worthwhile to go to the expense of broadcasting such auctions live on the Web. You can hear the auction via RealMedia (audio) and participate in the bidding via a form in the webpage. Although live auctions are not necessarily meant to be experimental, you should certainly view them that way. Jump in and experiment. Live auctions via the Web will have their place apparently.

Consult the Live Auctions section of eBay for specific instructions on participating and bidding. You must sign up ahead of time to bid in live auctions, and of course you must be an eBay registered and verified user. This provides you with an opportunity to participate in something a little different on eBay, even if you don't bid. To sell on Live Auctions, you must be a professional auctioneer. This privilege is not open to all eBay members.

Summary

Half.com is not an auction, but it complements eBay nicely with fixed-price inventory for a few types of standard merchandise (and more). Apparently it will not be incorporated completely into eBay but remains a separate selling mechanism. It's a special type of sales mechanism because it uses catalog databases for books, textbooks, music, movies, and video games. If you buy such merchandise, give it a try. Or, if you want to sell what you've got, give it a try.

Live Auctions have their place, but it's not a huge place. The items are limited to art, art objects, and similar things. It's more like going to Sotheby's to bid than it is like going to eBay to bid. eBay continues to experiment with live auctions, and perhaps someday it will accommodate a broader range of items.

26

eBay Stores and eBay Express

Don't go to sleep at this crucial point. This whole chapter is one big hot tip for you if you operate an eBay business. Your easy-to-use, low-cost Web storefront is now available. It's a way of selling and marketing that you need to consider carefully because it beats the alternative. It's the old golden opportunity knocking at your door.

Through the Third Edition of this book I advocated creating an ecommerce website and using it in conjunction with your eBay auctions. I no longer recommend such a strategy. Three factors have changed the eBay business environment to make this prior recommendation a less desirable alternative.

First, eBay no longer permits a link from your auction ad to your ecommerce website. Second, eBay now provides you with a storefront (eBay Store) and does your marketing for you. Third, auction management sevices now provide you with a checkout device for your eBay customers, and the eBay checkout is much improved.

If Not a Retailer

If you are not an eBay retailer, you can skip this chapter. People not selling as a retail business on eBay are not likely to need an eBay Store. For information about buying from eBay Stores, see Chapter 5.

Online Realities

eBay is still being invented. New twists in the invention process can quickly render useful techniques obsolete. In this case, eBay has evolved in a direction that is both restrictive and at the same time expansive.

The Magic Link

It used to be that eBay allowed a link from your auction description to your ecommerce website. This enabled you to promote (advertise) your website on eBay. In the spring of 2002 eBay disallowed this useful link, severely restricting your capability to promote your ecommerce website on eBay. Today eBay still allows a link to your ecommerce website from your *About Me* webpage. But it's not the same. It's too indirect.

Apparently, if I read the rule correctly, eBay doesn't even allow the URL for your ecommerce website to be published in your auction description. eBay characterizes it as a "static link," whatever that is. You will do well to review the rules about this if you have questions about it. Go *Help, Rules and Policies, Rules for Sellers, Listing Policies for Sellers, Links*.

The Website

Why have an ecommerce website in the first place? Well, it gives you a chance to put up an online catalog with fixed prices. It gives you another means of selling your merchandise. But it doesn't come free. A website costs time, effort, and money to create. It requires even more time, money, and effort to maintain. This is true if you can do it yourself. If not, you have to hire someone, and it costs even more.

If you already have a profitable website, great! Don't give it up as long as it's worthwhile for you to operate it. But many eBay businesses discover that having an ecommerce website is more trouble than it's worth. Before jumping into creating your own website, you need to give careful consideration to the alternative: eBay Stores.

The Checkout

A reason to have had your own website in the past was to provide a checkout procedure for your eBay customers. There was a time when the eBay checkout procedure was weak. Ineffective, really. Nonetheless, most ecommerce websites had capable checkout procedures. If you could steer your eBay auction winners to your ecommerce website checkout, you could handle them more efficiently, and they would see your website too.

Today eBay offers a much improved checkout procedure, although it's only capable if the seller sets it up properly. The auction management services' checkout procedures work well, and you can even use some of them on your ecommerce website in place of traditional ecommerce software. Consequently, today it's not important to have a website just to provide a capable checkout procedure.

Marketing Realities

The reality of operating your own ecommerce website is facing the great marketing problem. Marketing your website will take at least half the time, effort, and money you put into your business. Without being able to piggyback on eBay, you have the same marketing problem as any ecommerce website on the Web. The piggyback was the direct link from your eBay auction ads that eBay no longer allows. Without the link, the marketing effort required to make your online retail business successful is enormous. It's not any easier or less expensive on the Web than it is off the Web.

For instance, the search engines are probably the best marketing device on the Web. The reality is that you will have to hire an expert or a special service to analyze and restructure your webpages to be "found" by the search engines and put at the top of the lists. This will cost you $3,000 to $10,000 or more and will also require a lot of work on your part or require a lot of work by your website designer, an additional expense. There are other effective Web marketing techniques, too, but I don't know of any that don't require money or huge amounts of time.

The great thing about eBay is that it relieves you of the burden of doing anything but token marketing. That saves you considerable time, energy, and money.

Use the Stores

Now an eBay storefront can be yours for a reasonable fee. Granted, the eBay Stores aren't very pretty, but they improve from time to time. eBay has made changes recently to enable you to customize your Store to a greater degree than before. Granted, the eBay Stores aren't generating as much business as the auctions yet, but we can assume that they will eventually command an impressive retail market share. Granted, you can't do much with your eBay Store other than list items for sale in a catalog, but we can assume eBay will enable more refinements in the future. For instance, recently it created eBay Express (see below).

What the eBay Stores do today is present to you a grand opportunity to run an ecommerce website, in effect, without all the headaches, hard work, and expense. For most eBay businesses, an eBay Store will bring them more business immediately than an ecommerce website. And the best is yet to come.

Judge Separately

eBay auctions have grown so fast in the last 12 years that we tend to expect everything eBay does to perform just as well—or it's a failure. The fact is that eBay has had plenty of failures, and most of them aren't with us any longer. Nonetheless, it has plenty of submarkets that grow at a much slower rate than eBay auctions. That doesn't mean they're failures. It just means we need to judge them separately from the eBay auctions. Some eBay features, such as eBay Stores, will take a longer time to reach full fruition. But when they do, you'll want to be a part of the success.

eBay Stores is well on its way with over 730,000 participating businesses! Now that's a pretty good start.

Storefront

When you become an eBay Store, you get a storefront and a catalog.

You decorate the storefront, if you want to, and you fill the catalog with *Buy It Now* (fixed-price) listings.

Incidentally, Elance is a good place to find a low-cost but skilled webworker who will design a nice Store for you as well as a nice *About Me* webpage.

Special Features

Look for special Store features. For instance, eBay enables you to have your own custom search categories for searching through your Store items (once customers reach your Store). This becomes an increasingly powerful benefit the larger your Store gets.

Reports

eBay also gives you sophisticated monthly sales reports for your Store. These can be a powerful tool in analyzing your business and identifying opportunities for greater sales.

eBay Is No Slouch

Note that the auction management services offer you many features, some free and some for a fee. But eBay is no slouch. Although eBay may not be as inventive as the third-party service vendors, it eventually attempts to match their successful services feature for feature. The monthly reporting for Stores is a good example. (And, of course, eBay has invented a few things itself.)

The thing to watch with the auction management services, and with eBay too, is that they will experiment with a new service and offer it free. If it's successful, it often turns into a service for a fee. Nothing wrong with that. I encourage you to join the experiments. But you do have to watch the nickels and dimes. Your overhead can skyrocket quickly if you don't.

Items

A Store is a normal store idea. Its shelves, in effect, are stocked with goods selling at a fixed price. The listing for an item looks much the same as an auction listing, and you create and treat the listings much the same as you do an auction listing. One thing to keep in mind is that the Stores have their own general search mechanism and category classifications separate from the ones for auction listings.

The catalog of Store items looks much the same as an eBay member's list of pending auctions. Not very fancy but functional. It's only a matter of time before eBay will provide enhancements that will improve the appearance of the catalogs. It has done so incrementally already. The current benefit to you is that you can process your auction listings and your Store listings identically for all practical purposes, and the available software and services enable you to do so.

Cross-Promotions

Don't overlook the eBay Cross-Promotions. Go *Help, Selling, Marketing Tools, Cross-Promoting*. This is much like Andale's Gallery, which puts a mini-catalog of other items on each Store item ad. It's a terrific cross-marketing tool inside your Store.

Fees

The Stores operate on a different fee schedule than auctions, and that seems to be changing. The posting of items is longer (even unlimited) and the fees are generally lower. You can find the latest fee information at *eBay Stores, For Sellers, Subscriptions and Fees*.

Cross Marketing

Pay attention to cross marketing opportunities between your auctions and your Store. For instance, suppose you sell digital cameras in your eBay auctioning business. You can use your Store to sell accessories. Refer your bidders to your Store (including a link) specifically to purchase the accessories they need for successful digital photography (e.g., a camera bag).

Links

The key to making your Store successful is to use auctions to bring bidders to your Store. This is so important, let me say it again. *The key to making your Store successful is to use auctions to bring bidders to your Store*. To do so you need to link to your Store from within your auction ad and even suggest to bidders that they visit your Store. Don't rely on the opened red door icon link at the top of the auction listing.

If you have something specific to cross market, like the example in the previous section, that's fine. But beyond cross marketing, you will want to skillfully use your eBay auctions to promote your eBay Stores. Someday perhaps this won't be necessary for success, but today it is. The primary way to promote is to always include a link from your auction ad to your eBay Store and always tell bidders to visit your Store. And I will say again, don't rely on the red tag icon link at the top of the auction listing webpage.

Unique URL

Your eBay Store is your new website. You even get your own permanent unique URL! You can treat it just like your own website. You can even promote it outside eBay. It's your permanent Web address.

Dynamic Duo

Don't forget, your *About Me* webpage is also a unique URL. This is where you can do institutional advertising. This is more than it seems, even though it's just one page. It can be a gateway to something bigger as mentioned earlier in the book. The combination of your *About Me* webpage and your eBay Store gives you a powerful place on the Web. Make sure you have a lot of links going back and forth.

eBay Express

eBay Express is eBay's new department store (see Figure 26.1). It's a big online catalog filled with new, brand name, and hard-to-find products offered at fixed prices. Instead of dealing with multiple eBay Stores, you shop at one large store that includes a shopping cart. You can buy multiple items when you check out. Any eBay seller who meets certain criteria and sells items at fixed prices can participate. However, the inventory is limited to the eBay Express departments.

Departments

Instead of thousands of categories, eBay Express has a more manageable three dozen categories, which makes it seem more like a department store than a vast unlimited auction marketplace.

Search

The search function is quick and direct. Because the number of categories is smaller than eBay auctions, you can get to what you're looking for quickly. eBay Express displays the products with large photographs and includes prices and shipping costs.

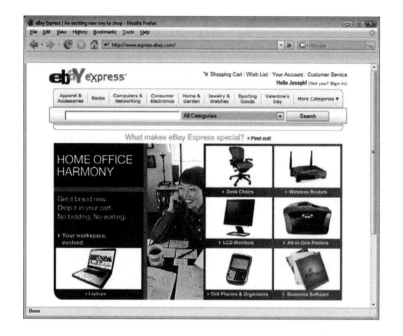

Figure 26.1 eBay Express. ©1995-2007 eBay Inc.

Customer Service

Customer service links are on every page to help consumers shop. One can even get customer service via chat or email as well as by online tutorials.

Printed Catalog

Not a printed catalog? Yes, indeed! eBay actually sent out a nice printed catalog for eBay Express in the fall of 2006. Whether it will do so in the future and which products it will include is a matter of conjecture.

Shopping Cart and Checkout

Unlike eBay auctions or Stores where you typically buy one item at a time, eBay Express enables you to put multiple items into a shopping cart and check out just once. This is a consumer convenience not available for eBay auctions or eBay Stores.

Sellers

Although no sellers who meet the eBay criteria for eBay Express are excluded, eBay Express is designed with eBay Store sellers in mind. This is another way to sell goods online. eBay Express looks more like Amazon.com than it looks like eBay. eBay Store owners will want to take a good look at how they can increase their sales using eBay Express.

eBay Express is not separate from from eBay. Your items for sale on eBay (that meet the eBay Express criteria) go right into the eBay Express catalog if you want them too. And it's free.

Summary

The eBay opportunities are expanding. The powerful threesome of your eBay auctions, eBay Store, and *About Me* provides you an exciting opportunity to sell to a huge market, an idea never contemplated in anyone's dreams just a few years ago. eBay's philosophy is to create a level playing field for all, large and small; that is, a democratic playing field. eBay Stores are another step (another opportunity) to take toward realizing success if you are a serious eBay retailer.

eBay Express is yet another opportunity to expand your market for goods you're already selling on eBay. It's a different experience for consumers, but it's little extra effort on the part of sellers.

27

eBay Motors

Does it make sense to buy a used car in Miami when you live in Omaha? It might. It depends on what you're looking for. The local market even in large cities tends to be thin when you're looking for something specific. There are so many brands and models.

Now if you're selling a popular car, you probably won't have any trouble quickly selling it locally. Unfortunately, most cars are not in high demand, and they can be difficult to sell locally. But expose them to a larger market, and you have more chance of finding a buyer who wants what you've got (see Figure 27.1).

With the above in mind, eBay makes a perfectly logical place to buy or sell cars. If you buy a car and live within 1,000 miles of the seller, you can hop on an airplane for less than $200 and drive the car home in a weekend. If you live 3,000 miles away, you can have the car shipped for under $900. If your prospective purchase is a good deal even after factoring in the cost of delivery from a distant city, why not buy it?

Indeed, eBay Motors sold about 3 million vehicles in 2006, and about

75 percent of those transactions took place across state lines. That's approximately one-fourth of eBay members' total sales for the year.

Figure 27.1 eBay Motors home page. ©1995-2005 eBay Inc.

Nice Car

We needed a third vehicle (late 2004) because our daughter got her driver's license. We had bought a 1999 Lincoln Towncar on eBay Motors in late 2003 (49,000 miles – $11,000 – excellent condition) in Eugene, Oregon, a day's drive from the San Francisco Bay Area where we live. A nice car and inexpensive when purchased used. So I decided to buy a similar car in late 2004, a Lincoln Continental.

A large portion of the American luxury cars sold on eBay seem to come from independent used car dealers in Florida or Texas. Consequently, I decided to look locally first in an effort to avoid the transportation costs. I drove long distances across town several times to look at cars for sale. That turned out to be a waste of time.

I bid and won the eBay auction of a Continental in Dallas, Texas. I had my wife's cousin's husband in Dallas check it out. It was beautiful and ran well. Unfortunately, an inspection of the undercarriage on the lift at an auto shop revealed that the car had been in a serious accident and welded back together. Since that had not been disclosed in the eBay auction ad, I did not complete the transaction. The seller, a dealer with a good feedback record, claimed that he did not know about the accident as he did not have a lift to inspect his cars. And the Carfax report did not show the car as having been in an accident.

I intended to be in Oklahoma City over Christmas and planned to drive any car that I purchased back home via New Mexico and Arizona where I had some business in January. Because of this false start in Dallas, I was running out of time before Christmas.

But I located several more nice Continentals on eBay. One, a 2000 Continental with 78,000 miles in excellent condition, fit my needs well. The seller, a dealer in Florida, had 100 percent postive feedback selling cars on eBay over four years.

The Continental had an $8,600 *Buy It Now* price, but there was weak bidding. The seller hinted that the reserve was low. I read between the lines to guess that the reserve was significantly lower than the Buy It Now price. I started my bidding at $7,400. When I got to $7,800, the reserve was met. Since the bidding had been weak, I stuck with this bid and eventually won the auction.

Because I was in a hurry, I made the blunder of failing to arrange with the seller to have the car inspected by a mechanic before completing the transaction. Not a good idea. But because the seller had such a good feedback record, I took a chance. I had the car shipped to Oklahoma City for $700. (For $900 I could have had it shipped all the way home.) There I had it inspected by a Lincoln Mercury dealer. Fortunately, it turned out to be in great shape, a very nice car. We used it for two weeks while staying in Oklahoma thus saving about $500 in rental car costs. Then I drove it home completing my business in New Mexico and Arizona en route.

The wholesale value for the car was $8,800 and the retail value was $13,200 (adjusted for mileage). Hence, I was pleased with my purchase (see Figure 27.2).

Figure 27.2 The author's used 2000 Lincoln Continental purchased on eBay.

As a seller, you can potentially generate more interest in a vehicle in the national market. eBay provides a cost-effective means of reaching that market.

Think Local Too

Even if you don't like the idea of a national market being a good place to buy or sell a used vehicle, don't forget eBay reaches local markets as well.

Buying a Car Nationally

Being a national marketplace, eBay often offers more choices, particularly when you want something specific or unusual. Researching the value of the vehicle provides you with the basic information you need to negotiate well. A possible drawback to an eBay purchase is your inability to inspect the vehicle before traveling to the seller's faraway city. But that might not be such a disadvantage with the proper safeguards agreed by buyer and seller before the auction is over.

Determining Value

Determining value is essential to intelligent negotiation. Vehicle values fall within certain ranges. If you know what those ranges are, you can do your best to purchase wisely. Otherwise, you're operating in the dark.

The Blue Books

The best way to determine the value of any car is to consult a publication containing the value data on a wide range of brands and models (see Figure 27.3 – Edmunds website).

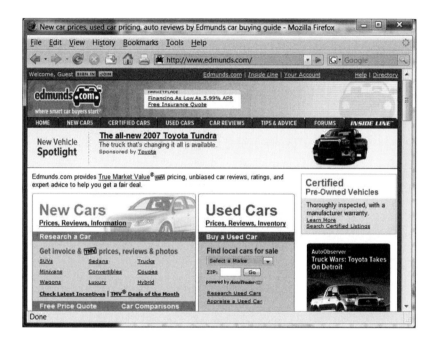

Figure 27.3 Edmunds website. ©1995-2007 Edmunds.com, Inc.

These are generically referred to as "blue books" and are published by several publishers:

Edmunds (*http://www.edmunds.com*)

Kelly, the original "Bluebook" (*http://www.kbb.com*)

NADA (*http://www.nada.com*)

They offer a wholesale (trade-in) value and a retail value for used cars. Somewhere between these two values is likely to be the purchase price of your next used car.

The Spread

What does the spread between wholesale and retail value mean? It's simply the markup a dealer seeks. A dealer acquires a vehicle at its trade-in value when a buyer buys a new vehicle and trades in the old one. Dealers also acquire used vehicles in auctions at wholesale (trade-in) prices. The dealer sells the vehicle traded in (or purchased at auction) to a new owner for a markup to cover expenses and make a profit. A dealer's expenses include the following:

- Preparation of the vehicle for sale
- Financing to carry inventory
- Dealership overhead
- Advertising
- Salesperson's commission

A private sale is not exactly the same. Typically, the seller in a private sale has lower expenses than a dealer. That's a primary reason that private sales tend to have a purchase price between wholesale value and retail value, usually closer to wholesale.

The Lender

A lender will usually loan the wholesale value of a vehicle or higher. In fact, some blue books list a loan value. That means that if you can purchase at wholesale instead of retail, you can get a 100 percent loan, assuming your banker has confidence in you.

How to Protect Yourself

How do you protect yourself against purchasing a defective vehicle? Well, how you do it for a local purchase shows how you might do it on eBay.

Local Purchase

The standard buying procedure is to visually inspect a vehicle. You can judge the exterior and interior condition reasonably accurately. But it's the engine that requires some expertise. I always take the vehicle to a mechanic who does inspections for car purchases. These inspections cost $50–$100.

Between your visual inspection and a mechanic's inspection, you will get a pretty good idea of the true condition of the vehicle. This procedure is not foolproof, but it's much better than sticking your head in the sand.

eBay Purchase

Alas, when you buy a vehicle on eBay in a faraway city, what can you do? First, you need to deal only with eBay sellers who have good reputations (solid positive feedback). Second, you need to get full information on the vehicle. Third, you need to see plenty of photographs, one from every angle, to do a preliminary visual inspection. Fourth, if these are not included in the seller's auction ad, you need to request them. If the seller won't provide them, forget the vehicle and move on to another. Fifth, there is free fraud insurance up to $20,000.

With honest information and a reputable seller, you can make a reasonably safe decision. It's not a risk-free decision, but it's workable. Remember, if the vehicle turns out to be as represented, you're stuck buying it. Better test drive one exactly like it at home before you commit yourself to some heavy bidding. If it's not as represented, the eBay Seller Guarantee program, if offered by the seller, may protect you.

Inspections

From time to time eBay has arranged a system of vehicle inspections with various auto services. For instance, Pep Boys, a national chain of auto service stores, was the soup du jour for a while. Check eBay for the current recommendation. (Regardless of the current eBay recommendations, Pep Boys and it's national competitors remain good choices.) The idea is that the seller takes the vehicle to a third-party mechanic for inspection (at seller's expense) and then uses the results of the inspection to help sell the car by providing the buyer with useful and presumably accurate information. In the alternative, the seller takes the vehicle to a third-party mechanic for inspection on behalf of the buyer (at buyer's expense).

If you arrive in the faraway city to find the vehicle is not as represented, you have reasonable grounds to back out of the deal, and you should do so. For that reason, you should, if possible, travel to the faraway city to inspect the vehicle immediately after the auction before the seller requires you to put down a deposit. Otherwise, in a dispute, you may lose your deposit. In any event, you will lose the cost of travel.

Test Drive and Engine Inspection

It's up to the seller whether to allow you a test drive or an engine inspection before completing the transaction. These inspections are your best protection against getting a lemon, and it seems silly to travel all the way to the seller's city to pick up the vehicle if the seller won't let you (an out-of-towner) do what most sellers will allow buyers in their locale to do. The honest seller takes little risk in allowing these inspections. After all, it's the buyer who travels at his or her own expense to make these inspections. It takes a serious buyer to do so. Consequently, if these post-auction inspections aren't allowed prior to the end of the auction, take a pass and go on to another vehicle.

Of course, if a seller pays for an inspection before auctioning the vehicle on eBay, she will probably not be inclined to accommodate your desire to have another inspection.

Before the Auction

Some sellers allow an inspection and test drive before the end of the auction but not after. This is obviously not workable for out-of-town buyers.

Victor Owens of Brooks Automotive, the chief mechanic who has taken good care of my family's cars for many years, recommends the following for an inspection:

- Ask for a pre-purchase check similar to one normally done during an oil change and lubrication, except more thorough. Check to see that everything on the vehicle both inside and outside works.

- Ask for a smog check (required upon transfer in some states). A successful smog check generally indicates that a vehicle operates properly, but it is not conclusive. (Keep in mind also that a smog test in one state is not necessarily valid in another state.)

- If a vehicle has over 80,000 miles, have each engine cylinder's compression checked manually. A compression check done on a scope saves time and sometimes costs a little less but is not as accurate as a manual check.

- Always have a vehicle checked in daylight, not at night.

- Have the mechanic do a test drive. In a test drive, a mechanic can uncover problems that others would miss.

A pre-purchase check costs $50–$100. A compression check is often extra and costs $50–$100. An emissions check is also extra, and the price varies from state to state.

Any Purchase

For any purchase, whether local or on eBay, you can collect paperwork to protect yourself. Don't miss this opportunity to make your prospective transaction as safe as possible. Get a Carfax Vehicle History Report (*http://www.carfax.com*), formerly known as the Lemon Check, to determine the history of the vehicle (see Figure 27.4).

Carfax reports the following in its Vehicle History Report:

- Salvage history

- Odometer fraud

- Multiple owners

- Flood damage

- Major accident damage

- Fire damage

Figure 27.4 Carfax website. ©1996-2007 Carfax, Inc.

eBay also offers a similar service arranged through a Carfax competitor for about $8. Click on the VIN (vehicle identification number) in the auction listing to get access to the service.

Not Conclusive

A Carfax or similar check is not conclusive. It can alert you to problems, but it cannot guarantee that problems do not exist. After all, it merely a check of the public records regarding a vehicle. Is it worth paying for? Absolutely! But a physical inspection of the vehicle is necessary too.

Warranty

Buying a warranty for the vehicle you purchase may be a good idea. You can purchase your own warranty, at the time you purchase the vehicle, from a firm such as Smart Auto Warranty (*http://smartautowarranty.com*). Warranties cost from $300 to $3,000 depending on the vehicle, what you want covered, and for how many miles or years you want coverage.

Your Take Your Chances

Vehicle warranty companies go out of business routinely, including at least one that was an eBay favorite a few years back. A warranty company from which I purchased a warranty online went bankrupt recently. Fortunately, my car is doing just fine. Going back 10 years, another company from which I purchased a warranty from a dealer also went bankrupt.

eBay Motors used to provide free warranty protection for 30 days after a purchase but no longer does so. It also used to feature a warranty provider on its website but no longer does so.

The moral of this brief story is that when you purchase a warranty, you take your chances.

eBay sponsors a Seller Guarantee program. Ask the seller to take part in the program. It provides additional assurances to buyers.

Consummating the Transaction

To complete the transaction, go with the seller to the Department of

Motor Vehicles (DMV) or whatever it's called in that state to complete the transfer of ownership and collect all the paperwork. Make sure all the seller's liens are removed from the title and that the title is free and clear. You pay sales tax and vehicle registration fees in your home state. If you are buying out of state, you will normally pay only nominal transaction fees, nominal temporary registration fees, and no sales tax. If you do have to pay sales tax, you will usually get credit for it when you pay sales tax (or use tax) the second time in your home state. Going through the transfer process at the DMV with the seller is your only assurance that everything is done correctly.

Don't forget to have your car insurance in place prior to the transfer of ownership. You are liable for your newly purchased vehicle. You can actually get auto insurance through the eBay Motors website too.

And what else? eBay will get you together with Dependable Auto Shippers (*http://pages.motors.ebay.com/services/das-shipping.html*) if you need to ship your newly purchased car home. eBay will also find financing for you if you don't already have it arranged. And finally, PayPal comes into the picture with a special Secure Pay service for car buyers. It is essentially an escrow service provided through Escrow.com. Not a bad group of services, all at the eBay Motors website. Where can you get this kind of service anywhere else?

Escrow

You may need to set up the transaction in escrow if:

> You cannot be present in the faraway city when the transfer of ownership takes place;

> There is a lender lien on the title (the seller owes on the vehicle);

> You are borrowing from a lender to make the purchase; or

> You just want to protect yourself.

This is extra paperwork that is sometimes tedious to arrange, but it may be necessary. Before the purchase funds are released to the seller, you must be satisfied with the vehicle.

Escrow.com

For a fee, Escrow.com (*http://www.escrow.com*) will provide an escrow transaction (see Figure 27.5). It will verify payment for the seller, and it will withhold payment from the seller until the buyer has inspected the vehicle and is satisfied. Although the fee seems reasonable, as the book went to press, this service was inadequate for many situations. For instance, it did not handle loan payoffs.

Through eBay you can get the Secure Pay arrangement (for vehicles) for $75, also provided by Escrow.com.

Figure 27.5 Escrow.com

Bank Escrow

An escrow agreement is particularly valuable when the seller still owes funds to a lender on the vehicle, and he or she will use your purchase money to pay off the loan. The escrow is your only assurance that the seller's loan gets paid off.

Perhaps the best place to arrange the escrow in the case of a loan payoff is the seller's lender. The seller's bank can adroitly handle the transaction because it can pay off the seller's loan instantly with the buyer's purchase payment.

Informal Escrow

Many lenders will do informal escrow arrangements. When two lenders (seller's and buyer's) are involved, you can expect them to work out the details of completing the transaction, sometimes without a formal escrow agreement.

Let the escrow agent worry about the transfer details. But don't overlook the problem of taking responsibility for the vehicle immediately after the transaction is complete. The escrow agent isn't going to put your vehicle in his or her garage until you get to town if you happen to be buying from afar.

Escrow Fee

An escrow arrangement is so germane to an eBay vehicle transaction that involves a seller's loan payoff, that the escrow fee should be split between buyer and seller. Indeed, this is true for most eBay vehicle transactions except where the seller can provide clear title and the buyer and seller can go to the DMV together to complete the transaction. eBay is not going to dictate the terms of agreement for a transaction, but as a practical matter and as a matter of fairness, the buyer and seller should split the escrow fee. Ask the seller to do so prior to the conclusion of the auction.

Dealer

Dealers do vehicle transactions every day as part of their business role. If the seller is a dealer, leave the details of the transaction to the dealer-seller and don't worry about an escrow arrangement. Dealers are regulated by the state and can lose their licenses for not handling transactions properly.

Escrow Fraud

Because vehicles are big ticket items, escrow fraud involving vehicles has widely proliferated online. Beware of escrow companies recommended (or required) by the seller. And vice versa. Make sure you use a legitimate escrow company.

Verification

To bid more than $15,000 on eBay, you have to either put your credit card on file or go through the ID Verify process (see Chapter 4). This is something to note because many vehicles will cost more than $15,000. This assures eBay and the seller that the bidder is a known person, not someone fraudulently hiding behind an alias and playing bidding games.

Agency

In some cases you will find that the seller doesn't really own the vehicle. He or she is selling it for someone else. Before you take a plane ride from Phoenix to Boston as the winning bidder to pick up the vehicle, you need to make sure that the auction is binding on the seller. The only way to do so is to get a copy of the agency agreement between the true owner of the vehicle and the person or company that auctioned it on eBay.

Mediation

Insist that the seller agree to mediation in regard to disputes that may arise from an auction transaction. SquareTrade, the eBay recommended service (see Chapter 8), is a great way to do this inexpensively and effectively. Vehicle purchases are financially large transactions. It's well worth it to have the most complete protection possible; mediation through an organization like SquareTrade can provide you with assurance that you will get treated fairly. In fact, SquareTrade thinks of itself as a type of insurance.

eBay Local Purchase?

Can you do a local purchase on eBay? Certainly. If a seller in your city sells your dream vehicle on eBay, it makes things simple for you. Treat such a purchase like any local purchase. You can insist on the proper protections covered in this chapter, and you're present to act in a timely manner to complete the transaction. Indeed, some eBay vehicle transactions are local transactions.

Seller "Maltactics"

Some sellers state that they reserve the right to cancel their auction at any time. That means they will sell the vehicle on eBay unless they get a reasonable offer locally in the meantime. This seems unfair but is a common practice.

eBay rules, however, state that sellers cannot cancel auctions unless they cancel all the bids first. To explain themselves, sellers need to give a credible reason for the cancellation, which potentially subjects them to angry bidders.

Impulse Buying

Americans love cars and trucks. It's easy to get carried away when buying one. And impulse buying for cars and trucks, unlike for other merchandise, tends to linger for days instead of hours or minutes. Don't let impulse buying affect your rational approach to buying a vehicle on eBay. Don't take shortcuts. They usually lead to unnecessary risks. Do what you have to do to protect yourself.

If you need a vehicle immediately and you insist on getting what you want, you will probably spend several thousand more dollars for the same vehicle than you will if you can shop for a vehicle casually.

Selling a Car Nationally

Selling a vehicle nationally potentially brings in more buyers than a local effort. More buyers mean a higher price, a quicker sale, or both. This is particularly true for unusual cars, antique cars, or classic cars, but it's also true for ordinary vehicles.

The best place to start finding out how to sell a vehicle on eBay is to read the section for buyers earlier in this chapter. That will give you some ideas about the plight of the faraway buyer. If you can accommodate the specific needs of faraway buyers, you're more likely to sell your vehicle for the highest price possible on eBay.

Three-quarters

As mentioned at the beginning of the chapter, three-quarters of the 600,000 vehicles sold in 2003 on eBay were in transactions that crossed state lines. In other words, only 25 percent of sales were in the same state, of which a smaller percentage were in the seller's locale.

Determining a Car's Value

Read the earlier section in this chapter on determining value. If you realistically want to sell your vehicle on eBay, you will need to sell it at a price that appeals to eBay buyers. It's not likely that you will sell it at full retail value for the following three reasons:

1. In the local market you will have a difficult time selling a vehicle at full retail. A typical private sale (not a dealer sale) in my experience is closer to wholesale than to retail value.

2. A normal eBay buyer has to spend $200–$900 to pick up the vehicle or have it delivered. That has to come out of the price, or what's the point of buying on eBay?

3. A buyer runs the risk of traveling to pick up the vehicle in a distant city, being dissatisfied with the misrepresented condition of the vehicle, and returning home empty-handed. That could cost as much as $500 or more, a substantial risk. It's not smart to take that risk and pay full retail too.

As a seller you might ask, What's the point of trying to sell a vehicle on eBay if sales prices are likely to be lower than full retail? There are several answers to that question:

1. A local sale is likely to be lower than full retail too.

2. A $200–$900 downward price adjustment looks less significant as the price of the vehicle increases.

3. Some vehicles will take a long time to sell in the local market, perhaps many months. It may be quicker to find a buyer on eBay.

4. For many vehicles, there are more potential buyers on eBay than locally. That means more possibilities and a greater likelihood of a successful transaction.

5. If you sell only via eBay, you are not likely to have a lot of people coming to your home to take a look at the vehicle.

6. Selling on eBay is an easier process than selling locally in many cases.

7. There are always potential eBay buyers who live in your city. Thus, an eBay auction has local possibilities.

8. You are likely to get more from an eBay sale than from a dealer trade-in or from selling to a dealer.

Perhaps a more relevant question is, What can you do to maximize the purchase price that an eBay buyer is willing to pay?

Winning Bid

To inspire the maximum winning bid, you need to lower the buyer's risk and make it easy for a buyer to purchase the vehicle from you. That's why reading the early part of the chapter is so important. If you see things from the buyer's point of view, you can make a purchase more appealing at little or no cost to yourself.

Do the following to entice potential buyers:

- Provide complete information on the vehicle (including good photographs).
- Permit a test drive and engine inspection after the auction and prior to making the sale final (for out-of-town buyers only).

The less risk the buyer has, the more the buyer will be willing to bid.

Verification

I believe ID Verify is essential to both buyers and sellers in vehicle transactions. The ID Verify costs you about $5 (one time only) and verifies to eBay and the world that you are who you say you are. eBay requires verification of sellers, or at least a credit card number and bank account number in lieu of verification. If as a seller PayPal (or eBay) has not required you to become verified, you should become verified anyway. It will build confidence with buyers.

eBay requires that a buyer who bids over $15,000 have ID Verify. This requirement is not good enough for vehicle transactions. Any winning bidder, regardless of the purchase price, should have ID Verify. And, as I say above, sellers should have ID verify too.

Title

Don't assume that because the buyer has paid for the vehicle he or she will carry through on the requisite paperwork, such as getting a new title. Buyers have many reasons why they don't get around to registering the transaction and officially taking title. One of the primary reasons is that they must pay sales tax when they officially take title to the vehicle.

Suppose a buyer sits on the paperwork and does nothing. As the seller, you still have your name on the title. If anything happens with that vehicle (e.g., an accident), you may be liable.

Therefore, walk buyers through the closing transaction at the DMV and make sure they have title to the vehicle before you bow out of the picture. Otherwise you might find yourself faced with a legal claim based on the fact that you're still the owner of record for the vehicle.

Mail-In Forms

Some states, such as California, have a mail-in transfer report that the seller can send to the Department of Motor Vehicles (DMV) after the transfer to report the transfer. As the seller, make sure you mail this to the DMV after the transfer, if you didn't do the transfer at the DMV.

Information Sells

This book continually stresses that information, not hype, sells merchandise on eBay. This is particularly important for big-ticket items such as vehicles. Provide prospective buyers with complete information on the vehicle that you auction. Take a look at some auction ads on eBay Motors to get an idea of what *complete* information means. If you provide anything less, you will lose potential bidders for each bit of information you don't include. The ultimate result will be a lower winning bid. Always include good photographs and a description (and photograph) of every defect.

I believe it's practically impossible to sell a normal vehicle on eBay for a good price without providing at least one very good photograph. The more, the better. Look at dealer auctions on eBay. They always include at least a half-dozen good photographs, and they're the expert sellers.

Seeing photographs is the primary way a potential buyer has of making a purchase decision. If you ignore this fact, you eliminate most potential buyers and make yourself look like an eBay rookie.

Check out Dealer Assist, available to all, a photography and presentation service offered by Auction 123 (*http://www.auction123.com*). They will come and take photographs of your vehicle for a reasonable fee and provide a professional Web presentation of the photographs.

Success

In the second edition of this book (written in 2001) I predicted, "I'm bullish on eBay Motors. It will evolve into a more secure and more dynamic vehicle marketplace over the next few years and gain a significant market share at the expense of local newspapers (classified advertising)." And so it has. eBay Motors is one of eBay's great success stories.

Summary

It works! Yes, it makes sense to buy and sell vehicles in the national vehicle marketplace that eBay enables. It's not perfect. Like any other means of buying or selling, it has its problems and its expenses, but it can work for you. This chapter explains how it can work for you, whether you're a buyer or seller, safely and with minimum financial risk. For more information, read my book *eBay Motors the Smart Way*.

If you don't believe in the national market for vehicles, eBay reaches the local vehicle market too. With over 200 million eBay members, there are plenty of members in your state or your locale to consititute a significant market. About 25 percent of eBay Motors transactions take place inside the seller's state, and a percentage of those are local.

eBay Motors will continue to evolve until it becomes a more convenient vehicle emporium for both buyers and sellers. But it works well already. Try it.

28

Business to Business

Businesses can auction new and used goods and equipment on eBay's specialty auction, the Business Marketplace. These types of transactions are known as B2B (business to business). They take place between businesses rather than between consumers or between businesses and consumers. Although eBay overwhelmingly dominates consumer (personal) auctions, it has focused its B2B efforts on small businesses. The big corporations have numerous B2B transaction hubs for particular industries in which they can participate. Small businesses are left out of many of those corporate B2B hubs, and eBay gives them a home on its Business Marketplace (see Figure 28.1).

The eBay Business site, previously called Business Marketplace and Business Exchange at various times, now just includes four major categories:

- Office Technology
- Office Supplies

- Industrial

- Professional Gear

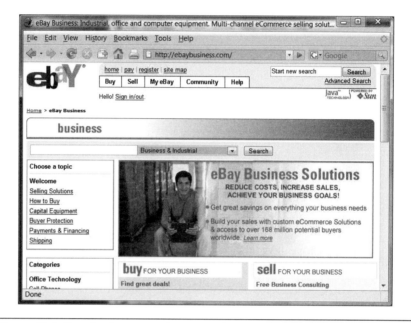

Figure 28.1 eBay Business Marketplace. ©1995-2005 eBay Inc.

Who knows what it will be called or what it will include by the time you read this? eBay continually experiments. You can find it at *http:// ebaybusiness.com*, or you might find a link to it from the eBay home page or elsewhere on eBay. B2B is growing on eBay, albeit not as fast as eBay overall. But eBay does demonstrate a commitment to it.

In addition, the Business and Industrial category in the categories on the eBay home page is similar to eBay Business except it's now called the Industry Marketplaces. It's somewhat confusing that there are two collections of business auctions. Alas, eBay isn't perfect yet. Both the eBay Business and the Business and Industrial category are subsets of the vast eBay auction listings database. Neither is really a separate auction.

Retailers don't overlook the Wholesale category on the eBay home page, which will take you to Wholesale Lots where you can buy merchandise in bulk to resell.

Basic Considerations

The eBay Business site auctions work the same as normal eBay auctions. eBay provides no special considerations or special mechanisms for conducting these B2B auctions. Thus, you need to examine the normal eBay auction buying-selling procedures to see how your business can make best use of the eBay Business site.

Review

Review the Risk and the Transaction Overhead sections of Chapters 2 and 3 to get a better feeling for how costs (buyer's or seller's overhead) may affect a transaction.

Opportunities for Buyers

Businesses, as buyers, need single items (e.g., equipment), and the eBay Business site is a good place to buy goods and equipment on which a business can realize a meaningful savings. Additionally, a business can buy the bulk merchandise it needs to fuel its everyday operations. That requires that the availability of such goods at the eBay Business site be dependable and that shipping not be a prohibitive expense.

Time Factor for Business Buyers

The time commitment for businesses to buy something is not favorable. An eBay transaction is a long process from a buyer's point of view. Whether it makes sense for a business to have an employee go through the procedure will depend on the size of the transaction and the potential for savings compared to other means of purchasing similar items. However, with the widespread use of fixed prices (*Buy It Now*), eBay has become more efficient from a business buyer's prospective. Of course, a steady diet of proxy bidding takes much of the time commitment out of buying on eBay too.

Supply for Businesses

The supply for buying at auction has yet to materialize for businesses, although there are certainly plenty of goods and equipment available at the eBay Business site and elsewhere on eBay. As eBay figures out how to make its local auctions and its Business site more useful, it will develop more potential to create a healthy and steady supply of the type of goods and equipment that businesses buy.

Individual Buyers

See Chapter 2 for similar considerations for individuals. But what works for individuals does not necessarily work for businesses.

Opportunities for Sellers

Businesses need to sell goods and equipment. Suppose you manage a small radio station that has four Sony TCM5000EV portable audio-cassette recorders (expensive field recorders for news reporters) in good condition. You are installing an all-digital studio system, and you can no longer use analog recorders even for field use. Where do you sell four TCM5000EVs? To another radio station perhaps, but beyond that, it might be tough. eBay provides a ready, willing, and capable market in which you can sell such equipment.

Businesses always have something to sell, such as depreciated industrial equipment, old office machines, old office furniture, and excess office supplies. eBay provides an appropriate place to sell such goods and equipment. Every business has these things. The primary drawback here is the shipping cost.

If you sell a heavy-duty copy machine for $2,000, the $150 for shipping isn't going to kill the deal. But if you sell a run-of-the-mill office desk for $100, the $120 for shipping will kill the deal.

This reveals one of the weaknesses of the eBay market: Large or heavy items that aren't worth much don't make good items to sell on eBay. The shipping costs will kill the deal. However, this also points out a hidden strength of eBay: A portion of the eBay market will always be local to a seller. It's not a stretch to think that you can find a local buyer via eBay who will buy your heavy office furniture and drive across town in a pickup truck to take delivery.

The Time Factor for Business Sellers

The tough consideration for businesses is: How much time does it take to sell something on eBay? An employee will have to do it. Will it ultimately be less expensive to haul the merchandise to the city dump than to attempt to sell it on eBay?

Auctions don't require much time. You need to create the advertising copy and create the eBay auction. Because the auction is a silent auction, no further action is required except to answer buyers' questions, if any. When the auction is over, you have to communicate with the buyer to arrange payment and shipping. The process seems manageable without a great deal of employee time. If buyers renege or other problems appear, the time expenditures by employees will increase. If multiple (identical) items are sold one at a time to different buyers, the time commitment also increases.

The Market for Businesses

The market for businesses will always be substantial. There are always new business start-ups looking for usable assets at reasonable prices. Many businesses need more office equipment or specialized industrial equipment each year. Even individuals need equipment for home offices and businesses.

When businesses need to get rid of something, it's often not just one item. It might be 10 cartons of $8\frac{1}{2} \times 11$ inch paper (100 reams) or 40 cases of 10W40 motor oil (480 quarts). The Business Marketplace is a good place to auction such surplus supplies to other businesses.

New Goods and Equipment

Just as in the normal eBay auctions, there are businesses selling new as well as used goods and equipment on the eBay Business site. This can make a good business for the entrepreneur who has enough capital to deal in high quantities, high-priced goods, or surplus goods.

Individual Sellers

See Chapter 3 for comparable considerations for individuals. What works for individuals, however, does not necessarily work for businesses.

Specialty Auctions

Below are a sampling of the B2B categories:

Agriculture

Construction

Food Services & Retail

Healthcare, Lab & Life Science

Industrial, Electrical & Test

Industrial Supply, MRO

Manufacturing & Metalworking

Office, Printing & Shipping

Other Industries

This list gives you an idea of what's included, but take a look at the eBay Business site and Industrial Marketplaces to get a better idea of what it has to offer. Some of the categories even have items listed by region. (This shows that eBay does in fact retain it's programming for local auctions and can feature local auctions where needed).

My Review

I reviewed the B2B marketplace in the first edition of this book soon after it started while it was still a little green. I was inclined to treat it humorously because the offerings were a little thin. Today, however, B2B on eBay is alive and well, even robust. But eBay needs to put more effort into promoting it.

The subsections below give you a flavor of this non-consumer marketplace. This is a down-to-earth business marketplace. Someday it will be much larger with a greater selection of goods. Nonetheless, it has already grown into a place quite useful to businesses.

Agriculture

Under *Agriculture & Forestry, Tractors & Farm Machinery* you will find tractors, about 625 items in the winter of 2007. See Figure 28.2 for a John Deere, which could be yours for about $17,000.

Figure 28.2 John Deere tractor.

Metalworking Equipment

Under *Manufacturing & Metalworking, Metalworking Equipment* you will find stuff that you will probably not buy for home use. Who needs a $25,000, 4-ton, vertical mill in the basement? See Figure 28.3.

Figure 28.3 A mill for all seasons.

Healthcare

In the first edition of this book I said, "It's not clear that eBay can get a good start in this category. The only two subcategories are X-ray Equipment and Stethoscopes, an odd selection." Boy, was I wrong. Today (eight years later, winter 2007) there are over 23,000 items for auction in many different subsections. This is not exactly setting the world on fire, but it's doing OK.

Restaurant

In the first edition, I said, "Restauranteurs are entrepreneurial. This could turn into a really robust B2B auction." Hey, I was right about something. The Food Services & Retail category is going crazy and has simmered into a smorgasbord of equipment, so to speak. See a nice range stove with oven in Figure 28.4.

Figure 28.4 Imperial 2000 Series range stove and oven.

A restaurant supply company in Atlanta decided to start selling used equipment on eBay. They couldn't make their efforts profitable, but they learned how to use eBay. Then they tried selling new restaurant equipment via eBay. Bingo! They developed a vigorous business selling expensive equipment to consumers with a large number of their orders coming in from California. Finally they started experimenting again selling used equipment, this time with some success. While this change in their business was taking place, they shut their doors—no more walk-in traffic—and sat at their computers. They did most of their business on eBay or over the phone.

Construction

I was talking with the owner of a metal fabrication company in Huntsville, Alabama, who told me he bought his metalworking machines on eBay at big savings. He was in the process of building a 3,000-square-foot metal building to expand his business. Naturally he looked to eBay to find construction materials. He purchased his drywall via eBay in a city a few hundred miles away because it was cheaper than buying the drywall in Huntsville, even after the shipping cost. He indicated that all together he saved about $30,000 by buying construction materials on eBay.

Warmed-Over eBay

Although included in eBay Business, *Office Products* (which includes computers and other office equipment) is an example of an auction category that is not specifically eBay Business stuff. It also appears elsewhere in eBay categories and is not unique to the eBay Business site.

Future B2B Auctions

What does the future hold for the eBay Business Marketplace? It's hard to tell. Clearly, eBay has captured the consumer-to-consumer market and the small-business-to-consumer market. Its hold on these markets is pretty tight.

The B2B market, however, is fragmented and specialized with plenty of competition. It may never be dominated by one Web auction the way eBay dominates the consumer markets. Nonetheless, eBay's B2B effort has enjoyed reasonable success and has tremendous potential for growing and for providing a useful outlet for used goods and equipment, for excess inventory, and even for new goods and equipment.

eBay is smart to focus on small business. Big business will continue to develop its own B2B transaction hubs and processes. Small business will look to eBay to establish smoothly functioning auctions to accommodate small business B2B needs.

Summary

eBay has established a solid foundation for its Business site. It's business will increase, although in smaller numbers than consumer activities. If eBay had strong local auctions, the B2B market would be better served (low-cost delivery for large or heavy items). But eBay hasn't figured out local auctions yet, and the B2B marketplace doesn't yet have the dramatic high volume enjoyed by the consumer auctions. This story isn't over yet, however. Stay tuned for further developments.

29

eBay Potpourri

No. This is not the leftovers. This is the odds and ends of eBay, mostly the relatively new stuff. And some of it is hot stuff. eBay services expand. eBay acquires new marketplaces. And eBay loses interest in marketplaces that don't grow rapidly. eBay evloves.

Marketplace Research

This is a new eBay feature, which enables you to easily research eBay sales for a particular item with up to 90 days of data (see Figure 29.1). There are three levels of fees:

- Fast Pass: $3 for two days
- Basic: $10 per month
- Pro: $25 per month

Marketplace uses Flash to display charts making the data easy to understand.

There are several auction management programs that provide similar data, and there are several dedicated research programs that do so too. They have used eBay data for several years. eBay has now joined the party and offers such research at competitive prices.

Who might use this service? A buyer of a big ticket item might feel that $3 is a reasonable fee to save perhaps ten percent on a $1,500 item ($150 savings). Most users, however, are eBay retailers who need to develop successful pricing strategies for their retail businesses. This research is invaluable.

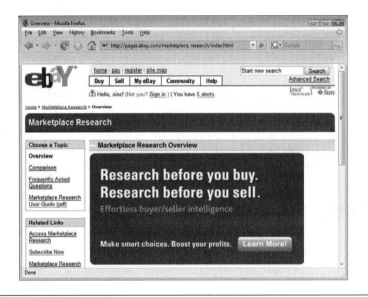

Figure 29.1 eBay Marketplace Research. ©1995-2007 eBay Inc.

Reviews and Guides

Buyers (consumers) write reviews and guides on a wide assortment of products and topics. On the eBay home page go *Reviews & Guides*.

Reviews

Searching for a review is similar to searching for a product on eBay. When you find the appropriate review, eBay gives you the average rating and the number of reviews on which the rating is based. For instance, the book *The South Beach Diet* had an average rating of 4.5 (out of 5) based on 58 reviews.

One set of reviews in which I am interested is for SLR camera lenses. eBay has done an excellent job of cataloging a huge number of lenses made by Canon, Minolta, Nikon, etc. Already many of the more popular lenses have been reviewed by multiple eBay members. This set of reviews has a long ways to go before it will be really useful, but it's well on its way. In a few years it could be the definitive lens review location on the Web. This type of information is difficult to find, even on the Web. But it is valuable information for prospective buyers of high quality (expensive) lenses.

Guides

Moving right along to guides, we find that the guides are written by knowledgeable volunteer eBay members. Naturally, I have read the one entitled *Camera Lens Buying Guide*, and it's a brief but pretty good guide. It would certainly help a novice make good choices in buying suitable lenses.

You find the guides much the same as you do other kinds of searches on eBay. It's quick and easy so long as you can think of some good keywords. If you're trying to buy something about which you know nothing, a visit to the eBay Guides may provide you with the expertise you need to make good buying decisions.

Solutions Directory

The Solutions Directory has been around for a long time with its link buried deep in the eBay website content. Today, however, there is a huge number of people doing a serious volume of selling on eBay. Thus, the link has migrated to the eBay home page. This directory contains software vendors and other vendors that assist eBay retailers in a variety of business activities. If you're an eBay retailer, it's a great place to find what you need to run your business.

Pro Stores

When you want to establish your own ecommerce website, you find a host ISP (Internet service provider) that offers the features you need to establish and maintain a productive site. eBay Pro Stores (see Figure 29.2) is a host ISP that offers functions aimed at online retailers. Pro Stores seem to have little to do with eBay. I'm not even sure why eBay is in this business other than it wants to provide a complete service to its top eBay retailers. Nonetheless, Pro Stores is a first rate service that makes it easy for anyone to set up and operate an attractive ecommerce website.

Figure 29.2 eBay Pro Stores. ©1995-2007 eBay Inc.

Apartments on Rent.com

Looking for an apartment or house to rent and occupy? Rent.com is the place to go (see Figure 29.3). On the eBay home page go *Apartments on Rent.com*. It works great in cities and large towns but not as well in medium to small towns. It has lots of features. It can even help you find an apartment mate. And it's nationwide, a terrific resource. It operates (and is licensed) in most states.

Or do you have apartment units or a house for which you want to find tenants? Again, Rent.com is a terrific resource. You can list your unit online. If the listing results in a lease, you pay eBay (Rent.com) $375. You can see it's designed for long-term rentals (e.g., one-year leases).

This is a relatively recent acquisition of eBay and demonstrates that eBay is interested in adding to its marketplaces with marketplace mechanisms that work well and are national in scope.

Figure 29.3 eBay Rent.com. ©1995-2007 eBay Inc.

Want It Now

eBay has had a Wanted section in the past, but it wasn't very popular. This is a reincarnation. It not only enables you to notify the world that you want something—that you're willing to buy something—but it even lets you place your request in a specific category. And it's free. What a deal!

Will it work this time around? Who knows? It seems to me that a beautification and categorization scheme isn't going to do much for this turkey. But what do I know? One thing I know for certain is that you should try it, just like you should at least try all new eBay ideas. You never know when something is going to click.

There's a link to *Want It Now* on the eBay home page. It will take you to the webpage where you can look at the listings posted according to the time last filed which shows at the top of the list.

You can also post your own wantings for the world to respond. But don't hold your breath.

In a more serious tone, I will say eBay deserves credit for continuing to experiment with this and other ideas that haven't worked yet. And I wish them good luck.

eBay Pulse

If you want to get your fingers on the pulse of eBay, this is definitely the place to go. Why anyone would want to do that, I have no idea, but if you do, click on the *eBay Pulse* link on the eBay home page. This is the eBay center for "Trends - Hot Picks - Cool Stuff."

The interesting feature about eBay Pulse is that it has categories. So for each category you get the top ten most popular search words and the Stores with the top five number of listings. In addition, you get the top ten most watched items. I don't know where all this gets you, but I guess if you check in to observe on a regular basis, you'll know what's hot and what's not. I would like to say I found all this somewhat useless except that I discovered a new camera Store in the Cameras & Photo category from which I made a purchase. So give eBay Pulse a try!

Giving Works

eBay has been active in encouraging charity activities from the early days. Many celebrities have donated items to be auctioned off to make money for charities, and so forth. With Giving Works, eBay is building an auction system to accommodate charity ecommerce. It facilitates not only the sale of items to raise money for charities but also enables convenient purchases for buyers who want to buy things in a way that will benefit charities. You can reach it by clicking on the Giving Works link on the eBay home page.

As a seller, you can designate a certain percentage of your sales revenue to go to the charity of your choice (picked from an eBay list). A blue and yellow ribbon icon indicates to buyers that your auction is a contributor to a charity. Sellers take part in the Mission Fish system, which offers the following:

- Verification
- Charity listing tool
- Donation processing
- Tracking
- Tax receipts

This system keeps you honest and accounts for the donated funds. It brings credibility to to the Giving Works system. You can make a contribution from one sale or all your sales. In other words, you can contribute as much or as little as you please.

Another way for charties to raise money is to sell direct to the public. Again Mission Fish enables nonprofits to make sales after going through a registration process. And Mission Fish provides donation processing and management services. This is a serious opportunity for charities that want to find a new way of raising funds.

How can buyers take part in this? You don't have to look through all the eBay listings to find the charitable icons. You can go to Giving Works and shop in the categories listed there. Only charitable auctions are in the listings at Giving Works.

All in all this new eBay center has lots of possibilities for benefiting nonprofits. That's something to keep in mind when you buy or when you want to raise money for your favorite charity.

Something Old – Elance

The Elance service (*http://elance.com*) had been affiliated with eBay for so long that I reported in the Second Edition that eBay had purchased it. Don't know where I read that, but it's not true. Today it no longer even has a link on the eBay home page as it did for many years.

The name stands for electronic freelancing. Today it is a successful, but not wildly successful, marketplace that offers certain professional services. That is, the sellers sell professional services, and the buyers buy and use such services. But Elance has a twist to it. The sellers do the bidding, so to speak.

How does this work? The buyer posts a project requiring services, and sellers bid to do the work. Theoretically, the low bidder gets the project. It's pretty straightforward, but it has a few gimmicks built in to insure that it works well.

Professional Services

First, this marketplace does not accommodate all professional services. Your service needs to be on the list before you can make this work for you. Second, this is really advertising and marketing for your skilled services, and as such it doesn't come free or even at a nominal cost. It will cost you real money to participate. Third, Elance doesn't guarantee your success. The low bidder isn't necessarily the winner.

This list will give you an idea of the categories in which you can participate:

1. Design
2. Programming
3. Websites
4. Writing
5. Other (e.g., accounting, photography, training)

To give you an idea of the depth of the categories, Administrative Support (under Other) had 20 subcategories in early 2007. You don't have to sift through these categories. You can also use the Elance search feature to find Elance services.

Elance changes constantly always attempting to identify categories that will work. But the categories are anything but open ended. Of all the services and consulting available, the Elance categories represent but a small percentage.

You might also wonder what the term "professional services" means. To Elance it means whatever they can define that generates some business. A more descriptive term might be "white collar" services. Clearly, Elance does not include "blue collar" services.

Seller's Cost

You are skilled and want to provide services working from home or in an office with a small staff. You understand that to keep busy you have to spend half your time marketing your services. Is there another way?

I doubt that Elance will solve your marketing dilemma. There doesn't seem to be enough work available on Elance to keep most freelancers busy. But if you can pick up some work with a minimum amount of marketing activity, you're further ahead. Elance can help you get that additional work.

Elance Fees

Elance charges fees to professionals. To be listed as a professional services provider, Elance offers a number of packages at different prices. Check the Elance website for the latest pricing.

Overhead

The Elance fees are not the only cost. For Elance, you must be ready to bid on projects quickly, accurately, and efficiently. This means you must be well organized, and you must be organized digitally. It takes time and energy to pursue a strategy of constant bidding on Elance.

How It Works

The buyer defines the work project. The sellers bid to do the work on the project in a reverse auction (low bid wins). Many of the projects are small and are often just fishing attempts for businesses.

What Buyers Do

The buyer has a work project. He puts it in writing. To use Elance he can take two approaches: He can review the resumes of appropriate service providers and choose a few to send his project to for bidding, or he can post it on Elance to open it to all for bidding.

What Sellers Do

Sellers put their best face forward and bid a price for a project. There is no obligation, however, to bid on anything.

A Buyer's Opportunity

Elance claims hordes of potential buyers (of professional services) visit Elance every week. It also claims thousands of freelancers ready to go to work. However, it appears to me that this is a buyer's market.

Sellers

As a seller, if you want to make something out of Elance, you'll have to hustle. There appear to me to be more people ready to work than there is work to go around. It's unlikely that you can rely upon Elance as your primary source of business. The real question is, Is it a worthwhile source of business?

To get business, you'll not only have to pay Elance but you'll have to get organized to efficiently work the Elance system. Only experimentation and hard work will reveal whether Elance is worth it for you.

Buyers

As a buyer, Elance provides you with an great opportunity to get high quality work done on the cheap. Let's take a look at how that works.

Working at Home

First, the market is unbalanced. There are apparently more sellers than buyers. Second, many freelancers work out of their home with minimal overhead and can do the work less expensively for you than people working in an office. Third, most freelancers don't charge enough. They establish fees based on what they need to make to get by and seldom cover the benefits they would get on a normal job. Such benefits typically add 10 to 40 percent to an employee's salary.

The bottom line is that you can purchase needed services at bargain rates. The question then becomes, How can I use these services?

Keep in mind that a considerable percentage of white collar workers work at home today. The Census Bureau shows Colorado with 4.9 percent of workers working at home while some communities have as high as 6.4 percent home workers according to the *Rocky Mountain News*, June 5, 2002. These are freelancers. These figures, however, don't take into account employees who work at home for employers, so-called "telecommuters."

The Maryland Department of Transportation did a survey that indicated 12 percent of the employees in the Washington metro area telecommuted in 1998 (for at least part of their work week).

What do these figures mean? Simply that a significant percentage of the national workforce works at home. With inexpensive telephone service, fax, cheap computers, and the Internet, one can work at home, do productive work for a business, and fit right in at the office from afar. In fact, my wife telecommutes two days a week for her employer (a major corporation) and gets several days' work done on each of those days with no meetings to distract her.

If you have a business and haven't tried using a freelance teleworker, Elance may provide a money-saving opportunity for you to experiment with out-of-the-office workers; that is, you can "outsource" the work. If you have an eBay business, you will need some kind of white collar work occasionally, if not regularly, and Elance may provide just what you need.

Hiring

Your first reaction might be that it's hard to hire people in distant places. You can't meet them. You won't have any local references for them. And they can't come into the office to do part of their work. That's all true and perhaps will prevent you from hiring some freelancers for some tasks. Nonetheless, for many tasks or projects, such considerations will not be a barrier.

First, although you can't meet them, you can have an extensive telephone conservation with them, perhaps more conveniently than meeting them. Second, you can review a freelancer's track record on Elance. It's perhaps easier to do via Elance than it is to do for a local freelancer. Third, email and the capability to attach a file to an email message greatly improves business communication. It means that you can expect to pass back and forth with a freelancer almost any type of information required for productive work. In addition, there are dozens of ways for workers to collaborate via the Internet. In fact, working with people you've never met and never see face to face has become commonplace.

Habit Breaking

What do you do when you want to make 10,000 entries in your database from electronic documents, and your staff is too thin to handle it? Do you ask around to find out if anyone knows someone? Do you run a classified ad? Do you call a temporary employment service? Do you post a Help Wanted ad at the local supermarket? It seems like using Elance might be the easiest way to get this task done.

It's not easy, however, to break old habits. You have to try something new and be successful. Elance provides you with a chance to try something new conveniently, get the job done, save money, and perhaps get even higher quality services than you might otherwise.

Give Elance a good look soon. You may find something there that you can use, even for small tasks and projects.

Ad Format

This is a strange name for an auction that is not really an auction but rather an advertisement. Real estate has been handled this way on eBay for a long time. Real estate auctions are not legally binding, although buyers or sellers who renege on auction results are begging for trouble. Such auctions are realistically advertisements and invitations to negotiate. This is specifically reflected in the special fees eBay charges, that is, high insertion fees and no final value fees.

Now this concept has been extended to other categories such as:

- Websites and businesses for sale
- Trade show booths
- Prefabricated buildings
- Travel
- Specialty services

It is this last category that is interesting in light of the fact that eBay doesn't provide a link to Elance any longer. It appears that the Specialty Services category under Ad Format is eBay's answer to Elance. It's not as robust yet, but it's on its way. Take a look at these subcategories:

- Advice & Instruction
- Artistic Services
- Custom Clothing & Jewelry
- eBay Auction Services
- Graphic & logo Design, Media Editing & Duplication
- Printing & Personalization
- Restoration & Repair
- Web & Computer Services

It's a start, and in the next edition of this book, we'll see how far eBay can carry this new endeavor. Keep in mind that eBay never figured out how to do local auctions. Otherwise, Craig's List wouldn't have wildly expended across the globe like it did. The provision of services for many types of services is strictly a local activity. Whether eBay is the proper place for a services marketplace remains to be seen.

Nonetheless, a national services marketplace is badly needed in this age of outsourcing. Elance hasn't captured this market. It's up for grabs, and eBay is taking a stab at it.

eBay Changes

eBay is not software that comes out with a new version each year. eBay evolves daily. When upgrades or new schemes are completed, eBay installs them immediately. eBay is an ongoing experiment. Today's latest eBay schemes are tomorrow's primary features. And some of the less popular features you find on eBay today may disappear overnight. eBay is exciting because of what it can do for you today—and tomorrow as well.

30

eBay International

eBay provides a smorgasbord of international buying opportunities. eBay operates auctions in over 32 foreign countries:

Australia (English)

Austria

Belgium

Canada (English)

Central America (Mercado Libre)

China

France

Germany

Hong Kong (English)

India (English)

Ireland (English)

Italy

Korea

Malaysia

Netherlands

New Zealand (English)

Phillippines (English)

Poland

Singapore (English)

Spain

South America (Mercado Libre)

Sweden

Switzerland

Taiwan

United Kingdom (English)

You can find the links to these auctions on eBay's home page.

This represents the results of an amazing expansion, which continues. Don't overlook the fact that PayPal continues to expand internationally too. Consequently, you can go shopping in many faraway places.

As a seller, a quick way to expand your market for your merchandise is to sell internationally (i.e., to foreign bidders) via eBay in the US.

Tally

My tally shows eBay serving a population of about 1.5 billion people in English.

Buying Far Away

With all those foreign auctions available, you can find something you want if you can navigate the auctions, or you can find something to import for sale in your retail business. You might be able to find some interesting, even exotic, merchandise on eBay's foreign auctions (see Figures 30.1 India and 30.2 Poland). They present a unique opportunity to shop abroad without ever leaving your home. You have five serious considerations, however, that might make foreign shopping difficult.

Figure 30.1 eBay India. ©1995-2007 eBay Inc.

Language

First, you must be able to search and find items. Then you must be able to pick out items in which you are interested. Finally, you must be able to read the auction ad. If you can't speak German, this is going to be difficult to do on eBay's auction in Germany. Try Babel Fish (*http://world.altavista.com*), or one of the other online translators, to translate the auction ads for you.

Communication

Once you want to bid, or are a winning bidder, you will have to communicate with the seller. Unlike most foreign buyers who buy on eBay US, you cannot count on the foreign sellers speaking English. You will most often have to communicate in the local language. Use Babel Fish to translate your email messages into a foreign language or translate a foreign-language email into English.

Figure 30.2 eBay Poland

Currency

The eBay auctions in other countries use the local currency. You will have to make arrangements to pay for the items you purchase in the currency of the auction. Some sellers may agree to take payment in US dollars, but it's not something you can count on. Some sellers may accept US credit cards. Some may accept international money orders. Some may accept PayPal, which has a built-in currency exchanger you can use. But it's up to you to find a practical means of paying that is acceptable to the seller.

Shipping

Shipping becomes a problem for purchasing in many foreign countries because distances are so long. You have to make a financial judgment as to whether the shipping costs preclude purchasing the specific item you want to buy abroad.

Taxes

You need to learn about taxation in the country in which you want to make a purchase. US citizens are used to considering the sales tax (paid to states). Similar taxation in foreign countries may seem abusive and financially unacceptable. Indeed, the local taxation may be complex or have multiple layers compared to the simple sales tax collected in the US. Probably, you will be exempt from such taxation, but that is something you need to determine.

Then there is the import tax (tariff). When you import something to the US, you may have to pay an import duty. There are certain exemptions, but the law is not simple, and you might get surprised. Some things are even banned for import.

What to Do?

If you are serious about buying in foreign countries on eBay, it will require some research on your part to be successful. Nonetheless, eBay will permit you to bid on its auctions abroad without obtaining special memberships, and foreign buying on eBay opens opportunities to you not easily available by other means. Of course, you can always travel abroad to buy items, but that's expensive.

If you're a retail seller on eBay, the capability to buy on foreign eBays presents a wonderful new opportunity. There is a huge amount of merchandise sold abroad that is not available in the US but that will sell well here. In buying such merchandise abroad for resale in the US, eBay gives you a cost-effective import opportunity unimagined before the Web. Although you probably can't buy enough merchandise at an eBay foreign auction to sell in volume, you can make contacts with foreign people who will help you import in larger quantities. Read my book *eBay Global the Smart Way* for more information.

Selling Internationally

This is a no-brainer. If you're willing to collect payment and ship abroad, you can expand your sales significantly.

For Occasional Sellers

This strategy is appropriate even for occasional sellers. It takes a little research to do it right, but buyers abroad are often aggressive bidders who can push up the bidding.

It's one thing to sell to people abroad via an eBay US auction. It's another to actually offer merchandise for sale on eBay auctions in foreign countries. If you do so, you will have many of the same problems as buyers, so read the earlier section *Buying Far Away*. You will have to consider language, communication, currency, shipping, and taxes in addition to discovering merchandise that will sell well. Keep in mind that foreign countries have cultural differences far greater than the differences between the states in the US. Generally, what sells well in Nebraska can be expected to sell well in North Carolina. What sells well in France may not sell at all in Germany.

For Retail Sellers

One reason sellers on eBay have been able to sell so well to people in other countries is that certain US merchandise is popular but unavailable or much more expensive.

Selling Via eBay US

Your job is to find out what merchandise sells well abroad. It is only a percentage of all US merchandise. What it happens to be in any particular country depends on local tastes, taxation, commercial customs, competing goods, and a variety of other considerations. It's your job to find out and meet the market by auctioning specific goods on eBay US.

Books about Computers and Software

Computer books sell many places in Europe for about three times the cost in the US. Why? That's a tough question to answer, but they do. That presents an opportunity for someone like me to sell computer books in Europe at a profit but also at a price considerably below the local market. Many high-tech personnel in Europe can read English, making the computer book market in Europe an attractive opportunity for US authors and publishers even for books in English.

But you don't necessarily have to find out anything to make foreign sales on a haphazard basis. Foreign buyers will come to you when you sell something they need or want. Indeed, such buyers are a constant presence in many categories of auctions, particularly auctions for consumer and high-tech items.

Specific Opportunities

For a retailer, occasional selling on eBay's foreign auctions is more trouble than it's worth for most items. The real opportunity is becoming a specialist in one country and making it a business.

With a little determination, you can learn to communicate in a foreign language (or use Babel Fish). That's perhaps the toughest part. Learning the commercial byways and the taxation aspects is almost certainly easier. Finding products that make sense to export is a matter of endless experimentation.

Certain US merchandise is popular abroad. If you can sell it on a foreign eBay auction profitably but at a lower cost than it is available locally, you have a cost-effective business opportunity not imagined before the Web. Go for it!

Get a Partner

Want to short-circuit the learning curve? Instead of learning the foreign language and byways, find a US resident (an immigrant from the target country) who knows the byways already. Form a partnership and start an import/export business using eBay.

An alternative and perhaps a long shot is to find someone in the target country to be your partner, that is, find him or her via the Internet (e.g., via eBay). It's difficult enough to form workable partnerships with direct personal contact. It's clearly a long shot to arrange a partnership with someone you don't know via the Internet. But virtual business organizations are becoming common.

The important thing to remember here is that most people will not do what is suggested here. The effort is simply too much. The entry to the import/export business is said to have a high *threshold* that will keep most people out. After all, how many people will learn French in order to sell American merchandise in France? If you're willing to cross that threshold, you may find it a challenging and profitable venture.

The Threshold Is Lower

The threshold to enter the import/export business remains high because of language barriers. But due to the Web, the capital requirements have dropped. Formerly, to enter the import-export business took significant capital for travel and communication as well as the personal effort to master the language learning curve. Today, due to the Web (specifically eBay) and Internet communications, the capital required to start an import/export business is potentially much lower even though the learning curve remains as high.

Who's the Competition?

If capital requirements are lower today, where is your competition? An immigrant to the US who speaks English and already knows the language and byways of the target country, is not only a potential partner but a potential competitor. By learning English and living in the US, immigrants potentially understand the two cultures well enough to make the import/export business work on eBay.

You need to be cautious about what you export. There are certain highly competitive export businesses that almost certainly will not be good opportunities for you. But these are usually major industries that are not the niche opportunities in which you are more likely to get involved. There are also some products banned from export. You don't want to get into trouble with the feds by exporting the wrong things.

Professional Exporting

If you want to be an aggressive seller, you can use eBay both at home and abroad to get yourself into the export business and still use eBay as your marketplace. To take the business seriously means you must learn the export regulations, get export licenses (if necessary), use customs brokers both in the US and abroad, and do a dozen other things to make your exporting successful.

Resources

A good source of import/export information is World Trade Press (*http://www.worldtradepress.com*). They provide everything from books to up-to-date specialized trade services via the Web that will keep you informed. If you need a customs broker, A&A Contract Customs Brokers, Ltd. (*http://www.aacb.com*), is looking for eBay business. For information on import/export with Canada, try Canada Post BorderFree (*http://borderfree.com*). And don't overlook my book *eBay Global the Smart Way.*

Don't Forget PayPal

In the first six months after eBay bought PayPal, it expanded to include 38 foreign countries and exchanged money in five currencies. When you learn more about the import/export business, you will realize what a fabulous service this is. Suffice to say, it makes taking payment much safer, something that many experienced eBay members can appreciate. PayPal is a big story on the international scene. Think of PayPal as an international bank that facilitates both sides of the transaction easily, quickly, and inexpensively. If you do so, you suddenly wake up to the fact that PayPal is going to take over the world, literally. It makes small business consumer import/export so easy that it's a no-brainer for anyone using eBay. And as a retailer, you can substantially expand your markets for your goods with a minimum of bureaucratic hassle.

Summary

The genius of eBay is that it creates a huge national market for goods and even services. But some goods sell well in the international markets as well. As the eBay foreign auctions grow and as foreign people bid in the US auctions, eBay will come to encompass a greater variety of goods and services and provide new markets. This evolution provides new opportunities for eBay members.

eBay's foreign auctions deliver the eBay magic to new markets. Such auctions also open opportunities for all eBay members as eBay takes on more of an international character. Although part of the eBay market has always been international, the new foreign eBay auctions, and PayPal as well, will rapidly expand the type of people-to-people and retail-to-consumer trade that eBay auctions support.

31

Shopping.com

Shopping.com, a comparative shopping ecommerce website, is the newest member of the eBay family. It adds yet another way for eBay sellers to sell their goods. It gives buyers an opportunity to compare product prices, product reviews, and vendor reviews. It's similar to the following programs:

Bizrate, *http://bizrate.com*

My Simon, *http://www.mysimon.com*

NexTag, *http://www.nextag.com*

PriceGrabber, *http://www.pricegrabber.com*

Pricescan, *http://www.pricescan.com*

Shopzilla.com, *http://www.shopzilla.com*

As you can see by the screen (Figure 31.1), the vendors are arranged on a list. In the first column is the name of the vendor. The second column contains a rating for the vendor based on reviews submitted by customers. As a consumer, with a quick review you can spot the lowest price and check out that vendor's rating. The product itself is also rated by consumers, and you can check out those reviews at the top of the page.

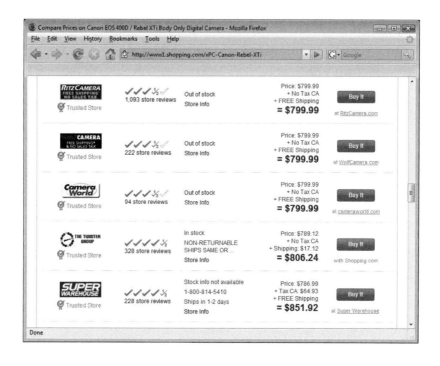

Figure 31.1 Shopping.com showing the comparisons for a specific model camera. ©2000-2006 Shopping.com

In the example above, the price for the camera ranges from $390 to $480. There are 19 vendor comparisons in all with four shown on the first screen. You enter your ZIP code in order for the listing to calculate your sales tax and shipping cost.

For Consumers

This is a wonderful and efficient way to shop for certain types of goods. The products are normally standard manufactured goods. If a product includes a guarantee from the manufacturer, it probably doesn't matter where you buy it. Why not buy it online from the vendor offering the lowest price—so long as the vendor has a good consumer rating? I buy a lot of products on eBay and Froogle, but I find comparative shopping websites a good place to buy products too; and Shopping.com is one of the best.

Below the listings you will find sponsored listings (See Figure 31.2). These are simply advertisements. Sometimes the sponsored listings include featured listing from eBay. And below that you will find Buyer Guides. These are at a variety of websites, relevant to products, and can be quite useful. In this case, one is the *Digital Camera Buying Guide* at eBay.

Figure 31.2 Shopping.com showing the sponsored listings and Buyer Guides. ©2000-2006 Shopping.com

Where?

Where do you find comparative shopping websites? I usually don't go to Shopping.com directly. I go to Froogle to look for a product. On the right side of the listing resulting from a Froogle (or Google) search are a number of text ads. There are usually several comparative shopping websites in the text ads. One might be Shopping.com. Click on the ad, and you go directly to the comparative shopping website featuring a product identical or similar to the one that's the subject of your Froogle search.

Perhaps the primary reason to shop the comparative websites is to get information about the quality of customer service practiced by individual vendors. Customer reviews tell the story. Another primary reason is to get the lowest price from a vendor one can trust (as indicated by the customer reviews).

Destination

You ultimately end up at a vendor's website where you can buy the product you seek. The website handles the transaction completely, and Shopping.com doesn't get involved. Shopping is just an advertising directory for products.

For Sellers

What does Shopping.com offer for sellers? It's one of the top three retail websites, and it delivers over 20 million customer leads to five thousand ecommerce retailers every months. (Those are 2004 figures.) Pretty impressive. And best of all, you can use a datafeed to insert your products or have your products automatically retrieved from your ecommerce website. You don't even have to do much to be a participant.

You pay per click; that is, every time someone clicks on the link to your online store, you pay Shopping.com a fee. It doesn't matter whether you make a sale or not. You pay for the "lead."

This marketing mechanism is not necessarily meant for the tens of thousands of eBay PowerSellers. Rather it is meant for high volume sellers selling standard products. Indeed, many of the leading high-volume national mail order retailers that now have websites are participants in Shopping.com. Consequently, if you have high volume sales and have experimented successfully with pay-per-click marketing, this may be the shopping portal for you.

Interestingly, some comparative shopping websites include occasional eBay retailers in their comparisons. Shopping.com doesn't seem to do that currently, but one speculates that it may do so in the future.

Summary

Comparative shopping websites provide valuable features to customers. Because they do, sellers find a lot of potential buyers when they participate in such ecommerce portals. It appears eBay hasn't done much yet to integrate Shopping.com into the eBay cosmos, but that is likely to change in the future.

32

Craig's List

eBay never figured out how to do local auctions effectively. When a seller lists an item, she indicates where she lives. The eBay listing database can thereby provide a listing of items according to place as well as according to category. One problem is that many sellers do not provide the correct information regarding place. For instance, many sellers indicate a general place such as the "United States," which doesn't enable the eBay database to place the listing in a local auction. Another problem is that not many buyers pay much attention to eBay's local marketplaces. Why would they? A national marketplace provides many more choices.

Yet some items cannot be sold in a national marketplace. Items that are too large or too heavy to be shipped inexpensively and are inexpensive too cannot be sold. For instance, a sofa worth $250 located in Portland, Oregon, is unlikely to be sold to a buyer in Joplin, Missouri, when the cost of transportation is $200 (by truck). On the other hand, the seller can probably sell the sofa to someone in Portland and the transportation cost will be nominal. The buyer is likely to borrow a friend's pick-up truck or van and drive across town to pick it up. Thus, it's clear that a local marketplace is needed for many items.

Waiting to Be Revived

Whatever the reasons, eBay has not found the magic formula for making local auctions work well. It has even ceased to offer local auctions, although the eBay database continues to have the capability to provide local auctions as it did in prior years. Perhaps someday local auctions will be revived.

Craig's List (*http://craigslist.com*), started about the same time as eBay in the mid 1990s, and flourished in the San Francisco Bay Area. Later it expanded to several other cities such as New York and Chicago. Unlike eBay's moribund local marketplaces, Craig's List local city marketplaces have prospered. Lately Craig's List has expanded into additional cities. The number is now up in the hundreds and growing.

In early 2004, I started reporting on Craig's List in my eBay books. Why? Because a book about eBay, in my estimation, is a book about the dominant online marketplaces. Clearly, Craig's List with its relatively recent expansion into hundreds of new cities (see Figure 32.1) has emerged as the predominant local online marketplace in most of the cities (and city regions) where it operates. Apparently eBay thinks so too. In August 2004, it bought a 25 percent interest in Craig's List.

Local Marketplaces

A Craig's List local marketplace online is strictly local. If you list an item on Craig's List in your home city, it won't be seen in another city. Thus, you are restricted to just one Craig's List city when you want to sell something.

How It Works

Craig's List is part local community online and part local marketplace online. Here I will cover just the marketplace aspect of Craig's List, but you might investigate the community aspect of Craig's List if you are so inclined.

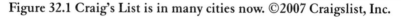

Figure 32.1 Craig's List is in many cities now. ©2007 Craigslist, Inc.

Listings

The listings are like classified listings in a newspaper. The latest listing entered is the first one that buyers see. A seller can create a listing free and enter it as many times as he desires. Consequently, as a buyer looks down through the long list of items for sale, he will find listings occasionally repeated.

Craig's List has only a few categories (compared to eBay's thousands of categories), but a buyer can search for items using keywords and effectively narrow the search. Thus, if you're looking for a Ford Taurus, you start with the category *cars+trucks* and then search using the keywords "Ford" and "Taurus." That will produce a list of Ford Tauruses for sale locally. For some items, the list will be short. For other items, the list may be many pages long (about 50 items per page).

As you might imagine, the kind of items you find on Craig's List are the type that don't sell well in a national online marketplace. The sofa mentioned above is an illustrative example of why Craig's List fills a need. The furniture market is big on Craig's List.

The Ford Taurus mentioned above is an example of an item that sells well in both national and local online marketplaces. You will find vehicles listed on both eBay and Craig's List.

Job Market

Craig's List also features local job "want" ads. This is a very popular feature but one beyond the scope of this book. But if you need someone to work for you or you're looking for a job, you will want to check out the Craig's List job marketplace.

Revenue

Craig's List doesn't charge for listings except for employers' listings. Thus, the revenue generated to operate Craig's List comes from employers looking for employees. That may change in the future, but currently listings are free for goods and services.

Drawbacks

Craig's List works surprisingly well but nonetheless has a few obvious drawbacks:

1. There are no instruction books on how to use Craig's List to sell. Consequently, many of the listings tend to be useless, for one reason or another, to prospective buyers.

2. Communication between sellers and prospective buyers is difficult. Mailing-list businesses regularly pirate sellers' names and contact information from Craig's List. Consequently, sellers are reluctant to include their direct contact information in their listings.

3. Photographs are not provided consistently by sellers. It always astounds me to see someone advertising a sofa for sale without including a photograph. Unfortunately, about a third of the furniture listings do not have photographs rendering them completely useless to prospective buyers.

4. Craig's List is not as easy to use as eBay for either buyers or sellers. This eliminates a lot of potential participants.

5. There are few rules for Craig's List participants. You are on your own. Of course, local laws apply as they do for local offline transactions.

6. There is no reputation system as there is on eBay. You take your chances. On the other hand, you are likely to have direct contact with the other party, and the exchange of money for goods is likely to be in person. You have local recourse for unfair dealings or fraud.

Sellers

For sellers, the principles are the same as for eBay. Provide plenty of text to describe your item in your listing and always provide a photograph(s). In addition, make it easy for prospective buyers to contact you. Unlike eBay, this is a marketplace in which buyers and sellers are likely to talk with each other and even meet each other as the transaction comes together.

Remember, when you relist, your listing goes to the top. It makes sense to relist your listing as things change or to add additional information based on market feedback. When your listing is many pages down the list, it's time to relist too. But don't relist too often. You will bore prospective buyers and give them the impression that you are desperate to sell.

Buyers

There are too many useless listings on Craig's List. Ignore them. Otherwise, you could waste a lot of your time. However, sometimes you are desperate to buy something that is not often available. In that case, contact the sellers of the useless listings and ask for more information.

After picking a category, use the search engine on Craig's List to narrow your search. That will make your search much more efficient and fulfilling.

There are more delivery possibilities than on eBay. Ask the seller to deliver. There may be a delivery service (e.g., for furniture) in the city that you can use for a reasonable fee (and you might find the delivery service on Craig's List). Borrow (or rent) a suitable vehicle to pick up an item. FedEx, UPS, DHL, and the Postal Services are seldom used for Craig's List purchases.

Make absolutely sure you have a solid purchase agreement (oral or in writing) before you go to take delivery. If you rent a truck to pick up a sofa and you get to the seller's house to find that she sold it to someone else yesterday, you probably have no recourse.

Keep in mind also that a lot of the assumptions you make about transactions on eBay may not apply to transactions on Craig's List. After all, there is no feedback system.

Retailers

Few retailers will find Craig's List an accommodating marketplace. You can only list in one city. Craig's List does not accommodate bulk listings. And Craig's List was not designed to promote retail listings. It's also clear that if Craig's List were inundated by retail listings, it would lose its effectiveness. Consequently, go easy on Craig's List if you're a retailer. It might be a good place for token advertising, but it's probably not a good place to sell a lot of merchandise.

Marketplaces

In the San Francisco Bay Area and the early cities, the Craig's List marketplaces are mature with lots of stuff for sale. In many of the new cities resulting from the recent dramatic expansion, the Craig's List marketplaces are not yet mature. Give them a few years to grow, and they will be much better places to buy or sell. You can find Craig's Lists in the following areas:

US

All 50 states and hundreds of cities

Abroad

Over 50 countries and hundreds of cities

This represents a huge expansion from just a few years ago. For instance under Colorado, a modestly populated state, Craig's List has five cities or areas:

Colorado Springs

Denver

Fort Collins

Pueblo

Rocky Mountains

Take a look at Canada. Craig's List is currently in 17 cities or provinces:

Calgary

Edmonton

Hamilton

Kitchener-Waterloo

London

Montreal

Newfoundland

Novia Scotia

Ottawa

Prince Edward Island

Quebec City

Saskatchewan

Toronto

Vancouver

Victoria

Windsor

Winnipeg

In France you will find Craig's List in:

Lyon

Marseille

Nice

Paris

China has Craig's List in three cities currently:

Beijing

Hong Kong

Shanghai

The next time you look at Craig's List, undoubtedly the list will be even more robust. This is a marketplace you will want to visit in your online shopping or use to make online sales that are appropriate only for your locale.

Kijiji

This is eBay's latest effort to establish local marketplaces. It is not offered in the US, presumably due to competition with Craig's List. (Remember, eBay has a 25 percent interest in Craig's List.) Nonetheless, Kijiji (*http://kijiji.com*), owned by eBay, is strong in Europe and Asia where it also competes with Craig's List.

Summary

The national market is not always the best place to sell certain types of items. Local markets can be robust and effective too. eBay's early efforts in local markets were lackluster. Now it owns Kijiji and has a 25 percent interest in Craig's List, both effective local marketplaces.

33

Google-Froogle

At one time not too long ago, the most successful means of retailing on the Web was to create a storefront website and get found by the search engines. What emerged in the early 2000s, however, was a large online marketplace called eBay that provided enormous retailing opportunities to online retailers. eBay had become a primary gateway to ecommerce. At the same time, Google with over half of the search engine traffic also emerged as a primary ecommerce gateway. At the end of 2002, Froogle was born. As a search engine, Froogle returns only products for sale at fixed prices, nothing else. It became a full-fledged feature of Google in the spring of 2004. Today eBay and Google-Froogle provide a gateway for perhaps 70 percent of all consumer online sales. (This is my estimate, my opinion, not a scientific measure.)

As mentioned in Chapter 32, eBay is essentially an online marketplace. When another online marketplace comparable in volume to eBay emerges, it is appropriate to cover it in this book. Consequently, Chapter 32 covers Craig's List, the preeminent local marketplace, and this chapter covers Google-Froogle, a large national marketplace (in effect) which together with eBay commands a huge portion (market share) of online consumer commerce.

Note that eBay is Google-Froogle's biggest advertiser. Consequently, eBay and Google-Froogle overlap.

In my first eBay books starting in 1999, I was encouraged by everyone to include information on the Yahoo and Amazon auctions. I didn't do so because eBay had a 90+ percent market share of online auctions. Yahoo and Amazon auctions were insignificant.

Amazon became very successful as an online department store. It even launched a marketplace for independent online retailers. But the scope of its merchandise offering is limited, and its marketplace of independent retailers has never seriously challenged eBay.

Early in the history of ecommerce Yahoo was the primary gateway to ecommerce. By the time eBay emerged as a primary online marketplace, Yahoo's dominance as a search engine had declined substantially. Google succeeded Yahoo as the dominant search engine and today has twice as much traffic. With such a reshuffling going on, it didn't seem appropriate to cover any online marketplace except eBay.

But times change. Today, whether you are a buyer or seller, if you find eBay useful, you may find Google-Froogle useful too. And other marketplaces may not be worth your attention. Consequently, I devote space to Craig's List and Google-Froogle.

Google

Using Google to find things to buy is fruitful for buyers. Thus, many online retailers have adopted a strategy of getting found by the search engines, and Google is the leading search engine (see Figure 33.1).

Buyers

Google is great for buyers. Plug in a keyword regarding a product you want to buy, and Google delivers the entire Web to you. The primary drawback when you're shopping is that Google may deliver a large number of non-commercial websites where you can't buy products. They are mixed in with the ecommerce websites, so you have to pick and choose. Still, Google is a very effective means of shopping.

Figure 33.1 A Google search page. ©2007 Google

Sellers

To sell through Google, your independent storefront website has to be found by Google and be in the initial Google pages, preferably near the top of the first page. Contrary to popular belief, this is difficult and expensive to accomplish. You have to be a successful online retailer to take this approach. It's not an approach for occasional sellers. But if you can afford the time and money to use a competent search-engine-optimization consultant (or take the time to learn it yourself – a substantial undertaking), you can make it work.

Another way to use Google for selling is to buy advertising via Google AdWords. For each word or phrase that you buy, Google will run your box advertisement on the right-hand side of the page that is returned by a search for that word or phrase. You pay for click-throughs.

Froogle

Using Froogle to find things to buy works well for buyers. As a result, many sellers have provided Froogle with a datafeed that puts their products into Froogle's pages (see Figure 33.2).

Buyers

Froogle is great for buyers. Plug in some keywords regarding a product you want to buy, and Froogle delivers a wealth of catalog entries to you. Most of the product listings appear with a photograph. There are no non-commercial returns to dilute your shopping effort. It's very robust already, and it continues to grow. Although Google comprises a huge marketplace, it's likely that Froogle will someday surpass it. In any event, Froogle is a more efficient way to shop.

Sellers

Since Froogle is, in effect, a huge online catalog, you have to send information (data) and a photograph for each product to Froogle. You do this with a datafeed as outlined in my book *Building Your eBay Traffic the Smart Way* (which also discusses Google AdWords). Although datafeeds are easy to do with the proper software and Froogle does not charge for entries into its catalog, this is a process for serious online retailers. Occasional sellers will likely find that managing this process is more than they want to do.

Figure 33.2 A Froogle webpage for a product search. ©2007 Google

Google Book Search

Yes, you can find books for sale on Google or Froogle. But you can find them in Google Books too. This is a new Google specialty marketplace. For buyers and sellers it works similar to Froogle.

Google Base (Beta)

Google Base (*http://base.google.com*) is like a free classified section. It is still being beta tested (pre-introduction user testing). The idea is overwhelming just considering the potential depth and scope of the enterprise. This is a new marketplace that buyers and sellers alike will want to experiment with and follow the progress of. Will it turn into the local marketplace that eBay couldn't invent? Will it displace Craig's List? Stay tuned.

Summary

If you're a buyer, don't overlook Google and Froogle as an effective means of shopping online. Then too, keep in mind that you don't have the built-in protections that you do in the eBay system, such as feedback.

If you're an occasional seller, Google and Froogle probably aren't for you. eBay is much easier. However, if you are an eBay retailer, you may want to consider taking the Google approach to ecommerce (getting found by the search engines), and you will certainly want to send datafeeds to Froogle to take advantage of Froogle's free listings and large marketplace.

Where Google Base will fall in the spectrum of online marketplaces has yet to be determined, but it will be interesting to watch it develop.

Epilogue

Whether you're a buyer, a seller, or an eBay retailer, you need to learn the basics well to maximize your effectiveness on eBay. This book will help you do that.

If you decide to become an eBay retailer—operate a retail business on eBay—there's a lot more to learn. Fortunately, there are several books on doing business on eBay that you will find useful. Take advantage of the eBay business information that's available in books. It will save you a lot of time, money, and mistakes.

And, of course, I recommend my book *eBay Business the Smart Way, Second Edition*. It provides the basics on eBay retailing.

Beyond the eBay business basics, however, there are more things to learn to make your eBay retail business as profitable as possible. I have written four more books you will find helpful. The first is *eBay Global the Smart Way*. It shows how to increase your sales significantly and inexpensively simply by accepting orders from buyers living abroad. It also provides information on importing products to sell. Ron Ubels, a Customs broker from Canada, is my very knowledgeable co-author.

The second is *Building Your eBay Traffic the Smart Way*. It shows you how to do datafeed marketing, an easy and inexpensive way to substantially increase your sales by selling on Froogle and other online marketplaces. It also covers other leading online marketing techniques giving my opinion for each as to its cost-effectiveness.

The third is *eBay Photography the Smart Way*. I had fun working on this book because I am an experienced amateur photographer and I co-authored the book with an old friend, Stan Livingston, who has been a product photographer for 40 years. Good photography is crucial to eBay retailing success, and mediocre photography is a handicap. So don't take your product photography lightly.

Finally, the fourth is *eBay Inventory the Smart Way*, a book about finding merchandise to sell. It also covers the retailer-wholesaler relationship so important for retail success. Jeremy Hanks, founder of Doba, is my co-author. Doba is an ecommerce leader in drop shipping retail.

An advanced eBay business book that I didn't write but that I recommend is *eBay Strategies* by Scot Wingo (Prentice Hall, 2005). It gives not only good retail advice but provides a series of systematic means of analyzing how your eBay retail is performing.

Whether you're a buyer, seller, or eBay retailer, I wish you the best of luck on eBay.

Appendix I Top 11 Tips

The top 11 tips for success on eBay for both buyers and sellers follow, not necessarily in order of priority:

1. Play by the Rules. The eBay rules were set to make sure that people deal with each other fairly. If you don't play by the rules, you may be unfair to others and undermine eBay. You may even break laws or incur legal liability.

2. Take eBay Seriously. eBay is not a game. It's a new international marketplace where valuable business is transacted.

3. Protect Yourself. Don't be paranoid, but don't be foolish either. Follow standard protective practices that make sense, just as you do offline.

4. Give Feedback. The core of eBay is trust. Feedback determines an eBay member's reputation. You want to make sure that the eBay members with whom you deal get the reputations they deserve so that eBay patrons will know who to trust.

5. Pay Attention to Detail. This means know eBay rules and procedures and follow them carefully. Provide plenty of detail on the items that you auction and on your sale requirements. For items on which you bid, review carefully the seller's auction and sales requirements. Whether seller or winning bidder, follow through diligently after the auction.

6. Research Market Value. Whether you're a buyer or seller, your best technique is to know the value of the item auctioned. With an accurate value, you can make smart decisions.

7. Keep a Cheerful Attitude. Buying and selling can be fun. No one likes to do business with a sourpuss, whether it's at a retail store or on eBay. Being pleasant can go a long way toward solving a lot of difficult problems.

8. Maintain Security. Online crime from overseas is running rampant. Protect yourself and those you deal with on eBay by following sound security practices.

9. Treat eBay as a Lifelong Asset. It's already ten years old, and it will be around for a long time. You will be able to use it profitably for longer than you think. Some pundits have said it's only a passing fad. Don't believe them.

10. Contribute to the eBay Community. A dynamic and successful marketplace is always a community. Sooner or later you will have opportunities to make a contribution to eBay or to other eBay members. Answer those opportunities.

11. Develop Your Own Approach. Only experience will lead you to auction practices with which you will be comfortable and successful. A book can be helpful, but what works for an author may not work for you. Invent a new eBay technique.

———

This top 11 list is not loaded with specific details that will make you an eBay wizard immediately. Nonetheless, it points out some things for you to consider in developing successful eBay practices.

Although this list does not provide the *details* you need for success on eBay, this book does. Read it through once. When you have a question later, use the book as a reference. Most authors, including me, write books they would like to use as references. When I buy and sell on eBay, I use this book as a reference for details that I have forgotten.

Appendix II Top 9 Tips

The top 9 tips for successfully auctioning items on eBay follow, not necessarily in order of priority:

1. Research the Market Value. This is the first and most important step in listing something for sale. If you set your minimum bid or reserve too high, no one will bid. If you set it too low, you will short-change yourself.

2. Pile It On. Put as much information about the item as you can gather in your auction ad—information, not hype. The Web is an informational medium, and there is no practical space limitation.

Lack of adequate information is almost certain to bring lower winning bids and in many cases no bids at all.

3. Always Include a Photograph. Pictures sell. Good pictures sell even better. There are a very small percentage of items that don't need a photograph. The rest do. Provide multiple photographs for expensive items (e.g., at least five or six sharp photographs for a vehicle).

Sellers Beware

I know of a woman in Sonoma County, California, who has an interesting eBay strategy. She buys items on eBay from auction listings that include poor photographs. She then takes good photographs of the items, relists them on eBay, and sells them for a profit. Great moneymaker.

4. State Your Requirements. Clearly state your requirements for sales to inform bidders of what to expect. Be sure to include everything that will cost winning bidders money.

Tell Them Before

If you intend not to sell to bidders with undesirable feedback, state that in your sales requirements. Then check the feedback on the leading bidders. If one is undesirable, email him or her before the auction ends to state that you will not accept the bid and ask him or her to retract it.

5. Remember the Search. Craft your auction *title* to include keywords for buyer searches and to be readable.

6. Answer Inquiries Immediately. Always answer bidder email inquiries immediately. If you wait, you may lose a bidder. A robust auction ad will help reduce bidder inquiries.

7. Follow Through. Most winning bidders will expect you to take the initiative to complete the transaction after the auction ends. Contact winning bidders by email within a half-day (a half-hour is better) after the auction ends and restate the details of your sales requirements. Keep a record of all documents, including the auction ad and all emails, for reference. Provide the buyer with a receipt. After the transaction is complete, don't forget to submit feedback on the winning bidder.

eBay Retailers

If you sell regularly on eBay, you will need to develop a system for handling auctions that will keep you well organized and responsive to buyers. It doesn't take more than two or three auctions at the same time to completely confuse you if you aren't organized to handle the action.

8. Use an Auction Management Service. If you sell routinely, use an online auction management service to manage your eBay business. The benefits far outweigh the cost.

9. Provide Good Customer Service. You are the seller, and the winning bidder is your customer. The customer is always right. Put customer service first. Keep a cheerful attitude. It's your responsibility to set a cheerful tone for the follow-through process. On eBay, customer service is the name of the game.

This top 9 list will help you focus on what's important for success in auctioning your items on eBay. Always keep in mind that excellent customer service has come to be expected online, and eBay is no exception.

Appendix III Top 8 Tips

The top 8 tips for successful bidding on eBay follow, not necessarily in order of priority:

1. Research the Market Value. There will always be alternative places to acquire at market value any item on which you bid. By researching market value, you know when you are getting a bargain and can move aggressively. You also know when there is no bargain to be had, and you can look elsewhere to obtain the item. Knowing the market value of the item is the single most important technique for successful bidding on eBay.

2. Save Your Insanity for Unique Items. Don't get carried away bidding on a Sony camcorder. There will be dozens more exactly like it available on eBay soon. However, when you bid on a unique item (e.g., an antique, eight-color, painted steel sign advertising the Monongahela Bakery), the market value of the item may be of less concern to you than your desire to have the unique item.

3. Check the Seller's Feedback. Once you check the seller's feedback, you will either develop confidence in dealing with the seller, or you'll avoid the auction.

4. Consider the Details. Review carefully the auction offering and the seller's requirements. Also consider the bidder overhead expenses (e.g., shipping costs). Factor these into your bid.

5. Look for Unsavvy Sellers. Look for auctions where the seller has not followed good eBay practices. The bids will be fewer, and the winning bids will be lower. You might find a bargain. Serious seller listing mistakes include a misspelling in the auction title, no photograph, a poor photograph, too little information, and the like.

6. Contact the Seller. Email the seller to get any additional necessary details you don't have in order to make a well-informed decision regarding whether to bid and what maximum amount to bid.

7. Develop a Repertoire of Bidding Techniques. No one bidding technique works best for all auctions. Learn and experiment with a variety of techniques and use them when appropriate.

8. Follow Through. Follow through in a timely manner after the auction. If the seller doesn't contact you within a reasonable time, take the initiative to contact him or her. Keep a record of all the auction documents; save the auction ad and all emails for reference. After the transaction is complete, don't forget to submit feedback on the seller.

———

This top 8 list does not guarantee success in every auction, but it will help you develop an intelligent and successful approach to bidding on eBay.

Put Defeat in Perspective

Being outbid almost always means that someone else was willing to bid more than you. It doesn't necessarily mean that your bidding skills are deficient. You will rebound to bid again another day.

Appendix IV   Web Authoring

An authoring software program is one that takes media and arranges them into a presentation. You can think of a word processor as a *text* authoring program. For the purpose of this book, we are interested in Web authoring programs. Because the Web is a multimedia medium, Web authoring programs are multimedia-authoring programs, which means they handle a variety of media.

Multimedia and the Web

The media generally used on the Web are text, color graphics (images), animation, streaming sound, streaming video, MIDI music, and embedded programs (e.g., Java applets). Of the greatest interest for running auctions on eBay are text and color graphics (digital photographs). Anything more may interfere with the efficient functioning and appeal of your auction ads.

Implied in digital multimedia is interactivity. The primary interactive device is the link. The link enables you to have choices. The simplest is stay where I am or click a link and go somewhere else. Links can be important for eBay auctions. With these simple ideas in mind, you can learn to author your own eBay auction ads, and even webpages, using a Web authoring program.

Netscape (*http://netscape.com* – current version is 8.0) offered Composer as its Web authoring program, and it came free with the Netscape browser, also free. Microsoft offered FrontPage Express when it competed with Netscape. Now that it monopolizes the Web browser market, it no longer offers FrontPage Express.

Nvu

Unfortunately, neither free Web authoring program seems to be available today, although Composer may be available free from a different source, Mozilla (*http://modzilla.org*), in a package called SeaMonkey. A new free authoring program, Nvu (pronounced N-View), is available at *http://www.nvu.com*. It is more powerful than Composer or Front Page Express.

Nvu is easy to use and is quite similar to both Composer and FrontPage Express. In fact, they were all designed as Web word processors, albeit word processors for Web text.

But remember, the Web is a multimedia medium. These Web authoring programs also handle other media competently. You will find using these programs about the easiest way you can do Web work without knowing HTML.

I do not encourage you to use more than one of these programs on the same webpages. You're just asking for trouble. Choose one and stick with it. Because they are so much alike, this chapter covers only one, Nvu. If you can understand Nvu, you won't have any trouble using Composer or FrontPage Express, if you can find them.

You will also find that using these authoring programs is incompatible with hand coding and editing. If you can code HTML, you can work more efficiently using an HTML editor or an authoring program, such as Adobe Dreamweaver (formerly Macromedia Dreamweaver), that does not change your HTML. Nvu, Composer, and FrontPage Express, however, do their own thing, and that can make subsequent HTML editing both tedious and inefficient.

Nvu

Open Nvu and start typing. It doesn't get any easier. It's just like using a word processor (see Figure A5.1). Want to add some headings? Do it. It's just as easy as using a word processor and virtually identical (see Figure A5.2).

Unless you know something about HTML, however, you may not fully understand how to format your headings and other typographical devices. For instance, <h1> is the largest heading, <h2> the second largest, <h3> the third largest, and <h4> the fourth largest. Few Web developers use <h5> or <h6> because you never quite know what you will get. Just understanding this HTML heading scheme will enable you to use Nvu better, even if you never do any HTML coding. When you use Nvu with templates too, it helps to know a little HTML.

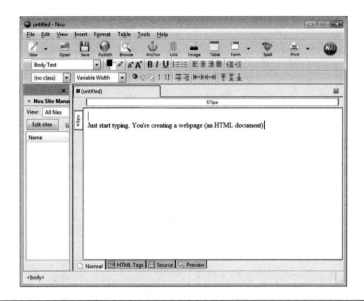

Figure A5.1 Open Nvu and start typing.

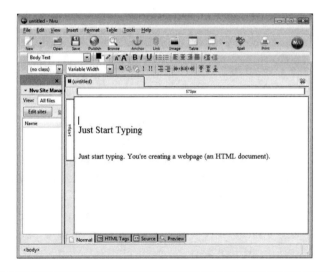

Figure A5.2 Add a heading.

Text

Don't do funny things with text. Keep it simple, readable, and well-organized. Unless you have something unique (e.g., a work of art), potential bidders just want to read quickly and move on. If you have what they want at a reasonable price, they will be likely to bid. If you don't, they won't. No amount of jazzing up your eBay auction ad is going to change that. Help potential bidders to quickly get the facts and information that they need from your auction ad.

Typesetting

Typesetting is pretty straightforward for an eBay auction ad. Browsers have Times New Roman or Times (serif fonts) for their standard font; they have Arial or Helvetica for their sanserif font; and they have Courier for their monospaced font. Beyond those, you're kidding yourself; not everyone will see anything else you use because not everyone has the requisite fonts installed on their computers.

Graphics

You can easily place digital photographs in your eBay auction ad. Just place the cursor where you want the photograph to go in the webpage and click on the graphics button (see Figure A5.3).

The image markup is *<img src=*"**[URL]**"*>*. You will need to enter the URL of the photograph as you learned to do in Chapter 11, and it will magically appear. (The photograph must be located on the Internet somewhere.)

Unfortunately, it may not appear on your computer screen unless you are online. Test your eBay ad while online. You can see your webpage text at any time in your browser on your own computer, but the photographs and other media will not show unless you are online (assuming you use URLs for photographs located somewhere on the Internet).

Figure A5.3 Inserting a photograph.

Links

You place a link (correctly called a hyperlink) just as you do a photograph. Click on the link button (see Figure A5.4).

Figure A5.4 Inserting a link.

In this case, however, the link has a beginning markup *<a href=*"[**URL**]"*>* and an ending markup *</a>*. Whatever is between these markups is the hot spot of the link. When someone clicks on the hot spot, he or she goes to the URL specified in the link markup.

You need to enter the URL for the link. Notice in your Web browser that the text that is in the hot spot of the link is a different color. That's how people find links.

Background Color

Changing the background color can prove attractive, but only if you are careful. Review Chapter 16, which covers browser-safe colors. Any colors you use that are not browser-safe may become slightly different colors in someone else's browser. Colors are not consistent unless they're browser-safe.

Keep in mind that you do not want to set the background color with the *<body>* markup for the entire webpage for your eBay auction ad. It will interfere with eBay's color scheme. That's practically suicidal. Use a table, and set the color background for the table. The Chapter 16 template shows how to limit your color changes to your portion of the entire webpage (i.e., inside the table that defines your auction ad).

You can have tables within tables. With different background colors, tables can provide a polished appearance to a webpage (see Figure A5.5).

Figure A5.5 Two tables—one inside the other—with different background colors in the template. A third innermost table contains the text.

Creating tables is beyond the scope of this book, but a book on Web authoring or HTML will teach you tables and more.

Browser

You can check your work at any time with your Web browser. Just open the auction ad HTML file in the browser. Before checking your work, *first*, save the HTML file in Nvu, and *second*, reload the webpage in your browser. You will see your latest up-to-the-minute work.

Chop It Off

Nvu makes webpages. You need only a portion of a webpage. Therefore, you need to chop off the head and foot retaining everything between the body markups <body></body> of the webpage before you can submit it to eBay as the body of your auction ad.

This is your last act of webpage developing. Don't do this before you're ready to submit your work to eBay. Save your webpage file and close Nvu. Open Windows Notepad or any other plain text editor. Load your webpage. Highlight the *<body>* markup and everything above it. Then delete it. Next go to the bottom of the webpage and highlight the *</body>* markup and everything below it, and delete it. Now you've got something you can copy and paste into the eBay auction input (*Sell Your Item*, *Description*) in the Sell section of the eBay website.

Summary

This Appendix gives you a small start on webpage development. Webpage authoring programs are easy to use. Use one to make a webpage. Chop off the top and bottom and enter it via copy and paste as you would any description of a product to be auctioned. The result can be a nicely formatted presentation that can be better and *easier to read* than the presentation resulting from the normal entry of text in the *Description* input in the *Sell Your Item* form.

Appendix V HTML Tutorial

You can learn Hypertext Markup Language (HTML) easily. It's not programming, although many Web developers now call it *coding*. This tutorial does not attempt to give you a comprehensive grasp of HTML. It does give you a good start on using HTML basics in the auction ad portion of your auction listing.

Sometimes when using a Web authoring program, you just can't get things quite the way you want them. If you know HTML, you can tune up your webpages more precisely. Sometimes you see an auction ad page you really like on eBay. You can copy it to your hard disk. If

489

you can read HTML, you can look at the markups to see how the auction ad is constructed. Although copying the content of someone else's auction ad may be a copyright infringement, copying layout and typesetting is not.

For a more thorough introduction to HTML, you might read *Teach Yourself HTML in 24 Hours*, Seventh Edition (SAMS, 2005) or any one of a number of similar books readily available in many bookstores.

The angle bracket characters (< >) indicate markups (also called "tags"). The markups instruct the browser how to display the content (text, graphics, etc.). The markups also enable some interactive functions such as links. Markups are not case-sensitive; that is, you can use either upper- or lowercase characters inside the angle brackets. As you can see, I prefer lowercase markups; I can read them faster.

Some markups stand by themselves.

```
<br>
```

Most require a closing markup.

```
<b>content</b>
```

The forward slant indicates the closing markup.

Spaces

HTML doesn't like spaces unless you specify them. Therefore, it will change two or more consecutive character spaces into one space. It will change redundant line spaces into one line space. See the * * markup later in this appendix for a way to increase spaces.

Refer to Chapter 12 for an example of an auction ad that goes into an auction listing. It uses only a few markups.

Markups Alphabetically

This section presents the most elementary HTML markups in alphabetical order.

<a href=" "></a>

You use a link to go to another webpage anywhere on the Web. For instance, suppose you want to go to the *Hike-Utah* website. You might use the following link.

```
<a href="http://www.hike-utah.com">canyon
trail maps</a>
```

This link will take you directly to the Hike-Utah website which features information on hiking and backpacking in Utah.

Notice that the opening and closing markups surround the words "canyon trail maps." In the webpage, these three words will be underlined with a different color to indicate that they are a link.

<b></b>

This is the markup which creates bold type. The browser will render the text inside the markups as bold. Consult Chapter 13 for the proper use of bold in typesetting.

*
*

Use this markup to create a line break. This differs from the <p> markup in that a blank line does not follow the line break.

```
Charlie Craft<br>
Wilderness experience: 21 years<br>
Canyon experience: 10 years<br>
779-341-8533 Ext. 409<br>
```

See Figure A4.1 to see how this looks in a browser.

Figure A4.1 Use *
* for line breaks not followed by a blank line.

<dl></dl>

This markup makes a list of terms and definitions like a dictionary with words and definitions. The <dl> markup creates the list. The <dt> markup marks the term. And the <dd> markup marks the definition of the term.

```
<dl>
<dt>term
<dd>definition
<dt>term
<dd>definition
</dl>
```

<dt>

This markup creates a term in a *<dl>* list. It is flush left. It must be used with the *<dl>* markup.

<dd>

This markup creates a definition in a *<dl>* list. It is indented. It must be used with the *<dl>* markup.

This makes a good markup to use for general layout purposes too. For instance, suppose you want to make an unnumbered and unbulleted list. You can use the <dl> and <dd> markups (see Figure A4.2).

```
<p>You will need the following 7.5 minute
topographical maps for the Slickhorn
trek.</p>

<dl>

<dd>Slickhorn Canyon East

<dd>Slickhorn Canyon West

<dd>Pollys Pasture

</dl>

<p>You can obtain these maps at your
nearest US Geological Survey office.</p>
```

Figure A4.2 An unnumbered unbulleted list.

Note that the indent is on the left side only, not on the right side.

<div> </div>

This division markup by itself is not much use. Its attributes make it useful. Use this markup (with attributes) to lay out a section of text. The section can be a heading, a paragraph, or multiple headings and paragraphs. For instance, one attribute is *align*. You can use this to center a heading or other text (see Figure A4.3).

```
<div align="center">Slickhorn - East
Slickhorn Loop, Utah</div>
```

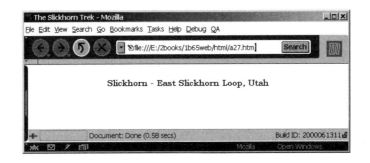

Figure A4.3 A heading centered with the *<div>* markup.

For other attributes of the *<div>* markup, consult an HTML book. Note that for the above example, you can also use the *<center>* markup, which may be discontinued by the HTML standards committee. Use the *<div>* markup instead with the *align* attribute.

<h1> </h1>

Use this markup for headings. It comes in six sizes: 1-6. For most uses, only sizes 1-3 prove useful (see Figure A4.4). Sizes 4-6 are too small for normal use.

```
<h1>Slickhorn - East Slickhorn Loop, Utah</
h1>
```

```
<h2>Slickhorn - East Slickhorn Loop, Utah</
h2>
```

```
<h3>Slickhorn - East Slickhorn Loop, Utah</
h3>

<h4>Slickhorn - East Slickhorn Loop, Utah</
h4>

<h5>Slickhorn - East Slickhorn Loop, Utah</
h5>

<h6>Slickhorn - East Slickhorn Loop, Utah</
h6>
```

Figure A4.4 Six different headings.

The headings display in bold with a blank line before and a blank line after.

<hr>

Use this markup to make a line (a rule) across the page. The attributes control how the rule looks (see Figure A4.5).

```
<hr align="center" size="2" width="300">
We took one five-gallon container out of
the vehicle at each trailhead and stowed it
in the bushes. This is an arid area. If
your car is stolen at the trailhead, you
don't want to come out of the canyon to
find no water.
```

Figure A4.5 Use the *<hr>* markup to create a rule.

The rule shown in Figure A4.5 is 300 pixels wide and 2 pixels thick.

<i> </i>

This is the markup which creates italic type. The browser will render
the text inside the markups as italics. Consult Chapter 13 for the
proper use of italics in typesetting.

<img src=" ">

To include an image in a webpage, use this markup. Place the URL of
the image file in the *src* attribute. The URL can be local or somewhere
else on the Web. The image displays at the location of the markup.

```
<img src="slickhorn23.jpg">
```

The *src* refers to an image file, which must be a GIF, JPEG, or PNG. Use the attributes of the *<img>* markup to control how the image displays in a browser (see Chapter 11). Note that the URL for the image file can be anywhere on the Web. It doesn't have to be at the same URL as the webpage.

<ol> </ol>

This markup makes a list of numbered items. You do not specify the numbers. The items are numbered in order. You must use the *<li>* markup to designate the list items.

```
<ol>
<li>item
<li>item
<li>item
</ol>
```

The list is indented. For example, the earlier unnumbered list displays with numbers when you use the *<ol>* markup (see Figure A4.6).

```
You will need the following three 7.5
minute topographical maps for the Slickhorn
trek.

<ol>
<li>Slickhorn Canyon East
<li>Slickhorn Canyon West
<li>Pollys Pasture
</ol>

You can obtain these maps at your nearest
US Geological Survey office.
```

<li>

This markup creates a list item in a numbered or bulleted list. It must be used with the *<ol>* or *<ul>* markups.

Figure A4.6 A numbered list.

<p> </p>

Use this markup for all your paragraphs. The difference between this and the <br> markup is that the <p> markup adds a blank line of space before and after (see Figure A4.7).

```
<p>To find the ruins, you have to
speculate. (It helps to know they are
there.) Look for a place where there might
be ruins (under an overhang). Then climb up
and look. In most cases, you will not be
able to spot the ruins from the canyon
floor.</p>

<p>We traveled about three and a half miles
for the day, not exactly a death-defying
pace. The wet potholes, although still
small, appeared more often. It's evident
```

that without recent rain, and particularly
in a drought year, there would be no water
in the canyon. Even with water present, we
topped off at almost every wet pothole not
knowing whether it would be our last.</p>

<p>We camped at another wide place in the
streambed with flat rock and small potholes
with fresh water. Ravens and lizards seemed
to be the only wildlife in the canyon.</p>

Figure A4.7 Use the <*p*> markup for all your paragraphs.

Note that today just the beginning markup <*p*> is enough, and you don't need the end markup </*p*>. But soon the browsers may require the end markup, too, and you don't want to have to go back and add the end markups.

<table> </table>

Use the *<table>* markup to create a table. The *<tr>* markup (table row) indicates a row (record), and the *<td>* markup (table data) indicates a column (field). The following is a two-column table with three rows.

```
<table>
<tr>
<td>data</td>
<td>data</td>
</tr>
<tr>
<td>data</td>
<td>data</td>
</tr>
<tr>
<td>data</td>
<td>data</td>
</tr>
</table>
```

For example, the following table shows three products (topographical maps) and their current prices (see Figure A4.8).

```
<table cellpadding="10">
<tr>
<td>Slickhorn Canyon East</td>
<td>$4.00</td>
</tr>
<tr>
```

```
<td>Slickhorn Canyon West</td>

<td>$4.00</td>

</tr>

<tr>

<td>Pollys Pasture</td>

<td>$4.00</td>

</tr>

</table>
```

Note that to create some space between the data of this table, you need to use the attribute *cellpadding* to add 10 pixels of padding within each cell. The default use of *<table>* uses no border as Figure A4.8 shows. To add the border, add the *border* attribute set to *1* (see Figure A4.9).

```
<table cellpadding="10" border="1">
```

Figure A4.8 The <table> markup makes attractive tables.

As you can see, the <table> markup is handy for tables, but most of us don't use tables very often. However, tables provide another tool in creating attractive layouts.

Figure A4.9 A table with borders.

As Chapter 4 explains, you can use tables to lay out a readable text column. The following one-cell table 480 pixels wide creates a convenient reading environment (see Figure A4.10).

```
<table width="480" align="center"><tr><td>

<p>To find the ruins, you have to
speculate. (It helps to know they are
there.) Look for a place where there might
be ruins (under an overhang). Then climb up
and look. In most cases, you will not be
able to spot the ruins from the canyon
floor.</p>

<p>We traveled about three and a half miles
for the day, not exactly a death-defying
pace. The wet potholes, although still
small, appeared more often. It's evident
that without recent rain, and particularly
in a drought year, there would be no water
in the canyon. Even with water present, we
topped off at almost every wet pothole not
knowing whether it would be our last.</p>
```

```
<p>We camped at another wide place in the
streambed with flat rock and small potholes
with fresh water. Ravens and lizards seemed
to be the only wildlife in the canyon.</p>

</td></tr></table>
```

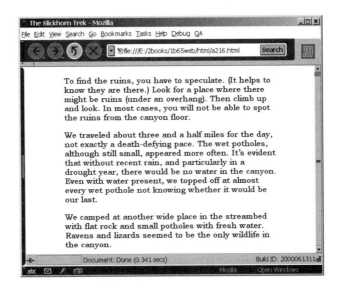

Figure A4.10 Use the *<table>* markup for special layouts such as a text column.

This is a good example of how with a little imagination you can use the *<table>* markup creatively to concoct a variety of layouts.

<tr></tr>

This markup creates a row (record) in a table. It must be used with the *<table>* markup.

<td></td>

This markup creates a column (field) within a table. It holds the data (content) for one table cell. Used with the *<table>* markup.

<ul></ul>

This markup makes a list of bulleted items. You must use the *<li>* markup to designate the list items. Figure A4.11 shows how the browser displays this list.

```
You will need the following 7.5 minute
topographical maps for the Slickhorn trek.
<ul>
<li>Slickhorn Canyon East
<li>Slickhorn Canyon West
<li>Pollys Pasture
</ul>
You can obtain these maps at your nearest
US Geological Survey office.
```

Figure A4.11 A bulleted list.

A browser eliminates redundant spaces between characters or between text blocks. In other words, a browser allows only one space between characters and only one blank line between text blocks. This particular markup establishes a space that will not be eliminated by a browser (see Figure A4.12).

```
Charlie Craft<br>

Occupation:    Wilderness Trekker
```

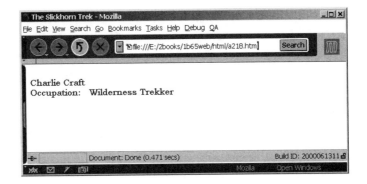

Figure A4.12 Use   to extend spaces.

<!-- -->

You can put this markup to good use. It marks text that does not display.

```
<!-- Change the color of this page to
offwhite when using it to display photos. -
->
```

You can leave instructions (reminders) to yourself or to others who will be working on the authoring of your webpages.

```
<!-- This article is not part of the series
of articles by the same author that appear
in the 4/97 monthly news archive. This
```

```
article belongs in the 2/99 monthly news
archive. -->
```

You can use the comment markup for almost anything, but it's not a good idea to use any other markups inside this markup.

Viewing the Webpage Source

Want to see the HTML in a webpage? You can do so with any webpage. In your browser go View, Page Source. You will be able to see the HTML markups together with the page text.

Viewing the HTML in webpages that you find attractive is a great learning technique. The next step is to use these webpages to help create your own templates for your own webpages. (One can copyright content but generally not standard typesetting and layout.)

Summary

This basic tutorial is designed to whet your appetite for understanding and using HTML. It doesn't include much information on attributes for the markups covered, and it doesn't include all the HTML markups. But it will get you off to a good start for making an eBay auction ad in an auction listing.

Index

The Definitive Series on eBay!

Comprehensive and Easy to Use!
Affordably Priced—A Lot of Information, All for $25 or less!

 eBay the Smart Way
Selling, Buying, and Profiting on the Web's #1 Auction Site, Fifth Edition
$17.95

 eBay Business the Smart Way
Maximize Your Profits on the Web's #1 Auction Site, Third Edition
$24.95

 eBay Motors the Smart Way
Selling and Buying Cars, Trucks, Motorcycles, Boats, Parts, Accessories, and Much More
on the Web's #1 Auction Site
$17.95

 eBay Global the Smart Way
Buying and Selling Internationally on the World's #1 Auction Site
$19.95

 Building Your eBay Traffic the Smart Way
Use Froogle, Data Feeds, Cross-Selling, Advance Listing Strategies, and More to Boost
Your Sales on the Web's #1 Auction Site
$17.95

 eBay Photography the Smart Way
Creating Great Product Pictures That Will Attract Higher Bids and Sell Your Items Faster
$19.95

eBay Inventory the Smart Way
How to Find Great Sources and Manage Your Merchandise to Maximize Profits on the
World's #1 Auction Site
$19.95

For more information about these titles, sneak previews of the contents, and updates
on forthcoming titles, check out **www.amacombooks.org/ebaysmartway**.

Available from your local retailer or online at Amazon.com, bn.com, and other
online bookstores.

Prices subject to change.